Luxembourg

the Bradt Travel Guide

Tim Skelton

edition
2

www.bradtguides.com

Bradt Travel Guides Ltd, UK
The Globe Pequot Press Inc, USA

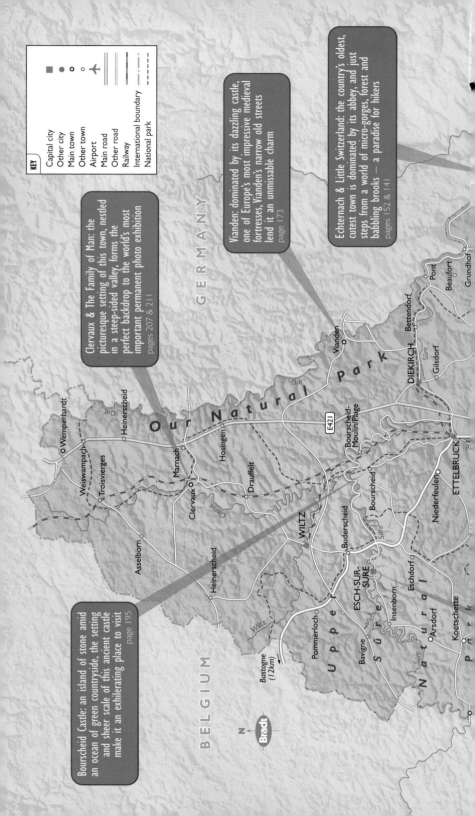

KEY

- ■ Capital city
- ● Other city
- ○ Main town
- ○ Other town
- ✈ Airport
- ═══ Main road
- ─── Other road
- ┈┈┈ Railway
- ─·─ International boundary
- ┈┈┈ National park

Clervaux & The Family of Man: the picturesque setting of this town, nestled in a steep-sided valley, forms the perfect backdrop to the world's most important permanent photo exhibition
pages 207 & 211

Vianden: dominated by its dazzling castle, one of Europe's most impressive medieval fortresses, Vianden's narrow old streets lend it an unmissable charm
page 173

Echternach & Little Switzerland: the country's oldest, cutest town is dominated by its abbey, and just steps from a world of micro-gorges, forest and babbling brooks — a paradise for hikers
pages 152 & 141

Bourscheid Castle: an island of stone amid an ocean of green countryside; the setting and sheer scale of this ancient castle make it an exhilerating place to visit
page 195

GERMANY

BELGIUM

Our Natural Park

Upper Sûre Natural Park

Wemperhardt
Weiswampach
Troisvierges
Heinerscheid
Asselborn
Marnach
Clervaux
Heinerscheid
Hosingen
Drauffelt
Vianden
Bourscheid-Moulin/Plage
Bourscheid
DIEKIRCH
Gilsdorf
Bettendorf
Pont
Beaufort
Grundhof
WILTZ
Buderscheid
Niederfeulen
ETTELBRUCK
Pommerloch
ESCH-SUR-SÛRE
Bavigne
Insenborn
Eschdorf
Arsdorf
Koetschette

Bastogne
(12km)

E421

N

Bradt

The Moselle Valley: with chocolate box scenery and scintillating taste sensations galore, Europe's smallest winemaking region makes a big splash on the global viticulture scene
page 107

Esch-sur-Sûre & Upper Sûre Lake: Luxembourg's tiniest town perches on a rock above the river, and is the gateway to the nation's largest lake, a beautiful watery haven in the heart of the Ardennes
pages 198 & 202

Luxembourg City: the capital city that works on many levels, from the shops and museums of the elegant upper town, on the rim of two gorges, to the lower town's buzzing nightlife districts
page 43

This map is based on the Philip's European database mapping from "Easyread Europe Atlas 2008" with permission.

GERMANY

BELGIUM

FRANCE

Trier (12km)

Girst

Moersdorf

Wasserbillig

Biwer

Grevenmacher

Wormeldange

Ehnen

Bous

REMICH

Schengen

MONDORF-LES-BAINS

Larochette

Reuland

Graulinster

Junglinster

Senningen

Sandweiler

Moutfort

Dalheim

Frisange

Cruchten

MERSCH

Wolferdange

Alzingen

Bissen

Ansembourg

Kopstal

Mamer

LUXEMBOURG CITY

BETTEMBOURG

DUDELANGE

Useldange

Saeul

Capellen

Dippach

Kayl

Redange

Hobscheid

Koerich

Grass

PETANGE

DIFFERDANGE

ESCH-SUR-ALZETTE

Steinfort

(under construction)

Moselle

Moselle

Sûre

Alzette

Eisch

A1

E29

E44

E29

A1

E29

E421

A6

E25

E44

A13

A4

A3

E25

A13

5km

5 miles

0

0

Luxembourg
Don't
miss...

Sightseeing in Luxembourg City
With an abundance of pleasant squares, great museums and centuries-old architecture, Luxembourg City is one of Europe's most charming cities (DR) page 43

The spectacular setting of Bourscheid Castle
Ringed by a great stone wall with 11 watchtowers, Bourscheid dominates the Sûre Valley in every direction (BL/A) page 195

Taking a hike in 'Little Switzerland'
Craggy outcrops, deep gorges and winding pathways abound in Luxembourg's very own 'Little Switzerland'
(TS) page 141

Stepping into history in majestic Vianden
Nestled in a steep valley on the banks of the Our River, Vianden is home to one of the world's most striking medieval castles
(RVPB/S) page 173

Sipping and savouring the locally produced wines
A visit to the Moselle Valley's stunning vineyards is a must for wine enthusiasts
(SS) page 107

above Separated from Luxembourg City's upper town by a soaring cliff, Grund feels like a village within a city (VY/S) page 46

left Interior of the imposing late-Gothic Notre Dame Cathedral (DR) page 74

below left Watch video clips of bank robberies in Luxembourg City's Banking Museum, housed in the impressive National Savings Bank (DR) page 81

below Overlooked by the Prime Minister's residence, place Clairefontaine is one of the city's prettiest squares (DR) page 73

right Resident of the Kirchberg business district, the Lange Banker ('Tall Banker') flaunts a giant umbrella and size 96 shoes (SS) page 80

below right Visit boutique shops and cafés on the rue du Marché aux Herbes, Luxembourg City (SS) page 33

The industrial south: take a tour through Luxembourg's industrial past on the Train 1900 [*top*] (TS) page 96, roam the underground passages at the National Mining Museum [*centre*] (LTO) page 102 and then finish the day with a relaxing soak in the mineral-rich Domaine Thermal Spa, Mondorf-les-Bains [*bottom*] (LBF/A) page 112

AUTHOR

Tim Skelton travelled extensively throughout Europe, Asia, the Americas and Australia before settling in the Netherlands in the mid 1990s, where he worked for the Dutch energy and environment agency. He now writes for numerous expat, energy and in-flight publications, has contributed to travel guides to the Netherlands and Belgium, and is a former finalist in the Bradt/*Independent on Sunday* travel-writing competition. He has been a fan of and regular visitor to Luxembourg for more than 20 years. In addition to *Luxembourg: The Bradt Travel*

Guide, he is also the author of *Around Amsterdam in 80 Beers* (Cogan & Mater, 2010).

AUTHOR'S STORY

Having lived for many years in Benelux I've taken every opportunity to explore its furthest regions. I soon realised its three member nations were markedly different from one another, and the only thing they had in common was they were all 'quite small'. As I gradually got to know Luxembourg I kept finding more and more things to do, and began to wonder what it was the country had done to deserve being deemed no more than an appendix or an afterthought to Belgium in most of the available guides. And all the feedback I've received from Luxembourgish people suggests they've long been curious about this as well. Thus it gave me the greatest of pleasure when Bradt offered me the chance to set the record straight, and to provide Luxembourg with breathing space in print that was long overdue.

The wealth of new things I discovered on my initial research trips, and have continued to find on all subsequent visits, coupled with the overwhelmingly warm reception I have received from people there – whether they knew the reasons for my being there or not – have done nothing but reinforce my previous feelings. In fact, I like it even more than ever and the fact that this book has been popular enough to warrant a second edition shows that I am not alone.

PUBLISHER'S FOREWORD   *Adrian Phillips, Publishing Director*

Rarely has the process of commissioning a Bradt author proved so simple. Tim Skelton attended our annual seminar on travel writing, and it was immediately clear he was of the right stuff – an excellent writer with a meticulous attention to detail and a passion for a place he knew well. Luxembourg was an intriguing suggestion. It doesn't feel as if it should be off the beaten track, and yet I know few people who've been there. Somewhere boasting Michelin-starred restaurants, good wine and romantic castles certainly deserved its own guidebook – and here we are now moving into a second edition. I hope Luxembourgers will agree that Tim has set things right in fine style.

Second edition published April 2012   First published July 2008

Bradt Travel Guides Ltd, IDC House, The Vale, Chalfont St Peter, Bucks SL9 9RZ, England
www.bradtguides.com
Published in the USA by The Globe Pequot Press Inc, PO Box 480, Guilford, Connecticut 06437-0480

Text copyright © 2012 Tim Skelton
Maps copyright © 2012 Bradt Travel Guides Ltd
Photographs copyright © 2012 Individual photographers (see below)
Project Managers: Anna Moores & Greg Dickinson

ISBN: 978 1 84162 424 2
British Library Cataloguing in Publication Data
A catalogue record for this book is available from the British Library

Photographs Alamy (A): Barry Lewis (BL/A), LOOK Die Bildagentur der Fotografen GmbH (LBF/A), Witry Pascal (WP/A), Wilmar Topshots (WT/A); Dreamstime (D): Chachas (C/D); Luxembourg Tourist Office (LTO); RLH Travel Photography/Luxembourg Tourist Office, London (RLH/LTOL); David Robertson (DR); Tim Skelton (TS); Shutterstock (S): Robert Paul Van Beets (RPVB/S), Victor Yuminov (VY/S); Superstock (SS); Ulterior Epicure (UE)
Front cover Clervaux Castle (DR)
Back cover Banking Museum, Luxembourg City (DR), Place du Marché, Echternach (DR)
Title page Bourscheid Castle (DR), Statue of William II (DR), Ripening grapes in the Moselle Valley (DR)

Maps David McCutcheon (compiled from Philip's 1:1,000,000 European Mapping (*www. philips-maps.co.uk*)
Colour map Relief map bases by Nick Rowland FRGS

Typeset from the author's disk by Wakewing, High Wycombe
Production managed by Jellyfish Print Solutions; printed in India

Acknowledgements

This second edition of the guide, just like the book that preceded it, would not have been possible without the efforts of a great many people.

Eternal gratitude must go first to my wife, Amanda, for all her patience, proofreading and tireless enthusiasm throughout the project.

As with the first edition, a big thank you goes to everyone at ONT, the Luxembourg National Tourist Office, and to LCTO, the Luxembourg City Tourist Office, for welcoming me to their homeland and for speedily answering what must have seemed at times to have been the most obvious of questions. Particular thanks for their support go to Serge Moes in London, to Brigitte Goergen and Lis Lorang of ONT in Luxembourg, and to Cathy Giorgetti and Jean-Claude Conter (both LCTO) for their hospitality, and for filling my head with facts, tips and recommendations. Also to Marianne Origer of the Echternach regional tourist office for giving up her weekend to guide me through Little Switzerland for the first edition, and to Dr Robert Philippart for plugging some gigantic holes in my knowledge of Luxembourgish and thus making it possible to complete the language appendix.

Thanks to British expat Steve Lyons for his local insight into Luxembourg City and for filling some gaps in my historical knowledge.

And thank you to everyone at Bradt for offering me this opportunity and supporting it throughout. In particular to Adrian Phillips and Hilary Bradt for making it all possible in the first place, to Emma Thomson for guiding me through the editing process for the first edition, and to Anna Moores and Greg Dickinson for the second. Thanks also to Alan Whitaker (first edition) and David McCutcheon (second edition) for their ability to decipher my hand-drawn maps, and to successfully turn them into plans to navigate by.

A big thank you also to those readers of the first edition who took the trouble to write in with comments and suggestions, all of which have been taken on board, and to the people of Luxembourg for having a country well worth getting to know better.

Finally, and most importantly, a great big heartfelt thank you to my dear departed mother (1941–2011), who was my biggest fan and greatest supporter of all, but who will sadly never get to read this second edition.

Contents

LIST OF MAPS

Introduction

Like many who grew up in Britain during the 1970s or before, my first introduction to Luxembourg was a crackly music station that entered my bedroom via a sea of white noise on a cheap hand-held transistor radio. It was only years later I discovered the radio station shared its name with a country, and that most people who lived there didn't really speak English with curiously chirpy DJ accents.

So imagine my delight on discovering during my first visit that this diminutive landlocked microstate was crammed with heritage, hills and castles – more of the last than any similarly pint-sized nation could decently be expected to possess. With everything so close at hand there are no tiring journeys here to make you weary of tourism before you've even begun. And to help you reflect on this wealth of history and nature, the wining and dining options are consistently great.

About that food: Luxembourg has more Michelin-starred restaurants per capita than any other country in the world. But even the legion of establishments that haven't received such accolades still pride themselves on producing the finest of dishes from the freshest of ingredients. Moreover, the nation's wines – which rate among Europe's best-kept secrets – are rather good, to say the least.

Luxembourg is no more immune to economic volatility than anywhere else, and there have been many changes since the first edition of this guide. A number of my favourite haunts have disappeared, but happily they've been replaced by exciting new alternatives, including two luxurious château hotels, and a theme park devoted to milk!

Yet as geographically close as Luxembourg is to the UK, it has somehow remained unknown to many, and stayed off the tourist radar. Fortunately, that's starting to change as people look for nearby and unusual spots for weekend breaks, and the environmentally minded choose destinations closer to home to reduce their carbon footprint. The British are waking up to the joys the Grand Duchy has to offer – and about time too.

Welcome to Europe's smallest big country. Yes, the old clichés are true and you can drive across it in an hour if you really must, but stop awhile to savour its delights and you may end up loving Luxembourg as much as I do.

Part One

GENERAL INFORMATION

Location Northwest Europe, wedged between Belgium, France and Germany

Area 2,586km²

Climate Temperate (mild winters, cool summers)

Status Constitutional monarchy

Population 512,000 (2011)

Life expectancy 80 (men 77.6, women 82.7)

Capital Luxembourg City (population 94,000)

Other main towns Esch-sur-Alzette, Dudelange

Economy Banking and financial services, steel, tourism

GDP per capita US$82,600 (2010 est), the third-highest in the world

Languages Luxembourgish, German and French

Religion Roman Catholicism, but all religions are tolerated and respected

Currency Euro

Exchange rate £1=€1.21; US$1=€0.78 (January 2012)

National airline, airport Luxair, Findel Airport

International telephone code +352

Time Central European Time (CET), GMT +1 (+2 in summer)

Electrical voltage 230V AC/50Hz

Weights and measures Metric

Flag Three horizontal stripes. From top to bottom: red, white and light blue. The national ensign has ten horizontal stripes, alternating light blue and white, with a red lion at the centre.

National anthem *Ons Hémécht* ('Our Homeland'), created in 1859 from a text by Michel Lentz, set to music by Jean-Antoine Zinnen. Unusually for a national anthem it's a hymn to peace rather than a call to arms.

National flower Rose

National bird/animal Goldcrest (*Regulus regulus*)/red lion

National sport Cycling: the one sport in which Luxembourg excels

Public holidays 1 January, Carnival (Monday before Lent), Easter Monday, 1 May, Ascension Day, Whit Monday, 23 June (National Day), 15 August, 1 November, 25 and 26 December

Background Information

GEOGRAPHY AND CLIMATE

GEOGRAPHY Luxembourg's land area, 2,586km², makes it the same size as a typical English county (larger than Cheshire, marginally more compact than Derbyshire). Despite this some people are surprised to learn it actually ranks as the sixth-smallest nation in Europe (there really are five smaller). The country divides naturally into two geographical parts: the northern uplands of the Ardennes and the rolling southern lowlands.

Ardennes Spilling across northern Luxembourg and eastern Belgium, the Ardennes form part of the Eifel: a range of low, ex-volcanic mountains covering the neighbouring regions of Germany. Also known as the Eisléck or Oesling, the Grand Duchy's share of these is a sparsely populated, forested world of high plateaux cut by deep river valleys, principally the Sûre and the Our. The few towns that are located here are principally tucked down in the valleys, which gives the higher elevations an even emptier feeling. The highest point in the country (580m) is also here, but as much of the region is above 500m you could easily drive straight past this without realising it is there. This ancient land formed as the bed of a Devonian sea some 380–390 million years ago. Its age makes it notably 200 million years older than the land further south.

Gutland The 'good land' that fills the southern two-thirds of the country is largely rolling farmland and woods. With an average height of 270m above sea level, it's lower lying and more densely populated than the north – all the towns of any significant size are here. Much of this gentle landscape is filled with arable fields and orchards, but Gutland also contains several tiny yet distinct sub-regions. In the northeast is the bizarre world of sandstone ravines known as the Müllerthal. To the east is the Moselle Valley, with a broad river and sloping hillsides perfect for growing grapevines. And in the southwest is an iron-rich soil that has been turned red by its mineral deposits.

CLIMATE Like much of northwest Europe, Luxembourg enjoys a temperate climate without extremes, not dissimilar to the UK. The sea is some 300km away, so its moderating influence is less than in Britain, and the 'continental effect' has marginally more impact. This makes winters slightly cooler and summers a bit warmer. January maximum temperatures in Luxembourg City average 5°C, while July maximums average 23°C. May and June are often the driest, sunniest months, while July and August are the hottest. It can rain at any time however, so come prepared – as with Britain, luck plays a major role in whether you stay dry, no matter what the season.

The Ardennes, being higher, is cooler than the south throughout the year. Winter often brings snow, although with less reliability than in past years. The north is also notably wetter.

Having said that, anyone who's experienced the vagaries of British weather in recent times knows weather trends are no longer as predictable as they once were. Summers may be scorching one year, miserable the next. One winter it might snow heavily and often, the next not at all – the once-thriving cross-country skiing industry (Langlaufen) in the Ardennes has all but vanished now conditions have become so unreliable.

Whatever else: expect the unexpected.

NATURAL HISTORY AND CONSERVATION

Luxembourg enjoys one of the highest proportions of woodland cover in western Europe, in an even mixture of deciduous and coniferous strands. The largest tracts of forest are in the Ardennes region – although most of these are now fragmented and have been modified to some degree. True wilderness no longer exists, as centuries of farming have altered the appearance of the land. Nevertheless, several areas have been afforded special protected status to preserve what remains for future generations, in particular the natural parks of the Our and the Upper Sûre. In total some 44,000ha is protected – 17% of the whole country.

Sightings of large wild mammals are rare – the wolves that once lived in the forests haven't been seen in more than a century. Wild boar and deer (red and roe) do still live in the Ardennes, but are shy and retiring and you're more likely to see them on restaurant menus during the hunting season than you are in their natural environment.

Birdwatchers on the other hand have far more to cheer about. A walk in the woods on most days will find buzzards, yellowhammers, chaffinches, treecreepers, woodpeckers, and more. Kingfishers frequent the many rivers, and wagtails seem to be common just about everywhere. In springtime swifts and martins gather in every town centre to nest, sometimes in huge numbers.

Even Luxembourg City can be a haven for wildlife-spotters. It lies on the spring and autumn migration route of the common crane (*Grus grus*), which flies overhead as it moves to and fro between summer breeding grounds in northern Europe and winter habitats in Spain and north Africa. Sometimes the cranes pass by in thousands, creating a marvellous spectacle. Peregrine falcons and eagle owls also nest in the craggy rocks around the Bock promontory, and can occasionally be seen hunting from there. Perhaps the most active conservation group within Luxembourg is the **Luxembourg Nature and Bird Protection League** (*Lëtzebuerger Natur- a Vulleschutzliga; Kraizhaff, rue de Luxembourg, L-1899 Kockelscheuer;* \ *29 04 04;* e *birgit.jacoby@luxnatur.lu; www.lnvl.lu*). The equivalent of the RSPB in the UK, LNVL – as they are known – have been involved since 1920 in the preservation of national wildlife habitats, not just for birds, but for all species. They actively campaign on conservation and nature issues, and organise educational programmes in schools. LNVL currently has around 13,000 members – almost 3% of the population.

Luxembourg's national bird is the tiny goldcrest (*Regulus regulus*), a diminutive creature representing a diminutive nation. But small as it is, you are more likely to spot one than you are the national animal, which is the red lion (*Inconspicuous nonexisticus*).

HISTORY

Luxembourg's geography is small and easily definable, but its history is far more complex. The story of the country is linked to a string of European power struggles from the expansion plans of the Habsburgs to the empire building of Napoleon and Hitler. Pretty much everyone who was anyone in Europe has at one time or other attempted to get their hands on this strip of land. The geographical area known as Luxembourg has been added to and had parts chipped off it with every change of management, although each upheaval has seen its political independence and sense of national identity grow.

ANCIENT BEGINNINGS The earliest evidence of human habitation dates back to around 5000BC. Almost nothing is known about who those people were, but when the Romans conquered the region in 53BC, two Belgic tribes – the Mediomatrici and the Treveri – were already there. The Romans built roads across the land, linking the cities of Reims and Trier. Two of these crossed in what became Luxembourg City, and the fortress built to guard the junction became its earliest known settlement.

The Roman Empire collapsed in AD500, and the country was dominated by the Franks for the next 500 years. It was during this period, in the late 7th century, that Northumbrian monk Willibrord arrived, founding the Benedictine abbey and the city of Echternach, helping to spread Christianity among the local population. He would later be honoured as the patron saint of Luxembourg.

THE ARRIVAL OF 'LUXEMBOURG' The first concept of a Luxembourgish nation emerged in AD963. Count Siegfried I of the Ardennes (a relative of King Louis II of France and Holy Roman Emperor Otto the Great) acquired the land in an exchange deal with the St Maximin Abbey in Trier. He turned it into an independent state, building a 'little fortress' – Lucilinburhuc – on the remains of the Roman fort, and making it his feudal seat. As a town developed around it, the castle became the focal point of a small but strategically vital nation. For a century Siegfried's descendants expanded their territory, using the classic medieval combination of treaties, marriages, inheritance and force. Then in 1060 a descendant named Conrad declared himself to be the first Count of Luxembourg.

FROM COUNTY TO DUCHY The new House of Luxembourg flourished, remaining an independent state within the Holy Roman Empire for 400 years. During its later years the dynasty provided some of the empire's leading figures: Count Henry IV became Emperor Henry VII in 1308, and Henry's son John the Blind (who died fighting the English at the Battle of Crécy in 1346), married into the royal family of Bohemia, linking the two households and cementing the position of both. In 1354, John the Blind's son, Holy Roman Emperor Charles IV, transformed the county of Luxembourg into a duchy, and declared himself the first duke.

BURGUNDIAN AND HABSBURG RULE By 1437, the imperial Luxembourg family had run out of male heirs. The duchy passed into the hands of Duchess Elisabeth of Görlitz, granddaughter of Charles IV. Three years later she made an agreement with her neighbour, Duke Philip the Good of Burgundy, that he would administer Luxembourg and inherit it after Elisabeth's death. Philip however, couldn't be bothered to wait for this and ousted Elisabeth anyway in 1443. The Bohemian half of the family, unhappy with the state of affairs, fought to retrieve their possession, but in 1467 Queen Elisabeth of Poland, their last surviving heir, abandoned the family claim, leaving the duchy as one of the 17 Provinces of the Netherlands.

With the marriage of Mary of Burgundy to Maximilian in 1477, all 17 provinces came under Habsburg rule. And when the abdication of Emperor Charles V in 1555 caused the Habsburg Empire to split into two, they became the Spanish Netherlands.

FRENCH INTERFERENCE – PART ONE The Spanish Netherlands were initially neutral in the Thirty Years War, which broke out across Europe in 1618, but France's intervention in 1635 meant Luxembourg and the other 16 provinces were inadvertently dragged into the fighting. This led to a period of hardship and famine, which only ended in 1659 when the Treaty of the Pyrenees ended hostilities between Spain and France – some 11 years after the Treaty of Westphalia had brought peace elsewhere.

In 1679, the French invaded. Louis XIV captured Luxembourg City in 1684, and set about strengthening its defences. But his aggressive actions caused alarm among France's neighbours. They formed the League of Augsburg and declared war, forcing France to give up the duchy, returning it in 1697 to the Spanish Habsburgs.

AUSTRIAN RULE After the War of the Spanish Succession in 1714, Luxembourg and Belgium again found themselves ruled by the Austrian Habsburgs, and in 1715 were integrated into the Austrian Netherlands. This led to unprecedented economic growth, and the ensuing 80-year period of peace is considered a golden age – many of the grand buildings in the capital today date from this time.

FRENCH INTERFERENCE – PART TWO Napoleon's invasion of Luxembourg in 1795 brought it under French influence for a second time, and heralded major and unpopular changes. The old duchy was divided among three French *départements*, state bureaucracy was introduced, secular ideals were imposed and the monasteries closed. The arrival of compulsory military service in 1798 was the final straw for the incensed local population. They revolted against the occupying forces in an action known as the Klëppelkrieg, but were brutally crushed.

A GRAND DUCHY Along with much of western Europe, Luxembourg's fate following the defeat of Napoleon was decided at the 1815 Congress of Vienna. It was elevated to a Grand Duchy and William I, Prince of Orange-Nassau and King of the Netherlands, became its first grand duke. Its status was complex however: it was legally independent, and technically only united with the Netherlands because it was the Dutch king's personal possession – its military importance meant Prussia refused to allow it to be fully integrated into the kingdom. Instead it was included under the German Confederation, which gave the Prussians a legal right to station a military garrison in the capital. This new Luxembourg was also greatly reduced in size, as all its territory east of the Our, Sûre and Moselle rivers was ceded directly to Prussia.

Despite nominal independence, the country suffered because William treated it as a colony, imposing heavy taxes on the population. This prompted most of them to join the Belgian revolt against Dutch rule in 1830. In October that year, the government of newly formed Belgium declared the Grand Duchy to be part of its land, although William still claimed it as his. The dispute remained unresolved for nine years, until the first Treaty of London reconfirmed the terms of the Congress of Vienna. However, the treaty also split the country in two, making the French-speaking western half part of Belgium (where it remains to this day as the province of Luxembourg), and leaving William only the eastern, Luxembourgish-speaking part.

The loss of so much territory caused severe economic problems. To solve this William negotiated a deal with Prussia, ratified by his son and successor William II in 1842. Luxembourg became part of the Prussian-led Zollverein (Customs Union), and soon reaped the benefits by transforming into an industrial powerhouse. The infrastructure improved immeasurably and the first railways were built.

THE LUXEMBOURG CRISIS In 1866, the German Confederation was dissolved, leaving Luxembourg a sovereign nation again. Napoleon III of France stepped in and offered to buy it from William III, the third grand duke. They even got as far as agreeing a sale price – five million florins – but William III reneged on the deal following pressure from Otto von Bismarck, the Prussian chancellor then emerging as central Europe's dominant figure. Events spiralled into a diplomatic stand-off known as the Luxembourg Crisis, and almost led to war between Prussia and France. A compromise deal was needed, and it came in 1867 in the form of a second Treaty of London. Prussia withdrew its garrison from the capital, the city's fortifications were dismantled, Luxembourg became a fully independent nation ruled by the House of Nassau, and was declared neutral 'in perpetuity'.

A BENELUX DIVORCE William III died in 1890 without a male heir, leaving his daughter Wilhelmina to succeed him. But Luxembourg's ascendancy laws prevented the new Dutch queen from becoming grand duchess, so the union with the Netherlands ended, and the Grand Duchy passed to Wilhelmina's cousin, Duke Adolphe of Nassau. Luxembourg was finally truly independent.

NEUTRAL? The German invasion at the outbreak of World War I made a mockery of Luxembourg's agreed neutrality. Nevertheless, Grand Duchess Marie-Adélaïde (Adolphe's granddaughter – the ascendancy laws having been rectified to allow female sovereigns) tolerated four years of illegal occupation, and in return was allowed to remain in office. This apparent act of collaboration was heavily criticised by the Allies, particularly France, and after the Armistice she was forced to abdicate in favour of her sister Charlotte.

When peace returned the Allies also urged Luxembourg to end its customs union with Germany. This meant the loss of its best customer for iron and steel, and its primary source of coal. The country tried to broker replacement ties with France, but as the French weren't interested it was forced to negotiate with Belgium. The Belgium–Luxembourg Economic Union (BLEU) was thus established in 1921, leading to customs and monetary union.

REMAINING WHAT WE ARE

Luxembourg's national motto *Mir wölle bleiwen wat mir sin*, translates as 'we want to remain what we are'. You may see it displayed in several places throughout the country, most prominently inscribed on a wall outside the Îlot Gastronomique restaurant complex in Luxembourg City. Considering the nation's traumatic history and the number of times it's changed hands and had other cultures imposed on it, this seems not an unreasonable plea to make.

I've asked many locals what it is that makes them feel most proud of being Luxembourgish. By far the best answer I've heard to date is, 'the fact that we still exist.'

I think that sums it up perfectly.

On 10 May 1940, the Nazis invaded. The defending army totalled just 425 soldiers, leaving the country no choice but to capitulate. This time the government refused to collaborate and, along with Grand Duchess Charlotte, it went into exile in London, via Portugal. The royal family were offered temporary asylum in the United States, but moved on to Canada in deference to America's (then) neutrality. Although she remained far away, Charlotte continued broadcasting messages of support via the BBC throughout the war.

Luxembourg remained technically 'under military occupation' until August 1942, but then was formally annexed by the Third Reich. French was banned and German made the only official language. Whether they liked it or not Luxembourgers became German citizens, and 13,000 were called up for military service – almost 3,000 would eventually die fighting against their will in the Wehrmacht.

Resistance was initially passive – such as a refusal to speak German. As French was forbidden, many people resorted to Luxembourgish, which led to a renaissance of the language. But measures to quell the opposition became increasingly brutal, and included forced labour, deportation to concentration camps, and execution. A general strike, called in September 1942 in response to the declaration of forced conscription, was violently suppressed. Twenty-one men were executed and hundreds more sent to concentration camps. Altogether, of Luxembourg's pre-war population of fewer than 300,000, an estimated 8,000 lost their lives during the hostilities.

MODERN LUXEMBOURG After World War II ended Luxembourg joined the new United Nations, and together with Belgium and the Netherlands formed the Benelux Economic Union. Realising its neutral status was barely worth the paper it was printed on, it also formally abandoned this, joining NATO in 1949.

The economy improved rapidly in the post-war years, particularly with the formation of the European Coal and Steel Community in 1952. Luxembourg was a founder member of that organisation's successor, the European Economic Community (later the EU) in 1957, and remains one of the strongest advocates of the European ideal. Several EU administrative offices are located here, and former prime minister Jacques Santer was head of the European Commission from 1995–99. In 2004, current prime minister Jean-Claude Juncker became semi-permanent president of the Eurogroup of finance ministers from the 17 countries that have to date adopted the euro. His enthusiasm for the common currency means he is known in some circles as 'Mr Euro'.

In the second half of the 20th century the country gained a reputation as a centre for private banking and financial services. This has kept the economy strong, and today it boasts the world's third-highest per-capita GDP.

The royal family also continues to be popular and held in high regard. The House of Nassau is supported by all major political parties and there's no abolitionist movement. The current grand duke, Henri (b.1955), became head of state in 2000 following the abdication of his father Jean (son of Charlotte) at the age of 79. Grand Duke Henri and his wife, Grand Duchess Maria Teresa, have five children.

That doesn't mean all is sweetness and light. With Luxembourg's economy dependent on banking, it was inevitably hit hard by the financial crisis of 2008. That same year the country also endured a constitutional schism. In February, the parliament passed a bill legalising euthanasia under strictly controlled conditions. In order to become law however, it needed the signature of Grand Duke Henri. But the staunchly Roman Catholic monarch's conscience would not allow him to sign.

In the end the situation was resolved when Henri backed another bill in December 2008, reducing his own role from constitutional to purely ceremonial. That allowed the controversial law to be passed after a second reading the following spring, without the involvement of the head of state.

GOVERNMENT AND POLITICS

The world's only Grand Duchy, Luxembourg is (like the UK) a constitutional monarchy. This means that in principle the grand duke has the power to hire and fire ministers, and to organise ministries and government departments as he sees fit, but in practice these tasks are left to the elected prime minister, usually the head of the largest political party in government.

Executive power is held by the grand duke, and a cabinet of 12 ministers led by the prime minister. Legislative power rests with the Chamber of Deputies, consisting of 60 members elected in a system of proportional representation by men and women aged over 18. Elections take place every five years – the next will be in 2014. Following the constitutional crisis of 2008, the signature of the head of state is no longer required for any parliament-approved bill to become law. Instead, it must be passed by a two-thirds majority in each of two readings in the Chamber of Deputies.

The last general election in 2009 saw a coalition government formed between the Christian Socialist Party (CSV) and the Socialist Worker's Party (LSAP), which between them won 39 of the 60 seats. Other parties representing the opposition in the Chamber of Deputies are the Democratic Party (DP), the Greens, the Alternative Democratic Reform Party (ADR), and the Left.

By and large the government and the people of Luxembourg are pro-European. In a 2005 referendum, 56% of voters approved the ratification of the European Constitution, even though the ill-fated document had already been scuppered by 'no' votes in France and the Netherlands.

Current prime minister Jean-Claude Juncker of the CSV came into office in 1995, when his predecessor Jacques Santer resigned to become President of the European Commission. Now in his fourth term, Juncker is currently the longest-serving premier in the EU, and a popular leader who's greatly respected as a statesman both at home and on the international stage. Despite this, a few critics are concerned by his authoritarian leadership style – one satirical magazine in Luxembourg once famously likened him to former African dictator and self-proclaimed 'Emperor' Bokassa.

In general however, Juncker runs an informal show. If you're passing his official residence – just off place Clairefontaine in Luxembourg City – at around lunchtime, he has been known to pop out and chat informally with tourists. Like many things in Luxembourg, politics is just that little bit more laid back and relaxed here.

ECONOMY

Luxembourg's per-capita GDP of over US$82,600 (2010 – CIA World Factbook) is the third-highest in the world after Qatar and Liechtenstein. It is however, a common misconception that the country's wealth originated from banking. Luxembourg actually became rich during the 19th century, when iron ore from national mines fuelled the steel industry, and a customs union with rapidly expanding Germany ensured a ready market for its output. At its peak it had the seventh-highest steel production in the world.

International finance only arrived in a big way in the 1960s and 1970s, when the Luxembourg government, seeking a way to shore up the economy during the decline of the European steel industry, introduced advantageous tax laws to lure foreign banks to relocate there. Despite this shift in emphasis, the presence of by far the world's largest steel company ArcelorMittal (formed when Luxembourg-based Arcelor merged with its giant rival Mittal Steel in 2006), shows that heavy industry is far from dead and buried. The last iron ore mine closed in the 1980s, but the steel industry continues to thrive – it accounts for around 29% of all national exports, and employs almost 4% of the workforce.

Banking has overtaken steel to become the largest sector of the economy. According to official figures compiled by KPMG for the report *Luxembourg Banks Insights 2011*, 147 banks (including PayPal) were registered in the Grand Duchy in 2010, the largest concentration in the EU. Of these, 109 are incorporated in Luxembourg, while the other 38 are branches of foreign banks. Together they employ 26,000 people, with thousands more working in related financial businesses. More than 9,000 holding companies are established here, and this is also the home of the European Investment Bank. The combined assets of all the banks is thought to exceed €750 billion (2010), markedly down from a peak of €900 billion just prior to the 2008 global financial crisis. The two biggest areas are the investment fund market (the second-largest in the world behind the United States), and personal banking. Some banks do operate in the domestic market, but the vast majority only deal internationally.

Why is Luxembourg a banking haven? It offers political stability (according to Transparency International, it's the world's 12th least corrupt nation), a location at the heart of Europe, well-educated multi-lingual staff, and it welcomes foreign investment. Of course, low corporate taxes and a tradition of banking secrecy haven't done any harm.

The 2008 downturn affected the sector badly, nearly bankrupting the two biggest private banks: Dexia (the country's oldest) and Fortis (formerly the Banque Générale du Luxembourg, or BGL). They were saved only as a result of concerted government intervention, making the state a major shareholder of both. Fortis reverted to its original name BGL and has since merged with another significant stakeholder, which is why it now trades in Luxembourg as BGL BNP Paribas.

Concern about secrecy laws haven't gone away either. In April 2009, Luxembourg's reputation as a tax haven led to the G20 adding it to a 'grey list' of countries with questionable banking arrangements. In order to get itself removed from this inventory of bad guys, in July of the same year the government adopted OECD standards on the international exchange of tax information.

Government policies have also promoted Luxembourg as a telecommunications hub. Radio-Television Luxembourg (RTL) is Europe's largest private broadcaster, while the government-backed Société Européenne des Satellites (SES) operates the Astra satellites and is the world's biggest satellite services company. Other high-tech multi-nationals with their European bases here include AOL, Skype, eBay and iTunes.

Another factor that has made Luxembourg an attractive investment opportunity is its healthy labour relations. Strikes are rare, and unemployment averages around 4%. Inflation was 2.1% in 2011, and also relatively stable.

But don't let this economic miracle fool you into thinking that everyone walks around with pockets crammed with gold. While there are plenty of wealthy people, property costs and rents in the capital are exorbitant, and international investment in the banking sector artificially distorts the official GDP figures, as does the fact that many people working in Luxembourg and contributing to the gross GDP live outside the country and don't count as inhabitants. People in lower-paid jobs can find it tough to make ends meet, and although there is a minimum wage (around €1,600 per month), for some it's barely enough to live on.

PEOPLE AND CULTURE

The population of Luxembourg is around 512,000 (2011 estimate), with the majority living in the south. Luxembourg City (94,000) is the country's sole significant urban area, while only three other towns – Esch-sur-Alzette, Dudelange and Differdange – have more than 10,000 inhabitants.

Migration and multi-culturalism have been at the core of the Luxembourg story for over 150 years. In the 19th century, and until as recently as World War I, emigration was the dominant force, as people were inspired by economic hardship at home to seek a better life overseas. Many headed for the United States, and around 70,000 settled in two states: Minnesota and Wisconsin. In fact, if you drive around 20km east from Green Bay, Wisconsin, you'll find yourself in the town of Luxemburg.

When industrialisation and the iron ore mines began bringing prosperity, foreign labourers were needed to bolster the workforce. Thousands of Polish, Italian and Portuguese families were the first to arrive, and integrated easily because they shared a Catholic faith with their hosts. The influence of the Italians and Portuguese in particular remains strong throughout the country, even though many of today's families are second-, third- or more-generation Luxembourgers.

Other waves followed, and immigration has risen again in recent decades with the booming economy. People of 150 different nationalities live and work here, comprising the highest proportion of foreign passport holders in the EU. Altogether, 40% of the population is non-Luxembourgish, and over 50% was born elsewhere. Despite this melting pot, race relations are very good, and if tensions do exist between the various communities they rarely become visible.

Another large section of Luxembourg's working population doesn't actually live in the country at all. Each weekday the capital more than doubles in size as 120,000 migrant workers from the neighbouring countries pour across the border, creating traffic jams on all arterial roads on their daily commute. In the evenings they go home again – and you wonder why the streets can feel quiet at night?

Like many countries in northern Europe, Luxembourg is an open and tolerant society in which pretty much anything goes – within reason. Crime rates are low, and as a result the atmosphere is generally relaxed. The Luxembourgish people are quietly spoken with a non-confrontational 'live and let live' attitude. They will accept almost any behaviour that doesn't impinge negatively on their own. In other words, 'respect' is a massively important byword here. Show the locals due respect and you will find them welcoming and friendly in return.

There is one thing to bear in mind if you want to avoid causing offence in Luxembourg. The royal family are widely revered and command a great deal of respect – most restaurants and shops have photographs of the grand duke and his family adorning their walls. The subject of abolishing the monarchy simply doesn't come up, and has never been an issue.

Food is another thing close to every local's heart – particularly at lunchtime, as you'll learn. When people return from visits abroad the first thing their friends and family usually ask is: 'What was the weather like?' But the second question is always: 'How was the food?' Perhaps the two most important hours in any local's day are those that fall between midday and two in the afternoon, and eating well is something that is considered a national obligation, not just a right. If you really want to make friends with a Luxembourger, take them out to lunch.

LANGUAGE

Luxembourg has three official languages – Luxembourgish (Lëtzebuergesch), German and French. Unlike neighbouring Belgium, which also has three official tongues, but few people who can actually speak more than one of them, people born and brought up here are nearly all trilingual. This can cause humungous confusion to the casual onlooker, as locals can and do switch randomly between idioms in mid conversation without blinking. The constitution gives all three equal status and upholds the right of Luxembourgers to use whichever they prefer. If you write to the government in any of the three, they are obliged to reply using the same one.

Luxembourgers tend to speak Luxembourgish among one another and in the home, and this is the language they are taught from birth and in preschool. German is introduced during the first year of primary school, and French a year later.

This early encouragement of multi-lingualism also helps many people become competent in other languages. Most have a good understanding of English, and those in regions like the Ardennes, where tourists from the Netherlands predominate, are often also able to speak a little Dutch. Thanks to the country's grab bag of cultures, Portuguese and Italian are widely understood as well.

Historically, French has always been the country's legislative language (largely because many laws are based on the Napoleonic code), although any language can be used for parliamentary debates. German was traditionally the language of the media, although most newspapers also contained random columns in French or Luxembourgish according to journalistic whims. More recently, government sponsorship has allowed several predominantly French titles to appear alongside the German papers. Luxembourgish remains a largely spoken language, and you won't see it written down that often, except on road signs, shop names, and at a more social level such as emails.

There are so many non-native Luxembourgers in Luxembourg City that the situation is slightly different there. Among the local population French is becoming the lingua franca, while in expat communities English is widely used. Since fewer people know Luxembourgish, even those that do sometimes use 'Bonjour' instead of 'Moïën' ('Hello') as a greeting to strangers, unless they're sure which languages they speak. You'll also hear more French spoken in shops and restaurants here than in other parts.

Luxembourgish is a distant cousin of German, but the two have been diverging for at least 1,000 years, and pure German speakers aren't able to understand it easily – unless they live in neighbouring regions of Germany where similar dialects are spoken. The language has become an important source of national pride and in recent years there's been an upsurge in interest. In 1984, it was awarded equal status as a national language, and a standard system of spelling was introduced for the first time. Many native speakers have also battened down the hatches as waves of immigrants and foreign workers, either unable or unwilling to learn it, threaten to turn French into the country's mother tongue.

To make the locals' day, try speaking a few words of Luxembourgish – *Appendix 1, Language,* page 221 contains a list of handy key words and phrases. You'll find a cheery '*Moiën*' to break the ice will usually guarantee a friendly response, even if you immediately switch to French or English – the simplest of efforts is always appreciated. Likewise, when leaving a restaurant or bar, etc, a quick '*Merci, äddi*' ('Thanks, bye') will leave a warm vibe wherever you go.

RELIGION

As you'll hear if expecting a lie in on Sundays, around 90% of the population was baptised as Roman Catholic – from early morning onwards, bells across the country chime out calling the faithful to Mass. Luxembourgers are more devout than those in most other northern European countries, although religion plays a far less obvious role in people's lives than it does in places further south, such as Italy or Spain.

Luxembourg is legally a secular state, but the government recognises and supports various denominations. This status was first afforded to the Roman Catholic Church in 1801, and the state also recognises Judaism, Greek and Russian Orthodox Christianity, and Protestantism as official religions.

Since 1979 it has been illegal to collect statistics on personal religious beliefs, so there are no precise figures. Nevertheless there are significant minority religions. Protestants form the largest of these, possibly 3% of the population. There are also thought to be around 6,000 Muslims, mostly recent arrivals from Bosnia-Herzegovina and Montenegro.

Religious studies and moral and social education are compulsory subjects in Luxembourg schools.

EDUCATION

Luxembourg is a highly educated country with literacy levels at, or close to, 100%. Early education can begin at the age of three, but isn't compulsory for all youngsters – it's largely designed to teach social skills, and to help the children of immigrants to integrate. Official preschool begins at the age of four, is taught entirely in Luxembourgish, and is compulsory for everyone. Primary education then lasts six years. Secondary education takes a further six or seven years, and is split into two streams: 'classic' secondary education focuses on core subjects needed to prepare pupils for university, while 'technical' secondary education offers vocational and practical training.

Until the University of Luxembourg was founded in 2003, most Luxembourgers had to travel abroad for their higher education, usually to France or Germany depending on linguistic preference. Students spend their first five years at university reading for a bachelor's degree, and often follow this with a master's.

2

Practical Information

WHEN TO VISIT

You can visit Luxembourg at any time, but bear in mind that the availability of services in some regions varies with the seasons. May, June and September are usually very pleasant months, as the weather is often at its most benign during late spring and late summer. July and August are also recommended, as they tend to be slightly warmer, if marginally wetter and busier.

In much of the Ardennes, mid-July to the end of August is considered 'high season', and it's only at this time of year that everything is fully open. Outside this period some museums or attractions may be closed, or have limited opening hours. Many smaller hotels and restaurants may shut during the winter months, limiting your eating and sleeping choices. Autumn, however, can be a wonderful time to travel in the north as the weather is not too bad, and the annual turning of the leaves provides a wonderful and free spectacle. Moreover, many country hotels have open fireplaces for warming your feet during colder evenings.

In Luxembourg City, restaurants, hotels and most attractions remain open all year. There's no specific high or low season for tourism, but one big advantage of arriving in July or August is that room rates, especially in top hotels, can drop dramatically as the business trade temporarily evaporates. Hotels tend to fill up around the National Day celebrations (22–23 June), so book ahead if you plan to be in town then. Winters are rarely severe, and indeed December can be a great time to visit the city as it allows you to check out the Christmas Market on the place d'Armes.

Several establishments listed in this guide have opening hours that become more limited 'out of season' (*hors saison*). With a few minor variations, this generally means the quieter tourist period running from mid-October to Easter.

HIGHLIGHTS

Tiny, but perfectly formed, Luxembourg has a little of everything to tempt visitors whatever they're looking for (unless that's golden sandy beaches): cities, castles, steam trains, mines, nature, wine, great food, and more castles. Here's just a small selection of what you'll find:

LUXEMBOURG CITY A small capital with a big heart. Not only is the old town on the UNESCO World Heritage List, it's also packed with great restaurants, and wedged between two spectacular gorges.

VIANDEN Guarded by one of Europe's most dazzling medieval castles, Vianden's cobbled streets could charm the socks off even the most jaded travellers. It certainly worked its magic on Victor Hugo: he loved it here.

ECHTERNACH The country's oldest town has a centre so delightful you want to take it home and introduce it to your parents.

LITTLE SWITZERLAND It may not look much like the Alps, but this enchanting landscape of sandstone micro-gorges, dense woodland and rushing streams has more than enough beauty of its own, and a network of walking trails for hikers of any ability.

CLERVAUX The castle in the heart of Clervaux is already pretty, but the fact that it also contains 'The Family of Man' – the most culturally important photographic exhibition in the world, bar none – should put it near the top of anyone's to-do list.

ESCH-SUR-SÛRE A tiny town to take the breath away. Esch's picturesque location, perched on a rock by the river, is what jigsaws were invented for.

FOND-DE-GRAS Ride on a century-old steam train and travel to Luxembourg's industrial past – a fun day out for children aged five to 105.

NATIONAL MINES MUSEUM Take a trip into the heart of an old iron ore mine in Rumelange, and learn about the lives of miners who once drove the economy and made the country what it is today.

STOLZEMBOURG COPPER MINE Another mine, but on a completely different scale. Time to get your hands dirty – you'll be glad of the rubber boots and the waterproofs they provide.

UPPER SÛRE LAKE Luxembourg's largest lake doesn't just provide half the country's drinking water, it's also a place for boating activities, and is surrounded by a network of hiking trails bringing you closer to the marvellous scenery of the Ardennes.

DIEKIRCH NATIONAL MUSEUM OF MILITARY HISTORY One of the country's largest and finest museums tells you everything you need to know about the Battle of the Ardennes.

BOURSCHEID CASTLE Sitting on a rocky outcrop in solitary splendour, this medieval ruin has arguably the finest view in the country.

THE MOSELLE Not one place, but a whole region of wine-growing excellence. Take a boat ride on the river, or relax and enjoy the view with a chilled glass of local produce. Or do both.

SUGGESTED ITINERARIES

ONE DAY Visit Luxembourg City, *or* try the Ardennes double-header of the 'Family of Man' in Clervaux in the morning, followed by Vianden and its castle in the afternoon and evening. Or visit Echternach in the morning, followed by an afternoon walk in Little Switzerland.

THREE DAYS Spend two days in Luxembourg City to enjoy it at a more relaxed pace. On the third day take in one of the two alternatives described previously.

ONE WEEK Spend three days in Luxembourg City to get a proper feel for the place. On the third day make an afternoon excursion to Fond-de-Gras (⊕ *Sun only*) or the National Mines Museum in Rumelange. Spend night four in Esch-sur-Sûre, with a side trip to the Upper Sûre Lake. On day five, head to Clervaux and the 'Family of Man' in the morning, then to Vianden in the afternoon and overnight. Move on to Echternach and Little Switzerland for day six. Spend the final day in the Moselle Valley sampling and stocking up on essential supplies, stopping overnight in Remich, and detouring to check out the delightful butterfly garden in Grevenmacher.

TWO WEEKS Two weeks will allow you to absorb the country at leisure. Spend a fourth night in Luxembourg City and trip out to both Fond-de-Gras *and* the National Mines Museum. On day five, head to Bourscheid, perhaps detouring via the Seven Castles Route (only recommended with your own transport). On day six, make the short hop to Esch-sur-Sûre. Stay in Esch on night seven, and take the day to explore the Upper Sûre Lake. On day eight take in Wiltz in the morning, before heading to Clervaux for the afternoon and evening. Spend nights nine and ten getting to know Vianden. On the tenth day, go on an afternoon excursion to the copper mine in Stolzembourg (⊕ *Sun only outside Jul/Aug*). On day 11, visit Echternach and stay for two nights. Spend day 12 exploring Beaufort Castle and walking in Little Switzerland. On day 13 visit the Museum of Military History in Diekirch, before moving to Larochette for the evening. Spend night 14 in Remich on the obligatory wine (and butterfly) tour of the Moselle.

One advantage of Luxembourg's size is that you could also base yourself in one or two of the above places, and make side trips to the rest.

THREE WEEKS You can pretty much cover everything in this book.

TOUR OPERATORS

Luxembourg's **tourist office** in London isn't exactly a tour operator, but it has an excellent website and is an invaluable source of helpful information and brochures before you travel.

Luxembourg National Tourist Office (UK)
Sicilian Hse, Sicilian Av, London WC1A 2QR; ✆020 7434 2800; e tourism@luxembourg.co.uk; www. luxembourg.co.uk; ⊕ 10.00–17.00 Mon–Fri

UK
Crusader Holidays ✆01255 425453; www. crusader-holidays.co.uk. 4-day coach trips to Luxembourg. Also Dec trips to Luxembourg City's Christmas Market.
Eddie Brown ✆01423 321246; travelcentre. eddiebrowntours.com. 5-day coach trips to the Grand Duchy.
Just You ✆0844 567 8844; www.justyou.co.uk. 5-day singles holidays by coach to the Grand Duchy.
Railbookers ✆020 3327 0800; www. railbookers.com. City breaks via Eurostar.

Russell Hafter Holidays ✆01946 861652; www.walking-in-luxembourg.co.uk. 7-day walking tours in the Luxembourg Ardennes, including accommodation & baggage transfer, with or without transport to/from UK.
Travelsphere ✆0870 240 2426; www. travelsphere.co.uk; ⊕ 09.00–20.00 Mon–Fri, 09.00–16.00 Sat, 10.00–15.00 Sun. 4- to 5-day coach excursions to Echternach & Vianden. Also Dec trips to Luxembourg City's Christmas Market.

Ireland
Arrow Tours ✆+353 41 983 1177; www. bookings.arrowtours.ie. Short breaks in Luxembourg City.
Breakaway City Breaks ✆+353 1 607 9900; e hols@breakaway.ie; www.breakaway.ie. Short breaks to Luxembourg City.

2

US

European Destinations ☎+1 877 267 2247; www.europeandestinations.com. Includes Luxembourg City on tours of Benelux.
Go Ahead Vacations ☎+1 800 590 1170; www.goaheadtours.com. Includes Luxembourg City on some whistle-stop tours of Europe.

Luxembourg

Voyages Emile Weber 15 rue d'Oetrange, L-5411 Canach; ☎+352 35 65 75 234; www.voyages-weber.lu. Will tailor tours to specific needs on request.

RED TAPE

Citizens of EU countries including the UK and Ireland can enter Luxembourg for visits of up to 90 days with a valid passport or national identity card. Nationals of the United States, Canada, Australia and New Zealand need a valid passport to enter for up to 90 days – passports must also be valid for three months after your intended departure date.

Citizens of most African states, including South Africa, and some Asian nations (but not Hong Kong, Japan, Malaysia, Singapore or South Korea, whose citizens require only a valid passport), need to obtain a **Schengen visa** before travelling. These entitle holders to enter one country and travel freely throughout the 15 countries of the Schengen zone (Austria, Belgium, Denmark, Finland, France, Germany, Greece, Iceland, Italy, Luxembourg, the Netherlands, Norway, Portugal, Spain and Sweden) for stays of up to 90 days within a six-month period.

If you intend only to visit Luxembourg, or Luxembourg is your main destination, you must apply for the visa at a Luxembourg embassy. Applicants living in countries where Luxembourg has no consular representation should apply at the Belgian embassy or consulate. Otherwise you must apply to the embassy of the country that is your main destination. If you intend to visit several countries, but don't have a main destination, apply at the embassy or consulate of the country that is your first point of entry. For more information, visit the website www.eurovisa.com.

Always carry a valid passport or ID card with you when travelling around Luxembourg, because you may be required to prove your identity. In practice, if you behave yourself this is highly unlikely to happen, but you never know.

EMBASSIES

ABROAD

UK (also for Ireland) 27 Wilton Cres, London SW1X 8SD; ☎020 7235 6961; ☼ londres.amb@mae.etat.lu; londres.mae.lu; ⊕ 09.00–17.00 Mon–Fri; visa section ⊕ 10.00–11.45 Mon–Fri
US (also for Canada) 2200 Massachusetts Av NW, Washington, DC 20008; ☎+1 202 265 4171; e luxembassy.was@mae.etat.lu; washington.mae.lu; ⊕ 08.30–17.00 Mon–Fri; visa section ⊕ 08.30–12.30 Mon–Fri
US (Consulate – New York) The Luxembourg Hse, 17 Beekman Pl, New York, NY 10022; ☎+1 212 888 6664; e newyork.cg@mae.etat.lu;

newyork-cg.mae.lu; ⊕ 09.00–17.00 Mon–Fri; passports & visas ⊕ 10.00–13.00 Mon–Fri
US (Consulate – San Francisco) 1 Sansome St – Suite 830, San Francisco, CA 94104; ☎+1 415 788 0816; e sanfrancisco.cg@mae.etat.lu; sanfrancisco.mae.lu; ⊕ 09.00–17.00 Mon–Fri; visas ⊕ 10.00–13.00 Mon–Fri
Australia (Consulate) 6 Damour Av, East Lindfield, NSW 2070; ☎+61 2 9880 8002; e luxembourgconsulate@bigpond.com; ⊕ 10.00–16.00 Mon–Fri

LUXEMBOURG **Australia**, **Canada**, **New Zealand** and **South Africa** have no diplomatic representation in Luxembourg. For consular issues contact the relevant embassies in Brussels, Belgium.

UK 5 bd Joseph II, L-1840 Luxembourg City; ☎ 22 98 64; ukinluxembourg.fco.gov.uk; ⊕ 09.30–12.00 Mon–Fri & 14.00–17.00 Mon–Fri by appointment, except UK & Luxembourg public holidays

US 22 bd Emmanuel Servais, L-2535 Luxembourg City; ☎ 46 01 23; luxembourg. usembassy.gov; ⊕ 08.30–17.30 Mon–Fri, except US & Luxembourg public holidays

GETTING THERE AND AWAY

With its handy location at the heart of the continent, reaching Luxembourg from the UK and other points in Europe is a straightforward matter. There is a wide range of transport options available that will get you to the Grand Duchy by plane, train or automobile in a matter of a few hours. From further afield, the lack of direct inter-continental air routes makes life slightly more complicated. Nevertheless, several European hub airports offer easy onward connections for far-flung arrivees.

BY AIR Luxembourg's Findel Airport (*www.lux-airport.lu*) has all the usual facilities, including a newsagent, bank, café/restaurant, and information desk. Arrivals are on level –1; check-in, departures and shops on level 0. Level 1 landside has a self-service restaurant with panoramic windows, and a more upmarket brasserie (⊕ *11.30–14.30 Mon–Fri*) that will refund two hours of parking. There are more bars and restaurants airside. The taxi rank is on the right as you exit; the bus stop (16 for downtown) to the left. The major car-rental firms have offices on level –1, on the left as you emerge through arrivals.

There are no long-haul passenger services directly into Luxembourg. Visitors from the US and elsewhere need to connect via one of the European hubs: London, Paris, Amsterdam and Frankfurt are arguably the most convenient. Another option is to fly into either Paris or Brussels and take the train from there.

There are also currently no plans to allow budget airlines access to Findel. The airport is geared towards business travellers and the prices of flights reflect this. A cheaper (but more time consuming) alternative is to fly via **Ryanair** (*www.ryanair. com*) into 'Frankfurt' Hahn Airport, and take the **flibco.com** bus (*www.flibco. com*) – prices start from €5 one-way; buy tickets online. The bus journey takes 1¾ hours and buses coincide with flight arrivals/departures. Services run via Trier in Germany. Some continue to Metz and Thionville in France.

Airlines The following airlines operate direct flights to Luxembourg airport from the UK. It is also possible to fly direct to Luxembourg from other European cities (see above), and additional operators include **Air France** (*www.airfrance.fr*), **Hahn Air** (*www.hahnair.com*), **KLM** (*www.klm.com*), **LOT** (*www.lot.com*), **Lufthansa** (*www.lufthansa.com*), **SAS** (*www.flysas.com*), **Swiss International** (*www.swiss. com*), and **TAP Portugal** (*www.flytap.com*).

British Airways www.britishairways.com. Flies from London Heathrow.
CityJet www.cityjet.com. Has flights from London City.

Luxair www.luxair.lu. Luxembourg's national carrier operates flights to Luxembourg from London City & Dublin, as well as numerous other short-haul European destinations.

BY BUS You can make the trip from London to Luxembourg on a Eurolines bus (*www.eurolines.com*), but this requires a change in Brussels and there's no convenient onward connection. I'd struggle to recommend such a buttock-numbing experience. One for masochists only.

BY CAR I'd love to be able to tell you to leave your car behind, but for now the most popular and practical way to reach Luxembourg as an independent traveller remains the car. Once you arrive it has the advantage of liberating you from sometimes-limited public transport connections, and fuel prices are relatively low (by northern European standards). On the downside, having your own vehicle may become a burden in Luxembourg City where parking is expensive. Driving times from the Channel ports should be around three hours, depending on traffic.

BY TRAIN To reach Luxembourg from the UK by rail you have two choices: one is to take the Eurostar from London to Brussels-Midi and change to an intercity; the other is to ride the Eurostar to Paris Nord, then take a TGV from Gare de l'Est. Both routes take the same time: 5½–six hours depending on connections. One slight disadvantage of travelling via Paris is that you need to transfer between main line stations to continue (an easy 500m walk, or five minutes by metro), whereas the transfer in Brussels is within the same building. Another point in favour of Brussels is you don't have to reserve on a specific onward train, whereas you do for the Paris TGV: if you miss your connection due to a delay you have to re-book.

A scenic but much slower way to arrive by train is via Liège in Belgium (disclaimer: Liège isn't scenic, but the countryside between there and Luxembourg City certainly is). Departures leave in either direction every two hours and the trip takes 2½ hours, passing through the central valleys of Luxembourg via Clervaux and Ettelbruck. International services also run to and from Trier in Germany.

HEALTH   with Dr Felicity Nicholson

There are no serious health issues to worry about, and no endemic diseases. As in other parts of northern Europe, influenza outbreaks can occur over the winter months. Elderly or vulnerable visitors arriving at this time may therefore wish to consider vaccination before travelling. Insect bites are perhaps the biggest risk in rural areas so it is worth taking an insect repellent. It is wise to be up to date with the standard UK vaccinations including diphtheria, tetanus and polio which comes as an all-in-one vaccination (Revaxis), which lasts for ten years.

If you do have an accident or fall ill, the level of healthcare is amongst the best in Europe (and by inference, the world). Residents of EU countries including the UK and Ireland should obtain a **European Health Insurance Card** (EHIC) before travelling, as this covers the costs of any standard medical treatment you may require. Everyone, including holders of an EHIC, should also take out travel insurance that includes medical costs, as the EHIC doesn't cover all eventualities, such as repatriation to your home country following an accident. This is available in the UK by calling ✆ 0845 606 2030, or online at www.ehic.org.uk.

EMERGENCY CARE In a medical emergency, dial ✆ 112 to call for an ambulance. The following are the major hospitals, both in Luxembourg City:

Centre Hospitalier de Luxembourg 4 rue Nicolas Ernest Barblé, L-1210 Luxembourg City; ✆ 44 11 11; www.chl.lu

Kirchberg Hospital 9 rue Edward Steichen, L-2540 Luxembourg City; ✆ 24 681; www.chk.lu

TRAVEL CLINICS AND HEALTH INFORMATION A full list of current travel clinic websites worldwide is available from the International Society of Travel Medicine on www.istm.org. For other journey preparation information, consult www.

tripprep.com. Information about various medications may be found on www.
emedicine.com.

DRINKING WATER Tap water throughout Luxembourg is of the highest standard
and perfectly safe to drink. In practice however, most locals prefer drinking bottled
mineral water simply, they say, because it tastes better.

SAFETY

Luxembourg is a very safe place in which to travel. The crime rate is low compared
with most places in Europe, and violence a rarity. You can wander round anywhere
without fear, although incidents aren't completely unknown so normal precautions
should be taken, particularly late at night. Lone women travellers seldom
experience problems, but again the usual common-sense rules apply. Attacks on
women do occur, but are rarer than in most western European countries. This is
also officially one of the world's least corrupt lands, so you shouldn't have to deal
with any 'requests for additional payments'.

Some streets in the immediate vicinity of Luxembourg City's main railway station
– including rue Joseph Junck, directly opposite the entrance – form the red light
district and have a local reputation for drug dealing and prostitution. In reality it's
pretty low key compared with larger cities elsewhere, which is just as well because
a lot of hotels are located there. Besides having to walk past a few seedy bars, you're
highly unlikely to be disturbed by anything other than loud music, and even here
single women are not in any significant danger. There are also a few down-and-outs
and winos in the same area, but they're generally harmless and far fewer in number
than you would find in other major capitals.

Of course, nowhere in the world is completely without risk, but a little due care
and attention to what's happening around you should keep you safe. If anything,
your biggest annoyance is likely to stem from the drunken behaviour of expat office
workers having one too many on their way home on a Friday evening. Antisocial
behaviour and assaults (usually alcohol-related) among the nation's youth are on
the rise – or so the national papers will have us believe – but again this is a minor
annoyance compared with most countries.

DISABLED TRAVELLERS

Luxembourg's efforts to make the country as convenient as possible to people
with mobility difficulties are as advanced as anywhere in the world, and disabled
visitors should not encounter any unexpected surprises. A large number of hotels,
restaurants and tourist sites are fully accessible to wheelchair users. There may,
however, be a few smaller hotels that do not have lifts, and some attractions – not
least of all castle ruins on rough ground – may be less easy to visit than others.

For specific queries and the most up-to-date information, contact **Info-
Handicap** (*65 av de la Gare, L-1611 Luxembourg City;* \ *+352 36 64 66; www.
info-handicap.lu*) Luxembourg's national association for the disabled. Their other
(French) website (*www.welcome.lu*) contains a searchable database of accessible
properties, including museums, hotels and restaurants.

The London-based office of the Luxembourg tourist office has a page on its
website dedicated to tips for disabled travellers (*www.luxembourg.co.uk/accessible.
html*). This page has links to several downloadable brochures produced by Info-
Handicap, containing listings of wheelchair-friendly transport, accommodation,

and other properties. The accommodation brochure has information in English, as well as French and German.

If in doubt, local tourist offices are also usually happy to assist with any special requests from disabled travellers. The LCTO website (*www.lcto.lu*) has ReadSpeaker voice synthesis, allowing visually impaired users to hear the contents of each page.

GETTING AROUND

By bus Local buses in Luxembourg City have low-level entrances for wheelchair-bound passengers. Note, however, that many regional and longer distance coaches do not.

By car If bringing your own car, Luxembourg City and all the main urban centres have many parking places reserved exclusively for disabled drivers. Parking elsewhere in the country is seldom a problem.

By taxi Most local taxis can take wheelchairs, but for any specific needs contact the Croix de Malte (*Maltese Cross;* \ *+352 691 38 91 94; lu.croixdemalte.org*). This organisation has a fleet of adapted taxis and ambulances, and staff are specifically trained in the use of wheelchair transportation.

By train Many mainline train stations are accessible to wheelchair users. If you require assistance at stations or aboard trains, call CFL (\ *+352 49 90 33 42;* e *st-tr-l2@cfl.lu*), Luxembourg national railway's helpline. Although help can be provided immediately, 24 hours' notice is always appreciated if you know your travel plans in advance. Luxembourg City's main railway station also has yellow telephones at various locations for requesting instant help.

GAY AND LESBIAN TRAVELLERS

Luxembourg's tolerance of homosexuality is reflected in the fact it has been legal here since 1792. It's an offence, punishable with a fine or prison sentence, to incite or indulge in acts of hatred, discrimination or violence based on sexual orientation. Gay and lesbian visitors are by and large treated with respect and accorded the same welcome as anyone else. The age of consent for everyone, gay or straight, is 16.

Owing to the country's low population as a whole, the gay scene is quite limited in scope. The website of the **Rosa Lëtzebuerg Gay and Lesbian Association** (*60 rue des Romains, L-2444 Luxembourg City;* \ *26 19 00 18; www.gay.lu*) has information about upcoming events in the Grand Duchy, and lists the addresses of gay (and gay-friendly) bars and restaurants. It's in French only, but easy to navigate.

SENIOR CITIZENS

Luxembourg's high-quality infrastructure and modern facilities make it easy to get around and an attractive destination for senior citizens. Discounts for travel and entry to many attractions are offered to people over 60 or 65 (the qualifying age varies).

FAMILIES

Travelling with younger children presents no problems in Luxembourg. The one complaint levelled by teenagers is that there are no large adrenalin-rush attractions along the lines of Disneyland to keep them occupied. Pre-teens however, will love the smaller-scale fun to be had at the Parc Merveilleux (see *Chapter 5, The Industrial South*, page 105). Children receive discounted (or free) entry to most sights and attractions, and reduced fares on public transport. Many hotels can provide additional beds or baby beds in rooms on request.

The Family Luxembourg Card (see box below) is a worthwhile – nay, vital – investment if travelling as a family and could save you a second mortgage in travel and entry fees.

STUDENTS AND YOUNG TRAVELLERS

The excellent chain of youth hostels across Luxembourg is an affordable sleeping and eating option for anyone, no matter what their budget.

Younger visitors have in the past bemoaned the country's lack of exciting nightlife, but this is changing now the University of Luxembourg has opened, and more university-age Luxembourgers are staying at home to study instead of moving abroad. The appearance of a home-grown student population has resulted in an upsurge of trendy clubs and bars aimed at a young crowd. Try Rives de Clausen in the lower town, or rue de Hollerich, near Luxembourg City railway station, for a few good choices. The situation is improving year by year.

WHAT TO TAKE

The fickle nature of northern Europe's weather means you should be prepared for rain no matter what the season – bring a waterproof jacket or umbrella. Except on the balmiest of summer nights, evenings can feel cool, so consider bringing a minimum of a fleece or pullover as extra protection.

For those who intend to go hiking in the hills, don't forget to pack walking boots and appropriate all-weather clothing. Remember that in general the north – which

THE LUXEMBOURG CARD

Anyone planning to visit more than one or two sights in Luxembourg should make this little baby their essential first purchase, either on arrival or before travelling. For a few euros per day this credit card-sized magic wand will get you unlimited free travel on all public transport throughout the country (second class on trains), plus free entry to most of the country's museums and attractions (and discounted entry to virtually all the others).

The cards are available from tourist offices throughout Luxembourg, from many hotels and some museums, and can be ordered in advance from the national tourist office's website (*www.visitluxembourg.lu*). One-person cards cost €10/17/24 for one/two/three days. Family cards (two to five people, regardless of age) cost €20/34/48 for one/two/three days. Seniors aged 60 and over receive 10% off the price of a one-person card.

When you buy the card you'll be given a booklet detailing all the available discounts. They are valid for the calendar year stated on the front, but you must also write the specific day and month on which you wish to use them in the space provided – note that two- and three-day cards don't have to be used on consecutive days.

If you do a lot of sightseeing it could save you a fortune. And no, I'm not on a commission for saying that.

is where the best trails are located – is wetter and cooler than the south. Additional safeguards such as carrying a pair of waterproof trousers in your daypack could help to avoid a lot of misery on longer treks. A compass could also simplify direction finding on some trails, although all the major routes are well signposted.

Horseflies are an occasional nuisance in rural areas – if you are planning to do a lot of hiking you may want to invest in insect repellent. Mosquitoes on the other hand are not that common, even in summer.

If you do forget something, there's nothing you might need that you can't find in Luxembourg City's shops.

Mains electricity is 230V AC, 50Hz. Standard northern European two-pin plugs are used – if you bring equipment such as phone chargers from the UK, the US or Australia you'll need an adaptor.

MONEY AND BUDGETING

MONEY The national currency in Luxembourg is the **euro**, which is also legal tender in 16 other countries across Europe. One euro consists of 100 cents. Euro coins come in one, two, five, ten, 20 and 50 cents denominations, and also as one and two euros. Notes come as five, ten, 20, 50, 100, 200 and 500 euros. Higher-value notes (sometimes 100 euros, but particularly the 200 and 500 versions) are rarely seen and many establishments won't accept them because of concerns about counterfeiting. Try to use notes with a maximum value of 50 euros if you can. Many shops in tourist areas may also be happy to accept your pounds or US dollars, but the exchange rates they offer will favour them and not you, and buying goods this way isn't recommended.

Major **credit cards** (a minimum of Visa and MasterCard, and usually also Diners Club and American Express) are almost universally accepted, except in some smaller bars and shops. Payment is always made electronically, using a four-digit PIN code for security – make sure you know what yours is.

Travellers' cheques have become an endangered species in recent years, and are no longer as widely accepted as they once were. You may find them more of a burden than an asset.

Since banking is the national sport, you'll rarely be far from a branch. Opening hours vary, but are typically 09.00 to 16.30 Monday to Friday. Those in smaller towns may close for an hour at lunchtime. Most have **ATM**s outside, available 24/7. They usually work on the Maestro and Cirrus system, and will accept Visa, MasterCard, and passes from many foreign banks. Even though you may pay a small charge for this service, it often works out as the most economical way of getting cash.

BUDGETING How much your visit will cost depends very much on the levels of comfort you require. If you camp, cook for yourself, steer clear of bars, and make

COSTS OF EVERYDAY ITEMS	
Bottled water (1l) from a shop	€0.75
Bottled water (50cl) from a café or bar	€2.50–3.50
Beer in bar or café	€2–3.50
Glass of wine in bar or café	€1.80–3.50
Loaf of bread from a supermarket	€1.50–2
Pizza or pasta dish in restaurant	€8–12
A litre of unleaded petrol	€1.28

use of the Luxembourg Card to cover transport and museums, you can get by quite easily on less than €30 per person per day. But if you need pampering, travel by taxi, and demand the finest wines and foods, there is almost no limit to what you could spend. To eat out well and still save money, have your main meal at lunchtime; on weekdays most restaurants offer a very reasonable *plat du jour* or *menu du jour* (dish or menu of the day).

Drinks in bars, and other similar items rise in price the closer you get to the centre of Luxembourg City and the place d'Armes, where you can expect to pay around 50% more than you would in the countryside. Even there, however, wine is still quite cheap compared with elsewhere in northern Europe.

The estimations in the three higher budget ranges below assume two people sharing a hotel room – add a little more for a single room. Some hotels offer slight discounts for long stays (three or more days) and at weekends – if in doubt, ask.

Luxury: €250+ per person per day Stay in the country's very top hotels, take that taxi to the Michelin-starred restaurant, and even choose something from the wine list once you've got there. There's still no excuse to leave the Luxembourg Card behind when visiting museums however.

Expensive: €140–250 per person per day With this much to spend you can move into a good four-star hotel in Luxembourg City, or just about any hotel you like elsewhere. You will also be able to pick from almost any restaurant menu with impunity.

Mid range: €65–140 per person per day Around €35–40 per person will get you a cheap double room in Luxembourg City, or something very comfortable elsewhere. Adding in simple dining and a Luxembourg Card gets you into the lower reaches of mid-range. Moving into a more comfortable Luxembourg City hotel will push the daily bill up, as will splashing out a little more on the evening meal and perhaps rounding off the evening in a bar.

Shoestring: €30–65 per person per day At the lower end of this range you'll need to sleep in a tent (up to €10), buy and cook your own food (say €10), use a Luxembourg Card (€8), and make your own entertainment in the evenings. Serious ascetics could get by on slightly less. Staying in a youth hostel (€17–20), eating simple meals in cafés or brasseries (€10 each), and enjoying the occasional glass of wine or beer (€2.50 each) will push you towards the upper end of this bracket.

TIPPING Service and taxes are included in the total on restaurant bills, and adding a fixed percentage extra is far less widespread than it is in the UK and (especially) North America. Instead, the usual practice is to round up the bill to the nearest convenient amount. If paying by credit card, pay the exact amount and leave a few euros in coins on the table to show your appreciation.

Tipping elsewhere such as in taxis isn't common practice, but they're unlikely to refuse you if you offer.

GETTING AROUND

BY BIKE Cycling has historically been the one sport at which Luxembourg competes on equal terms with the world's best. François Faber (in 1909) was the first non-Frenchman to win the Tour de France, and Nicolas Frantz (1927 and 1928) and Charly Gaul (1958) have also won the coveted race. Half a century later, the country's two latest heroes, brothers Fränk and Andy Schleck, could soon emulate these past legends, and their exploits have sparked a new wave of interest in cycling across the country (see box, page 28). It isn't surprising then that there's an extensive network of cycling and mountain-biking routes for you to choose from if you want to get around under pedal power. Be warned, however, that if you get tired you aren't allowed to take your bike on the bus. Tourist offices sell a map (*Luxembourg by Cycle*, €4.90) showing every dedicated cycle path in the country.

BY BUS AND TRAIN Getting around by public transport is very cheap, and simple in all but the remotest areas – see the specific chapters for travel to and between individual places. On quieter routes the regularity of service tails off dramatically on Sundays – bear this in mind if you need to do much travelling then. For short journeys buy a **'short duration' ticket** (*billet 'courte durée'*), valid for two hours. These can be bought for €1.50 each, or in packs of ten (*carnets à dix billets*) for €12. If you travel a lot, go for the **'long duration' ticket** (*billet 'longue durée'*) for €4 (€16 for five), valid all day and until 08.00 the following morning. On Saturday and Sunday a **'Weekend' ticket** (€6) is good for up to five people travelling together, and valid on the day of issue until 03.00 the following morning. All tickets can be used on any bus or train, including transfers. Travel on all buses and trains (second class) is free with a Luxembourg Card.

If you plan to make lots of trips, for convenience you may wish to consider an **e-Go** card, not dissimilar to London's Oyster Card. This credit card-sized ticket is available free from bus and train stations, and can then be loaded with up to six at a time of any *one* of the ticket types listed above (for example, six *carnets à dix billets* would entitle you to make 60 short journeys), and topped up when needed. However, you can't mix-and-match ticket types on one card, and there's no cost saving involved, so its appeal is somewhat limited for short-term visitors.

For specific times of connections through the country, visit the national transport website (*www.mobiliteit.lu* or *www.autobus.lu*).

Night Rider This is effectively a nationwide late-night taxi network, and vehicles can take a maximum of four passengers. It operates between 18.00 and 05.00 Friday and Saturday and because of its popularity and the limited number of vehicles, it's best to book in advance by calling ✆ 8002 1010 (⊕ *08.00–20.00 Mon–Thu, 08.00–05.00 Fri–Sat*), or by going online (*www.nightrider.lu*). If booked between Monday and Thursday, journeys cost €12 per person one-way and €18 per person return for the first three passengers – the fourth passenger rides for free. If booked on Friday or Saturday, rates rise by one-third to €16/24 per person single/return.

BY CAR Driving distances are never that great in Luxembourg, the roads are in excellent condition, and with your own vehicle you can see a lot in a little time. The winding roads and sparse traffic in the north are also particularly popular among motorcycling enthusiasts.

Having said that, the fact that international borders are so close at all times seems to exert an unusual subconscious force on the brain. Whenever I come here with a car for more than a day or two my sense of scale alters perceptibly. I look upon simple 20km journeys – something I might walk in an afternoon back home – and find myself thinking: that's such a *long* way. It may get to you too.

Speed limits are 50km/h in urban areas, 90km/h on single-carriageway country roads (rising to 110km/h on short stretches with an overtaking lane), and 130km/h on motorways (dropping to 110km/h in the rain). As you enter almost any built-up area a helpful radar-controlled sign may light up and tell you exactly how fast you're travelling.

Fuel is around 20% cheaper than in neighbouring countries (which is why queues build up around border petrol stations), but more expensive than North America.

All major car-rental companies have offices in Luxembourg City and at Findel Airport. Some are also represented in Esch-sur-Alzette, but are a rare find elsewhere. Expect to pay €35–40 per day and up, depending on size of car and length of hire.

If visiting during the colder months, note that Luxembourg has adopted similar safety legislation to that already in force in Germany. As of October 2012, cars must be fitted with winter tyres during periods of snow, slush, ice or frost. Failure to comply risks a fine of €49.

ON FOOT A great way to get a feel for the countryside is to walk through it. There are hundreds of hiking routes available, ranging from a couple of kilometres to several hundred. If you hit the trails during the week, then even in summer you may find yourself alone with the skylarks. In all regions, short walks are waymarked with letters; medium-length routes with numbers; and long national paths with symbols. Tourist offices throughout the country carry walking maps for their region.

CFL, the national railway company, produces a book of 40 station-to-station walks called *Luxembourg Train and Tour* (available from bookshops in Luxembourg City). These are signposted with unique 'CFL' waymarkers, generally follow a course of intertwining trails for up to 25km, and are designed so that you finish at a station and can easily return to your starting point by train. The book includes detailed maps and easy-to-follow directions in English.

There's such a maze of walking paths that the biggest problem you may face could be trying to pick out your marker from among a host of other signs. At busy trail junctions the posts containing the route signifiers get crowded, and include letters, numbers, and the odd blue lozenge, red triangle or green squiggle. All in all however, if you know what you're looking for you won't go far wrong.

One of the joys of the rumpled topography is that you don't need to head very far out of almost any town to feel you're in the heart of the countryside. And you can walk past some towns almost without realising they're there.

For more information on outdoors activities, including both hiking and biking, see www.hiking-in-luxembourg.co.uk.

ACCOMMODATION

There's accommodation to suit every pocket in Luxembourg, from simple campsites, youth hostels, holiday apartments and *gîtes*, to the most luxurious of five-star hotels. The one thing that's relatively unknown here is the bed and breakfast concept as you might understand it: a family house with two or three rooms let out to overnight guests. There are a few, but most places that advertise bed and breakfast accommodation are actually small hotels. The national tourist office produces separate brochures containing listings of campsites, hotels (and some restaurants) and holiday apartments. These are available from tourist offices or can be ordered online at www.visitluxembourg.lu.

HOTELS Unless otherwise stated, assume the rates listed in these pages include breakfast, that rooms are equipped with a minimum of bed, telephone and colour television, and that they have en-suite bathrooms.

Many hotels in Luxembourg City are owned by international chains, and you pretty much know what level of service to expect before you walk in. The city's role as an international banking centre means business guests usually outnumber tourists during the week, keeping occupancy levels up and prices high. On the flip side rates often drop at weekends (sometimes dramatically) and in low season, which in Luxembourg's business community means July and August.

Most hotels outside the capital are privately owned, and some have been family run for generations. They're more geared up for tourists, and as competition for customers is fiercer than in the city, they offer better value for money. Discounts are sometimes offered for stays of three or more days.

Hotels are rated from one to five stars under the Benelux rating system. One-star hotels seem to exist in name only – I have yet to find one here. Two stars ensures a basic but clean room with few frills beyond those mentioned above. A simple breakfast is usually included, but little else. Move up a notch to three stars and rooms improve considerably. Four stars may only up the comfort ante very slightly on this, but will add peripheral extras such as room service. Some four-star places are very luxurious indeed, and may only miss out on a fifth star on a technicality such as lack of valet parking. Five stars is no-holds-barred luxury, with every service imaginable on tap.

A refreshing number of Luxembourg's hotels have taken the environmental message to heart. You'll often encounter suggestions not to launder towels every day and reminders to turn off lights. And some conscientious front-runners have even installed rainwater collection systems for flushing the toilets.

GÎTES AND SELF-CATERING APARTMENTS For economic stays of a week or more, consider renting a holiday apartment. These usually sleep two to eight people and have kitchens for self-catering. Often they are former farmhouses, while some are found in unusual locations such as the medieval watchtowers in Echternach's city wall (see *Chapter 7, The Müllerthal*, page 156). Get hold of the national tourist office's free brochure for a full list.

THE 'SCHLECK EFFECT'

When it comes to Luxembourg sport, only two names are currently worth mentioning. The two Schleck brothers, Fränk and Andy, have risen to the top of world cycling and grab all the national headlines. Andy has been runner-up in the Tour de France three years in a row, from 2009 to 2011, and in 2011 his elder sibling joined him on the podium in third place. Earlier that same year the Luxembourg-based Team Leopard Trek (which merged with rivals Team RadioShack in 2012, becoming the awkwardly named RadioShack-Nissan-Trek Professional Cycling Team) was established to develop and get the most from their potential, and it seems likely that one or other – probably Andy – will win the coveted yellow jersey outright very soon. Expect them both to feature prominently for several years to come.

The brothers' success is widely appreciated by other Luxembourgers, and has generated the so-called 'Schleck effect', as more and more people across the country are dusting off their old bikes, or buying new ones, and getting into the saddle hoping to emulate their heroes.

HOSTELS For those on a budget Luxembourg has a superb system of youth hostels (*www.youthhostels.lu*), which between them provide 1,100 beds. Non-YHA members are welcome, but must buy a guest card costing €3 per day. Many of the ten countrywide locations are either new or recently refurbished, and the facilities in all are excellent. Prices always include breakfast and bedding, meaning you don't need to bring sheets or sleeping bags. In some establishments, two people can rent out smaller dorms as doubles for a slight premium. The hostels also have cafeterias offering daily menus, which can be a real bargain. Advance booking can be done online, and is recommended as they do fill up.

CAMPING There are good clean campsites all over the country, offering great value for money. Sometimes they may be large-scale sites geared up to receive caravans, with electrical hook-ups, supermarkets, tennis courts and swimming pools on site. Nonetheless many are also in idyllic riverside or wooded spots, and may have a quiet corner where individual campers can pitch their tents away from the mêlée. Fees are usually charged per person and per pitch. By and large you avoid the latter if all you have is a small tent.

✖ EATING AND DRINKING

For those with deep pockets, the good news is that Luxembourg has more Michelin-starred restaurants per head than anywhere else in the world, with truly outstanding cuisine and wine lists to die for. But you don't need to break the bank in order to eat very well anywhere. Most places, even the top ones, offer a special *menu du jour* at lunchtime on weekdays, which may include up to three courses sold at a fraction of the à la carte prices.

The biggest influences in Luxembourg restaurant food tend to come from the south, and many dishes are French-inspired. Despite the proximity to Germany you won't find sausage very often (apart from at festivals), although a central European influence is visible in the regular appearance of veal in tourist areas – particularly in the triumvirate form of *veal cordon bleu* (stuffed with ham and cheese, and fried in breadcrumbs), *veal escalope* with cream and mushrooms, and *escalope viennoise*, also known as *wienerschnitzel*. These latter dishes pander to tourist rather than local demands however, so can't really be classed as 'typically Luxembourgish'.

One thing Luxembourg shares with its neighbour Belgium is that while food is prepared with French finesse, it's often also served in huge portions to suit Teutonic appetites. Brace yourself: one thing you're unlikely to do here is go hungry.

Luxembourg City's restaurants cover every aspect of world cuisine, but countryside eating options are sometimes more limited. Smaller villages may only have a brasserie serving a combination of French/Luxembourgish/tourist fare, and perhaps a bar for snack foods such as *croque monsieur* (ham and cheese toastie) and burgers. Most towns also have pizzerias, and maybe a Chinese outlet with a couple of Japanese or Thai choices.

Vegetarians face a tougher time. In many traditional restaurants, meat-free is still an alien concept – you might have to develop a taste for warm goat's cheese salad, or choose somewhere with a pasta and pizza menu. The availability of meatless dishes usually improves the further upmarket you go. There are several dedicated vegetarian restaurants in Luxembourg City.

The range of salads on restaurant menus, available either as starters or mains, is regularly excellent, although even most of these contain meat. And an example of the Italian influence on the country is that even in non-Italian restaurants, *carpaccio* has become a standard item – some places offer half-a-dozen variations involving different meats and fish.

The vast majority of menus are written in French, some with a German translation underneath. In tourist areas an English version is also usually available.

In many smaller towns, restaurants are also hotels and vice versa. Unless you've booked a special 'gastronomic arrangement' including meals, you're under no obligation to eat in the same place as you stay.

Smoking in restaurants is banned, but at the time of writing you can still smoke on terraces, and in bars where no food is served. However, a blanket indoor ban will come into effect sometime in 2012.

LUXEMBOURG SPECIALITIES The national dish is *judd mat gaardebounen* (the 'j' is pronounced like the 's' in measure): smoked neck of pork, served on a bed of stewed broad beans and accompanied with potatoes sautéed in bacon. It's hearty, tasty, and the portion sizes often verge on the titanic. Another favourite is *bouchée à la reine,* also called *paschtéitchen* – chicken and mushrooms in a puff-pastry case. A large *vol-au-vent* in other words.

Many eateries pride themselves on their use of fresh local ingredients. Ardennes ham (*jambon d'Ardennes*) features regularly, particularly in the north. Usually this is served cold, with a side order of chips and a simple green salad. In the autumn, hunting season game from the Ardennes is very popular, including wild boar (*sanglier*) and venison (*chevreuil*).

Grilled sausages appear on restaurant menus in the form of the slender *weinzossis,* served with mashed potatoes and a mustard cream sauce – the Luxembourg equivalent of bangers 'n' mash. Chunkier *mettwurst* and *grillwurst* are sold from outdoor stalls during festivals and other events. You may encounter the latter billed as *Luxemburger grillwurst, Lëtzeburger grillwurscht, Luxringer,* and other regional alternatives such as *Ouringer* (in Vianden), but all are essentially the same thing: variations on the classic Germanic *bratwurst.*

As Luxembourg is landlocked, freshwater fish have had a greater impact on national cuisine than seafood. Trout (*truite*) is seen everywhere, cooked in a variety of ways, often *au Riesling,* with a wine/cream sauce. Near the Moselle, two regional specialities to look out for are pike (*brochet*) in Riesling sauce, and *friture de la Moselle*: a plate of Moselle river fish of various descriptions and sizes, deep-fried. Eat the latter with your fingers: with larger specimens, chew the flesh off the bone; smaller ones are designed to go down whole in the same way as whitebait.

Not a Luxembourg original, but one increasingly available dish is *tarte flambée* (also called *flames,* or

RESTAURANT PRICE CODES	
Average price of main meal:	
€€€€€	€30+
€€€€	€22–30
€€€	€15–22
€€	€8–15
€	< €8

Flammkuchen). This Alsace speciality is effectively pizza, with cream replacing tomato as the topping base. They are as filling as they sound.

DRINKS When ordering in a bar, the bill usually arrives with the drink and is left on the table for you to pay at your convenience – only in busier establishments might you be asked to pay immediately. On Friday and Saturday nights some more popular places offer what's known as *nuit blanche*, which loosely translates as 'all-nighter'. Basically, if the customers are buying and the landlord is happy, there's no closing time, although officially it's 03.00.

Water You can drink the tap water, but many locals claim not to like the taste (personally I find nothing at all wrong with it) and stick to the bottled stuff. In bars and restaurants, mineral water is ordered by brand name. Sparkling water comes mainly in the form of the local Rosport Classic or Rosport Blue (it's actually written in English on the label, but usually ordered in French as Rosport '*bleu*'). The latter is treated to remove harsher mineral tastes and partially de-carbonated to make the bubbles softer; and it is by far the most popular mineral water even though it costs a little more than other brands. German Gerolsteiner and Italian San Pellegrino are also widely available. Locally sourced Viva and French Vittel are the most common brands of still water.

Wine Luxembourg's home-produced Moselle wines are frequently excellent – refer to *Chapter 6* for more extensive and detailed eulogising on this subject – and several of the larger wineries have *caves* (literally cellars) that can be visited on a tour for a small fee, usually including a tasting. Almost every café and restaurant stocks at least a small selection alongside its imported (predominantly French) choices. The only exceptions tend to be upmarket Italian restaurants, which may stock only wines from that country.

Local wines sold by the glass in traditional bars and cafés cost €1.80–3.50 depending on grape variety (Elbling and Rivaner are cheaper, Riesling more expensive) and location. The vessel in question is often the distinctive 20cl engraved bowl with a green stem that's common in the nearby German Mosel. I've also come across a curious unwritten rule that appears to stipulate that each and every one of these must have a small chip out of its base (restaurant glasses and those in more upmarket bars are always posher and usually arrive intact).

Beer Surprisingly perhaps, given that Luxembourg is wedged between Belgium and Germany – two of Europe's greatest brewing nations – their influence hasn't really rubbed off. Beers are widely produced and drunk, but the vast majority are lager-style pilsners created for the mass market and without much attention paid to flavour. If you just ask for a beer in a bar, this is what you'll end up with – the strength of most offerings hovers in the 5% abv region. Ordering a *mini* will get you a 25cl glass of draught beer; a *humpen* is a 33cl glass; and a *grande bière* 50cl.

The two biggest breweries are Bofferding and Brasserie de Luxembourg (Mousel-Diekirch), the latter being owned by corporate multi-national AB InBev. Besides their flagship brews, Diekirch also produces a medium-strength amber ale called Grand Cru (5.5%), which is slightly sweet. Bofferding Pils (5%) is a simple lager, not too bitter. Their Battin Gambrinus (5%) is a full-bodied malty pils, while Battin Extra (6.6%) is a stronger, sweeter version of the same.

Less widespread than its larger rivals, the Simon brewery in Wiltz (founded in 1824) is worth seeking out and supporting because it's the last full-sized independent family-run brewery in the country. They produce several different brews: Simon

Dinkel is an unfiltered beer made from rare spelt grain; Simon Noël is a strong brown ale, only available (as the name implies) around the festive season. They have also resurrected two brands once made by another long-defunct brewery, Okult No1 Blanche (5.4%), which is an organic wheat beer flavoured with orange peel and coriander; and Okult 'Quaffit' Stout (5%), also organic with hints of coffee, and in my book Luxembourg's best beer – you can indeed Quaffit.

Simon also owns the Ourdaller microbrewery in Heinerscheid (see page 216), which produces Wäissen Ourdaller (4.6%), a honeyed unfiltered wheat beer with hints of citrus; Wellen Ourdaller (6.5%), an unfiltered amber beer; and Hengeschter (4.5%), their unfiltered pils, which is not as gassy as many lagers.

Brasserie Béierhaascht is a microbrewery based in Bascharage. You can visit and stay overnight there (see *Chapter 4, Around Luxembourg City*, page 86). Their Hell (5.1%) and Donkel (6.3%) are modelled on German-style light and dark lagers. The Ambrée (5.2%) is a maltier amber beer, while Weess Béier (5.3%) is a refreshing wheat brew. There's also a seasonal dark Winterbier (5.0%).

Elsewhere, the Clausel brewery occupies part of the former Mousel brewery in Luxembourg City, and their output (primarily pils) is served in the neighbouring bars of Rives de Clausen (see page 65). Den Heischter from Heiderscheid in the Upper Sûre Natural Park produces Blanche (5.2%), a blonde wheat beer, and De Grënner (6.5%), a palatable brown wheat beer. Rarest of all is Spelzbéier (5%), a spelt beer produced in tiny quantities in the Upper Sûre Park.

Most other beers you'll encounter (apart from in 'English/Irish' pubs) will be Belgian or German, which is no bad thing. Of the former, Duvel and Orval are widely available and Bitburger is the most widespread German brand. AB InBev beers (in addition to Diekirch and Mousel, that means Leffe, Stella Artois, Hoegaarden and others) are widely seen, but a triumph of marketing over taste, and usually avoided by connoisseurs.

Other drinks Luxembourg produces numerous liqueurs and *eaux de vies*. The latter often contain 45–50% alcohol and may strip the lining from your throat as you swallow, but they go down rather well as *digestifs* with coffee after a meal. Popular varieties include *quetsch*, *vielle prune* and *mirabelle* (all distilled from plums), *framboise* (raspberry), *Poire William* (pear) and *kirsch* (cherry). *Marc de Gewürztraminer* is derived from the residues of wine grapes, *spelzdrëpp* is a white spirit made from spelt, and *hunnigdrëpp* is a sweetish honey liqueur. Elsewhere, Beaufort Castle produces a very fine blackcurrant liqueur known as *cassero*, a stronger version of it fortified with *kirsch*, and *framboise des bois*, a lovely raspberry liqueur; the National Mines Museum in Rumelange sells an apple-based liqueur called *galeriewasser* (don't take them too seriously if they claim it was a traditional miner's tipple); and Vianden is partial to its sweet walnut liqueurs (*nësslikör*) and walnut schnapps (*nëssdrëpp*), both sold in quantity during the October nut festival (see page 181).

PUBLIC HOLIDAYS AND FESTIVALS

PUBLIC HOLIDAYS

1 January	New Year's Day
Carnival	late February or early March – pre-Lent festivities in which people take the opportunity to have a party and let their hair down before the impending fast. In practice however, not many people actually observe Lent any more.
Easter Monday	(9 April 2012, 1 April 2013, 21 April 2014)

1 May	Labour Day
Ascension Day	40 days after Easter
Whit Monday	May or June
23 June	National Day – see box, page 34
15 August	Assumption
First Monday in	Luxembourg City Kermesse (*Schueberfouer*) – local only. This
September	is a special holiday to give those in the capital a chance to
	enjoy a day out at the country's biggest annual funfair.
1 November	All Saints' Day
25 December	Christmas Day
26 December	Boxing Day

FESTIVALS Besides its **National Day**, Luxembourg holds festivals throughout the year in different locations and for different reasons. These are outlined in more detail in the appropriate chapters.

One of the most traditional is the mysterious and bizarre hopping ritual known as the **Echternach Dancing Procession**, held on Whit Tuesday since medieval times and now UNESCO-listed.

Burgsonndeg on 13 March is said to have Pagan origins. In villages across the country people light bonfires to welcome spring and the return of the sun.

Despite its name, the **Vianden Medieval Festival** in early August can trace its own roots back, ooh, at least five or six years. It's a lot of fun nonetheless.

Also in Vianden, the mid-October **Nut Market** will teach you more uses for walnuts than you could possibly ever imagine existed.

Several towns along the Moselle Valley host **wine festivals** in late summer to celebrate the harvest, which sometimes involve the town fountain flowing with wine. The most popular event is held in **Grevenmacher** over the second weekend in September. The **Riesling Open** held at several locations the following weekend also attracts big crowds.

Christmas markets are popular throughout the country, and offer ample opportunities to hum carols in tune to brass bands as you sip *glühwein*. The largest takes place on place d'Armes in Luxembourg City throughout December until Christmas Eve.

Several musical events are also held, most providing a mix of classical music, jazz and dance. The largest is Wiltz's **Festival de Wiltz** in July. The **Echternach International Festival** fills that town from mid-May to the end of June. Meanwhile, Luxembourg City's three-month **Summer in the City Festival** takes place – well, in the summer, and in the city.

SHOPPING

Needless to say, the capital presents the best opportunities for picking up souvenirs, and the available options are detailed in that chapter. If you want porcelain or glass, look no further than the **House of Villeroy & Boch** – their factory outlet in the suburbs offers 'seconds' goods at lower prices than the top-of-the-range items on display in the city centre.

Most of Luxembourg's best souvenirs are either edible or quaffable. A bottle of sparkling crémant wine from the Moselle costs around €7–12 in the shops or bought from the wineries themselves. Still wines start at around €3, and even top brands rarely cost more than €10. A bottle of Beaufort Castle's cassero is around €16. If you want to take home an *eau de vie*, it'll set you back €10–12.

2

Held on 23 June to mark the grand duke's 'official' birthday, Luxembourg's biggest party might more accurately be dubbed the National Days, since the fun cranks up well beforehand. Around this time flags appear everywhere in abundance, musical events and street processions take place, and the beer and wine flow freely.

Parties are held across the country, but the main events are centred on the capital. On the birthday eve, formalities kick off with a wreath-laying ceremony on place de la Constitution in the presence of the grand duke, followed by a changing of the guard ceremony outside the royal palace. Members of the royal family then disperse to other towns, before reconvening on place Guillaume II at 22.00 to watch a torchlight parade: a spectacular march-past of clubs, societies, fire brigades, and just about every scout and guide in the country. Everyone carries a flaming torch in 'angry rioting mob' style – though of course the celebratory mood is nothing of the sort. It's an impressive sight as the flickering flames light up the encroaching darkness.

Citywide pre-festival jollities culminate at 23.30 with a massive musical firework display around Pont Adolphe. And I do mean massive: this is a great example of how to blow up one million euros in under 20 minutes. The streets get very crowded around this time, so arrive early to bag a good vantage point (place de la Constitution is the best spot, or south of the Pétrusse Valley). If the wind blows in the wrong direction you may find a shower of smuts, ash and still-smouldering embers raining down on you as the sky literally fills with fire. Meanwhile, street stalls ply the masses with beer, and blare out loud music, and there's a convivial carnival atmosphere. Other stalls sell beer, popcorn, beer, hot dogs, beer … You get the idea – many bars remain open all night and the revelry goes on loud and long, so either join in or find a quiet hotel. While there are a few elements of tradition on show, the whole is at heart just a big excuse to party.

At 10.30 next morning things turn solemn again. Firstly the grand duke's family – along with foreign diplomats and invited guests – attends a Te Deum service in the Notre Dame Cathedral in Luxembourg City; then everyone decamps to a stand in front of the ArcelorMittal Building on avenue de la Liberté. This is where the real pomp in the nation's circumstance comes to the fore, as the grand duke and grand duchess take the salute, and a military parade containing what appears to be Luxembourg's entire national armed forces marches and drives past accompanied by military music. Needless to say, in a country this size, it doesn't take that long.

For chocolate delights try the products of **Oberweis** or **Namur**, both more than a match for their Belgian counterparts taste-wise. For something a bit different, there's also Oberweis's mini *bamkuch*: a handily shrunken version of a giant 'tree cake' traditionally eaten at Luxembourg weddings. It consists of a moist almond sponge with an apricot and lemon glaze, and in its small-scale guise resembles a stack of ring doughnuts.

There has been a resurgence in shops selling local produce (*produits du terroir*), from herbal infusions to spirits, and from spelt products to soaps, honeys and beyond. Wherever they have a reasonable selection I have tried to include them

– Esch-sur-Sûre, Heinerscheid and Müllerthal are all happy hunting grounds. The interactive www.foodmap.lu (in French) can help you find what you seek.

Opening hours vary from one shop to the next and are impossible to pin down. Most remain closed on Sundays, although many places in Luxembourg City now remain open until 20.00 on Saturdays.

ARTS AND ENTERTAINMENT

MUSIC The country's most important musical ensemble is the **Luxembourg Philharmonic Orchestra** (*www.philharmonie.lu*), based in the beautiful Philharmonie Concert Hall in Luxembourg City. The hall also hosts countless events by touring artists – see the website for the full agenda. Several towns and cities in Luxembourg hold (primarily classical) musical festivals over the summer months, with performances often taking place on outdoor stages – see *Festivals*, page 33.

The Rockhal (*www.rockhal.lu*) in Esch-sur-Alzette attracts international stars of the rock and pop world, and Luxembourg is finally starting to register on the modern music map as well. Elsewhere, rock music shows are generally lower-key events featuring minor artists, and take place in smaller venues including bars and clubs.

FILM There isn't much of a domestic film industry (national output is around one per year), but the government offers tax credits to lure in big international companies. As a result it's sometimes used as a 'European' location for Hollywood movies. Despite being set elsewhere, parts of *Girl with a Pearl Earring* were shot here, as were *Shadow of the Vampire* and *An American Werewolf in Paris*.

Cinema-going is a popular pastime in Luxembourg, and there are around a dozen theatres and multiplexes across the country. See www.cinenews.lu for up-to-date listings of what's showing and where.

THEATRE The National Theatre of Luxembourg (*www.tnl.lu*) stages performances in all three national languages, and even occasionally in English. Check the agenda listed on their website for up-to-date information about forthcoming events.

MEDIA AND COMMUNICATIONS

NEWSPAPERS AND MAGAZINES Weekly English-language magazine *352* (*www.352luxmag.lu*) provides a handy news digest for expats, and a guide to what's going on in the Grand Duchy. It no longer publishes a paper version, but can be downloaded free from the website. The website of the *Luxemburger Wort* newspaper (*www.wort.lu*) has an English-language section with domestic and international news stories, as does the web-only service News 352 (*hello.news352. lu*). The monthly *Delano* magazine (*www.delano.lu*) covers business stories, but also features culture and nightlife. *Business Review* is a monthly English-language magazine – you can probably take a wild guess at its subject matter.

Elsewhere, the American Chamber of Commerce (*www.amcham.lu*) publishes *Connexion*, a free quarterly magazine distributed to hotels, aimed primarily at US businesspeople. Another (mainly French-language) freebie aimed at the business sector is *Paper Jam* (*www.paperjam.lu*), published ten times per year. *Luxuriant* (*www.luxuriant.lu*) is a free quarterly arts and culture publication – largely in French, but interviews with artists are often printed in their original language.

The main Luxembourg press is subsidised (but importantly, not controlled) by the government. This forward-thinking approach allows a range of publications with differing viewpoints to operate and co-exist in a market that would otherwise be too small to support everyone. The papers were once mainly in German (with a few articles in French and Luxembourgish), but newer ones have appeared that are predominantly in French (with a few articles in German and Luxembourgish). German-language titles include *Tageblatt* and the aforementioned *Luxemburger Wort*, while French versions are *Le Quotidien* and *L'Avenir*. *Télécran* is a weekly television guide and family magazine, largely in German.

There are several free 'Metro-style' papers, mainly found in the city: *L'Essentiel* (in French), *.24* ('Point 24', in French and German), and the weekly *Contacto* (Portuguese).

RADIO For most people outside the country, there has only ever been one name worth mentioning in the Luxembourg radio world, especially as far as those of us (cough) above a certain age are concerned (see box opposite). For those within Luxembourg, Radio ARA (103.3 and 105.2 FM, *www.ara.lu*) broadcasts in English from 06.00 to 14.00 Monday to Friday.

TELEVISION The majority of channels on cable television in Luxembourg are in either German or French, and culled mainly from neighbouring countries. English-language choices in most places are limited to CNN and BBC World. Those with access to satellite television will find their options expand greatly – lest we forget, Luxembourg is home to the owners of Astra satellites, without which Sky TV would need another route into British homes.

TELEPHONE The international access code for Luxembourg is ☏ +352, which should be added at the beginning of the numbers in this book when calling from abroad. There are **no local codes** (and no initial zero) – just dial the number quoted in these pages when phoning within the country.

Somewhat confusingly, there's no standard number of digits in local telephone numbers. Older ones may only have five, most have six, while others have seven, eight, or even nine. Mobile phones have nine-digit numbers, generally starting with a '6'.

In an **emergency** call ☏ 112; for the police dial ☏ 113. The number for the emergency breakdown service is ☏ 45 00 451.

The three domestic **mobile** network providers are **Orange** (*www.orange.lu*), **Tango** (*www.tango.lu*) and **Luxgsm** (*www.luxgsm.lu*). All three give good coverage at reasonable rates. If you're going to be in Luxembourg for more than a few days consider getting a local SIM card, as calls will be a lot cheaper.

POST Postboxes in Luxembourg are easy to find as they're bright yellow. Postal rates for standard letters (up to 50g) are: €0.60 within Luxembourg, €0.85 to Europe, and €1.10 to the rest of the world.

INTERNET Most hotels now offer **Wi-Fi** access to guests. Some provide this service free; others may charge up to €10 per hour. **ADSL** connections may be available and a few hotels have internet terminals accessible to guests in the lobby.

Internet cafés are a rarity, but many bars offer free Wi-Fi. The terminals in Luxembourg City's library are also free. **Hot City** is a pay-to-use Wi-Fi network accessible throughout the capital. Rates are €3.90/7.90 for two/five non-contiguous hours, or €7.90/14.90 for unlimited use over a two- to 30-day period, if paying by credit card or internet subscription. Add €1 if buying scratch cards with access codes (available from stations and supermarkets among others). For help call ✆ 27 11 5000, or see www.hotcity.lu/www_laptop_en.

BUSINESS

Luxembourg's attractive investment climate makes it a popular choice in the international business world. Many global companies have at least a European

RADIO LUXEMBOURG

As someone who grew up in the 1960s and 1970s I'm just one of possibly millions of Britons who spent their formative years listening to transistor radios, normally furtively and under the bedclothes to muffle the sound and prevent my parents finding out I wasn't sleeping in readiness for school. The object of my secrecy was an attempt to pick out the 'Top 20' singles countdown on Radio Luxembourg, which somehow entered my bedroom via a poor signal through a barrage of background interference. All I heard was hiss most of the time, but it remains a cherished childhood memory nonetheless.

'Two-oh-eight' was arguably Britain's best-loved radio frequency before the arrival of BBC Radio 1 in 1967, and it retained that title long afterwards for some. Elsewhere, behind the Iron Curtain, before the Berlin Wall fell in 1989, many young people preferred the pop sounds of Radio Luxembourg to politics, and it had a huge influence on their cultural identity.

The station first went on air in English in 1933, taking advantage of the fact it had access to Europe's most powerful transmitter. For many years it was the only independent commercial music station available in the UK, and many preferred it to the stuffier BBC because it had a relaxed style and played what people wanted to hear.

On the other hand, the British government considered this foreign invasion of the airwaves an outrage, and tried to have it blocked through diplomatic channels. For their part, the BBC described it as scandalous and British newspapers, worried about competition for advertising revenue, refused to publish Luxembourg's schedules for decades.

Forced off the air by war in 1940, the radio station's frequency was used to broadcast Nazi propaganda, including the voice of William Joyce, also known as 'Lord Haw-Haw'. Returning in happier times it broadcast Britain's very first 'Top 20' countdown in 1948, and turned the show's DJs, Teddy Johnston and Pete Murray, into household names.

Then in 1951, English programmes switched from long wave to the legendary 208 metres medium wave. The transmission signal quality suffered immeasurably, but audiences kept on growing. Radio Luxembourg was soon the only place for aspiring young DJs to cut their teeth. Many big names who later switched to the BBC got their first break here, including Jimmy Savile, Noel Edmonds, Tony Blackburn, Jimmy Young, and dozens of others.

But the good times didn't last, and audiences drifted away throughout the 1980s. With financial losses mounting up, the station ended transmission almost unnoticed in 1992.

That wasn't quite the end though. In 2006, a new Radio Luxembourg reappeared, reborn in digital and online format as a 'Classic Rock' station. If that's your thing, you'll find it at www.radioluxembourg.co.uk.

base here, including such leaders of the e-commerce world as PayPal, iTunes and AOL. But although the national business world continues to diversify, the bulk of the booming economy is still driven by banking and steel, just as it has been for the last three decades. As of 2011 there were 147 national and international banks based in Luxembourg, although of these only one – the National Savings Bank (aka Banque et Caisse d'Epargne de l'Etat Luxembourg, aka Spuerkeess) – is still 100% in Luxembourgish hands. All the others are either partly or completely under foreign ownership. The massive number of multi-national corporations that are represented in the country has given rise to a large and thriving expat community of office workers, who are living primarily in Luxembourg City either on a temporary or permanent basis (as opposed to immigrant groups, who have poured into the country for other socio-economic reasons).

If you're in Luxembourg on business, arrive on time for meetings as punctuality is considered important. If you are going to be more than a few minutes late, call ahead to apologise and explain.

BUYING PROPERTY

Property in the centre of Luxembourg City is phenomenally expensive, even by over-inflated British standards. Many expats who work in the capital prefer to commute from the countryside, where prices are lower. Others live across the border in Belgium, France and Germany where land is even cheaper.

Buying property is relatively straightforward, but finding one that's for sale is not, as 'for sale' boards are not commonly used – you need to keep your ear to the ground. Once you've identified a place you want to buy, a legally binding written contract, or 'sales agreement', can be drawn up and matters can proceed. For ease of buying, always employ the services of a local solicitor familiar with the correct legal procedure to follow.

On top of the purchase price you also need to pay registration fees and transcript taxes amounting to around 7% of the house value.

CULTURAL ETIQUETTE

Luxembourgers are friendly, tolerant and easy-going, and you should have little problem avoiding causing offence.

A casual 'Moiën' or 'Bonjour' is the usual greeting between friends and business associates. Men invariably shake hands on meeting and on leaving, as do men and women who don't know each other well. Two or three kisses on the cheek is the normal greeting among friends when at least one of them is a woman.

Dressing up for dinner is not essential, though some may like to anyway if it's a special occasion.

For information on tipping, see *Money and budgeting*, page 24.

TRAVELLING POSITIVELY

If you enjoyed your stay in Luxembourg, why not show your appreciation by donating to the **Mentor Foundation** (*249 Derby Rd, Loughborough, Leics LE11 5HJ, UK;* ☏ *01509 221622;* e *secretariat@mentorfoundation.org; www.mentorfoundation. org*), a charity of which Grand Duke Henri and Grand Duchess Maria Teresa are honorary trustees. The foundation's mission is to prevent drug misuse and promote the health and well-being of young people worldwide.

The guiding principle of another, Luxembourg-based, royal charity, the **Fondation du Grand-Duc et de la Grande-Duchesse** (*8 An der Sang, L-7739 Colmar-Berg, Luxembourg;* \ *+352 31 70 311;* e *fondhmt@pt.lu; www.fondation-grand-ducale.lu*), is respect for human dignity. The foundation works in two key areas domestically: providing social assistance to those in need, and helping those with physical, psychological or social difficulties. It also works internationally, supporting UNICEF projects in Burundi.

Part Two

THE GUIDE

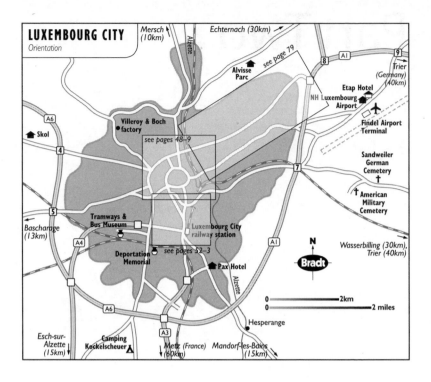

LUXEMBOURG CITY
Orientation

Mersch
(10km)

Echternach (30km)

see page 79

Alzette

Trier
(Germany)
(40km)

Alvisse
Parc

Etap Hotel

NH Luxembourg
Airport

Findel Airport
Terminal

A6

Skol

Villeroy & Boch
factory

see pages 48–9

Sandweiler
German
Cemetery

American
Military
Cemetery

Bascharage
(13km)

Tramways &
Bus Museum

Luxembourg City
railway station

see pages 52–3

Deportation
Memorial

Pax Hotel

Wasserbilling (30km),
Trier (40km)

N

Bradt

Alzette

0 ————————2km
0 ————————2 miles

Hesperange

Esch-sur-
Alzette
(15km)

Camping
Kockelscheuer

Metz (France)
(60km)

Mandorf-les-Bains
(15km)

3

Luxembourg City

'Gibraltar of the North', one of Europe's smallest capitals, or Eurocrat heaven. Think of it how you will, Luxembourg City is many things to many people. But put it all together and what you find is a place of manageable scale, with abundant charm and one of the most stunning settings of any urban area in Europe. At the confluence of the Alzette and Pétrusse rivers, both of which have cut deep gouges into the sandstone plateau, it's the old town's spectacular location, perched on a cliff edge, which grabs your attention right away. Its 'Gibraltar of the North' tagline actually refers to the fortifications dug into the rock – in appearance I think 'Edinburgh of the Continent' is more apt (although I concede it doesn't scan as well). Lacking the overwhelming scale of London or Berlin, this is a city you can navigate on foot, with plenty of pleasant squares, surprising amounts of green, great museums and intact centuries-old architecture. In short, it's a delightful place, and UNESCO clearly agrees: it awarded the old town World Heritage status in 1994.

Quaint and appealing as it is, the city also has a hard-working business and administrative side, which has made it wealthy. It's a major centre of international banking, the seat of several significant European institutions, and (along with Strasbourg and Brussels) one of three capitals of the EU. Despite its permanent metropolitan population being just 94,000, these roles have turned it into the most multi-cultural of cities – around 60% of the residents are of foreign origin. The population also more than doubles every working day, when 120,000 migrant workers flood in from Belgium, France and Germany. When everyone goes home in the evening it can feel strangely empty in the centre, with only tourists and the remaining locals left to frequent the bars and cafés.

This is the only place to have become European Capital of Culture twice, having held the honour in both 1995 and 2007. The title may have since passed on, but its legacy is in plain view, as large sums of public money were poured into creating prestige sites such as the MUDAM Museum of Modern Art and the neighbouring Philharmonie Concert Hall, both gems of modern architecture.

New and old, there's more than enough here to keep you occupied for days.

HISTORY

In essence, the story of Luxembourg the city *is* the story of Luxembourg the nation. It isn't the oldest town, but the whole concept of this country came about when it was founded.

The Romans knew a thing or two about location, and had already spotted the strategic importance of the site. They made it the crossroads of two Roman roads, and built a fortified tower to guard the junction. But nothing much happened to make them want to expand such a remote outpost of empire.

Things changed in AD963 when Count Siegfried I of the Ardennes acquired the land. He too saw the defensive potential of the sandstone outcrop called Bock Fiels ('rock', cleverly enough), built a castle there, and named it Lucilinburhuc – 'little fortress'. God arrived 24 years later in 987, when Egbert, Archbishop of Trier, blessed the altar in the Church of the Redemption (later St Michael's). Then a small market appeared at the junction of the two former Roman roads, and the three necessary foundations for the building of a city – government, religion and commerce – were in place.

Siegfried wasn't the last to get all possessive about this location. It was fought over, fortified, expanded, taken, demolished and rebuilt with monotonous regularity for most of the ensuing 1,000 years. By the late 12th century the city had expanded west to the St Nicholas Church (on the site of the current Chamber of Deputies), and a city wall was constructed. It was extended during the reign of John the Blind in the 14th century, and his fortifications remained in place until 1867.

Yet walls weren't always sufficient to keep the city safe. Despite the fact it was one of the most heavily fortified sites in Europe (and increasingly so, as each successive landlord added to the work of their predecessors), Philip the Good of Burgundy's arrival in 1443 triggered a 400-year merry-go-round that saw ownership pass back and forth like 'pass the parcel' at a children's party between Burgundians, Spanish Habsburgs, Austrian Habsburgs, French and Prussians. The longest period of peace (around 80 years) came under the Austrian Habsburgs in the 18th century, and much of the old town stems from this 'golden age'.

The 1867 Luxembourg Crisis, a confrontation between Prussia and France, prompted a radical redesign. Under the terms of the Treaty of London, which declared the Grand Duchy neutral, all the city's fortifications were dismantled, and eventually replaced by the parkland you see today to the north and west of the centre.

Despite its neutrality, the trauma wasn't quite over. The city was occupied in August 1914 when General Helmuth von Moltke moved his headquarters to be closer to his armies at war in France – it played host to the German high command for the next four years. When the war ended in 1918 it then became the setting for an unlikely revolution. On 9 November, communists declared a new socialist republic in Luxembourg. It turned out to be one of the shortest-lived countries in history, as the rebellion was crushed within hours.

In May 1940, Germany invaded a second time in the form of the Nazis, who remained until the city was liberated on 10 September 1944. But it recovered quickly after the war, and in 1952 became the headquarters of the European Coal and Steel Community, the foundation stone of the European Union. It remains the seat of the European Parliament's secretariat, as well as the European Court of Justice, the European Investment Bank and the European Court of Auditors, along with parts of the European Commission. In the late 20th century the city also became a thriving financial centre, thanks to banking laws that kept investors' identities confidential and allowed the accounts of foreign nationals to earn interest tax-free.

GETTING THERE AND AROUND

BY AIR Findel Airport is 6km east of the city centre, at the far end of route de Trèves. Direct flights land here from short-haul destinations across western Europe, including several times daily from London.

Getting to and from the airport Taxis hang around in front of the terminal (to the right as you exit), but are expensive compared with the bus. A typical journey into the city could set you back as much as €25–40 depending on destination, traffic and time of day (fares go up at night and on Sundays). For a cheaper alternative, bus 16 departs from outside the terminal building (left as you exit) and takes you into the centre for €1.50 (€4 for an all-day ticket, or free if you already have a Luxembourg Card). It travels along a useful route via the Kirchberg Plateau, the old city, and the railway station – you may find line 16 becoming a familiar friend by the end of your stay. Buses operate between 05.30 and 23.00 Monday to Saturday (four to six per hour) and between 07.00 and 23.00 on Sundays (twice hourly). All major car-rental companies have offices at the airport.

BY BIKE All over the city are banks of sturdy blue **Vel'oh!** bicycles, offering an environmentally friendly, pedal-powered way to get about. Mainly aimed at residents, this bike-borrowing scheme is slightly less practical for visitors as you must subscribe before you can use it (€1 for between one and seven days, €15 for one year). A quick ride (less than 30 minutes) is free; after that it costs €1 per hour, up to a maximum of €5 for 24 hours. You pay a deposit of €150 when you sign up, which you forfeit if you fail to return a bike within 24 hours. See www.veloh.lu or call \ 80 06 11 00.

BY BUS Bus services fan out across the country, serving practically every community not connected by train. Most leave from outside the railway station – timetables are posted rather unobtrusively on a yellow board to the left as you exit, and are tricky to decipher unless you know the end destination on your route. Detailed travel information for both regional buses and trains can be obtained from the travel bureau inside the station, or from www.mobiliteit.lu. They'll print timetables for any route on request, for free. The LCTO office on place Guillaume II [58 A4] has timetables for city lines. The maximum fare on any domestic bus or train is €4 for an all-day ticket.

The **CitySightseeing Luxembourg** (*www.sightseeing.lu; departs Apr–Oct every 20mins 09.40–17.20 daily, mid-Jun to mid-Sep every 20mins 09.40–18.20 daily; adult/child €14/7, valid 24hrs, 30% discount with Luxembourg Card*) bus tour is an open-top, hop-on/hop-off affair with commentary in eight languages, which stops at eight popular points between the central station and Kirchberg. Buy tickets from hotel receptions, on board, online, from the city tourist office, or from the ticket office on place de la Constitution [58 A6]. If you're mad enough to want to ride on top when it's raining, rain capes are included.

BY CAR Driving into the city is easy, but parking in the old town can cost €25 or more per day. If you're prepared to walk, you can save money by looking for the green parking meter zones just outside the central old town. You can pay to park here for up to five hours Monday to Friday between 08.00 and 18.00. Outside these times, parking is unlimited and free. Beware of meter zones with orange signs, as these are also free on Sundays, but not Saturdays. The LCTO website (*www.lcto.lu*) has real-time updates of the available spaces in all city centre car parks.

BY TRAIN If you arrive by train you'll come into the central station, Luxembourg Gare [53 G5]. There are direct international services from Brussels (hourly; three hours), Paris (six per day; 2¼ hours), Liège (every two hours; 2½ hours), and Trier in Germany (hourly; 45 minutes). Domestic trains depart at least hourly on routes east to Wasserbillig, north to Ettelbruck, Clervaux and Wiltz, and south and west to Bettembourg, Pétange (for Fond-de-Gras) and Esch-sur-Alzette.

Join the **Pétrusse Express** (*www.sightseeing.lu; departs Apr–Oct every 30mins 10.00–18.00 daily, tours last 50–60mins; adult/child €8.50/5, 30% discount with Luxembourg Card*) **miniature 'train'** for an easy ride down into the Pétrusse Valley and around Grund. It departs from place de la Constitution [58 A6].

ORIENTATION

The city is compact, and the central areas quite manageable **on foot**, even if there are a fair few hills involved. **Taxis** are expensive, but a comprehensive network of city **buses** covers the centre and outlying districts. There are two main bus hubs, and every route passes through at least one of these, often both. One, outside the train station [53 G5], is referred to on bus signs as *gare centrale* (central station). On exiting the station building, turn right for city lines, left for regional services. Straight ahead is bay 9, where bus 16 stops. This handy route runs at least four times every hour to the old town, past the MUDAM, the European District, the Auchan shopping mall, and out to the airport. Many southbound services (away from the centre) leave from stops across the road from the station.

The old town bus station is on place Hamilius [48 C4], usually called 'Centre Hamilius'. From the train station, any northbound bus (ie: on the station side of the main road) numbered between 1 and 16 will get you there. Coming back, any bus that stops at platform (*Quai*) 6 in Hamilius will do the job, as will most of those at platform 5 – they pass every minute or two throughout the day. Tickets valid for two hours cost €1.50; €4 will buy you unlimited travel for the day. With a Luxembourg Card, ride free to your heart's content. Most routes operate on a regular basis between 05.45 and 23.45 Monday to Saturday, starting slightly later on Sundays. Three night bus routes (CN1–3) operate until 03.30, which can prove useful when sampling the nightlife. There are plans to redevelop the Hamilius area in the future and turn it into a pedestrianised precinct. If this happens the bus station may be relocated. Check the city website (*www.vdl.lu*) for up-to-the-minute information.

The parts of the city of most interest to tourists can be divided into several convenient areas; see below.

UPPER OLD TOWN The UNESCO-listed upper old town is the effective centre of Luxembourg City, and the heart of the action as far as tourists are concerned. It clusters around a series of key squares, including place d'Armes [58 A4], place Guillaume II [58 B4], and the oldest of them all, Marché Aux Poissons [49 E4]. The Grand Ducal Palace, Notre Dame Cathedral and many other historic buildings are here, as are most museums, restaurants, shops, and a number of hotels. Navigating your way around can sometimes be confusing as street signs are thin on the ground, and you may not always know which road you're walking along. But you can't stray too far without reaching the park to the north and west, or the dramatic gorges to the east and south. As well as the long-standing lift down to Grund (below), a second is under construction leading from the end of boulevard Royale to Pfaffenthal (near Clausen). No-one knows, however, when it will be finished. There is also talk of a third lift, from place de la Constitution to the Pétrusse Valley, but at the time of writing this was still under discussion.

GRUND The lower old town, or Grund, is cut off from the upper town by a soaring cliff, and feels like a village within a city. This area fell into decline when the former abbey here was used as a prison, but in the last 20 years it has received a major facelift. It has become gentrified, and once again *the* place to live and be seen. The narrow streets have many trendy bars and are a centre of local nightlife. You can walk up and down between the upper town and Grund, but the easiest way is via the **lift** [49 F5], which makes the 70m ascent through the rock in less than a minute (*operates 06.30–02.00*).

CLAUSEN Next to and just north of Grund, this area has become a centre for the expat community, and has several themed pubs to keep homesick Brits content. The Rives de Clausen [49 H3] is a multi-million euro development on the site of the former Mousel Brewery, containing bars, clubs, restaurants and the Clausel microbrewery.

GARE The area around the railway station will be your first introduction to the city if arriving by public transport, and you may end up staying here as it's home to several hotels. It's a 15-minute walk, or five-minute bus ride, south of the old town, and separated from it by the deep Pétrusse Valley. The area around the station is a little seedy, but things improve rapidly as you move north along avenue de la Liberté.

CENTRE EUROPÉEN AND KIRCHBERG Two newer districts stretch out in a long line to the east and north of the old city, accessible via the Pont Grande-Duchesse Charlotte, aka the 'red bridge'. Close to the bridge the Centre Européen is home to various EU institutions, and also the MUDAM [49 G1] and the Philharmonie [49 H1]. Further out, a new business district has sprung up (and is still springing up) across the relatively flat Kirchberg Plateau. Many banks are headquartered here, and it's also the site of the large Auchan shopping mall.

TOURIST INFORMATION AND LOCAL TOUR OPERATORS

☒ Luxembourg City Tourist Office (LCTO) [58 A4] 30 pl Guillaume II; ☎ 22 28 09; e touristinfo@lcto.lu; www.lcto.lu; ⊕ Apr–Sep 09.00–19.00 Mon–Sat, 10.00–18.00 Sun & public holidays; Oct–Mar 09.00–18.00 Mon–Sat, 10.00–18.00 Sun & public holidays. LCTO can help book accommodation & arranges interesting guided tours that start from its office. The most popular is the City Promenade (*Nov–Mar at 14.00 Mon, Wed & Sat–Sun, Apr–Oct in English at 13.00 daily adult/child €7/3.50*), a 2hr walk around the upper town. Also fun for children is the City Labo (☎ 47 96 27 09; mid-Jul to mid-Sep 14.30 Tue, Thu

Sat–Sun; €6pp; advance reservation requested), a 2hr educational adventure tour designed for young would-be scientists, with experiments along the way. The tourist office also sells tickets for hop-on hop-off sightseeing buses, & for concerts & events (tickets for which can also be bought from *www.luxembourgticket.lu*).

☒ Luxembourg National Tourist Office (Office National du Tourisme, ONT) ☎ 42 82 82 20; e info@visitluxembourg.lu; www. visitluxembourg.lu. ONT no longer has a public tourist office, but its website remains an invaluable source of information.

For trips further afield, there are a couple of handy travel agents in the city centre.

Sotour 15 pl du Théâtre; ☎ 46 15 141; ⊕ 09.00–18.00 Mon–Fri, 09.00–12.00 Sat

Voyages Flammang 17 bd Royal; ☎ 46 87 871; ⊕ 09.00–18.00 Mon–Fri, 09.00–12.00 & 13.30–17.00 Sat

WHERE TO STAY

With so many international companies based here, business guests usually outnumber tourists during the week. This often means hotels are full Monday to Thursday, and

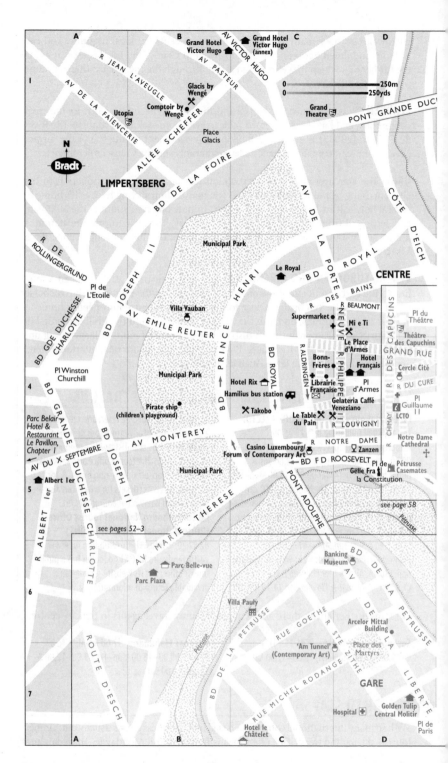

A

B

C

D

AV VICTOR HUGO

Grand Hotel Victor Hugo

Grand Hotel Victor Hugo (annex)

AV PASTEUR

R JEAN L'AVEUGLE

1

Glacis by Wengé

Comptoir by Wenge

Utopia

AV DE LA FAÏENCERIE

ALLÉE SCHEFFER

Grand Theatre

PONT GRANDE DUC

0 ────── 250m
0 ────── 250yds

Place Glacis

Bradt

N

2

LIMPERTSBERG

BD DE LA FOIRE

AV DE LA PORTE ROYAL

CÔTE D'EICH

R DE ROLLINGERGRUND

Municipal Park

Le Royal

CENTRE

3

Pl de L'Etoile

JOSEPH II

AV EMILE REUTER

Villa Vauban

PRINCE HENRI

R DES BAINS

BEAUMONT

Supermarket

Mi e Ti

Pl du Théâtre

Théâtre des Capuchins

DES CAPUCINS

BD GDE DUCHESSE CHARLOTTE

Le Place d'Armes

R NEUVE

R PHILIPPE

Hotel Français

GRAND RUE

Cercle Cité

Pl Winston Churchill

4

Municipal Park

Hotel Rix

Hamilius bus station

BD ROYAL

R ALDRINGEN

Bonn-Frères

Librairie Française

Pl d'Armes

R DU CURE

Pl Guillaume II

LCTO

BD GRANDE DUCHESSE CHARLOTTE

BD JOSEPH II

Pirate ship (children's playground)

Takobo

Gelateria Caffé Veneziano

Le Table du Pain

R LOUVIGNY

R CHIMAY

Notre Dame Cathedral

Parc Belair Hotel & Restaurant Le Pavillon, Chapter 1

AV DU X SEPTEMBRE

AV MONTEREY

Municipal Park

Casino Luxembourg/ Forum of Contemporary Art

R NOTRE DAME

Zanzen

BD F D ROOSEVELT

Gëlle Fra

Pl de la Constitution

Pétrusse Casemates

5

Albert 1er

R ALBERT 1er

see pages 52–3

AV MARIE-THERESE

PONT ADOLPHE

see page 58

Pétrusse

see pages 52–3

6

ROUTE D'ESCH

Parc Belle-vue

Parc Plaza

Villa Pauly

Pétrusse

Banking Museum

BD DE LA PETRUSSE

AV DE LA PETRUSSE

BD DE LA PETRUSSE

RUE GOETHE

R STE ZITHE

Arcelor Mittal Building

Place des Martyrs

'Am Tunnel' (Contemporary Art)

GARE

7

RUE MICHEL RODANGE

Hospital

Golden Tulip Central Molitir

Pl de Paris

Hotel le Châtelet

A

B

C

D

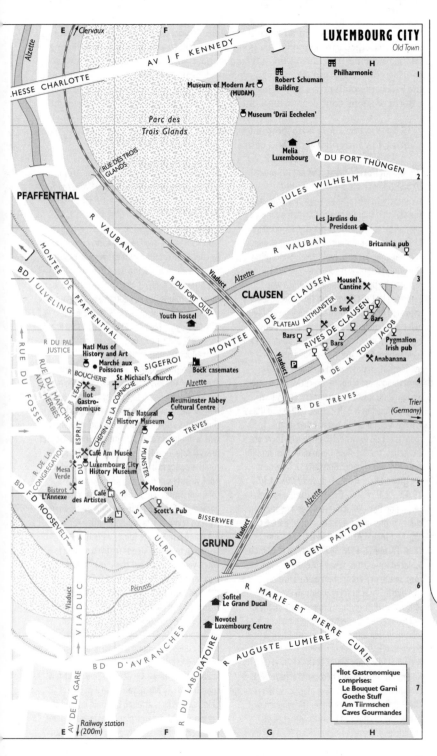

LUXEMBOURG CITY
Old Town

E / Clervaux
AV J F KENNEDY
HESSE CHARLOTTE

Museum of Modern Art (MUDAM)
Robert Schuman Building
Philharmonie

Museum 'Dräi Eechelen'

Parc des Trois Glands

Melia Luxembourg

RUE DES TROIS GLANDS

R DU FORT THÜNGEN

R VAUBAN

PFAFFENTHAL

R JULES WILHELM

Les Jardins du Président

R VAUBAN

Britannia pub

MONTEE DE PFAFFENTHAL

BD J ULVELING

Viaduct
Alzette
R DU FORT OLISY

CLAUSEN

Mousel's Cantine

DE CLAUSEN

Le Sud

Youth hostel

PLATEAU ALTMÜNSTER

Bars

RIVES DE CLAUSEN

Bars

R DU PAL JUSTICE

Natl Mus of History and Art
Marché aux Poissons
BOUCHERIE
R SIGEFROI
St Michael's church

MONTEE

Bars
Bars

Pygmalion Irish pub

R DE LA TOUR JACOB

Anabanana

RUE DU MARCHE AUX HERBES

Bock casemates

Alzette

R L'EAU
Îlot Gastronomique

Neumünster Abbey Cultural Centre

R DE TRÈVES

Trier (Germany)

RUE DU FOSSE

CHEMIN DE LA CORNICHE

The Natural History Museum

R DE TRÈVES

R DE LA CONGREGATION

R ST ESPRIT

Café Am Musée
Luxembourg City History Museum

R MUNSTER

Mesa Verde

BD F D ROOSEVELT

Bistrot L'Annexe

Café des Artistes

Mosconi

Alzette

R ST ULRIC

Lift

Scott's Pub

BISSERWEE

Viaduct

GRUND

BD GEN PATTON

Viaduct

Pétrusse

Sofitel Le Grand Ducal

R MARIE ET PIERRE CURIE

6

Novotel Luxembourg Centre

VIADUC

BD D'AVRANCHES

R DU LABORATOIRE

AV AUGUSTE LUMIÈRE

AV DE LA GARE

E / Railway station (200m)

*Îlot Gastronomique comprises:
Le Bouquet Garni
Goethe Stuff
Am Tiirmschen
Caves Gourmandes

Luxembourg City WHERE TO STAY

3

49

keeps prices up – book in advance if possible. If you arrive without a reservation, the tourist office can help out. The good news is that rates in many establishments fall at weekends and during the July and August 'low season'. There is, however, a shortage of budget and shoestring accommodation, with the glowing exception of the excellent youth hostel. If you need to save your pennies but don't want to sleep in a dorm or a tent, consider staying a little out of town, where rates drop considerably.

EXCLUSIVE For those with bottomless wallets, there are plenty of luxury hotels catering to your every whim and desire.

⌂ **Grand Hotel Cravat** [58 A6] (61 rooms) 29 bd F D Roosevelt, L-2450; ☎ 22 19 75; e contact@hotelcravat.lu; www.hotelcravat.lu. The stylish if slightly quaint Cravat is a family institution in the heart of the city, founded in 1895 by the grandfather of the current owner. The manager, her son, is effusively welcoming. The original hotel was torn down in 1933 & replaced by this 1938 building, which was extended in 1953 & again in 1964. Because it appeared in stages, room sizes vary greatly – older ones are huge. All the elegantly furnished bedrooms have minibar. Some bathrooms still have fittings from the 1960s, but a gradual modernisation programme is under way. For something more modern, executive rooms are designed for business customers. These have wooden finishes & half-carpet, half-wood floors. Wi-Fi is free here, but not in other rooms. 1 room is set up for wheelchair guests. There are 2 eateries: the 1st-floor Normandie Restaurant & the slightly cheaper Brasserie La Taverne on the ground floor (both ⊕ daily 12.00–14.30 & 19.00–22.30; €€€–€€€€). The big lure of the Le Trianon bar – which resembles a gentlemen's club – is the open fire, lit in winter. €€€€€

⌂ **Le Place d'Armes** [48 D4] (28 rooms) 18 pl d'Armes, L-1136; ☎ 27 47 37; e info@hotel-leplacedarmes.com; www.hotel-leplacedarmes.com. In the perfect spot on place d'Armes, this plush 5-star hotel occupies an exquisitely renovated 18th-century property – actually 7 interconnected properties, explaining why it's a warren with many stairs (there are lifts), & floors on various levels. There's a lovely conservatory, & several reception rooms in the stone cellar. Rooms are individually decorated & have Wi-Fi & broadband. Bathrooms have marble washbasins. The 3rd-floor rooms are under the wooden roof eaves. The Crystal Suite comes with its own chandeliers. There is valet parking (€26 per day),

& you may enter the pedestrian zone to drop off luggage & passengers. Alternatively, call & someone will meet you. The 1st-floor Cristallerie Restaurant (⊕ 12.00–14.00 & 19.00–21.30 Tue–Fri, 19.00–21.30 Sat; €€€€€) is elegance par excellence – the French *haute cuisine* created by chef Alain Straub includes specialities such as turbot with verbena. Brasserie Plëss (⊕ 07.00–22.00 daily; €€€€) is also French-inspired, but more affordable. It has a terrace, which is a great spot for an aperitif. B/fast €29pp. €€€€€

⌂ **Le Royal** [48 C3] (210 rooms) 12 bd Royal, L-2449; ☎ 241 61 67 56; e reservations@leroyalluxembourg.com; www.leroyalluxembourg.com. At the top of the heap in every way, the Royal is the city's (& the country's) most exclusive hotel, located by the park & a few mins' walk from the old town. White marble & shiny brass abound here. Rooms are equipped with a minimum of AC, internet, minibar, trouser press & safe. Besides that it has everything you could wish for in a luxury hotel: heated indoor pool, beauty salon, sauna, *hammam*, massage, solarium, fitness club, shops & underground garage. Wi-Fi is available in public areas. There are also several restaurants, a garden terrace & a piano bar. Service comes with all the attention to guests' needs that you'd expect when you're forking out this much. B/fast €22pp (continental)/€28pp (buffet). €€€€€

⌂ **Les Jardins du President** [49 H3] (7 rooms) 2 pl Sainte Cunégonde, L-1367; ☎ 26 09 071; e jardins@president.lu; www.jardinspresident.lu; ⊕ mid-Jan to mid-Dec. The 'President's Gardens' is down in Clausen. Surrounded by trees & in a cul-de-sac that only leads to the church next door, it's one of the few spots in the city where you stand a chance of being woken by chattering birdsong instead of beeping traffic or cargo planes taking off. Rooms have been individually styled by someone with enormous taste, & come with minibar, trouser press, internet & safe. In a former private house, the biggest selling point is the beautiful garden at the back, which looks out onto roses & a cascading water feature. You won't stay in many city hotels where, if the front door is closed, a sign will explain, 'We are feeding our ducks – please ring the bell.' The restaurant (⏰ *19.00–21.30 Tue–Sat;* €€€€–€€€€€) features Kobe beef among its many delights. €€€€€

🏠 **Parc Beaux-Arts** [58 D3] (10 suites) 1 rue Sigefroi, L-2536; 📞 52 26 86 761; e reception.beauxarts@goeres-group.com; www.parcbeauxarts.lu. For pampering on a more intimate scale, this sumptuous boutique hotel hits all the right notes. Located beside the National History & Art Museum there are no mere rooms here, just individually decorated suites. Each contains a living room & bedroom with stripped wooden floorboards. The walls are hung with works of art by local artists – with the amount you're already spending you'd think they'd be included in the rate, but they'll cost extra if you want to take them home. Some of the immaculate white-tiled bathrooms have baths, some showers. Pay attention to where you're going otherwise you may get lost in the maze of staircases inside the 240-year-old building. There's a small b/fast room, a restaurant next door for lunch & dinner, & a lounge bar on the top floor. The Goeres family classify their 4 hotels in the capital as economic, business, executive & exclusive. Can you guess which this is? They say the other 3 are there to pay the bills, & this is their plaything. €€€€€

🏠 **Parc Belair** [48 A5] (53 rooms) 111 av du X Septembre, L-2551; 📞 44 23 231; e reception. belair@goeres-group.com; www.parcbelair.lu. The Goeres Group's 2nd-tier hotel still sneaks into the exclusive category. This is the one they call 'executive'. At the back the modern building opens onto Merl Park, in a quiet residential district 1.5km west of the old town. Some rooms have balconies with this rustic view. Built in the 1990s, the hotel is modern & sleek from the

UPMARKET

🏠 **Mercure Grand Hotel Alfa Luxembourg** [53 G5] (141 rooms) 16 pl de la Gare, L-1616; 📞 49 00 111; e H2058@accor.com; www. mercure.com. Directly opposite the station in

outside, but the chic interior harks back to the golden age of luxury travel. The lounge area, with its dark ruby shades, exudes particular charm & sophistication. Sumptuous rooms have Wi-Fi, minibar & safe. There are several in-house restaurants & bars, & also a sauna & solarium. €€€€€

🏠 **Sofitel Le Grand Ducal** [49 F6] (128 rooms) 40 bd d'Avranches, L-1160; 📞 24 87 71; e H5555@accor.com; www.sofitel.com. Luxury accommodation that will take your breath away when you look out of the window. Ultra-modern rooms here have AC, safe, minibar & Wi-Fi. Those on the upper floors at the front have a panoramic vista across the Pétrusse Valley to the old town, as does the restaurant. It's possible to enjoy the view even if you're not staying in the hotel, by taking the lift to the 8th-floor bar. *B/fast €27pp.* €€€€€

🏠 **Sofitel Luxembourg Europe** [see map, page 79] (104 rooms) 6 rue du Fort Niedergrünewald, L-2015; 📞 43 77 61; e H1314@ accor.com; www.sofitel.com. Sofitel's original contribution to the Luxembourg hotel scene is located on the Kirchberg Plateau, near the Centre Européen. A focal point here is the building's stunning central plant-filled atrium, around which all rooms are arranged. The glass ceiling looks like the upturned hull of a ship. Adding to the illusion, the window cleaners' gondola hanging below it resembles a lifeboat. Modern & well-appointed bedrooms have AC, safe, minibar & Wi-Fi. *B/fast €25pp.* €€€€€

🏠 **Albert 1er** [48 A5] (40 rooms) 2a rue Albert 1er, L-1117; 📞 44 24 42; e hotel@ albertpremier.lu; www.hotelalbertpremier.lu. Just west of the old town, this elegant hotel has undergone major expansion & modernisation. Older Classic rooms are still decorated with lovely antique furniture brought in from England & Italy, & are cosily appointed with a homely appeal. Other rooms are modern, sleek & minimalist. All have safe, refrigerators, & Wi-Fi. A sauna & fitness room are also available. Rates plummet at w/ends. Parking costs €22 per night. *B/fast €22pp.* €€–€€€€€

a noisy area, but they can afford reasonable soundproofing here. The beautiful 75-year-old Art-Deco building is the best-looking one on the station square. Large, modern rooms have

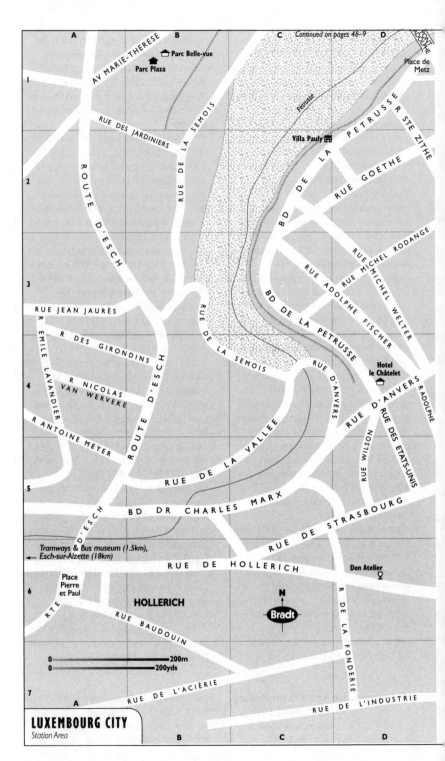

Continued on pages 48–9

PONT ADOLPHE

Place de Metz

Parc Belle-vue

Parc Plaza

AV MARIE-THERESE

RUE DES JARDINIERS

RUE DE LA SEMOIS

Petrusse

Villa Pauly

BD DE LA PETRUSSE

R STE ZITHE

ROUTE D'ESCH

RUE GOETHE

RUE MICHEL RODANGE

RUE ADOLPHE FISCHER

RUE MICHEL WELTER

BD DE LA PETRUSSE

RUE JEAN JAURÈS

R DES GIRONDINS

RUE DE LA SEMOIS

RUE D'ANVERS

Hotel le Châtelet

R EMILE LAVANDIER

R NICOLAS VAN WERVEKE

ROUTE D'ESCH

R ANTOINE MEYER

RUE DE LA VALLÉE

RUE D'ANVERS

RUE D'ANVERS

R ADOLPHE

RUE DES ETATS-UNIS

RUE WILSON

BD DR CHARLES MARX

RUE DE STRASBOURG

D'ESCH

Tramways & Bus museum (1.5km),
← Esch-sur-Alzette (18km)

RUE DE HOLLERICH

Den Atelier

Place Pierre et Paul

HOLLERICH

N

Bradt

R DE LA FONDERIE

RTE

RUE BAUDOUIN

0 ——————— 200m
0 ——————— 200yds

RUE DE L'ACIÉRIE

RUE DE L'INDUSTRIE

LUXEMBOURG CITY
Station Area

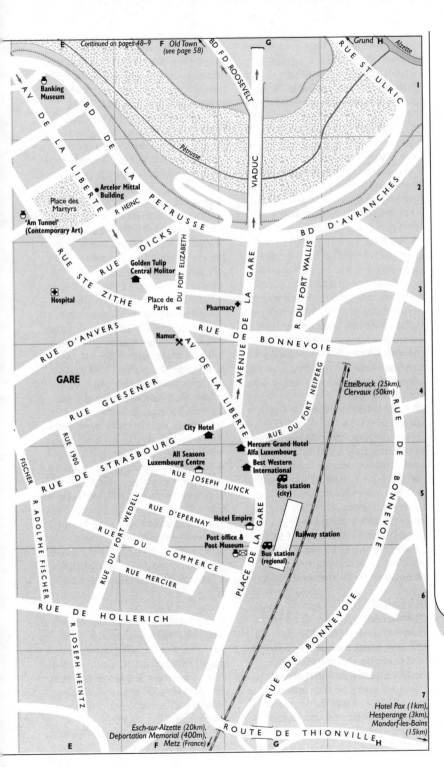

E Continued on pages 48–9 F Old Town (see page 58)

G

Grund H Alzette

RUE ST ULRIC

I

Banking Museum

AV DE LA LIBERTE

BD DE LA PETRUSSE

Pétrusse

VIADUC

BD FD ROOSEVELT

2

Arcelor Mittal Building

Place des Martyrs

R HEINC

BD D'AVRANCHES

'Am Tunnel' (Contemporary Art)

RUE STE ZITHE

DICKS

R DU FORT ELIZABETH

R DU FORT WALLIS

3

Golden Tulip Central Molitor

Hospital

Place de Paris

Pharmacy

RUE DE BONNEVOIE

RUE D'ANVERS

Namur

AV DE LA LIBERTE

AVENUE DE LA GARE

R DU FORT NEIPERG

Ettelbruck (25km), Clervaux (50km)

4

GARE

RUE GLESENER

RUE 1900

RUE DE BONNEVOIE

FISCHER

City Hotel

RUE DE STRASBOURG

Mercure Grand Hotel Alfa Luxembourg

RUE DU FORT NEIPERG

R ADOLPHE FISCHER

All Seasons Luxembourg Centre

Best Western International

5

RUE JOSEPH JUNCK

Bus station (city)

RUE D'EPERNAY

RUE DU FORT WEDELL

Hotel Empire

PLACE DE LA GARE

Railway station

6

RUE DU COMMERCE

Post office & Post Museum

Bus station (regional)

RUE MERCIER

RUE DE BONNEVOIE

RUE DE HOLLERICH

R JOSEPH HEINTZ

7

Hotel Pax (1km), Hesperange (3km), Mondorf-les-Bains (15km)

Esch-sur-Alzette (20km), Deportation Memorial (400m), Metz (France)

E F ROUTE DE THIONVILLE G H

AC, safe, minibar & Wi-Fi, while the bar & other public areas stylishly & more accurately reflect the hotel's age. *B/fast €18pp.* €€€€

🏠 **Novotel Luxembourg Centre** [49 F6] (150 rooms) 35 rue du Laboratoire, L-1911; ✆24 87 81; e H5556@accor.com; www.novotel.com. This swanky hotel has a convenient yet quiet location across the Pétrusse Valley from the old centre. Spacious rooms have AC, kettle, minibar, Wi-Fi & spotless bathrooms with radio. Sofas in some rooms turn into additional beds. The downstairs lounge bar is an ultra-stylish space in a tri-chromatic blend of black, white & red. There's also a gym. *B/fast €20pp.* €€€€

🏠 **Parc Plaza** [48 B6] (89 rooms) 5 av Marie-Thérèse, L-2132; ✆45 61 411; e reception.plaza@goeres-group.com; www.parcplaza.lu. Holding up the 'business' corner of the Goeres quartet, this modern, almost motel-style hotel perches on the northern precipice of the Pétrusse Valley with a suitably grand view. Rooms are light, bright & comfortable with restrained elegance. Some have scenic balconies. Wi-Fi is available in public areas (plus broadband in bedrooms). 3 rooms are accessible to guests with limited mobility. Rates drop at w/ends. €€€€

🏠 **Grand Hotel Victor Hugo** [48 B1] (61 rooms, 5 suites) 3–5 av Victor Hugo, L-1750; ✆26 27 440; e info@grandhotelvictorhugo.lu; www.grandhotelvictorhugo.lu. Just north of the centre, 2 sister hotels face each other across the street (the other shares the name, but loses the 'grand' part). Both are friendly & comfortable & run by the same management. As the more chic option, the Grand is plush & modern with an ultra-stylish lounge, & the staff friendly & efficient. Striking red 'arty' furnishings & tiled floors abound throughout. Rooms have (free) Wi-Fi, AC & minibar. Guests also have free use of the fitness

MID RANGE

🏠 **Alvisse Parc** (271 rooms) 120 route d'Echternach, L-1453; ✆43 56 430; e info@parc-hotel.lu; www.parc-hotel.lu. Another out-of-towner, 3km along route d'Echternach (bus 100 to Diekirch, & the 110/111 services to Echternach all pass by). Get a room at the back if you want to enjoy peace & quiet. This vast, sprawling edifice looks at first like a throwback from the 1970s. Some of the enormously long corridors could do with a little TLC, but things improve in other areas.

room. Tellyholics will be ecstatic to learn the satellite TV in the bedrooms has access to 1,000 channels – see if you can find 1 that's worth watching. Rooms across the road in the hotel's annex are slightly cheaper. €€€–€€€€

🏠 **Novotel Kirchberg** [see map, page 79] (260 rooms) 4 rue Fort Niedergrünewald, L-2015; ✆42 98 481; e H1930@accor.com; www.novotel.com. Next door to its sister the Sofitel Luxembourg Europe on the Kirchberg Plateau, modern, clean & comfortable rooms here have AC, safe, minibar & Wi-Fi access. There's a restaurant & bar downstairs, & these & other sleek public areas are brightened by colourful abstract art. One advantage of staying out here is the ample parking. *B/fast €18pp.* €€€–€€€€

🏠 **Suite Novotel** [see map, page 79] (110 suites) 13 av J F Kennedy, L-1855; ✆27 040; e H7206@accor.com; www.suitenovotel.com. Somewhere for people who want more than just a box to sleep in. Rooms are decked out in cream, grey & purple. Bathrooms come with shower & bathtub. Kitchenettes have fridge, sink, coffee & tea facilities, & a microwave – the lobby shop sells ready meals if you want to eat in, sitting on your sofa. In-room entertainments include free Wi-Fi, & a keyboard allowing you to surf the net via the TV. The latter has free movie, games & music channels. There are also more internet terminals in the lobby. There's a gym with WiiFit & WiiSport; a 24hr ironing room (if you need to get those annoying creases out of your shirt at 03.00); free coffee & tea in the lobby; & a bar. The hotel will even lend you a digital camera, & send 20 prints to your home, while those staying 4 nights or longer can borrow a Smart car (free up to 4hrs a day). The Fri midday to Mon midday w/end rate is exceptional value, & includes b/fast. Otherwise the latter costs €12. €€€–€€€€

The large rooms have been modernised, & have comfy beds, free Wi-Fi, safe, minibar, & – at the rear – a view of nothing but trees. If you're feeling sporty there are tennis courts, indoor & outdoor pools, a sauna & a gym. Massages are available for a fee. There's also a free internet terminal in the lobby. The hotel's restaurant serves decent French–Luxembourgish fare (€€€). €€€

🏠 **Best Western International** [53 G5] (70 rooms) 20–22 pl de la Gare, L-1016; ✆48 59 11;

e info@hotelinter.lu; www.hotelinter.lu. Another hotel opposite the station, but this is also sound-insulated. Modern rooms have bright décor, Wi-Fi access, minibar & safe. Some have AC. Cheaper rates apply at w/ends. €€€

🏠 **City Hotel** [53 F4] (35 rooms) 1 rue de Strasbourg, L-1021; ✆ 29 11 22; **e** mail@ cityhotel.lu; www.cityhotel.lu. Around the corner from the railway station, rooms here are modern & individually styled, & equipped with minibar, safe & Wi-Fi. Public areas are bright & welcoming. Elsewhere is a fitness room with sauna & solarium. Underground parking is available for €12 per day. €€€

🏠 **Golden Tulip Central Molitor** [53 F3] (36 rooms) 28 av De La Liberté, L-1930; ✆ 48 99 11; **e** reservations@goldentulipcentralmolitor. com; www.goldentulipcentralmolitor.com. Thanks to its Dutch chain owners, this friendly old hotel's name is a real mouthful, but there's no doubting the appeal of its location & price: midway between the station & the old town on both counts. The busy road outside quietens down at night so you shouldn't be bothered. Large rooms are lightly decorated with pine furnishings & comfortable Germanic duvets, & come with fan, free Wi-Fi, kettle & minibar. The downstairs brasserie has a reasonable range of Luxembourg & international standards, with discounts for overnight guests. The bar area has large leather armchairs that you feel belong in the smoking room of an exclusive men's club. €€€

🏠 **Hotel Français** [48 D4] (21 rooms, 4 apts) 14 pl d'Armes, L-1136; ✆ 47 45 34; **e** info@hotelfrancais.lu; www.hotelfrancais.lu. If your wallet stretches to 3 figures for a double, this exceptionally friendly, family-run hotel occupies a prime spot on place d'Armes & is the closest thing to a budget hotel in the old town. Green-&-white furnishings give the place an elegant feel that reflects the owner's love of art. Room 51 (top floor, at the back) has a terrace. Free Wi-Fi access is available for guests. €€€

🏠 **Hotel le Châtelet** [52 D4] (40 rooms, 8 suites) 2 bd de la Pétrusse, L-2320; ✆ 40 21 01; **e** contact@chatelet.lu; www.chatelet.lu. In a quiet residential neighbourhood, this friendly family-run affair with 40 years of history behind it occupies several buildings at the west end of the Pétrusse Valley. Only the main house where the reception is located has a lift. Just 500m west

of the station, it's a class apart in neighbourhood terms. Fee parking is available. Rates drop at w/ends & in summer. Some rooms have tiled floors; others wooden floors. The tiled floors can be a bit noisy if your neighbour is walking around in heels. Wi-Fi is available throughout. The hotel has its own sauna & a contract arrangement with a nearby gym. €€€

🏠 **Hotel Rix** [48 C4] (20 rooms) 20 bd Royal, L-2449; ✆ 47 16 66; **e** info@hotelrix.lu; www.hotelrix.lu. Within a few steps of Hamilius bus station, this friendly family-run establishment is on the western edge of the old town. Rooms are spacious & comfortable, with light-coloured furnishings. Very grand common areas, with chandeliers & mock-Grecian columns in the dining room, add a dash of modernity by having Wi-Fi access. There's free parking for guests out front – an important consideration in this city. €€€

🏠 **Hotel Simoncini** [58 A5] (35 rooms) 6 rue Notre Dame, L-2240; ✆ 22 28 44; **e** simhotel@pt.lu; www.hotelsimoncini.lu. Michel Lentz (1820–93), the poet most famous for writing the Luxembourgish national anthem, was born, lived & died in a house at this address – as a plaque outside will remind you. Today it's a friendly chic 'gallery/hotel' in a great location off place Guillaume II. It has a lovely clean, white décor throughout in both the bedrooms & public areas. Rooms have laminate floors, free Wi-Fi, & spotless bathrooms. There's an art theme throughout, with paintings in the rooms & sculptures in the lobby, & the adjacent gallery is also visible through glass screens. Rates drop at w/ends. €€€

🏠 **Hotel Vauban** [58 B4] (17 rooms) 10 pl Guillaume II, L-1648; ✆ 22 04 93, **e** info@ hotelvauban.lu; www.hotelvauban.lu. The Vauban is another mildly affordable option in the heart of the old town. The rooms are bright & airy (some might say 'orange') & just a short stroll from the sights. Free Wi-Fi is available in all rooms. Bathrooms are smallish, but very clean. €€€

🏠 **Melia Luxembourg** [49 G2] (161 rooms) 1 Park Dräi Eechelen (10 rue Fort Thüngen, L-1499; ✆ 27 33 31; **e** melia.luxembourg@ solmelia.com; www.melia-luxembourg. com. Friendly & stylish, this is perfect for culture vultures who can't get enough of the Philharmonie or the MUDAM – it sits between them on Kirchberg Plateau. From the outside it looks like a giant cube in a patchwork of greys with apparently random windows (making it remarkable how ordered the rooms inside are). As large as it is, it is dwarfed by the 250m façade of the conference centre next door. Depending on how you approach, you may enter via the 'ground-floor' bar & restaurant on the 2nd-floor – the reception & another bar are 2 floors below on the 'real' ground floor. Rooms are modern, sleek, decorated in tasteful light shades & come with Wi-Fi (not free), safe, minibar, comfortable beds (choose from the 'pillow menu' to ensure the ideal headrest), & views of various monuments from the windows. Bathrooms have walk-in showers. There's a gym & sauna on the 7th floor. B/fast is €20pp, but probably the best I've had in the Grand Duchy. €€€

🏠 **Parc Belle-Vue** [48 B6] (58 rooms) 5 av Marie-Thérèse, L-2132; 45 61 411; e reception.bellevue@goeres-group.com; www. parcbellevue.lu. Completing the Goeres team, the 'economic' Belle-Vue is hardly slumming it. It shares an address, a car park & a tremendous view with the adjacent Parc Plaza – you'll also have to go to that hotel's reception to check in. Rooms have Wi-Fi & are only slightly smaller than the Plaza, but just as stylish. Rates drop at w/ends. €€€

🏠 **Skol** (8 rooms) 268 route d'Arlon, L-8010 Strassen, 3km northwest of the city centre; 31 13 60; e info@skol.lu; www.skol.lu. Run by style guru & designer Marc Hobscheit, the Skol is 3km west of the centre in the suburb of Strassen (bus 248 gets you there). What it lacks in location it gains in the value for money stakes, offering free Wi-Fi & parking, as well as lower prices for the equivalent standard. Modern rooms have chocolate-brown furnishings, wooden floors, fridges, & good bathrooms. The adjoining bar & restaurant (see *Where to eat*, page 60) are very popular. €€€

🏠 **All Seasons Luxembourg Centre** [53 F5] (68 rooms) 30 rue Joseph Junck, L-1839; 49 24 96; e H1458@accor.com; www.all-seasons-hotels.com. Almost a budget hotel near the station, at least at w/ends when rates are lower. The street is home to several less than salubrious bars, clubs & other 'exotic' outlets. Nevertheless there's no hassle & when I stayed there even the lone women travellers didn't seem unduly bothered by the location. The neighbourhood can get noisy however, so bring earplugs, or try to get a room at the back. Rooms are comfortable & have free Wi-Fi. Bathrooms are clean, if a little small. €€–€€€

BUDGET Most of the few decent budget options are in the station area, which is also the red light district. Although it's not at all dangerous compared with some of its counterparts elsewhere, it can be noisy at night. Extra disturbance is provided by this location being on the flight path of Cargolux cargo planes, which take off from Findel Airport with exasperating regularity. Those who can afford it might prefer to stay in the old town, or pay a little extra for a hotel with decent sound insulation.

🏠 **Hotel Empire** [53 G5] (35 rooms) 34 pl de la Gare, L-1616; 48 52 52; e info@empire.lu; www.empire.lu. The Empire has been renovated in recent years, turning it into arguably the station district's best budget option. Rooms are of a reasonable size, simply furnished & comfortable, & the bathrooms clean. There's a free internet terminal in the lobby. €€

🏠 **Hotel Pax** [53 H7] (15 rooms) 121 route de Thionville, L-2611; 48 25 63; e info@hotelpax.

SHOESTRING

🏠 **Youth Hostel** [49 F3] (240 beds) 2 rue du Fort Olisy, L-2261; 22 68 89 20; e luxembourg@ youthhostels.lu; www.youthhostels.lu. The saviour

lu; www.hotelpax.lu. Cosy & friendly budget option above the 'La Locanda' Italian restaurant. The only negative aspect of this place is it's 2km south of the centre, but what you lack in locality you gain in price. Rooms are simple, but have been renovated, with wooden furnishings, laminate floors & free internet. Bus 16 (southbound) will get you there from the station (don't board from bay 9, the southbound stop is over the road) – ask the driver when to get off. €€

of many a budget-conscious traveller, this large, bright & clean hostel is the only option for those wanting to stay in the heart of the city, but watch the cents. Dorms have 4 or 6 beds, & are accessed using key cards for security. All 4-bed & some 6-bed rooms have en-suite bathrooms. Rooms have lockers – bring your own padlock. Free Wi-Fi is available in communal areas; use of the laundry facilities is €7.50. The terrace at the back has one of the best views around, & you don't have to stay here to make use of the cafeteria (see *Where to eat*, page 64). Bus 9 from the station passes close by, & continues to the airport. The hostel also offers a shuttle service to the station – call for pick-up. *€19.70pp (shared bath), €20.70 (en suite), inc bed, b/fast, & bedding, plus €2 returnable key deposit. Non-members pay €3 extra.*

Å Camping Kockelscheuer (161 pitches) 22 route de Bettembourg, L-1899 Kockelscheuer; ☎ 47 18 15; e caravani@pt.lu; www.camp-kockelscheuer.lu; ⊕ Easter–Oct. The nearest campsite to the city is 4km to the south in a quiet location. Facilities include clean showers, washing machines & dryers, a shop & 2 restaurants. To get there, take bus 18 southbound from the railway station (board on the far side of the road) – it's 1 stop before the end of the line (the Park & Ride). Bus 200 to Bettembourg also gets you there. If driving, the site is signposted. It's 400m off the main road. *€4pp, plus €5 per pitch.*

AIRPORT If you have problems finding a suitable room in the centre of the city, staying out by the airport provides an interesting alternative. It can also be handy if you land late at night or have an early departure. Buses 9 and 16 connect the airport with town on a regular basis from early morning until late evening.

🏠 NH Luxembourg Airport (148 rooms) route de Trèves, L-1019; ☎ 34 89 31; e nhluxembourg@nh-hotels.com; www.nh-hotels.com. Part of a Spanish chain, the modern, swish & stylish NH is a relative newcomer to the airport fold, a few mins' walk from the terminal. Staff are friendly, but efficient & businesslike. Comfortable, clean & sound-insulated rooms have AC & minibar. Even if you don't stay here, the hotel's Signature Restaurant (€€–€€€) provides a tasty alternative to airport catering before a flight, in relaxing surrounds. Good w/

end deals are available that push room prices well into the 'budget' range. *B/fast €20pp.* **€€–€€€**

🏠 Etap Hotel (61 rooms) route de Trèves, L-2632; ☎ 42 26 13 10; e H3579@accor.com; www.etaphotel.com. The Etap offers a genuine affordable option for budget travellers, with room rates borderline shoestring. Rooms are simple & small, but clean, comfortable & – crucially – soundproofed against nearby airplane movements. There's no restaurant, but you can eat next door at the Ibis. *B/fast €7pp.* **€**

✕ WHERE TO EAT

Luxembourg City has by far the biggest range of dining options in the country, with something to suit everyone. The following personal selection represents only the tip of the available iceberg, as to list everything would fill the entire book. Eating out at weekends is popular, so booking ahead is recommended. Restaurants can also be surprisingly busy on weekday lunchtimes. On the other hand, on a Monday evening – the quietest night of the week – you may be dining alone and wondering if the city's been evacuated without your knowledge. Tuesdays are also quiet, although the bars continue to do a brisk trade with the office crowd in the early evening. Things start to wind up again for the weekend from Wednesday on.

EXPENSIVE

✕ Clairefontaine [58 D6] 9 pl de Clairefontaine; ☎ 46 22 11; www.restaurantclairefontaine.lu; ⊕ 12.00–14.00 & 19.00–21.30 Mon–Fri, closed 1 week around Christmas. On one of the upper town's most

delightful squares, award-winning chef Arnaud Magnier serves up Michelin-starred wonders in quietly opulent surrounds, brought to your table by attentive staff. While very much influenced by classic French cuisine, the superb food also has a

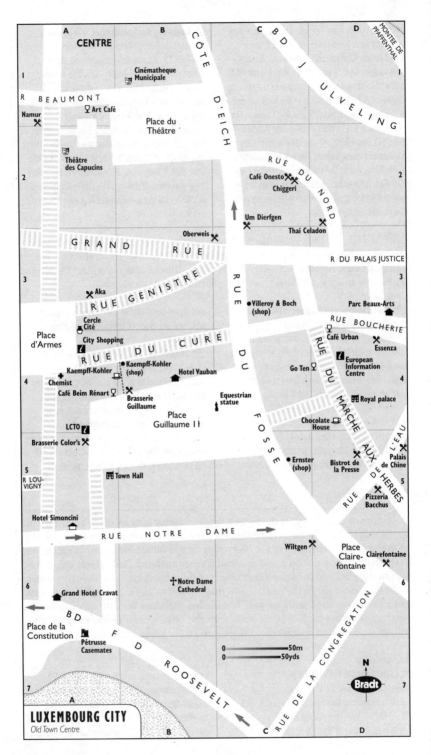

A **CENTRE** B

1 Cinémathèque Municipale

R BEAUMONT

Namur Art Café

Place du Théâtre

CÔTE D'EICH

2 Théâtre des Capucins

BD J ULVELING

RUE DU NORD

Café Onesto
Chiggeri

Um Dierfgen
Thai Celadon

GRAND RUE Oberweis

R DU PALAIS JUSTICE

3 Aka

RUE GENISTRE

RUE

RUE DU

Villeroy & Boch (shop)

Parc Beaux-Arts

RUE BOUCHERIE

Place d'Armes

Cercle Cité
City Shopping

RUE DU CURE

Café Urban
Essenza

Go Ten

European Information Centre

4 Chemist

Kaempff-Kohler

Kaempff-Kohler (shop)

Hotel Vauban

RUE DU FOSSE

Royal palace

Café Beim Rénart
Brasserie Guillaume

Equestrian statue

Place Guillaume II

Chocolate House

RUE DU MARCHE AUX HERBES

5 LCTO

Brasserie Color's

Town Hall

Ernster (shop)

Bistrot de la Presse

Palais de Chine

RUE

Pizzeria Bacchus

R LOU-VIGNY

Hotel Simoncini

RUE NOTRE DAME

Wiltgen

Place Claire-fontaine

Clairefontaine

6 Grand Hotel Cravat

Notre Dame Cathedral

BD F D ROOSEVELT

RUE DE LA CONGREGATION

Place de la Constitution

Pétrusse Casemates

0 ——— 50m
0 ——— 50yds

N

Bradt

7

LUXEMBOURG CITY
Old Town Centre

A B C D

MONTEE DE PFAFFENTHAL
R DU NORD
L'EAU

light modern touch. It's not cheap of course, but comes with all the starched linen you can handle, plus a secluded terrace. €€€€€

✗ **Le Bouquet Garni** [49 E4] 32 rue de l'Eau; ☏ 26 20 06 20; www.lebouquetgarni.lu; ⊕ 12.00–14.30 & 19.00–21.30 Tue–Sat. On 2 floors of the multi-storey dining experience known as the Îlot Gastronomique, are 2 restaurants both run by top chef Thierry Duhr. The Michelin-starred Le Bouquet Garni, on the upper floor, serves classic French cuisine in the finest of white linen settings, surrounded by bare stone walls. The emphasis here is on seafood & seasonal produce. For details of the other, the Caves Gourmandes, see below. €€€€€

✗ **Le Sud** [49 H3] 2 rue Emile Mousel; ☏ 26 47 87 50; www.le-sud.lu; ⊕ 12.00–14.00 Tue–Sat, 19.30–22.00 Tue–Fri. Occupying the 4th floor of the former Mousel brewery, there are hints of industrial heritage in the bare brick walls of this spacious dining room, but the ascetic nature ends there – the rest is all linen & chandeliers. This is not only a cut above the rest of Rives de Clausen in style; it's physically high enough that the windows look out onto wooded hillsides. The open-plan design means that the kitchen is on view, leaving no hiding place even for award-winning chef Christophe Petra. The French-inspired menu changes daily, except for the house signature dish: pigeon fillet *en croute*, with duck foie gras, cabbage stuffing & truffle

UPMARKET

✗ **Bistrot L'Annexe** [49 E5] 7 rue du St Esprit; ☏ 26 26 25 07; bar ⊕ from 07.00 for b/fast, restaurant ⊕ 12.00–14.00 & 19.00–22.00 Mon–Fri. 'The Annex', a secondary outlet of the Michelin-starred Clairefontaine, is a very pleasant place to eat in its own right, serving excellent French food. The stylish interior has unfussy tiled floors & simple furnishings, while floor-to-ceiling windows on one side look down over Grund & the Bock promontory. Service is friendly & efficient, & a good choice for those who want a little pampering without a crippling bill. The lunchtime *plat du jour* for just €11.50 represents extraordinary value for money, given the quality that comes with it. €€€–€€€€

✗ **Caves Gourmandes** [49 E4] 32 rue de l'Eau; ☏ 46 11 24; www.caves-gourmandes.lu; ⊕ 12.00–14.00 & 19.00–22.00 Mon–Sat.

mash – as good as it sounds. And if you think the cheese trolley is impressive, wait until you see the *tour des desserts*: 9 miniature puddings mounted on an afternoon tea platter, with a sorbet garnish bringing the total into double figures. As the waiter said to me on delivering mine, good luck! The 5th-floor bar & terrace is accessible to anyone reasonably dressed (⊕ *11.00 Tue–Sat*), & is great for an aperitif. €€€€€

✗ **Mosconi** [49 F5] 13 rue Münster; ☏ 54 69 94; www.mosconi.lu; ⊕ 12.00–14.00 Tue–Fri, 19.00–22.00 Tue–Sat, closed 1 week at Christmas, 1 week at Easter & 3 weeks in Aug. At the upper end of the scale in almost every sense, this restaurant in the heart of Grund was one of the first Italian restaurants outside Italy to earn a 2nd Michelin star. It's easy to see why as soon as you enter the light airy dining room & are welcomed by the owner, Simonetta Mosconi. The delightful food prepared by her husband Ilario has an exquisite lightness of touch, meaning you can savour multiple courses without feeling stuffed. Service is as unobtrusive, yet as thoroughly attentive, as you could wish for. The homemade pasta seems to melt in your mouth, & the 'tuna ice cream' is delicious, whatever you might think before tasting it. There's even a leafy terrace outside for alfresco aperitifs. Reservations are essential for evenings, but you may get in unannounced on a w/day lunchtime, when fabulous 4-course feasts are served for around €40. €€€€€

This bistro is in the stone cellar of the Îlot Gastronomique, directly below Le Bouquet Garni (see above), with a menu 'designed & inspired' by the latter's much-garlanded chef Thierry Duhr. There's a tiny terrace out front, but the real star is the dining room, deep in the underbelly of this medieval tower of gastronomic treats, with stone walls & parquet flooring. It's an atmospheric way to enjoy fine dining without hurting the finances … too much. The house speciality is slow-cooked lamb (€50, 2 people), which takes 7hrs to prepare – for obvious reasons, order in advance. The *dos de cabillaud* (cod) is also excellent. €€€–€€€€

✗ **Comptoir du Skol/Table du Skol** 268 route d'Arlon, Strassen; ☏ 31 13 60; www.skol.lu; ⊕ 12.00–14.00 & 19.00–22.30 Mon–Sat. 3km west of the centre is this enormously popular bar/restaurant. The Comptoir is a sleek wooden-floored dining area with black walls, slate-tiled bar, black tables, & an open kitchen, with lounge music to up the chicness. The adjoining Table is similar, without a bar & kitchen, & more formal with linen. The menu is the same in both, & seasonal produce is used. Meat & fish dishes are to the fore, including *carpaccio*, Black Angus *steak tartare* & hamburgers. The latter costs more than you'd pay in a fast-food joint, but the difference is on show – the burger's huge & made from Black Angus steak. The covered outdoor terrace even has log-effect gas fires for colder days. €€€–€€€€

✕ **Essenza@Apoteca** [58 D4] 12 rue de la Boucherie; 26 73 771; www.essenza.lu; ⊕ 12.00–14.00 Mon–Fri, 19.30–22.00 Mon–Sat. In the 1st edition of this guide I raved about this place in its former guise as Apoteca. I mention this here because the original name still crops up in various places & can confuse, although the style has changed radically. Today, Essenza is a straightforward but delicious Italian restaurant, more upmarket than your average pizzeria. The building remains a fascinating labyrinth of staircases & rooms going off every which way, including a terrace on the 1st floor (if you can find it), but the wow factor in the food has diminished. €€€–€€€€

✕ **Glacis by Wengé** [48 B1] 21–25 Allée Scheffer; 27 47 59 30; www.wenge.lu; ⊕ 12.00–14.30 & 19.00–22.30 daily. On the north side of place Glacis, this stylish brasserie serves French–Luxembourgish fare with a modern slant. The décor is far more chic than the description 'chocolate brown' implies. Its location close to several banks makes it popular with the business crowd on w/days, & the speed & efficiency of the service reflect the fact many customers have limited time. Don't be intimated by the suits at the other tables however – I was caught in a downpour before my visit, & went in looking (& probably smelling) like a wet dog. No-one batted an eyelid. The lunchtime menu (w/days only) is good value. There's a smart terrace out front, a separate bar (⊕ *from 10.00 daily*), & even a deli next door (⊕ *08.00–20.00 Mon–Sat;* €) if you prefer a sandwich, salad or wrap to take away (see *Shopping*, page 69). €€€–€€€€

✕ **Mi e Ti** [48 D3] 8 av de la Porte Neuve; 26 26 22 50; ⊕ 12.00–14.00 Wed–Sat, 19.00–22.15 Mon–Sat. You may walk right past 'Me & You' without realising. The bistro annex of the Mosconi Restaurant is so low-key it doesn't announce its name on the outside. Instead, look for the sign saying *bottega/ristorante*, & don't be thrown off by the chocolate shop (Les Chocolats d'Edouard) downstairs – head up the stairs to the 1st-floor dining room. Whilst big brother Mosconi veers towards classical Italian, Mi e Ti has been given free rein to develop its own character. The décor – bare floorboards, minimalist black furniture in the middle, & more indulgent purple banquettes with olive-green cushions around the walls – comes together beautifully. Attentive service & exquisite food prepared using the freshest ingredients make this a place to seek out & savour. A glass window on one side allows you to watch the goings-on in the kitchen. €€€–€€€€

MID RANGE

✕ **Am Tiirmschen** [49 E4] 32 rue de l'Eau; 26 27 07 33; www.amtiirmschen.lu; ⊕ 12.00–14.00 Mon–Sat, 19.00–22.30 Tue–Sat. Another Îlot Gastronomique offering, this too comes with stone walls & tiled floors as standard. The classic Luxembourgish dishes prepared here are given a modern slant that takes the heaviness out of that mountain of *judd*. Although the carnivore-heaven menu offers little refuge for vegetarians, they do claim to be able to cater to your needs if you ask, & if you book in advance they'll design a menu to suit your tastes. €€€–€€€€

✕ **Café 'Am Français'** [48 D4] 14 pl d'Armes; 47 45 34; www.hotelfrancais.lu; ⊕ 11.30–23.00 daily. Arguably the best dining option on place d'Armes. They do a reasonable *menu du jour* here, as well as a wide array of Luxembourgish classics & central European crowd-pleasers, plus a good range of salads. In addition to the passing tourist trade, the Français attracts a regular clientele of elderly locals, who obviously know a thing or two. €€€–€€€€

✕ **Chiggeri** [58 C2] 15 rue du Nord; 22 99 36 (restaurant), 22 82 36 (Resto-Café); www.chiggeri.lu; ⊕ 09.00–01.00 Mon–Fri, 11.00–03.00 Sat, 11.00–01.00 Sun, kitchen: 12.00–14.00 daily, 19.30–22.00 Sun–Thu, 19.30–22.30 Fri–Sat. This popular & sprawling eatery offers a range of dining options to suit all tastes & wallets. On the 2nd floor, the top-notch French restaurant (booking is essential at w/ends) is elegant & chic, with prices reflecting the high quality of the food & service. They claim to have more than 2,000 different wines available in their cellar. More down to earth both literally & financially, the 1st floor houses the Resto-Café & the ground-floor Winter Garden (Jardin d'Hiver, & open all year despite the name). Both offer the same menu of French & Belgian specialities, served up to a soundtrack of trendy rock music. Choose from a décor of dimly lit astral-themed motifs (in the former) or foliage (in the latter) according to your mood. The terrace overlooks Clausen. If your arteries are up to the onslaught, the *tartiflette* – a cholesterol-filled orgy of meat, cheese & cream – is a must-try here. €€€–€€€€

✗ Mesa Verde [49 E5] 11 rue du St Esprit; ☎ 46 41 26; www.mesa.lu; ⏰ 12.00–14.00 Wed–Fri, 18.30–23.30 Tue–Sat. Blue & turquoise patterns adorn the walls in the elegant interior of this mecca for vegetarians: one of the few completely meat-free restaurants in the land. Do pay attention to what you order as one side of the menu is devoted to fish (apparently this qualifies as vegetarian for some people). The inventively chosen & tasty selections are clearly demarcated however, so you shouldn't be in for any unpleasant surprises. €€€–€€€€

✗ Le Pavillon [48 A5] 111 av du X Septembre; ☎ 44 23 231; www.goeres-group.com; ⏰ 12.00–19.00 daily. The Goeres Group's pavilion restaurant has a beautiful location by a lake in leafy Merl Park, about 100m from the Parc Belair Hotel, run by the same company. The waterside terrace is a tranquil retreat from the city in summer & a good place to enjoy a range of international meat dishes, pastas or filling salads. €€€

✗ Mousel's Cantine [49 H3] 46 Montée de Clausen; ☎ 47 01 98; www.mouselscantine.lu; ⏰ 12.00–14.00 Mon–Fri, 18.00–22.00 Mon–Sat. Down in Clausen, this 'canteen' in the Mousel brewery (in name only – their beer is produced in Diekirch), is a back-to-basics all-wooden affair, serving a fine range of traditional Luxembourgish dishes in a friendly atmosphere. €€€

✗ Takobo [48 C4] 18 av Monterey; ☎ 46 90 05; ⏰ 11.45–22.45 Mon–Fri, 18.00–22.45 Sat–Sun. An excellent pan-Asian outlet offering a choice of Thai, Vietnamese, Chinese or Japanese dishes – mix & match as you please or select from set menus. You enter through a forest of bamboo & sit in tropical colonial splendour on bamboo & rattan furniture, surrounded by a miscellany of Asiatic bric-a-brac. As an authentic taste of the Far East the experience is a little Indiana Jones, but the food is both very good & popular. €€€

✗ Thai Celadon [58 D2] 1 rue du Nord; ☎ 47 49 34; www.thai.lu; ⏰ 12.00–14.30 Mon–Fri, 19.00–22.30 Mon–Sat. Elegant minimalist surrounds with starkly contrasting black furnishings & creamy white décor greet you in this intimate & friendly Thai restaurant. The food is excellent & there are several veggie options. Book ahead as the restaurant is both popular & rather small. €€€

✗ Um Dierfgen [58 C2] 4–6 Côte d'Eich; ☎ 22 61 41; www.umdierfgen.lu; ⏰ 11.30–14.30 & 18.00–22.00 Mon–Sat. This is a good place to chow down on a hearty Luxembourgish feast. The owner's brother runs a butcher's around the corner, so you know their meat will be fresh. The light-coloured interior brightens the otherwise standard wooden furnishings, which are guarded here by a collection of gargoyles on the windowsills that stare down whilst you dine. Alongside the *judd mat gaardebounen,* the appearance of sausage, sauerkraut & potato salad on the menu implies they're expecting a largely German clientele. Portions are hearty – nay, huge – & very tasty, but heavily meat-biased. €€€

✗ Brasserie Guillaume [58 B4] 14 pl Guillaume II; ☎ 26 20 20 20; www. brasserieguillaume.lu; ⏰ 11.00–midnight daily. A bright, high-ceilinged café/brasserie with red velvet curtains everywhere, on the city's biggest square. This is where you'll find some of the best seafood in town – a tank of live lobsters awaiting their fate by the door as you enter testifies to this fact. Wet fish is displayed on a bed of ice in the window so you can judge the freshness for yourself. The menu covers every price bracket from cheap to expensive. At the upper end, the Guillaume is *the* place to come for *fruits de mer* & oysters. For simpler meals there are *carpaccios* in various styles, served alone as a starter or with chips & salad as a main. Service & turnover are brisk, but friendly. Stop in the bar area for an aperitif – you can eat here if the restaurant is full, but tables are smaller & it feels more cramped. There's also a terrace on the square. Booking is advisable at w/ends. €€–€€€€€

CHEAP AND CHEERFUL

✗ **Aka** [58 A3] 3 rue Genistre; m 661 73 73 73; www.aka.lu; ⊕ 12.00–14.00 Mon–Fri, 19.00–22.00 Mon–Sat. Above the library, this stylish Japanese restaurant features Luxembourg's first 'sushi train', where you sit on high chairs around a long bar (there are separate tables) as the sushi & sashimi come to you on a conveyer belt. Each dish costs €5–10, but you'll need several to make a full meal. Other dishes are available. €€–€€€

✗ **Anabanana** [49 H4] 117 rue de la tour Jacob; m 691 92 52 56; www.anabanana.lu; ⊕ 12.00–14.00 Tue–Fri, 19.00–22.00 Tue–Sat. For full-on vegan food, head to this place in Clausen. The restaurant describes its dishes as 'vegan fusion', & the ingredients are 100% organic. The menu changes regularly & is influenced by seasonal availability. €€–€€€

✗ **Brasserie Color's** [58 A5] 5 rue Chimay; ☎ 26 20 28 03; ⊕ 09.00 until late daily. The eclectic mix of cuisines on the menu here encompasses Moroccan *tagine*, tapas & pasta. There's also an impressive array of *carpaccio* choices, plus *weinzossis* with puréed potato (Luxembourg's comfort equivalent of bangers 'n' mash). In addition to having tables on place Guillaume II at the back, there's a 2nd terrace above it for loftier dining & what would be a great view in summer – if it wasn't largely obscured by a row of leafy trees. To keep you on your toes, Color's has 2 entrances on different levels: enter through the bar on rue de Chimay & the brasserie is on the 1st floor; enter through the brasserie on place Guillaume II, & the bar is in the basement. €€–€€€

✗ **Goethe Stuff** [49 E4] 32 rue de l'Eau; ☎ 22 85 85; www.espaces-saveurs.lu; ⊕ 12.00–14.00 & 19.00–23.00 Wed–Sun. Old-fashioned décor meets modern food creations in this excellent choice on the top floor of the Îlot Gastronomique culinary labyrinth. Stone walls, stained-oak ceilings, tiled floors & wooden furniture combine to create a welcoming cosy interior. Needless to say there is a Goethe theme running throughout, with a bookcase containing old editions of his work. There's even a speech by Mephistopheles on the wall. So is there a genuine connection? Well yes – the poet apparently stayed here once during a visit to Luxembourg. The menu offers Alsace classics such as quiche, *boudain noir* (black pudding) & *choucroute*, all washed down with a choice of Luxembourg or Alsace wines. Reservations recommended at w/ends. €€–€€€

✗ **Palais de Chine** [58 D5] 18–20 rue de l'Eau; ☎ 46 02 83; www.palaisdechine.lu; ⊕ 12.00–14.15 & 18.30–23.30 daily. The menu here offers Cantonese dishes from sweet & sour to black bean sauce, covering all stops in-between. The food is tasty, if unspectacular, but the elegant setting & friendly welcome more than compensate. The interior has had a minimalist makeover, with sparse wooden furnishings. While the corny 'dial-a-Chinese-restaurant-interior' (think willow pattern, dragons & Buddhas) hasn't been entirely eliminated, it has at least been kept to a minimum. There's also a fair range of *dim sum* available as starters. €€–€€€

✗ **Pizzeria Bacchus** [58 D5] 32 rue du Marché Aux Herbes; ☎ 47 13 97; ⊕ 12.00–14.30 & 18.00–midnight Tue–Sun. Buzzing & popular, this busy pizzeria is a big hit with families, & one of those efficiently run joints that's always full, yet can always accommodate more guests. Wood ovens give the delicious thin-crust pizzas extra flavour. The dining area is bright, with white tiled floors & gaily coloured abstract art on the walls, bringing a slice of the Mediterranean into the city. Plenty of other options are available if you don't want pizza. There's a take-away service if you fancy a picnic. €€–€€€

✗ **Bistrot de la Presse** [58 D5] 24 rue du Marché aux Herbes; ☎ 46 66 69; ⊕ daily until late. Opposite the Grand Ducal Palace, this cosy café is a popular place to eat or just hang out for a drink. The interior walls match the locality & are festooned with patriotic photos of royalty past & present. There are also works by local artists, with price tags if you're smitten & feel the need to take one home. Daily specials are available on w/day evenings for just €11. Other food varies from sandwiches & cheap snacks to heartier mains including pasta. During the week this place has a convivial 'local' feel, when friends of the landlord gather around the bar debating the state of the nation. The Luxembourg press club meets on the 1st floor – hence the name. €€

✗ **Café Am Musée** [49 E5] 14 rue du St-Esprit; ☎ 26 20 25 95; www.goeres-group.com; ⊕ 10.00–18.00 Tue–Wed & Fri–Sun, 10.00–20.00 Thu. The City History Museum's café is worth visiting for its views alone – it occupies the perfect spot for spectacular views over Grund. You don't have to enter the museum to eat here as you can access it through a side gate leading into the peaceful stone & grass gardens. It's a popular lunch spot, so if you want to eat outside (highly recommended on fine days) book in advance. The salads are large, & meals in themselves. Or come here for afternoon tea & cakes to enjoy the setting. €€

✗ Café Onesto [58 C2] 11 rue du Nord; ✆ 22 38 18; ⏱ 11.45–14.00 & 18.30–23.00 Mon–Sat. Another cheap-&-cheerful, no-frills pizzeria, with wooden tables, red vinyl banquettes & stone floors, Onesto has similar prices & food to the Bacchus. The welcome here is no less warm & friendly. Pastas & pizzas dominate the menu – the latter prepared in an authentic wood-fired oven, & substantial in size. There's also a nice terrace at the back. €€

✗ Art Café [58 A1] 1a rue Beaumont; ✆ 26 27 06 52; www.goeres-group.com; ⏱ 12.00–19.00 Mon–Sat, 12.00–14.00 out of season. Want an authentic 'bordello' feeling as you sup or dine? On a quiet little square behind place du Théâtre, this sumptuously decadent café-cum-boudoir is bedecked with plush red tasselled velvet drapes, candelabras, floor-to-ceiling mirrors, a chessboard-tiled floor & leopard-skin covered chairs (although I'm fairly confident the fur has never seen any animal, let alone the Serengeti). All in all it's tackily wonderful. The food is excellent, the prices raise an eyebrow because of how reasonable they are given the décor, & the mood is enhanced by the eclectic mix of unobtrusive world music piped through the speakers. Choose from salads, wok dishes, pasta, a *plat du jour,* pizza baguettes or *tarte flambée.* Note that the full menu is only served until 14.00, after which you're limited to bread-based options. Alternatively, just recline on a chaise longue & sip an aperitif. €–€€

✗ Kaempff-Kohler [58 B4] 18 pl Guillaume II; ✆ 26 86 861; www.kaempff-kohler.lu; ⏱ 08.00–18.00 Mon–Sat. A 1-stop delicatessen, cheese shop, patisserie & confectioner since 1922, the café also does a more substantial *plat du jour.* €–€€

✗ La Table du Pain [48 C4] 19 av Monterey; ✆ 24 16 08; ⏱ 07.00–19.00 daily. A bakery first & foremost, there are tables here where you can sit & order filled rolls, quiche & other light meals. It offers free Wi-Fi access to customers. The 'Bread Table' also has another city-centre outlet at 37 av de la Liberté (✆ 29 56 63). €–€€

✗ Namur [58 A1] 27 rue des Capucins; ✆ 22 34 08; www.namur.lu; ⏱ 11.40–18.00 Mon, 07.45–18.00 Tue–Sat. Oberweis's main competitor is another delightful patisserie that makes its own chocolate. It too has a couple of outlets in town (*another is at 44 av de la Liberté, near the station;* ✆ 49 39 64). Their city-centre shop first opened in 1863 & much of the interior is original (even though the building itself is not). Even if you aren't hungry, stop by to check out the marble floors, glass chandeliers, ornately carved wood & shiny mirrors. The tearoom beside the shop serves light meals & afternoon tea. Or just sit with a coffee, bite down on a deliciously indulgent pastry & kiss goodbye to your waistline. €–€€

✗ Oberweis [58 C3] 19–21 Grand Rue; ✆ 47 07 03; www.oberweis.lu; ⏱ 10.30–18.15 Mon, 07.30–18.15 Tue–Fri, 07.00–18.15 Sat. The central & original location of Luxembourg's renowned pastry & chocolate family has a 1st-floor tearoom above its narrow shop, where you can enjoy light meals & salads at lunchtimes, or pig out on mouth-watering cakes & pastries through the afternoon. When weather permits there are tables on the tiny square out front. There are several other Oberweis outlets throughout the city, including a take-away in the main railway station. Note that sometime in 2012 Oberweis will relocate to new premises on the Grand Rue, directly opposite the old place. The street number will change; other details won't. €–€€

✗ Wiltgen [58 D6] 46 pl Guillaume II; ✆ 26 20 20 94; www.wiltgen.lu; ⏱ 10.00–18.30 Mon, 08.00–18.30 Tue–Sat. A mouth-watering patisserie/chocolatier on the southeast corner of pl Guillaume II that also has a dining room, serving a *plat du jour,* plus simpler but tasty fare including burgers, salads & sandwiches to eat in or take away. And then of course there are those cakes & chocolates … €–€€

ROCK BOTTOM If you really can't live without a fast-food burger, you'll find what you're looking for on place d'Armes [58 A4].

✗ Chocolate House – Nathalie Bonn

[58 D4] 20 rue Marché aux Herbes; ☏ 26 26 20 06; ⏰ 07.00–20.00 Mon–Fri, 09.00–20.00 Sat, 10.00–20.00 Sun. Downstairs is a chocolate & cake shop, with homemade goodies created on the premises, plus ice creams. Upstairs is a wooden-floored café, where you can eat the aforementioned. But the main highlight could only loosely be described as 'food'. Choose from 40 flavours of 'chocolate spoon', wooden spoons with blocks of chocolate on the bottom that you drop into hot milk & stir to melt. €

✗ Gelateria Caffé Veneziano [48 C4]

14–16 rue Philippe II; ☏ 22 08 58; ⏰ daytime only, daily. Just off Grand Rue, head here to administer to your ice-cream cravings. You can take away or sit at one of the tables inside or out. Prices start from €1 per scoop. €

✗ Youth Hostel [49 F3] 2 rue du Fort Olisy;

☏ 22 68 89 20; www.youthhostels.lu; ⏰ daily. The youth hostel's cafeteria attracts budget-conscious diners from far & wide. Set menus are served all day while stocks last (they sometimes run out in the evenings), & go for just €10 (€9 for YHA members). In summer, dine on the terrace at the back. €

ENTERTAINMENT AND NIGHTLIFE

The city abounds with cafés and bars where you can drink into the small hours. The highest concentrations are around place d'Armes [58 A4] in the upper town, down in Grund [49 G6], around the railway station [53 G5], and in Clausen [49 G3]. Leafy place d'Armes is a pretty place to sit out in fine weather, and therefore a tourist magnet – the people who set the menu prices here know this too. Many bars fill up with after-office drinkers on weekdays in the early evening, and then quieten down later. For reasons unknown, Wednesday is the most popular weekday night – I guess it breaks up the week. To find out what's on pick up the free monthly *City Magazine* (*citymag.lu*), available across the city. Each issue is named after the cover star, so it may be titled 'Anne's City Magazine', or similar. *352 Magazine*'s website (*www.352luxmag.lu*) also carries cultural listings, as does *Agendalux*, published in paper form or downloadable from www.agendalux.lu.

BARS AND CLUBS

Grund

☿ Café Des Artistes [49 E5] 22 Montée du Grund; ☏ 46 13 27. This discerning bohemian's drinking hole has candlelit tables, poster-strewn walls (& ceiling), & rather more chairs & tables than the space can support. The cluttered little pub conveys a convivial feel that's both quiet & arty. There's live piano music Wed–Sat evenings, but even that fails to overwhelm the conversation. It attracts couples and arty types in equal numbers.

Upper town

☿ Art Café [58 A1] 1a rue Beaumont; ☏ 26 27 06 52; www.goeres-group.com. Gloriously overdressed, this not just a good place to eat, it's also a cool spot to hang out for a drink (see *Where to eat,* page 63). Unfortunately it's no longer open evenings, & closes at 19.00 – even earlier in 'low season'.

☿ Scott's Pub [49 F5] 4 Bisserwee; ☏ 22 64 75; www.scotts.lu. One of the city's biggest drinking institutions, popular with younger visitors, expat residents & locals. Situated by the Alzette River in central Grund, it manages to be both loud & cosy – 'pubby' in fact, right down to the dartboard. Live music is hosted on a regular basis – check the website for the agenda. The riverside terrace is great for a relaxing chat with friends & has a fabulous view to boot.

☿ Bistrot de la Presse [58 D5] 24 rue du Marché aux Herbes; ☏ 46 66 69. An 'almost local' in the city centre, this cheap, cheerful no-frills pub doesn't feel the need for gimmicks (see *Where to eat,* page 62).

☿ Café Beim Rénart [58 A4] 20 pl Guillaume II; ☏ 22 49 28. A traditional, plain & unpretentious bar in the centre of the upper old town, which has the attraction of being less overwhelmed with tourists than some of the neighbouring establishments on nearby place d'Armes – which is odd considering it's 25m from the tourist office. This is as close as you'll come to a locals' pub in the centre.

Café Urban [58 D4] 2 rue de la Boucherie; 26 47 85 78; www.urban.lu. By the royal palace, this is enormously popular with the young after-work crowd & fills up quickly when offices in the area start to close. The large TV

screen showing predominantly British sports betrays this place as a hangout for expats.

Go Ten [58 D4] 10 rue du Marché aux Herbes; 26 20 36 52; www.goten.lu. The Japanese-inspired décor in this chic drinking joint creates a sense of serenity by going for the forested, wood bark look. This is a rare opportunity to enjoy Simon beers in the southern half of the country.

Zanzen [48 D5] 27–29 rue Notre Dame; 26 20 18 22; www.zanzen.lu. Very popular with local workers, it tends to get busy after office hours.

Clausen Another centre of drinking life can be found in the lower town area of Clausen, to the north of Grund and close to the youth hostel. Anglophone visitors may think they've entered some kind of parallel universe or twilight zone. Within a few staggering steps of each either are the **Britannia** English pub [49 H3] (*69 Allée Pierre de Mansfeld;* 43 32 33) and the **Pygmalion** Irish bar [49 H4] (*19 rue de la Tour Jacob;* 42 08 60). Both attract a largely expat crowd, and after a while here you may wonder if you've actually left home at all. If that's too much, seek refuge in the more traditional **Mousel's Cantine** [49 H3] (*46 Montée de Clausen;* 47 01 98), a stone's throw from all three (see *Where to eat,* page 61). Or head the extra few steps to Rives de Clausen [49 H3].

Rives de Clausen The site of the old Mousel brewery in Clausen has been redeveloped into an entertainment district catering mainly to a young trendy crowd, who like to drink cocktails while shaking their thing to boomingly loud music.

Although the original brewery has gone, a **microbrewery** (Clausel) has appeared in its place. Most bars and clubs listed below serve its beer, and a restaurant [49 H3] (*Big Beer Company; 12 Rives de Clausen; www.bigbeercompany.lu*) has opened in the former steam room, selling its own house beers, and somewhat overpriced Luxembourgish food. Rives de Clausen is also home to the exquisite Restaurant Le Sud (see *Where to eat,* page 59).

Most places have terraces, quieter than the thumping interiors, but their future is uncertain, as local residents have complained about their failure to keep the noise down after 23.00. The majority of the bars are open similar hours: Tuesday to Saturday, evenings only (some are also closed Tuesday), usually from 17.00 or 19.00 until 01.00 or 02.00, and until 03.00 on Friday and Saturday. I offer brief descriptions here, but they're all in a row so if one doesn't suit your tastes the next is seconds away. There are no cover charges. Since Rives de Clausen isn't technically a road, and all these places officially share the same street address (2 rue Emile Clausen) I have used their unofficial Rives de Clausen numbers for clarity. They are listed in the order you'll come across them. See www.rivesdeclausen.eu for news of upcoming events.

There is on-site parking, or take the free shuttle bus (*Navette*) from the east end of place Glacis [49 G4], where there is also a large car park (except during the annual *Shueberfouer* funfair) on Wednesday, Saturday and Sunday. It returns there into the early hours until 03.00.

Rock Box 3 Rives de Clausen; m 661 20 26 26. No-frills bar with loud rock music.

Space Bar 5 Rives de Clausen; 26 26 25 26. The same as Rock Box above, but with more, er, space for dancing.

♀ **Água de Côco** 7 Rives de Clausen; ☎ 26 27 08 04; www.aguadecoco.lu. Goes down the Brazilian route, with grilled meats served. Brazilian dance lessons are held 19.00–21.00 Tue.

♀ **Life Bar** 9 Rives de Clausen; ☎ 26 86 45 88; www.lifebarclausen.com. Filling 3 floors, Life Bar has white vinyl seating & more chandeliers than you can shake a stick at.

♀ **TromBar** 13 Rives de Clausen; ☎ 26 26 22 66; www.trombar.lu. Narrow cocktail bar with neon, barstools, tapas, lounge music, & all-you-can-eat chicken wings on Tue nights.

♀ **King Wilma** 15 Rives de Clausen; ☎ 691 112 339; www.kingwilma.lu. Has a Flintstones theme, with a large (plastic) dinosaur skeleton hanging from the ceiling. Music courtesy of DJs plays into the early hours.

♀ **Sins City** 16 Rives de Clausen; ☎ 26 20 17 64; www.sinscity.lu. More beer, cocktails & loud music. Possibly no more or fewer sins than anywhere else though.

♀ **Verso** 17 Rives de Clausen; ☎ no phone. Same again: beer, cocktails & music.

♀ **Ikki** 19 Rives de Clausen; ☎ 49 69 40; www.ikki.lu. The most chic bar here, with neon & velvet. It offers sushi finger food & serves main meals in the €€€–€€€€ range.

MUSIC, CINEMA AND THEATRE
Music

Brasserie Neumünster [49 F4] Neumünster Abbey Cultural Centre, 28 rue Münster; ☎ 26 20 521. Hosts free jazz brunch concerts (billed as Apero's Jazz) every Sun at 11.30. Performances are usually inside the brasserie, but move out onto the expansive terrace if weather permits. You don't have to eat here to come down & enjoy the music.

Den Atelier 54 rue de Hollerich; ☎ 49 54 851; www.atelier.lu. A live music venue that hosts rock concerts & dance events.

Philharmonie [49 H1] 1 pl de l'Europe; tickets and information ☎ 26 32 26 32; www.philharmonie.lu. For something quieter, the most prestigious classical music events are held at here. The season runs mid-Aug to mid-July; check the website to see what's on. The Philharmonie's La Clé de Sol Restaurant (☎ 26 68 73 94; www.cle-de-sol.lu) is a great spot for pre- or post-performance dining. It's also popular, so reserve well ahead.

Cinema For movies, head to the ten-screen **Utopolis** (*45 av J F Kennedy;* ☎ *42 95 95; www.utopolis.lu*), out in Kirchberg beside the Auchan shopping mall (see map, page 79). Some films are shown in their original language and subtitled, others are dubbed into French or German, but the posters tell you which – look for the magic letters 'VO' signifying 'original version'. If in doubt, ask. The same group also runs the five-screen **Ciné Utopia** [48 A1] (*16 av de la Faïencerie;* ☎ *22 46 11; www.utopolis.lu*). Elsewhere, the **Cinémathèque Municipale** [58 B1] (*17 pl du Théâtre;* ☎ *29 12 59 or 47 96 26 44*) shows arthouse movies and re-runs of old classics. Call ahead or see the local press for listings.

Theatre The theatre season generally runs from September or October until June or July. Prices and times vary. **Grand Théâtre** [48 C1] (*1 Rond-point Schuman;* ☎ *47 96 39 00; www.theatres.lu*) stages musicals, ballet, opera, etc. The smaller **Théâtre des Capucins** [58 A2] (*9 pl du Théâtre;* ☎ *47 96 39 00; www.theatres.lu*) puts on more plays, and occasional music events.

FESTIVALS AND EVENTS

The multi-cultural **Festival de l'Immigration** (*www.clae.lu*) takes place in March at the LuxExpo in Kirchberg, and is where NGOs and cultural associations representing every nationality gather for music, dancing, art expos and world food.

A festival of jazz and world music, **Printemps Musical** (*www.printempsmusical.lu*) fills several venues across the city from March to May.

Every Easter Monday the **Emaischen** pottery market is held on the Marché au Poissons. Stalls sell food and other items, but the top-sellers are *péckvillchen*, glazed hand-painted terracotta whistles shaped as birds (originally from Nospelt, see page 90). Any small child will show you how to get the maximum noise from one.

Mainly centred on place Guillaume II, the **All American Music Festival** (*www. allamerican.lu*), with jazz, gospel, Dixieland and reggae acts playing over the Whitsun weekend, marks the official start of the open-air season.

The **Fête de la Musique** (*www.fetedelamusique.lu*) fills the days running up to the National Day (see below). Free concerts take place across the country in bars and on public squares. The biggest event is the Luxembourg Philharmonic Orchestra performing on place Guillaume II.

The **National Day** (Fête National) festivities on and around 23 June are celebrated with particular vigour in the capital. As well as the traditional ceremonies, a series of free concerts (rock, classical and jazz) are performed on place Guillaume II (see *Chapter 2, Practical Information*, page 34, or check with the tourist office for more details).

Summer in the City (*www.summerinthecity.lu*) is a three-month programme of musical events that take place across the city throughout the summer. Pick up a brochure from the tourist office to find out exactly what's on and where. The festival includes a host of free outdoor performances.

On the Saturday (usually the first in July) before Rock um Knuedler (below) is **World MeYouZik** (*www.meyouzik.lu*). It's a festival of world music and culture with gigs at several locations, including place Guillaume II.

Rock um Knuedler (*www.rockumknuedler.lu*) takes place on three stages on place Guillaume II on the first Sunday in July. This free open-air rock festival attracts around 8,000–10,000 visitors.

Blues'n Jazz Rallye (*www.bluesjazzrallye.lu*) is a free festival with around 50 concerts held at several locations – open-air stages and cafés – in Grund and Clausen on the third Saturday in July.

For visual entertainment, the **Streeta(rt)nimation** (*www.streetartnimation.lu*) festival in mid-August attracts around 70 acts including mimes, clowns, acrobats, wandering minstrels and performance artists to the city centre. It's free.

La Nuit des Musées (*www.statermuseeen.lu*), or Museums Night, occurs on the second Saturday in October, when all major museums and galleries in the city throw open their doors from 18.00 until 01.00. Each participant puts on special events to lure in the public, and a free shuttle bus ferries visitors between locations.

In late August and early September the Champ des Glacis just north of the centre – normally a car park – transforms into the massive **Schueberfouer** funfair (*Kermesse*). Plenty of eateries spring up in-between the tacky thrill rides, and many locals go there to dine. It's very popular and draws a million visitors during its 2½-week run. The first Monday in September – the midpoint of the fair – is a local public holiday in the city. This day is also the occasion of the **Grande Braderie** citywide sales (see *Shopping*, below).

Luxembourg Festival (*www.luxembourgfestival.lu*) is a combined music and theatre event organised jointly by the Philharmonie and the Grand Théâtre in October/November.

During the last weekend in November, from Thursday to Sunday (afternoons only), **La Fête des Vins et Crémants** takes place in a large tent on place Guillaume II. Forty Luxembourg winemakers take part, with tasting being the central theme. Admission is free, but glasses and wines are not.

Winter Lights (*www.winterlights.lu*) is a citywide celebration with concerts, exhibitions and other events in the month leading up to Christmas. Most events revolve around the centrepiece, the **Christmas Market** on place d'Armes.

SHOPPING

Shops in Luxembourg City have varying opening times. Most are open from 09.00 until 19.00 Monday to Friday and 09.00 until 18.00 Saturday, give or take an hour at either end. A few bigger shops trade until 20.00 on Saturday. Some remain closed on Monday morning; others remain open until 21.00 on one or two weekday evenings. Most are closed Sundays, except in the run up to Christmas, and many smaller shops close for an hour or two at lunch, commonly from 12.00. Bakeries are sometimes open earlier in the morning, and on Sunday.

For all your shopping enquiries, visit the **City Shopping Info Point** [58 A4] (*2 pl d'Armes;* 26 27 02 70; *www.cityshopping.lu;* 10.00–18.00 *Tue–Sat*). They can advise on where to get this or that, which shops are hot, which not, and they have a handy free booklet (more of a book really) filled with useful addresses.

Buses are free at weekends when there are sales on. The sales season starts on the first Monday in September (a citywide public holiday) with the **Grande Braderie** (*08.00–18.00*), during which some 400 shops in the centre offer bargains sold from stalls on the street. Many shops also open on the previous Sunday afternoon for 'pre-Braderie' sales.

ART AND ANTIQUES There are several antique shops along the rue des Capucins [58 A2]. On the first Saturday of the month from April to October, an **arts market** is held in Grund [49 G6] – only professional artists can set up stalls here, which generally guarantee the quality of the work.

BOOKSHOPS

Chapter 1 [48 A5] 42 rue Astrid; 44 07 09; www.chapter1.lu; 10.00–18.00 Mon–Sat, 08.30–13.00 Sun. Luxembourg's first specialist English-language bookshop, in the suburb of Belair, 1km west of the centre. They also stock English magazines, cards & DVDs. It's on a residential side street close to the Parc Belair hotel.

Ernster [58 C5] 27 rue du Fossé; 22 50 771. Ernster has a reasonable range of English-language books and is in the city centre. **Librairie Française** [48 C4] 2–4 rue Beck; 22 00 67. A good bookshop in the old town. They stock a small selection of English-language paperbacks.

CLOTHES Thanks to high rents and space restrictions, you won't find many large chain stores in the old town. The main downtown shopping street, **Grand Rue** [58 B2], is pedestrianised, and the majority of premises are exclusive boutiques selling fashionable designer clothing, shoes, handbags, jewellery and perfume. There are too many to list them all, but if those items are what you seek, that's where you need to head. There are also those tremendously expensive shops that only seem to stock a handful of arty knick-knacks, which they would never taint by applying price tags. You know very well that if you have to ask how much, you're in the wrong shop.

HOUSEHOLD ACCESSORIES Perhaps the *grande dame* of all the city's shops, **Bonn-Frères** [48 C4] (*9 rue Philippe II;* 22 32 01), just west of place d'Armes was founded in 1855, and is the place to look for upmarket household furnishings and designer artefacts created by Armani et al.

FOOD For everyday needs and more familiar high-street names, try the out-of-town shopping malls. Handiest is **Auchan shopping mall** (*Centre Commercial*; *www.auchan.lu*) in Kirchberg, with no fewer than 60 retail outlets under one roof – including the huge Auchan hypermarket itself, which sells pretty much everything *including* the kitchen sink (see map, page 79). Bus 16 will drop you outside. Prices inside are much the same as elsewhere in northern Europe, but higher than the US. About the only supermarket in the centre is **Alima** [48 C3] (*off rue de la Porte Neuve, behind No 11*). It's open from 08.30 until 18.30 Monday to Friday, and 08.00 until 18.00 Saturday. For more down-to-earth shopping, a fruit, vegetable and flower market appears on place Guillaume II [58 B4] on Wednesdays.

Comptoir by Wengé [48 B1] 21–25 Allée Scheffer; ☎27 47 59 20; www.wenge.lu; ⏰ 08.00–20.00 Mon–Sat. A mouth-watering delicatessen with everything from chocolates & patisserie to pâté & teas. They also sell take-away food designed & produced in the restaurant next door (see *Where to eat*, page 60).

Kaempff-Kohler [58 B4] 18 pl Guillaume II; ☎26 86 86; www.kaempff-kohler.lu. Spread over several premises between the place d'Armes & place Guillaume II, Kaempff-Kohler has been a one-stop delicatessen, cheese shop, patisserie & confectioner since 1922.

Little Britain 1C, route d'Arlon, Capellen; ☎26 31 08 56; www.littlebritain.lu; ⏰ 08.00–18.00 Tue–Sat, 09.00–14.00 Sun. A haven for homesick Brits as it stocks an extensive range of British food. In addition to teapots, books, cards & newspapers, there's a tearoom at the back for a cuppa. Technically it's not in the city at all, but about 10km west in Capellen.

Namur [58 A1] 27 rue des Capucins; ☎22 34 08; 66 av de la Liberté ☎49 39 64; www.namur.lu. The chocolates here & in Oberweis (see below) are available in pre-packaged boxes, or you can make your own selection.

Oberweis [58 C3] 19–21 Grand Rue; ☎47 47 03; moving across the road to an even-numbered address in 2012; in the railway station; ☎47 47 03; & in the Auchan shopping mall; ☎42 94 09; www.oberweis.lu. For sheer chocolate indulgence.

OTHER PRACTICALITIES

PHARMACIES When the pharmacies below are closed they will normally display the address of the nearest open alternative (*pharmacie de garde*) on the door. These are open from 08.00 until 20.00 on specified days – visit www.pharmacie.lu for a list of which pharmacy is on duty on any given day. Other pharmacies are generally only open normal shop hours Monday to Friday, and Saturday mornings. Many also close for an hour at lunchtime.

✚ **Pharmacie du Cygne** 11 av de la Porte Neuve; ☎ 22 23 14; ⊕ 09.30–18.30 Mon, 07.45–18.30 Tue–Fri, 07.45–12.15 Sat. Also stocks homeopathic medicines.
✚ **Pharmacie G Schroeder** 23 rue Aldringen; ☎ 26 20 17 18; ⊕ 07.30–18.10 Mon–Fri, 08.00–12.00 Sat

✚ **Pharmacie Goedert** 5 pl d'Armes; ☎ 22 23 991; ⊕ 08.00–18.15 Mon–Fri, 08.00–18.00 Sat
✚ **Pharmacie Lugen** 18 av de la Gare; ☎ 48 83 671; ⊕ 08.00–18.15 Mon–Fri, 09.00–12.30 & 13.30–18.00 Sat

BANKS Luxembourg City is one of the world's banking capitals. There are so many branches dotted around that in some areas you can't throw a stone without hitting one. To list them all would fill much of this book – they occupy six pages of the local telephone directory. Rest assured that in the city centre you're unlikely to be more than 200m from an ATM – there's one on virtually every street corner. **Rue Aldringen** and **Grand Rue** in the old town have several, as do **avenue de la Gare** and **avenue de la Liberté** in the station district. Opening hours may vary slightly from one branch to the next, but in general they are open from 08.30 until 16.30, Monday to Friday.

POST OFFICES

✉ **Post office (old town)** [48 C4] 25 rue Aldringen; ☎ 47 65 44 51; ⊕ 07.00–19.00 Mon–Fri, 07.00–17.00 Sat

✉ **Post office (station)** [53 G5] 38 pl de la Gare; ☎ 40 88 76 00; ⊕ 06.00–19.00 Mon–Fri, 06.00–12.00 Sat

CHOCOHOLIC'S DELIGHT

Purveyors of the finest chocolate since 1964, the Oberweis family business (it's currently run by the founder's two sons and their wives) started life as a cottage industry, but today employs over 100 staff. They've long been a favourite pleasure of the royal household: to the extent that they can officially label their products as 'by Royal Appointment'.

Co-owner and creative designer Jeff Oberweis has taught himself to recognise the best cocoa plants, and visits the growing countries personally to source the finest beans, bought directly from the farmers in fair trade deals. He also likes to push back the boundaries of chocolate manufacturing, mixing styles by combining Germanic truffles with Swiss pastilles and Belgian pralines to produce something uniquely Luxembourgish. The family philosophy is always to look forward and develop new ideas, rather than to rest on traditional laurels and become stuck in the past like some of their more internationally known competitors. One top-seller reflecting this trend is a range of very high quality dark-chocolate bars sourced from single countries: the Dominican Republic, Papua New Guinea, etc. Be tough on yourself, and try them all – I did.

WALKING TOURS Luxembourg City tourist office produces a number of good walking-tour pamphlets covering various routes through different aspects and quarters of the city (also available as pdf files from the LCTO website, www.lcto. lu). The most comprehensive of these, the **City Promenade**, takes in most sights of historical interest. Beginning from the place Guillaume II [58 B4], the walk passes (amongst others) the royal palace, place d'Armes, place de la Constitution, the Pétrusse casemates, Notre Dame Cathedral, the Corniche and St Michael's Church, before leading you down into Grund and back up via the Pétrusse Valley. The total distance is about 4km and takes a minimum of half a day – longer if you stop to absorb everything along the way.

Another interesting walk is the **Wenzel Route**, also billed as '1,000 years in 100 minutes'. The 'Wenzel' after whom it's named is Wenceslas II, who was Duke of Luxembourg from 1383–1419 (but *not* the 'good king' we sing about at Christmas – that was one of his ancestors). This trip leads you around what remains of the city's fortifications in the upper and lower towns, and is signposted on the ground with crown symbols. As the name suggests it follows a journey through time that should take under two hours to complete. Informative boards along the way explain both the history and the wildlife you might encounter, but explanations are only in French and German so the tourist office's leaflet comes in handy.

A host of other self-guided routes are available, depending on your area of interest. The **Vauban walk** covers points related to the city's development as a defensive stronghold, thanks in no small part to the efforts of French fortress builder, Sebastien Le Prestre de Vauban. There's a fair amount of up and down involved, so be prepared or don't go on a hot day. Note also that this may not follow exactly where it's marked on the map. The bridge over the railway was closed for renovation at the time of writing and the only way to cross the tracks was to detour (marked on the pamphlet) via rue Trois Glands. The bridge should reopen during the lifetime of this book. The **Schuman walk** links together important sites in the life of Robert Schuman, founder of modern Europe. There are also no fewer than three separate **architectural walks**: one in the railway station district (Art-Deco and Art-Nouveau buildings from the late 19th and early 20th centuries); one in the heart of the city (Modernist buildings from the 1930s to the 1960s and more recent); and one through Kirchberg (all new). For a greener circuit, the **gardens and parks walk** follows a 5km loop down the Bock promontory, along the Alzette and Pétrusse rivers, and up into the municipal park.

For something different (and more energetic), the **Eich walk** offers a taste of both the countryside and Luxembourg's industrial past. It's quite long (10km) and there are few facilities along the way, so bring water. Half the route is through forest or parkland, but this bills itself as an industrial heritage trail because the valley was once full of iron and steel foundries. Little remains of the latter other than a few brick chimneys, so you'll need to use your imagination. Along the way you pass two beautiful old châteaux once owned by foundry magnates. Today, stark evidence of the shifting sands of global power, they house the Russian and Chinese embassies. The latter has a lake and is particularly grand. You can reach the start of the walk on foot, but that adds 1.5km each way. Otherwise take bus 5 to Dommeldange station.

A shorter cultural walk is **Museumsmile** (*www.museumsmile.lu*), covering around 1.6km and passing seven museums: Villa Vauban, Casino Luxembourg, the City History Museum, the National Museum of History and Art, the Natural History Museum, the Dräi Eechelen and the MUDAM. See their individual entries for more information.

UPPER OLD TOWN The centre of the old town as far as most visitors are concerned is **place d'Armes** [58 A4]. This leafy plaza, bursting with cafés and lime trees, has formed the hub of the city since 1671. As with central squares in other capitals the restaurants and bars that line it come with inflated prices, and service with a sneer may be the order of the day. For better value for money look elsewhere, though you will miss out on the ambiance and the lovely view. There is no spectacular architecture on show, and little to do other than sit on the terrace and enjoy a drink, but there's no harm in that and it's an exceedingly pleasant place for hanging out and doing nothing. In summer it fills completely with tables, and free concerts are performed on the bandstand in the middle.

Joined at the hip to place d'Armes, **place Guillaume II** [58 B4] is larger and more open than its neighbour, making it feel less crowded even though it too contains numerous cafés and bars. The square is named after William II, the second of three Dutch kings who owned Luxembourg in the 19th century – his **equestrian statue** watches over everything from a plinth in the centre. On the south side is the neoclassical **town hall**, built between 1830 and 1838. To that building's left is another small statue, this one devoted to Michel Rodange, who is the nation's greatest literary hero. Rodange's most famous creation *Renert the Fox* sits atop the monument, gazing down at its creator's head.

To most Luxembourgers place Guillaume II is known as *Knuedeler*, meaning 'knot'. This is a reference to the fact that the site was once a monastery, and the knot in question was located on the belts worn around monks' robes. The monastery was dismantled in 1829 and some of the stones from it were used in the construction of the town hall.

Just east of place Guillaume II, the **Grand Ducal Palace** [58 D4] (*Palais Grand-Ducal; 17 rue du Marché aux Herbes; information & tickets from the city tourist office* ⟍ *22 28 09;* ⊕ *for guided tours mid-Jul to Aug Tue–Thu, tours in English begin at 15.00 & 16.00; adult/child €7/3.50*) was constructed in 1573, replacing an earlier building destroyed in a gigantic gunpowder explosion some 20 years earlier. It was originally the town hall, and only became the royal residence in 1890. When the Nazis occupied the city during World War II, the high command in Luxembourg used the palace as their headquarters. Sadly they trashed the place in the process – to such an extent that when Grand Duchess Charlotte returned from exile and saw the state it was in, she no longer wanted to live there. Since that time the palace at Colmar Berg has been the principal royal residence, and this building is only used for ceremonial purposes and state occasions. Nevertheless, the interior is fabulous, having been meticulously restored to its former beauty, replete with vaulted ceilings (during World War I the German high command whitewashed over the original 16th-century frescoes on these, but restoration work has managed to salvage some), period furniture, sweeping staircases and chandeliers. The strikingly beautiful green vases on the main staircase are Siberian malachite, a souvenir from a state visit to Tsarist Russia. The cobbles inside the front entrance are wooden: Grand Duke Adolphe had the former stones here replaced as he liked a nap in the afternoon, and was being kept awake by the sound of horses' hooves making deliveries. The 45-minute tour starts from behind the palace and takes in the official rooms on the ground and first floors.

The building adjoining the palace to its right is the **Chamber of Deputies**, Luxembourg's lower house of parliament. It was built as an annex to the palace in 1859. More recent additions to the Marché aux Herbes are the floodlights, each with a golden face, which illuminate the palace at night – they were created by Munich-based designer Ingo Maurer.

The **European Information Centre** [58 D4] (*Europäeschen Informatiounszenter; 7 rue du Marché aux Herbes;* \ *43 01 37 833;* ⊕ *13.00–17.00 Mon, 09.00–18.00 Tue–Fri, 11.00–16.00 Sat; free*) is located by the Grand Ducal Palace in an 18th-century mansion. This is where you'll find answers to all the questions you never wanted to ask about your rights in Europe and the running of the EU. You can pick up brochures here on aspects of the Union you hadn't even considered existed. But if it does exist, you can bet someone has spent your tax money compiling a detailed factual document about it – make their job worthwhile by picking up a copy.

Little **St Michael's Church** [49 E4] (*Eglise St Michel; 12 rue Sigefroi;* ⊕ *Easter–Oct 10.00–17.00; Nov–Easter 10.00–17.00 Sat–Sun, except during services; free*) sits on the oldest occupied site in the city, where the castle chapel of the Counts of Luxembourg once stood. Destroyed and rebuilt many times, the current building dates from 1688. Subsequently damaged and repaired in various styles, it's now a mix of Gothic, Romanesque and Baroque architecture. As you look up at the tower from below, there's a strange metal object embedded in the wall. Tour guides will tell you it's a cannonball from a city siege, but no-one actually knows this for sure.

Just outside the church is the crossing point of the two Roman roads that signified the beginnings of the city, and across the way is its oldest square, the **Fish Market** (Marché aux Poissons) [49 E4]. Heading downhill towards Clausen and the Alzette Valley is the Bock promontory, which has stupendous views on both sides.

The **Bock casemates** [49 F4] (*Casemates du Bock; Montée de Clausen;* \ *22 28 09;* ⊕ *Mar–Oct 10.00–17.00 daily; adult/child €3/2.50*) are cut into the Bock promontory, and are a maze of rock tunnels that helped defend the city against marauding invaders – their original use was to allow safe underground passage between the city gates. The first underground caverns in the city were dug in 1644 during the Spanish era – they were later expanded by the French, and a century later by the Austrians. These on the Bock promontory date from 1745. At their peak there were 23km of galleries, which could house thousands of soldiers, along with all their equipment and support teams. As part of the Treaty of London in 1867 the casemates were supposed to have been destroyed, but it would have been impossible to blow them up without demolishing the city as well. Instead, the entrances were sealed and 17km of tunnels, opened to the public since 1933, remain. At the entrance, the first gallery you enter is the **Archaeological Crypt**, where excavations have uncovered some of the earliest buildings in the city, showing part of the castle belonging to the first Counts of Luxembourg. Beyond it are the tunnels themselves, which you can explore at leisure. There isn't much to see inside, but windows in the rock, once handy for cannons, now provide great views over Grund and Clausen.

The casemates are closed in winter to avoid disturbing the population of greater mouse-eared bats (*Myotis myotis*) that hibernate there. If you're fortunate, you may also catch a glimpse of the peregrine falcons hunting from the rocks outside.

Leading south along the ridge from the Bock casemates is **Chemin de la Corniche**, which affords fabulous views along its entire length. Thanks to the sheer drop beyond the railings on one side it's usually referred to in tourist bumf as 'the most beautiful balcony in Europe', and it's difficult to argue with that description.

Halfway between the royal palace and the cathedral, **place Clairefontaine** [58 D6] is one of the city's prettiest squares. In the middle is a statue erected in honour of Grand Duchess Charlotte (1896–1985), one of the nation's most beloved monarchs. The rather modest buildings through the railings on the west side house the prime minister's residence and several ministries.

3

The imposing late-Gothic **Notre Dame Cathedral** [58 B6] (*Cathédrale Notre-Dame; rue Notre Dame & bd F D Roosevelt;* ☉ *10.00–12.00 & 14.00–17.30 daily, except during services; free*) was founded in 1613, originally as a Jesuit church. Towards the end of the 18th century it became the Catholic Church of the Virgin Mary, and in 1870 Pope Pius IX elevated it to cathedral status. Having survived two world wars, disaster struck in 1985, when (ironically, cynics might say) on Good Friday the spire caught fire and collapsed. It has since been rebuilt. The interior of the cathedral contains the tomb of John the Blind, King of Bohemia and Count of Luxembourg from 1310–46. Several members of the royal family are also buried in the crypt. An Octave pilgrimage is held here for two weeks from the third Sunday after Easter.

At the heart of **place de la Constitution** (Constitution Square) [58 A6] is the **Golden Lady** (Gëlle Frau) [48 D5], standing on a 12m-tall granite obelisk. The gold-plated monument, created by Luxembourgish artist Claus Cito, was installed in 1923 to honour the Luxembourgers who died in World War I. The Nazis pulled it down in 1940, and it was only restored to its original glory in 1985. Today the lady represents freedom and resistance, and embodies the national pride at still being an independent nation against the odds. She's also a memorial to the fallen of all wars. Catch her on a sunny day and she reflects the light in a quite breathtaking way. As a sign of the times, she now has her own Facebook page, and in 2010 she went 'on holiday' to China, as the star attraction of Luxembourg's pavilion at the Shanghai Expo.

Equally stunning is the **panoramic view** from the southern edge of the square, down into the Pétrusse Valley and across to the Adolphe Bridge, and the National Savings Bank on the far side.

The **Pétrusse casemates** [58 A6] (*Casemates de la Pétrusse; pl de la Constitution/ bd F D Roosevelt;* ☏ *22 28 09;* ☉ *Easter, Whitsun & Jul–Sep 11.00–16.00; adult/child €3/2.50*) have the same origins as those on the Bock promontory (see page 73), although they are older, and formed part of the original excavations in 1644 (later expanded by successive conquering forces). They are essentially a labyrinth of long, narrow stone corridors, and contain 450 steps, so you'll get a good work out if you explore them all. The cannon in the lowest chamber is a Prussian original, dating from 1834.

The long ribbon of green hemming in the old town on its northern and western edges is the **municipal park** [48 B4]. Designed in 1900 by Edouard André it replaced the city fortifications that were dismantled as a condition of the 1867 Treaty of London. It's a lovely and tranquil maze of interlocking paths, which criss-cross between trees and lawns and encircle small ponds – in other words a great place to amble about if you get tired of museums and monuments. At its southern end, near the junction of boulevard Prince Henri and avenue Monterey, is a giant climbing frame in the shape of a pirate ship: a popular spot for mothers to bring young children and allow them to run riot. Nearby Lambert Redoubt is the last remnant of the old fortifications, and shows how the entire west and north of the city was once defended, albeit rarely successfully.

Museums and galleries
National Museum of History and Art [49 E4] (*Musée National d'Histoire et Art; Marché aux Poissons;* ☏ *47 93 301; www.mnha.lu;* ☉ *10.00–18.00 Tue–Wed & Fri–Sun, 10.00–20.00 Thu; adult/child €5/free*) The highlight of this excellent if schizophrenic museum is a huge Roman mosaic depicting the Muses. Believed to date from around AD240, the 60m² floor was discovered in Vichten in 1995 and brought into the city two years later. Another Roman treasure here in remarkably

good nick is a wooden water pump from around AD260. In general, the 'history' half of the building is the more interesting of the two – the lower down you are, the further back in time the collection travels. On the lowest floors, mock-up Bronze-Age dwellings go back as far as 12,000BC. Elsewhere, the 'arts' galleries also contain some gems. One high point is *Bacchus, Venus and Love*, painted in 1531 by Renaissance artist Rosso Fiorentino. The collection is also strong on Flemish masters, and has a small figurine created by Auguste Rodin in 1877. The on-site **Green Art café** (↘ 27 47 88 77; *www.greenart.lu*; ⏲ *museum hours*) has a large terrace and an all-you-can-eat salad bar, a healthy option for a light meal. It isn't exclusively veggie, but uses organic fair trade produce where possible.

Luxembourg City History Museum [49 E5] (*Musée de l'Histoire de la Ville de Luxembourg; 14 rue du St Esprit;* ↘ 47 96 45 00; *www.mhvl.lu;* ⏲ 10.00–18.00 Tue–Wed & Fri–Sun, 10.00–20.00 Thu; *adult/child €5/free*) The modern glass façade at the entrance of this fascinating museum contrasts well with the four residential houses it occupies, which date from the 17th to 19th centuries. Inside, the expansive displays cover the history of the city from its founding in AD963 to the present – each level deals with a different era, and wooden models show what it would have looked like at various stages. In one gallery is a circular life-sized panorama of a street scene, based on the Marché aux Herbes in 1655. Walking into it transports you to another time – quite a disconcerting experience. The museum is an architectural triumph, which is cut deep into the rock, yet even the lowest level opens onto the cliffs so it feels light and airy and never claustrophobic. The floors are linked by a massive glass lift that rises gracefully between the open galleries (insert your own 'travelling through time' metaphor here) – the lazy can also use it as a shortcut between the upper town and the Corniche, accessible via the museum's back entrance on level 0. Try to time your visit to allow a stop in the museum's restaurant, and enjoy the most scenic dining in the city (see *Where to eat*, page 62).

Villa Vauban [48 B3] (*Musée d'Art de la Ville de Luxembourg; 18 av Emile Reuter;* ↘ 47 96 45 52; *www.villavauban.lu;* ⏲ 10.00–18.00 Wed–Mon, 10.00–21.00 Fri; *adult/child €5/free*) This grand white villa surrounded by manicured lawns and flowerbeds feels like an idyllic escape, even with traffic passing barely metres away. It was built between 1869 and 1873 by a wealthy glove manufacturer, on top of the city's old fortifications. Bought by the city in 1949, from 1952–59 it was the Court of Justice of the European Coal and Steel Community – the forerunner of today's European Court of Justice. Then a gallery for several decades, extensive renovation has turned it into a state-of-the-art home for the city's collection of old masters. Inside are works by Van Dyck, Jan Steen and Canaletto, among others, juxtaposed with photography and paintings on similar themes by contemporary artists. It also hosts changing art exhibitions, plus a permanent exhibit detailing the building's restoration and transformation – a story worth telling in itself.

Casino Luxembourg – Forum of Contemporary Art [48 C5] (*Forum d'Art Contemporain; 41 rue Notre Dame;* ↘ 22 50 45; *www.casino-luxembourg.lu;* ⏲ 11.00–19.00 Wed–Mon, 11.00–20.00 Thu, 11.00–18.00 Sat–Sun; *adult/child €4/free*) There's no gambling any more in this grand old casino building – you'll have to head to Mondorf-les-Bains to lose your shirt (see page 116). Instead, Casino Luxembourg plays host to ever-changing contemporary art exhibitions – consult the website to see what's on. The building is closed in-between exhibitions, but entry is free if you roll up after 18.00 on Thursdays.

3

Cercle Cité [58 A3] *(pl d'Armes;* ✆ *47 96 51 33; cerclecite.lu)* Re-emerging in 2011 after a decade-long restoration, this complex comes in two conjoined packages. The neoclassical (with Art-Nouveau hints) **Cercle** *(hours vary; free)*, contains the former Ratskeller, and was originally built in 1909. It was once home to the city's literary circle, and their name stuck even when it became municipal offices. The building's prominent location meant the Nazis used it for propaganda stunts during the occupation, and it later became a rallying point for the liberated city. Its other claim to fame is that in 1952 it hosted the first meetings of the High Authority of the European Coal and Steel Community, a body that would evolve into the European Commission. The interior is used for temporary exhibitions, but arguably the most striking feature is the frieze on the façade, created by Pierre Federspiel (1864–1924). It depicts Countess Ermesinde giving liberty, in the form of a letter of franchise, to the people of the city in 1244.

Part of the same complex, but across the street (the two are linked by a glass footbridge, not open to the public), is the **Cité**, now the city library *(Bibliothèque Municipale; 3 rue Genistre;* ✆ *47 96 27 32;* ☉ *10.00–19.00 Tue–Fri, 10.00–18.00 Sat)*. Between 1958 and 1997 it was the Ciné Cité cinema – hence the name. Covering several floors, it has books in English, and also free internet terminals. Occasional free concerts are held in the auditorium above.

GRUND Simply walking around Grund is a pleasure in itself. The charm of its narrow streets is enhanced no end by the spectacular sight of the Bock promontory and upper town looming above – they are visible from virtually everywhere. Because the area is hemmed in by vertical rock walls it's been unable to expand, allowing it to retain a village atmosphere. The high cliffs on either side also channel water, and in the days before proper river management arrived, this often had disastrous consequences. Take a look at 14 rue St Ulric, near the bridge. On the wall are two **plaques** indicating the height floodwaters reached in 1756, and again in 1806 – they're about 5m off the ground, which certainly gives one pause for thought.

If you fancy a semi-rural excursion in the midst of a national capital, a walk beside the **Alzette River** makes a pleasant diversion. From the lower entrance to the lift, follow rue Plaetis down and to the left (opposite the Café des Artistes). After 200m you emerge onto a quiet footpath beside the river. After another 200m, opposite Neumünster Abbey, you'll need to do a little climbing: take the steps up and over the old city wall, then descend the spiral staircase on the opposite side back to river level. The path then leaves the city behind and continues through quiet leafiness for another 1km. There's a good chance you'll see grey heron fishing here, and moorhens paddling about doing, well, whatever it is moorhens do. Eventually you'll emerge by the bridge in Clausen, where there are several options to rest and refresh yourself before continuing. You can then continue up Monteé de Clausen to the upper town, wait for bus 6 or 9 from the stop opposite the pub or retrace your steps to Grund.

Museums and galleries

Natural History Museum [49 F4] *(Musée National d'Histoire Naturelle 'natur musée'; 25 rue Münster;* ✆ *46 22 331; www.mnhn.lu;* ☉ *10.00–18.00 Tue–Sun; adult/ child €4.50/3)* This is one of the highlights of a visit to Grund. The expansive collection – interesting for adults and children alike – concentrates its message of conservation on two fronts. On the ground floor, the main gallery contains the taxidermied remains of all the animals you probably won't see when visiting the Ardennes, largely because someone saw fit to shoot them all and place them in museums. There are deer, wild boar, owls, wild cats, badgers, otters, stoats, polecats, red squirrels and more besides. The displays also explain the complexity of the forest ecosystem and the important role played by even the smallest of insects in keeping everything in balance. The first floor widens the scope and focuses on global biodiversity, passing through time from the cooling of the planet, through fossils, to another room full of stuffed ex-animals, in which Asian tigers casually rub shoulders with African ostriches and Antarctic king penguins.

Neumünster Abbey Cultural Centre [49 F4] (*Centre Culturel de Rencontre Abbaye de Neumünster; 28 rue Münster;* \ *26 20 521; www.ccrn.lu;* ⊕ *11.00–19.00 Mon–Fri, 10.00–18.00 Sat–Sun*) Just beyond the natural history museum, the abbey has led a chequered life. The original 'new' abbey was founded in 1606 and constructed over the cemetery of the older Altmünster. The buildings were badly damaged in 1684 by Louis XIV's besieging army, when only the church tower survived. A century – and another French invasion – later in 1796, the abbey was closed by Napoleonic decree. It spent the next two centuries performing a string of secular costume changes, becoming prison, police barracks, orphanage, hospital, and finally prison again. When the prison closed in 1985 it became an arts centre, and has played a crucial role in the rejuvenation of Grund.

You're free to look around. Entering from rue Münster you first reach the **Agora**: once a courtyard, now a striking glazed atrium. Inside, the first floor of the abbey **cloister** (⊕ *13.00–18.00 Sat, 11.00–18.00 Sun, other times on request*) contains works by sculptor Lucien Wercollier (1908–2002), who was imprisoned here in 1942 for participating in the National Strike against the occupation, before being sent to a concentration camp. Through a door to the left of reception is the **Baroque staircase** – a slight misnomer since the staircase is new and only the banister is original. Around the walls are photographs of the building during its prison days (see box, page 78), while on the second floor – through the door on the left at the top of the stairs – are two wooden cell doors, preserved as a reminder of the bad old days. The abbey also hosts regularly changing temporary exhibitions.

The cultural centre's **Brasserie Neumünster** is a popular place for Sunday brunch, when free jazz concerts are held (see *Music*, page 66).

CENTRE EUROPÉEN AND THE KIRCHBERG PLATEAU
The European district and Kirchberg are linked to the old town by Grand Duchess Charlotte Bridge. Don't get confused however: this is how it's clearly marked on every map, but locals refer to it simply as the *pont rouge* ('red bridge'), for reasons that become patently obvious when you see it. Our old friend bus 16 will get you to all the sights mentioned in this section, or you can walk across the bridge for giddying views over the district of Pfaffenthal below.

As the name suggests, the Centre Européen is where the city's European institutions are based. This is no small-time operation: since the membership of the EU increased from 15 countries to 27, the number of employees here has shot up. Around 12,000 work in the various offices, busying around and maintaining Robert Schuman's dream. Some older buildings are currently undergoing a much-needed major facelift.

Museums and other places of interest
Museum of Modern Art (MUDAM) [49 G1] (*Musée d'Art Moderne Grand-Duc Jean; 3 Park Dräi Eechelen;* \ *45 37 851; www.mudam.lu;* ⊕ *11.00–18.00 Wed–Mon, until 20.00 Wed; adult/child €5/free*) Built at vast expense, the museum is a

Between 1869 and 1985 the buildings of Neumünster Abbey served time as Luxembourg's principal men's prison. The location here, overlooked by the upper town, meant that relatives of the inmates could watch the goings on inside from the Corniche, and could wave down at their loved ones whenever they were allowed out to exercise in the central courtyard. Conditions inside were never easy, but the bleakest period occurred during World War II, when the occupants were mainly political prisoners, arrested by the Gestapo and held captive before transfer to concentration camps. Some 4,000 men and women passed through its doors during the occupation, among them members of the Luxembourg resistance, Italian anti-fascists, and other opponents of the Nazis. The photos on the walls of the abbey today mainly show the prison during its last years, but even then it looked like a medieval jail – it's only when you peer more closely and spot the lewd girlie posters in the background that you realise these scenes date from barely a quarter of a century ago.

superb architectural statement, which not without reason has been described as the most ambitious construction project ever undertaken in Luxembourg. The building is a mix of white limestone (chosen because it feels warm and light even on overcast days) and glass, which together create a beautiful whole. They form a series of pyramids, reminiscent of that in the Louvre in Paris – no coincidence since they share a common architect: Chinese-American I M Pei. Pei wanted to link his design with history, so the museum has the same arrow shape as neighbouring Fort Thüngen, forming a symbolic link between it and the Euro institutions on the other side (War and Peace, get it?). His creation also represents the city in miniature: the pyramids are church towers; the central atrium the main market square; and an internal balcony mimics that on the royal palace (and is the only spot from where the real city is visible). Overall the museum generates a wonderful sense of space and openness complementing the displays by various contemporary artists – you never know what you might see as even this expansive building is far too small to house the whole collection. Nothing is on permanent show and exhibits appear on a rotating basis. In the basement is a videolab with an array of screens, showing images themed to the changing exhibitions.

Even if you have no interest in modern art, come here anyway to admire the architecture – if you coincide your visit with a time when the exhibitions are being changed, the building remains open but there's no entry fee. The museum restaurant (⏰ *museum hours*) is also worth checking out if you get peckish. There's a stunning view back across Clausen and Pfaffenthal to the Bock casemates from the terrace to the left of the entrance.

Museum 'Dräi Eechelen' [49 G1] (*5 Park Dräi Eechelen*) Fort Thüngen, aka the 'Three Acorns' sits behind the MUDAM, guarding the Alzette Valley from its eastern slopes. Currently being renovated, projections suggest it may open in autumn 2012, but this is already way overdue, so don't hold your breath. You can get inside (as far as the first casemate) on free guided tours, departing the middle Saturday of the month in summer – check with the tourist office for times. When it does eventually open, the museum will be a record of Luxembourg's national identity and among the exhibits will be a model of Luxembourg City (*Maquette*

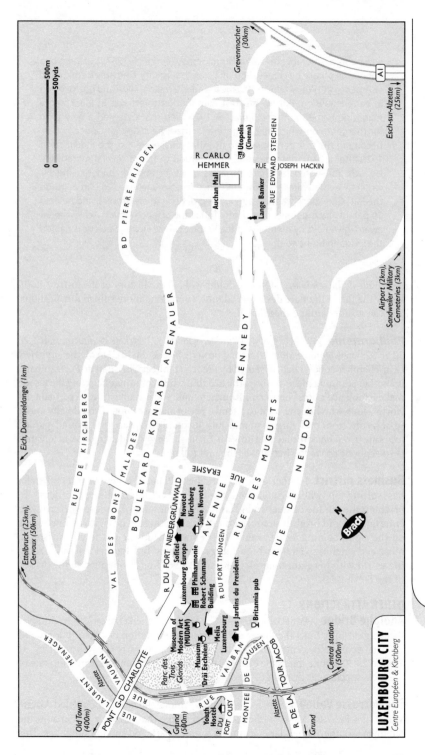

LUXEMBOURG CITY
Centre Européen & Kirchberg

Labels on map:

Grevenmacher (30km)

A1

Esch-sur-Alzette (25km)

R CARLO HEMMER

Utopolis (Cinema)

RUE EDWARD STEICHEN

RUE JOSEPH HACKIN

Auchan Mall

Lange Banker

BD PIERRE FRIEDEN

Airport (2km), Sandweiler Military Cemeteries (3km)

BOULEVARD KONRAD ADENAUER

J F KENNEDY

RUE DES MUGUETS

RUE ERASME

RUE DE NEUDORF

Eich, Dommeldange (1km)

RUE DE KIRCHBERG

VAL DES BONS MALADES

N
Bradt

R DU FORT NIEDERGRÜNWALD

Sofitel

Novotel Kirchberg

Suite Novotel

AVENUE

Philharmonie

Luxembourg Europe

Robert Schuman Building

R DU FORT THUNGEN

Les Jardins du President

Britannia pub

Etelbruck (25km), Clervaux (50km)

RUE LAURENT MENAGER

PONT G-D CHARLOTTE

RUE G-D CHARLOTTE

RUE VAUBAN

Alzette

Old Town (400m)

Grund (500m)

Youth Hostel

R DU FORT OLISY

Parc des Trois Glands

Museum of Modern Art (MUDAM)

Museum 'Drai Eechelen'

Melia Luxembourg

VAUBAN

MONTEE DE CLAUSEN

RUE TOUR JACOB

R DE LA TOUR JACOB

Alzette

Grund

Central station (500m)

0   500m
0   500yds

de la Ville de Luxembourg). Other exhibits will tell the history of the fortress itself. Below the fort is the **Parc des Trois Glands**, containing more ruined fortifications. You can wander around these at will.

Philharmonie [49 H1] (*1 pl de l'Europe;* \ *26 02 271, tickets & information* \ *26 32 26 32; www.philharmonie.lu*) Sitting proudly beside the MUDAM, the city's new twin-chamber concert hall, designed by French architect Christian de Portzamparc, is another stunning piece of work. The 823 thin white columns encircling the façade make it look like a cross between a Roman temple and a giant white harp. Again, it's worth a look whether you want to attend a performance or not. If you do, the music season runs from mid-August to mid-July. If you just want to nose around, guided tours are given on Saturday mornings at 10.30 – it's a good idea to book in advance (by telephone or via the website) as they get full up.

Business district Further east on Kirchberg Plateau, a new business district has sprung up where you'll find no end of commercial head offices. To brighten the parade of steel and glass the buildings are often interspersed with entertaining and brightly coloured modern sculptures. The first you encounter on the right, coming along avenue J F Kennedy from the old town, is also the most eye-catching. The 8m-high **Lange Banker** ('Tall Banker') stands facing the world with his giant umbrella and his size 96 shoes from outside the offices of the Deka Bank.

OTHER ATTRACTIONS

Adolphe Bridge (Pont Adolphe) [48 C5] Spanning the Pétrusse Valley, Adolphe Bridge gracefully links the upper old town with the station district. Built around 1903, it becomes the centre of festivities on 22 June, the eve of the National Day. At around 23.30 a quite infeasible quantity of fireworks are launched from it in one of the most spectacular displays of pyromania you'll ever see.

The Pétrusse Valley [see map, pages 48–9] Unlike the heavily populated Alzette Valley, the Pétrusse Valley – the spectacular gorge that abruptly demarcates the old town's southern boundary – contains forested parkland and few buildings. This makes it an absolute joy to stroll through. To reach the valley floor take any of the several paths leading down from boulevard F D Roosevelt. Within a few metres you'll feel like you've entered another world, as the chattering of birdsong starts to drown out the traffic thundering across Adolphe Bridge. The Pétrusse River that lends its name to the valley can hardly be described as a mighty torrent: it spends most of its life no more than 50cm wide – if you were that way inclined you could easily step across without getting wet. It is, however, prone to occasional floods, which is why it's channelled through a none-too-pretty concrete culvert. Because of this unusual appearance it's often described as a drain or sewer, but this doesn't detract from the enjoyment of a walk along its banks – a forest hike in the heart of a European capital. It's also a cool retreat in midsummer as the paths are sheltered and tend not to heat up as much as the streets above, making it a favourite haunt of joggers, cyclists and dog walkers. If you follow the trails downstream you eventually appear in Grund, where you can stop for refreshments, catch the lift back to the upper town or continue along the adjoining Alzette Valley (see *Grund*, page 76). In April a **Duck Race** is held on the river, in which 10,000 numbered plastic yellow quackers are launched into the water to see which navigates the stream fastest. There are two events: one for adults, one for kids, both raising money for good causes. See www.duckrace.lu for dates and times.

'Am Tunnel' Contemporary Art Gallery [53 E2] (*Galerie d'art contemporain 'Am Tunnel' & Espace Edward Steichen; 16 rue Ste Zithe;* \ *40 15 24 50; www.bcee. lu;* ⏰ *09.00–17.30 Mon–Fri, 14.00–18.00 Sun; free*) This gallery, owned by the National Savings Bank, has one of the more unusual locations of any exhibition space: inside an underground tunnel built to link the bank's various premises south of the Pétrusse Valley. It's only 5m wide at most points, but around 300m long – yes, a corridor in fact. Bank employees can enter and leave via any of the buildings linked to it, but visitors must enter through the rue Sainte Zithe office, across the rose garden from the ArcelorMittal Building. Sign in at the front desk and then be whisked by lift down to basement level -4. The bulk of the space has changing exhibits by local artists, while the far end is a secret world that makes the effort worthwhile: a permanent collection of photographs by Edward Steichen, the person responsible for the Family of Man exhibition in Clervaux. Despite the latter being the work for which he is remembered, he only took four of those 503 photographs. This display allows his own pictures to shine, highlighting a career spent photographing the rich and famous during the 1920s and 1930s. There are portraits of stars from Joan Crawford, Mary Pickford and Clark Gable, to Henri Matisse and Franklin D Roosevelt – to name just a few.

Banking Museum [53 E1] (*Musée de la Banque; 1 pl de Metz;* \ *40 15 24 50; www. bcee.lu;* ⏰ *09.00–17.30 Mon–Fri; free*) The National Savings Bank doesn't operate one museum, but two. As you enter this, the bank's headquarters, you'll also have to sign in before being allowed to visit the museum. You'll find the usual numismatic collection of old coins and notes here, including a complete history of the now-defunct Luxembourg franc. But what sets this collection apart is its ability not to take itself quite as seriously as you'd think a bank would. On one side a projection room decked out as a bank vault shows video clips and photomontages of real and cinematic bank robberies. Alternatively, enter the mock stock exchange and watch helplessly as your share portfolio rises and falls on the display screens. There's nothing at all to spend your money on, but in case you've found yourself caught short, there's also a fully functional ATM.

2 Place de Metz [53 E1] Next to the National Savings Bank, 2 place de Metz is more noteworthy for what it represents than for what it is today. Now just another of the bank's many properties in this area, this unassuming building has a lot to answer for – or its former occupants do. It was the original headquarters of the European Coal and Steel Community, formed on 10 August 1952. The name doesn't mean much to you? Well, in 1957 it became known as the European Economic Community, and today we call it the European Union. Yes folks, this is where it all began. Now you know who to blame. The building was also the Allied headquarters following the liberation of Luxembourg in 1944.

Villa Pauly [52 C2] (*57 bd de la Pétrusse*) A short walk west along the south side of the Pétrusse Valley from place de Metz, Villa Pauly is an imposing *Munsters*-style building that's also mainly notable for its history. During the Nazi occupation it was the Gestapo headquarters and many prisoners were tortured here, including leaders of the resistance. Today it houses the offices of various organisations whose task is to collect and document information about the resistance movement, and to co-ordinate the national memory of the events.

Post Museum [53 G6] (*PostMusée; corner pl de la Gare/rue d'Epernay;* \ *40 88 88 40;* ⊕ *13.00–17.00 Mon–Fri; free*) Located in the post office directly opposite the main railway station, this museum tells the history of post and telecoms in Luxembourg. Besides the inevitable array of stamps, there's also a small collection of old equipment, documents and photos. The entrance is via the 'Téléboutique' shop on the corner.

Deportation Memorial [53 F7] (*Mémorial de la Déportation; Gare de Hollerich, 3a rue de la Déportation;* \ *48 32 32;* ⊕ *14.00–17.30 Thu except public holidays; free*) This small but significant museum tells several tragic tales of World War II. In documents and photos it relates the plight of Luxembourg citizens who were forced to serve in the Wehrmacht, and of those who were deported to labour and concentration camps for refusing to co-operate. It also highlights the story of Luxembourg's small Jewish population during the war years. The museum is south of the centre, in the former Hollerich railway station. Any southbound bus 18 will drop you outside.

Tramways and Bus Museum [52 A6] (*Musée de Tramways et de Bus; 63 rue de Bouillon;* \ *47 96 23 85; www.autobus.lu;* ⊕ *13.30–17:30 Thu, 10.00–18.00 Sat, Sun & public holidays; free*) This museum mainly covers the history of the city's long-defunct tram system. The core of the collection is a workshop containing restored vehicles, the most interesting of which is a horse-drawn contraption taken out of service in 1908 when electricity took over (disclaimer: although the carriage is original, the horses you see may not be). The museum is 2km west of the centre through an unappealing industrial suburb. Buses 12 and 17 run from the old city to 'Bouillon Park & Ride', while buses 1 and 15 will get you to the same spot from the station. The museum is 200m further along. The fact there are no buses on Sundays is slightly ironic considering that not only is this a museum about public transport, but the site is also the depot for Luxembourg City transport – empty buses run to and fro all day at the ends of their shifts.

American Military Cemetery (*50 Val du Scheid, Hamm;* \ *43 17 27; www.abmc. gov;* ⊕ *09.00–17.00; closed 25 Dec & 1 Jan; free*) The war veterans whose comrades fell during the Battle of the Ardennes get fewer in number with each passing year, but this is still a place of pilgrimage for many American families, who come over to visit graves or find out what happened to fathers and grandfathers. The cemetery, covering 20ha in a peaceful wooded location, was established in December 1944 when the city was the headquarters of General Patton's US Third Army. It contains the remains of 5,000 American serviceman, including Patton himself, who was buried on Christmas Eve 1945, three days after being killed in a road accident in Germany. Initially lying alongside his troops, due to the overwhelming numbers of visitors paying homage (an estimated 200,000 in 1946 alone), Patton's grave was moved to a more prominent location in 1947, where he remains to this day. Also here are five of the celebrated Band of Brothers, whose heroic actions were immortalised in the Steven Spielberg-produced TV miniseries. One victim lying here won the 'Medal of Honor', the highest decoration the US government awards its servicemen and women. The Cemetery is in Hamm, 5km east of the city centre, close to the airport. If driving, follow the signs to 'Cimetières Militaires'. Bus 15 will get you closest from the main train station. Go to the end of the line then follow the white signs – about a 15-minute walk.

Sandweiler German Cemetery (*Sandweiler;* \ *35 50 07;* ⊕ *08.00–18.00 daily; free*) Just a hop and a skip further east is this cemetery, where the remains of 5,600 German victims of the same conflict were also interred by the US Army Burial Service after the war, and 5,300 others joined them from sites across Luxembourg in 1952. They now lie with the same quiet dignity as their former foes. If you're arriving here after visiting the American cemetery, this can seem smaller- scale. But then you discover that four soldiers are buried beneath each headstone, and around 4,900 more are interred in a common grave marked by a giant cross. Oak trees among the graves provide mottled shade in summer, creating a sense of serenity.

THE FATHER OF EUROPE

Robert Schuman was born in Clausen in 1886, to a Luxembourgish mother and a father from Lorraine. They spoke Luxembourgish at home, but since Lorraine had been annexed by Germany in 1871, he was technically German, and took advantage of this to gain a law degree in Berlin. At the end of World War I, when Alsace-Lorraine returned to France, Schuman changed citizenship and became active in French politics. He spent much of World War II serving with the resistance movement there.

After World War II he was briefly Prime Minister of France, before becoming its foreign minister in 1948. While in this role, seeking to eliminate a major source of tension between France and Germany, he adopted a scheme proposed by fellow politician Jean Monnet. In a statement made on 9 May 1950, later known as the Schuman Declaration, he suggested that the two countries manage their coal and steel industries together. This formed the basis of the European Coal and Steel Community, which eventually morphed into the EU. When he became the first president of the European Parliamentary Assembly from 1958 to 1960, he was hailed as the 'father of Europe'. So what if the original idea actually belonged to the relatively forgotten Jean Monnet? The result has been the longest period of sustained peace western Europe has ever known. And for that we should be grateful.

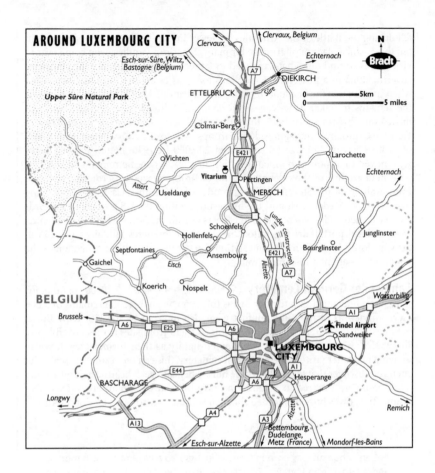

AROUND LUXEMBOURG CITY

N

Bradt

Clervaux, Belgium

Clervaux

Echternach

Esch-sur-Sûre, Wiltz,
Bastogne (Belgium)

A7

DIEKIRCH

Upper Sûre Natural Park

ETTELBRUCK

Sûre

0 _____ 5km
0 _____ 5 miles

Colmar-Berg

Larochette

E421

Echternach

Vichten

Vitarium

Pettingen

Attert

Useldange

MERSCH

Schoenfels

(under construction)

Junglinster

Hollenfels

Septfontaines

Ansembourg

E421

Bourglinster

Gaichel

Eisch

A7

Koerich

Nospelt

Wasserbillig

BELGIUM

A1

Brussels

A6

E25

A6

Findel Airport

Sandweiler

LUXEMBOURG
CITY

A1

E44

Hesperange

BASCHARAGE

A6

Longwy

Alzette

Remich

A13

A4

A3

Esch-sur-Alzette

Bettembourg,
Dudelange,
Metz (France)

Mondorf-les-Bains

4

Around Luxembourg City

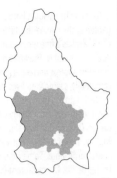

The countryside surrounding Luxembourg City is known as Gutland – literally 'Good Land' – thanks to its local reputation as a particularly fertile area. This is a lush green region of gently rolling hills dotted with apple orchards and laced with picturesque meandering rivers. And more castles than you can shake a stick at.

Yes, the attractions here consist mainly of an infeasible number of stone ruins in varying states of disrepair. You may see bigger and more spectacular fortresses in other parts, but you won't find quite so many in such a small area as this – it can seem at times like visiting a medieval housing estate.

Most people will opt to do their sightseeing using Luxembourg City as a base, but there are several excellent places to stay, plus a unique chance to sample some of Luxembourg's finest *haute cuisine* inside one of its actual castles.

GETTING THERE AND AROUND

Despite their proximity to the capital, the sights in this chapter are actually further off the beaten track and less visited than many of those further afield. **Bus** connections along the Seven Castles Route in particular are irregular at best, and by far the most efficient way to see this region is with your **own vehicle**. Those travelling by public transport should perhaps consider places of interest in the other chapters, such as Echternach, Remich, Vianden or Clervaux, where bus and train connections are more readily available.

Some places are easily accessible without a car. Mersch is linked to Luxembourg City by regular trains and buses. **Trains** also run hourly between Bascharage and the capital. Bourglinster and Junglinster are both linked hourly in each direction by bus 100, which passes through both villages on its way between Luxembourg City and Diekirch, via Larochette.

Taxis are few and far between in the countryside. A few companies, usually single-person operators, offer a service. More often than not taxis are sent out from Luxembourg City, with all the increased expense this entails.

TOURIST INFORMATION

The region's main **tourist office** is in Mersch Castle (*Château de Mersch;* 📞 *32 50 23; www.mersch.lu;* ⏱ *08.30–11.30 & 13.30–16.00 Mon–Fri*).

WHERE TO STAY

📍 **Hotel de la Gaichel** (12 rooms) Maison 5, L-8469 Gaichel-Eischen; 📞 39 01 29; **e** gaichel@ | relaischateaux.com; www.lagaichel.lu. Luxury is very much the watchword in this family-run hotel, perched on the Belgian border with a large green garden at the rear. With a history stretching back to 1852 it has a fine reputation to live up to & does so admirably. The building's façade is bright pink, but a forest of creepers smothers it almost completely, saving your eyes from the glare, offset by the bright red geraniums in the window boxes. Guest rooms are individually decorated in bold colours (the outside wall should have warned you), with slightly fussy but very elegant 'country house' furnishings. Some rooms have balconies. There's no lift. The restaurant (⏱ *12.00–14.00 & 19.00–21.30; closed Sun dinner, Mon, & Tue lunch;* €€€€–€€€€€) serves full-on French gastronomic treats, & has deservedly earned a Michelin star, with the pampering levels cranked up just that little notch higher. Overlooking the tranquil garden is a quiet tree-shaded terrace. €€€–€€€€

🏠 **Auberge de la Gaichel** (17 rooms) Maison 7, L-8469 Gaichel-Eischen; ☏ 39 01 40; e auberge@lagaichel; www.lagaichel.lu. If your wallet can't quite handle the Hotel de la Gaichel, the nearly as good but slightly cheaper auberge is next door to its upmarket sister & run by the same couple. Between them the 2 buildings comprise half the hamlet of Gaichel. Even if that wasn't the case, the bright pink walls of the auberge (no helpful creepers here, but flowery window boxes soften the blow) make it impossible to miss. Bedrooms are tastefully & individually decorated, with hints of the exterior pink, but toned down so it won't keep you awake at night. There's no lift here either. Rooms at the back look out over the same beautiful gardens as the neighbouring hotel. Given that the nearest settlement of any size is Arlon, 5km into Belgium, it comes as no surprise that this is where the bulk of the customers originate. The cosy restaurant (⏱ *12.00–14.00 & 19.00–21.30; closed Tue dinner, Wed, & Thu lunch;* €€–€€€) makes a fantastic place to start or finish the Seven Castles Route, with excellent French food & friendly efficient service. In summer, eat out on the beautiful terrace. €€–€€€

🏠 **Hotel-Brasserie Béierhaascht** (28 rooms) 240 av de Luxembourg, L-4940 Bascharage; ☏ 26 50 85 50; e info@beierhaascht. lu; www.beierhaascht.lu. This sage green building may resemble a motel from the outside, but how often do you get the chance of a sleepover in a brewery? The hotel has been awarded the

Luxembourg EcoLabel for sustainability within the tourist industry. Rooms are squeaky clean & comfortable, with wooden floors. All have Wi-Fi, & 1 has disabled access. You can also arrange a tour of the microbrewery (☏ *26 50 85 50;* e info@ beierhaascht.lu) without staying at the hotel. They don't just make beer here, they also have a farm & cure hams, sold in the on-site shop (⏱ *07.00–23.00 daily*) – *béierhaascht* means 'beer & smokehouse' by the way, even if the curing is actually done elsewhere. In the large restaurant (⏱ *11.30–14.30 & 18.00–22.30 Tue–Sat;* €€), the brewery's own beers are used to flavour its regional food. Other house specialities include *fondue bourguignonne* & raclette. The bar, dominated by large copper brew kettles, resembles a German *Brauhaus* – perfect for sampling the house beers, the first of which is offered as a welcome drink to overnight visitors. When the restaurant is closed, hotel guests can pre-order evening meals. €€

🏠 **Hotel Gulliver** (70 rooms) 58 rue Nicolas Meyers, L-4918 Bascharage; ☏ 50 44 551; e info@gulliver.lu; www.hotel-gulliver.com. This hotel on the outskirts of Bascharage is business-oriented, meaning rates drop at w/ends. It's also conveniently close to Fond-de-Gras (see page 95). Rooms are clean, with tiled floors, safe, minibar, & Wi-Fi (not free). It has sheets & blankets on the beds, an increasingly rare find in this age of the duvet. The bar is a locals' hangout & you can eat from a limited menu here at any time. For more elaborate fare, the restaurant (⏱ *12.00–14.30 & 18.30–23.00 daily;* €€) serves large portions (my *Salade Niçoise* starter would have done as a main). Pizzas & pastas are specialities, although the menu covers many bases besides Italian. €€

🏠 **Hotel Parmentier** (10 rooms) 7 rue de la Gare, L-6117 Junglinster; ☏ 78 71 68; m 621 17 10 24; e restparm@pt.lu; www.parmentier.lu; ⏱ closed 3 weeks in Aug. A friendly hotel offering comfortable lodgings in the heart of Junglinster. Rooms have been renovated & have modern furnishings with laminate floors. No lift. The restaurant is excellent value (see *Where to eat,* opposite). €€

🏠 **Bourglinster Youth Hostel** (53 beds) 2 rue de Gonderange, L-6161 Bourglinster; ☏ 26 78 07 07; e bourglinster@youthhostels.lu; www. youthhostels.lu. Offering a great-value way to stay in the heart of Luxembourg, this hostel occupies a renovated townhouse (classified as a historic monument) in the village centre. Rooms have 2–8 beds; toilets & showers are down the hall. There's a relaxing garden at the back. Packed lunches & special meals available on request. The hostel is often full with local youth groups, so book early. *€17.50pp inc bed, b/fast & bedding. Non-members pay €3 extra.*

🏠 **Hollenfels Youth Hostel** (103 beds) 2 rue du Château, L-7435 Hollenfels; \30 70 37; e hollenfels@youthhostels.lu; www. youthhostels.lu. An ultra-clean hostel in a grand pink building by Hollenfels Castle, at the heart of the Seven Castles Route. Rooms have 2–10 beds. Bathrooms are on the ground floor, with extra toilets on other floors. Special meals & packed lunches are available on request. There's a free internet terminal in the lobby. Evening meals cost €10 (€9 to members). *€17.50pp inc bed, b/fast & bedding. Non-members pay €3 extra.*

⛺ **Camping Simmerschmelz** (140 pitches) 1 rue de Simmerschmelz, L-8363 Septfontaines; \30 70 72; e info@campingsimmer.lu; www. campingsimmer.lu. Just outside Septfontaines, this campsite is ideally placed on the Seven Castles Route. There's a café, a swimming pool & a playground for kids. The owners are Dutch, so expect caravans in abundance. *€5.50pp, plus €10 per pitch.*

✗ WHERE TO EAT

✗ **Restaurant La Distillerie** Bourglinster Castle, 8 rue du Château, Bourglinster; \78 78 781; www.bourglinster.lu; ⊕ 12.00–14.00 & 19.00–21.00 daily; closed Sun dinner, 3 weeks in Aug & 2 weeks in Nov. Ever had the urge to dine in medieval splendour in a castle, but didn't want the tacky tourist experience such an evening usually entails? Well, come here then. This is no mock 'Disney in armour' show with buxom serving wenches dishing out platters of chicken & flagons of ale. The dining room here is only medieval from the waist up: in the setting itself with stone pillars holding up the half-timbered ceiling. From the waist down – see the tables decked out in fine linen – this is exquisite *haute cuisine* dining with contemporary finesse. Belgian head chef.René Mathieu was once head chef in the royal palace, & was Gault Millau's Luxembourg Chef of the Year in 2010. He gained his first Michelin star in 2012. Dining here is all about lightness of touch, both with the attentively restrained service & with the food. The prices of the à la carte mains featuring duck, lobster & turbot seem to know no bounds, but arrive on a w/day lunch & you can sample one of the best-value 3-course set menus you'll ever taste. Chef likes to experiment with flavour combinations, often to surprising effect. The menu changes constantly, but my *amuse bouche* with tuna & white chocolate, or main course of duck with peaches & nougat, should give you an idea. As weird as that may sound, the combinations actually work beautifully. €€€€–€€€€€

✗ **Brasserie Côté Cour** Bourglinster Castle, 8 rue du Château, Bourglinster; \78 78 781; www.bourglinster.lu; ⊕ 11.30–13.00 & 18.30–21.30 Wed–Sun; closed 2 weeks in Nov. Next to La Distillerie, & still in the castle, this offers a slightly cheaper alternative to its elegant neighbour, but the menu is also 'designed' by René Mathieu. The décor is more homely & marginally more modern. €€€–€€€€

✗ **Parmentier** 7 rue de la Gare, Junglinster; \78 71 68; m 621 17 10 24; www.parmentier.lu; ⊕ 12.00–14.00 & 18.00–22.00 Thu–Mon; closed 3 weeks in Aug. In the friendly Hotel Parmentier (see opposite), you can eat in the front bar area (with brown & cream modern décor, placemats not tablecloths, & abstract art), or in the more traditional restaurant (tablecloths, stone arches & older art). The menu is the same in both. The Mon & Thu/Fri *plat du jour* is tremendous value, not least because despite the name you get 2 courses. Other dishes include traditional Luxembourgish (*bouchée à la reine*) & homemade lasagne. €€

OTHER PRACTICALITIES

JUNGLINSTER

➕ **Pharmacie de Junglinster** 7 route d'Echternach; \78 00 25; ⊕ 08.30–12.30 & 13.30–18.30 Mon–Fri, 08.30–12.30 Sat

$ **BGL BNP Paribas Bank** 2 route de Luxembourg; \42 42 20 00; ⊕ 09.00–12.00 & 13.30–16.30 Mon–Fri

$ Caisse Raiffeisen Bank 1 route de Luxembourg; ☎78 00 35; ⊕ 09.00–12.00 & 13.30–16.45 Mon–Fri

MERSCH
✚ Pharmacie Centrale de Mersch 29 rue G-D Charlotte; ☎32 01 66; ⊕ 08.30–12.00 & 14.00–18.30 Mon–Fri

$ BGL BNP Paribas Bank 1 rue d'Arlon; ☎42 42 20 00; ⊕ 09.00–16.30 Mon–Fri
$ Dexia Bank 37 rue G-D Charlotte; ☎32 02 881; ⊕ 08.30–12.00 & 13.15–16.45 Mon–Fri
⊠ Post office 3–7 rue G-D Charlotte; ☎32 99 70 32; ⊕ 08.00–12.00 & 13.00–18.00 Mon–Fri, 09.00–12.00 Sat

WHAT TO SEE AND DO

HESPERANGE CASTLE (*Château d'Hesperange;* ⊕ *always open; free*) Once a town in its own right, Hesperange is slowly being swallowed up as a suburb of Luxembourg City – if you drive southeast in the direction of Mondorf and Remich in the Moselle, you're likely to pass through. Alternatively, take bus 192 or 194 from outside the Hotel Empire, opposite the railway station. The trip takes just seven minutes and there are regular departures.

Hesperange sits in the Alzette Valley and is dominated by the ruin of its small castle. Built originally between 1190 and 1277, little evidence of the earliest structure remains. It was mainly noteworthy for being one of the main defensive strongholds on the southern approaches to the city, and was badly damaged in several wars as a result. Today a number of houses have been built on and around what little remains, using the castle walls as a support.

THE SEVEN CASTLES ROUTE Don't follow this 40km drive expecting grand Loire-style country estates. With the notable exception of Ansembourg's new château, you won't find those here. What you will encounter instead are a large number of small ruins – and with a few short detours there are considerably more than seven. Some are in a sorry state and on the verge of being reclaimed by nature. In others, more effort has been made to preserve them for future generations. Taken as a whole, the route is a relaxing meander through the pretty, wooded Eisch Valley, and a chance to indulge in some low-key, off-the-beaten-path tourism in the heartland of the Grand Duchy. The drive between Koerich and Mersch in either direction takes around half a day, depending on how many side detours you make. These descriptions follow the route from west to east, but you can just as easily start at the other end. For more information (in German), including suggested hikes, see www.septchateaux.lu.

There's no practical way to make this journey on public transport – with no direct service linking all the castles you'd have to keep backtracking via Luxembourg City. If you have time and energy to spare however, it can be covered on foot or by mountain bike.

At the southwest end of the route in Koerich, **Grevenburg Castle** (*Château de Grevenburg;* ⊕ *always open; free*) lies at the centre of the village. Originally established in the 12th century, time has not been kind to it. The impressively high outer walls allude to something grander, but today it's a mere shell of crumbling stone. You can enter the grounds and wander around freely, but some parts are off-limits whilst extensive restoration work is under way – it's going to take some time by the look of it. Behind the castle, atop a small mound lifting it conveniently closer to Heaven, is the picturesque **St Remy Parish Church** (Eglise St Remigius). Worth a look inside and out, this quaint little house of God was completed in 1747. The belfry dates from 1727, while the onion-dome spire appeared somewhat later. It's one of the prettiest Baroque churches in the country. The interior is surprisingly ornate, with an elaborate marble altar and a white-and-yellow vaulted ceiling.

Septfontaines Castle (*Château de Septfontaines; not open to the public*) is best viewed from the eastern side, from where its hilltop location looking down over the village and the valley can be most appreciated. Built during the 12th century, it was enlarged several times, and a square keep added around 1600. The castle has been in a pretty poor state since it was gutted by fire in 1779, and some 20th-century attempts at restoration actually made matters worse. Today, it's an overgrown wreck and privately owned. The owner has expressed a wish to renovate, but lacks the funds to do anything major. Below the castle, the little **parish church** is an unusual mix of Romanesque and Gothic styles. There are also a couple of small **cafés** in Septfontaines if you need to sit down after all that excitement.

The original 12th-century **Ansembourg Fortress** (*Vieux Château d'Ansembourg; not open to the public*) sits high above the valley, obscured by the trees that surround it, and hard to spot from the road. Its biggest claim to recent fame is that in 2000 it was used as a setting for the film *Shadow of the Vampire*. But one 17th-century lord had already decided he didn't like living there. He felt a need to be lower down the valley, where more space was available, and so built the rather grander **Ansembourg Castle** (*Nouveau Château d'Ansembourg; 10 rue de la Vallée, Ansembourg; castle not open to the public, gardens ⊕ 11.00–13.00 & 15.00–18.00 daily; free*) beside the main road. The original building was erected in 1639 and has been enlarged several times since. It's now huge, rivalling the grand châteaux of the Loire in scale. Unfortunately it's also privately owned and not open to the public, but you can visit the lavish 3.5ha gardens. One previous occupant in particular – Count Lambert-Joseph d'Ansembourg (1706–68) – made these a place of wonder, introducing exotic plants and landscaping the ground into terraces. There's a grand staircase, paths lined with statues of mythical figures, neatly clipped hedges, and of course a fountain. Four other statues represent the four continents that were known in the 18th century. Be sure to walk right around the back for a superb view of the château façade as it was meant to be seen – you don't get the full idea of just how large it is from anywhere else.

The forces of topography and road design seem to combine to prevent you reaching **Hollenfels Castle** (*Château de Hollenfels; ⊕ visits to the tower by appointment – information from the youth hostel opposite; free*) via the direct route by car. Approach from the west and you'll probably miss the turning to the left as it's hidden by a bend in the road. In fact, you may not even realise you've missed it until you see the hulking castle in the rear view mirror. Once on the steep road leading up to the village, keep your fingers crossed that you meet no-one coming down the narrow 1km lane as there's little room to pass and a scary vertical drop on your side. Take care. If you prefer, there's also a longer but wider route up the hill: that turning is 1km further east. The journey is worth it, however, as picturesque Hollenfels is on a ridge with a fabulous view. The 14th-century castle is very small, but also one of the best restored in the region, with a tiled roof and a 39m-high keep.

Over in the adjacent valley to the other castles, the bizarrely shaped **Schoenfels Castle** (*Château de Schoenfels; not open to the public*) is easy to find, but right next to a busy main road. Only the keep remains – the rest was pulled down by the French in 1684. Tall and absurdly thin for its height, it appears as though a giant hand has squeezed it like a tube of toothpaste to make it taller. It's a cute tower with round turrets in each corner and stepped gables, which together make it appear half Dutch townhouse, half Dracula's castle.

Compared with everywhere else along the route, Mersch comes across as a thriving metropolis. It's a bustling crossroads town with a motorway running down one side and a railway passing through the middle. With such transport links, getting here is a breeze. Fortunately the area around **Mersch Castle** (*Château de Mersch; place St Michel;* \ *32 50 231; not open to the public, except for the town hall*) has managed to maintain a modicum of Old-World charm against this onslaught of modernity. The castle itself, founded in the early 13th century, is still in use today, and is where you'll find the town hall and the **tourist office**. Over the road on the market square is the **tower** of the former St Michael's Church. The main building has long since disappeared and this is all that remains. Next to the tower is a small **fountain** shaped like a dragon. It's not old and it doesn't have any special history, but is there to play up the myths and legends that you know should belong in this world of castles, even if they are all made up.

Other places of interest If seven castles aren't enough for you, detour north from Septfontaines for a peek at **Useldange Castle** (*Château d'Useldange;* \ *23 63 00 511; www.useldeng.lu;* ⊕ *08.00–19.00 daily; free*). This impressive feudal ruin was created around 1100 and now sits in the middle of the sleepy village sharing its name. After years of painstaking restoration work, it is now accessible to the visually impaired. The tall square keep tower has a 'tree' sculpture rising up through four floors of the stairwell, telling the history of the castle. The captions are only in French and German, as (I suspect) are the Braille translations on the flip side of the caption boards, but an English audio commentary is available on each floor. There's a marvellous view from the roof (eighth floor), once you've recovered your breath. Back down on the first floor, a door leads via a footbridge to a second tower, which depicts a typical year in medieval life, told month by month.

Also interesting is the walk around the castle exterior (⊕ *always open*). To the left of the entrance are a series of recreations of various styles of medieval gardens to make Alan Titchmarsh teary-eyed with nostalgia: raised bed, box hedged, giant pots housing aromatic herbs, and so on. The rest of Useldange is a charming place straddling the gushing Attert River – many houses have shuttered windows and are painted in various pastel shades. For the peckish, the castle is directly opposite the village bakery.

A few kilometres north of Useldange is Vichten, worth a quick stop if you're passing through. Between the village church and the municipal offices next door is an exact copy of a **Roman Mosaic** (⊕ *always open; free*) that was unearthed here in near-perfect condition in 1995. The original is in the National Museum of History and Art in Luxembourg City (see page 74).

NOSPELT POTTERY MUSEUM (*Musée de la Poterie; 12 rue de Poterie;* \ *30 03 07;* ⊕ *Easter, Jul–Aug 14.00–18.00 Tue–Sun, other times by prior arrangement; adult/ child €2/1.50*) Nospelt is a working village in the middle of nowhere (or so it feels), a few kilometres south of Septfontaines. It was once home to a thriving pottery industry, which lasted from 1458 until the last kiln cooled in 1914 – at its peak in the 1820s there were no fewer than 17 here. If you're passing nearby it's worth (sorry) pottering into this small museum, created in memory of the town's former breadwinners. It's in the building occupied by the very last pottery, which was owned by a man named Nicolas Schneider. Besides the expected rooms filled with cracked, glazed pots, there are also dioramas showing the potter at work, and a rare chance to stick your head inside a bread oven and a kiln without any risk of cooking yourself. The top-sellers that made Nospelt famous throughout the land were glazed hand-painted terracotta whistles shaped as birds, which warble when blown. Known as *péckvillchen*, they have long been a hit with children at fairs and festivals, and you still see them on sale (and loudly demonstrated by youngsters) at events today, including Vianden's medieval festival, and the Emaischen pottery market, held every Easter Monday on the Marché au Poissons in Luxembourg City.

PETTINGEN CASTLE (*Château de Pettingen;* ☎ *32 50 231;* ⏰ *always open; free*) At 4km north of Mersch, Pettingen Castle is one of Luxembourg's smallest castles, built in 1243 by Arnold von Pettingen as the family seat. Although it's a ruin like many of its neighbours, most of the outer walls and some corner towers are intact, and the whole does at least look like a complete building from the outside. The castle is totally lacking on the door front, so walk in any time you like and stroll around the interior courtyard, which is devoid of features, but a grassy and pleasant place to wander nonetheless. If you enter from the village, be sure to walk through to the far side by the river valley and railway and admire it again, as it's notably prettier from there. The remains of the moat (now dried up and grassed over) are plainly visible from that angle.

North again from Pettingen, the village of **Colmar-Berg** is also dominated by its **château**. Forget about getting too close to this one, however, as it's the current residence of Grand Duke Henri and his family, and very much off-limits to the general public.

VITARIUM (*On N7, 3km south of Colmar-Berg, near Roost/Bissen;* ☎ *25 02 80 222; www.vitarium.lu;* ⏰ *09.00–20.30 daily, last visit at 18.00; adult/child €14.50/8*) Opened in 2010, this may have an odd address, but it's by the main road and easy to spot – it's part of the Luxlait dairy, which employs 260 staff and processes more than half of Luxembourg's milk. It's a huge place designed to remind (primarily) children that milk comes from cows, not the supermarket. There are initial hands-on 'education stations', then you watch a short 3D film before entering the dairy proper. The route carries you around a walkway above (but sealed off from for hygiene purposes) the production areas, while interactive videos and audio guides explain how the various processing steps work. At the halfway point is a museum showing pictures of the dairy around 1930. Following a second film you return to the interactive zone, where kids (and adults) can play games, or don a set of artificial udders to learn how much they weigh (a lot). Finally comes a chance to try the products – and to buy, of course. Visits (guided) generally take around 2½ hours.

JUNGLINSTER A nondescript village between Luxembourg City and Echternach, Junglinster's most immediately striking features are the three giant red-and-white Radio Luxembourg masts that stand like sentinels guarding the entrance to the town. If you're passing through, do check out **St Martin's Church** (*Eglise St Martin;* ☎ *78 00 43;* ⏰ *afternoons daily; free*). The building was constructed in 1772–74, and isn't in itself that exciting, although it appears disproportionately large for the small parish it serves. Go beyond the front door, however, and find the highlight of the late-Baroque interior (most of which pre-dates the exterior): a massive altar created in 1634 by the German sculptor Johann Manternach. Around the choir, embedded in the walls, are delicately carved gravestones that date back to the mid 16th century. For centuries the Lords of Linster, occupants of Bourglinster Castle, were interred here.

Salt grotto (*Salzgrotte; 31 Um Räilend, Junglinster;* ☎ *26 78 27 30; www.salzgrotte. lu;* ⏰ *09.00–20.00 Mon–Sat, 10.00–14.00 Sun, advance reservation only; adult/child*

€15/8) Junglinster is also home to possibly Luxembourg's most bizarre attraction. A temple to relaxation, this artificial salt grotto is in the basement of a house on an anonymous estate, 500m east of the centre (one stop on bus 100, 110 or 111). There's no sign from the main road: turn right onto Um Räilend (opposite the radio masts), left at the mini roundabout, then it's the second yellow house on the right. Forty five-minute treatments are designed to provide all the health-giving benefits of a bracing day at the seaside, without actually going there (handy since Luxembourg has no coastline). The grotto walls are thickly coated in salt from the Dead Sea, creating a microclimate in which you relax and apparently absorb healthy minerals, whilst being bathed in warm-coloured lights.

BOURGLINSTER At 3km from Junglinster, the sight of **Bourglinster Castle** (*Château de Bourglinster; 8 rue du Château, Bourglinster;* \ *78 78 781; www. bourglinster.lu; free*) on a rock in the centre makes this village, with its peaceful cobbled streets, altogether more appealing than its larger neighbour. Hemmed in on two sides by craggy outcrops, it seems the perfect spot to build a defensive fortification. No surprise then that someone did precisely that in the 10th and 11th centuries. Regular renovations have ensured the turreted and pointy-roofed edifice is still in pretty good nick today. Arts exhibitions and concerts take place here, and it's home to two highly recommended restaurants (see page 87). Tours are possible by prior arrangement, but a much easier and tastier way to peek inside is to eat here.

BOFFERDING BREWERY (*Brasserie Bofferding; 2 bd J F Kennedy, Bascharage;* \ *23 63 63; www.bofferding.lu;* ⊕ *group visits only; adult €4, inc drink, free with Luxembourg Card*) The only reason to come to the industrial town of Bascharage is to visit one or both of its breweries. The eco-friendly Béierhaascht microbrewery is covered previously (see *Where to stay*, page 86), but you can also drop by its burly big brother. Wherever you look in southern Luxembourg, green-and-white Bofferding pub signs are everywhere – the brewery owns 1,100 cafés in the Grand Duchy, and many more in Belgium. The tour leads you round the brewing process, and yes it will drop you in the tasting room at the end. Group visits require a minimum of ten people, but if you call to check when one is leaving you may be able to join in.

5

The Industrial South

Whereas much of central and northern Luxembourg remained quaint and pastoral throughout the 19th century, the south knuckled down, donned a blue collar and rolled up its sleeves. This relatively flat region is where most of the money that made the country rich was generated, and it came from heavy industry. You'll also notice how much more crowded it is than elsewhere. One-third of the country's entire population lives here, and six of the seven largest urban areas are crammed into this small tract of land, known as the Minett.

Two thousand years of iron extraction have left an indelible mark on the landscape. Long-abandoned opencast mines have been reclaimed by nature, and the region is strewn with the ore-laden boulders that give it its nickname: *terre rouge*, or 'land of the red rocks'.

What make this area most interesting are the places that directly reflect its human past, in particular the fascinating National Mining Museum, and the industrial heritage park of Fond-de-Gras, with its working steam trains that are fun for everyone. There's also Parc Merveilleux, which is a veritable wonderland for pre-teens.

You can cover all the sites here in easy day trips from Luxembourg City. Or for a change of pace, decamp to the laid-back regional capital, Esch-sur-Alzette.

HISTORY

Contrary to what many people believe, Luxembourg's status as a wealthy nation wasn't founded on the strength of its banks. It was iron ore mining and the consequent development of a hugely prosperous steel industry that put the Grand Duchy on the map during the 19th century.

The iron ore seam itself stretches away into northern France and covers an area of more than 1,000km². Only 3.7 of these actually lie in Luxembourg territory, but geology gave the country a tremendous advantage. The seam slopes downwards towards the south, and at its southern end is 1km below the surface. French miners faced a long ride in a lift to reach the workplace, and extracting the iron was painstaking and expensive. But the same vein of rock breaks the surface here, making it easily accessible and possible to remove in huge quantities by road and rail.

The region's industrial history goes back further than this, however. The discovery of ancient galleries cut into the rock show that the Romans and Celts were both aware of, and tapping into, its potential. Nevertheless, their knowledge was lost in the murk of the Dark Ages when Barbarians overran the land. It fell into decline, and the iron-rich soil was only noticed again in 1838. At first the ore's high phosphorous content limited its use in the steel industry, but when a system for removing this was developed in Britain during the 1870s, commercial mining

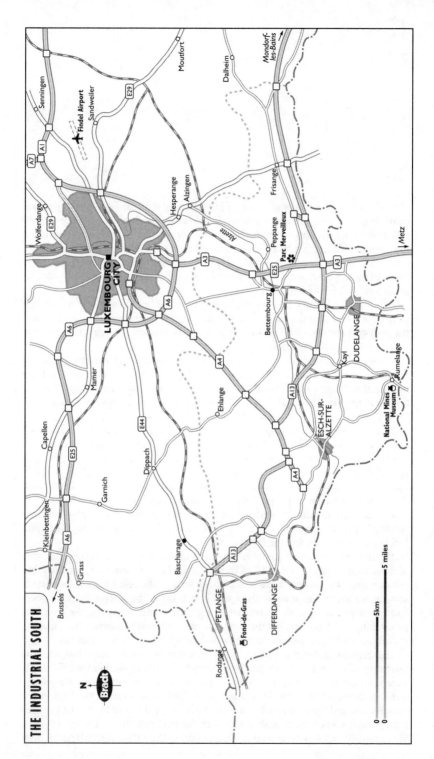

THE INDUSTRIAL SOUTH

The map labels include: Senningen, Moutfort, Dalheim, Mondorf-les-Bains, Sandweiler, Findel Airport, E29, A1, A7, Wolferdange, E29, Hesperange, Alzingen, Frisange, Alzette, Peppange, Parc Merveilleux, LUXEMBOURG CITY, A3, E25, A3, Metz, A6, A6, Mamer, Bettembourg, DUDELANGE, A6, A4, A13, Kayl, Capellen, E44, Ehlange, ESCH-SUR-ALZETTE, Rumelange, National Mines Museum, E25, Dippach, A4, Kleinbettingen, A6, Garnich, Bascharage, A13, Grass, PETANGE, Fond-de-Gras, DIFFERDANGE, Rodange, Brussels, 5km, 5 miles, N, Bradt

THE INDUSTRIAL SOUTH

became a viable money-spinner. Further boosts came when a railway was built, and Luxembourg joined its biggest market, the German Customs Union.

Unprecedented wealth flooded into the south, reshaping its cities and changing the face of its population. Esch-sur-Alzette became dotted with mansions, mainly built in the Art-Deco and Art-Nouveau styles that were all the rage during its peak around 1900. Meanwhile, thousands of migrant workers were brought in from southern and eastern Europe to cope with demand.

The south escaped much of the catastrophic annihilation of World War II that affected the north, and this meant its steel industry could restart almost as soon as the fighting ended, going a long way to rebuild the country in the post-war years. The boom times lasted until the 1970s, which saw a sharp decline in the European iron and steel industries. That setback sounded the death knell for mining, which was unable to compete with cheaper imports and ended for good in the early 1980s. But the steel business soldiered on, and is once again thriving (see box, below).

GETTING THERE AND AROUND

This region's relatively dense population means transport links are better than anywhere elsewhere in the country. **Trains** cover the ground several times an hour between Luxembourg City and Esch-sur-Alzette, Dudelange, Bettembourg and Pétange. Occasional trains or half-hourly **buses** travel to Rumelange. Even tiny Peppange has a regular bus service into the city. Nowhere is more than 30 minutes from the capital.

The only time you may want to use your own wheels is to reach Parc Merveilleux. You can get there on public transport, but this requires a change from train to irregular buses, so **driving** yourself is a good way to avoid a host of complaints from impatient youngsters.

FOND-DE-GRAS

At the end of the 19th century, the Chiers Valley, at the point where Belgium, France and Luxembourg all meet, was not just a driving force of the Luxembourg economy, it was one of the industrial powerhouses of northern Europe. The iron ore mines that created the boom times are now closed, but a new tourism industry has sprung up in its place to preserve the legacy of the past.

STEEL DID-YOU-KNOWS

I doubt many people outside the business would think immediately of Luxembourg when it comes to steel, but a merger in 2006 between Luxembourg-based Arcelor and its Rotterdam-headquartered competitor Mittal Steel created ArcelorMittal, by some considerable margin the world's largest steelmaker. And the company's reputation for producing high-quality metal has made its products sought after in many high-profile construction projects around the world.

Did you know, for example, that the 24 giant steel girders – each weighing 807 tons – that will hold up the new Freedom Tower in New York are made from Luxembourg steel? Or that part of the raw materials for the world's tallest bridge, Sir Norman Foster's 'bridge in the sky' across the Tarn Valley in France, also came from ArcelorMittal plants?

5

Fond-de-Gras is a loose term connecting several intriguing heritage sites in the Pétange–Rodange region. Numerous industrial relics from around the country have been moved here and restored. They are linked to one another by not one, but two privately run steam-train networks. Although these are operated by separate groups of enthusiasts, their timetables co-ordinate just enough for you to see everything in one day.

GETTING THERE The easiest way to visit on public transport from Luxembourg City is to take the regular **train** as far as Pétange (two per hour; 25 minutes; €5). You can also **drive** directly to Fond-de-Gras in about 20 minutes, or park by Pétange station and board a **steam train** there. The car park and departures are behind the main line and signposted.

The 13.26 train from Luxembourg City gets you to Pétange at 13.51, well in time for the first steam departure at 14.15. You'll need to catch this one if you want to take in all the sights and make it back on public transport. If you do miss the last return steam train, the town of Rodange, where there's a main line station, is only 30 minutes' walk from Fond-de-Gras.

The starting point of the Train 1900 steam locomotive in Pétange is just 100m from the main station. Turn left at the bottom of the platform steps (ignore the signs to 'centre'). On emerging from the underpass, head up the ramp immediately to your right and the Train 1900 ticket office is 50m straight ahead. If the train is already waiting its location is abundantly obvious – just aim for the billowing black smoke. There's little point in arriving too early as the ticket office won't be open and there are no facilities. There are a few cheap-and-cheerful bars and pizzerias on the town side of the main line station, but little to be recommended. You can also board Train 1900 in Rodange, but this is impractical without a car as the station is 3km uphill from the main line, on the road to Lasauvage.

✗ WHERE TO EAT You can bring a picnic or try:

✗ Bei der Giedel Fond-de-Gras; \58 05 83; ⊕ 11.00–midnight daily. Once in Fond-de-Gras, this pleasant café is right by the Minièresbunn station & the old grocery. There's a pretty terrace where you can sit & watch the steam trains busying about. In former times it was a favourite hangout of local miners. €–€€

WHAT TO SEE AND DO

Train 1900 The impossibly cute Train 1900 (\ *58 05 81; www.train1900.lu; departs Pétange for Fond-de-Gras May–Sep 14.15, 16.15 & 18.10 Sun only, departs Fond-de-Gras for Pétange at 13.55, 15.52 & 17.52; adult/child €8/5 in second class, €11/8 in first, 30% discount with Luxembourg Card*) was built in (how *did* you know?) 1900. Driven by steam, it huffs and puffs and chunters its way at a dizzying 20km/h along an 8km route through the woods between Pétange and Rodange, leaving a whiff of coal smuts and nostalgia in the air. For anyone hankering after the golden age of train travel, this is as unmissable as it gets. Twenty minutes into the half-hour journey it stops in the heart of Fond-de-Gras, allowing you to step off and check out the sights there.

Another train, a single-carriage diesel 'autorail', also plies the same route. See the website above for departure times – the timetable makes it clear which departures are pulled by which train.

Fond-de-Gras Until 1955, Fond-de-Gras (\ *26 50 41 24; www.fond-de-gras.lu; sites ⊕ May–Sep Sun only, from arrival of 1st train to departure of last; free*) was the loading station for locally mined iron ore. It has now become a gathering place for restored old buildings, which have turned it into an open-air museum. The **railway station** itself dates originally from 1875.

L'Epicerie Binck This grocer's shop dates from 1919. It was once located in the nearby town of Differdange, before being taken apart brick by brick and meticulously reconstructed here, and stocked with period goods for that authentic look.

Paul Wurth power station (centrale électrique Paul Wurth) Named after a local engineer and entrepreneur, the power station dates from 1913. It once generated electricity for the Hollerich suburb of Luxembourg City, before being moved here in 1988. The massive steam-powered generators inside are the originals.

The Minièresbunn (⟍ *26 50 41 24; departs Fond-de-Gras May–Sep 14.55, 15.05, 16.00 & 17.00 Sun only; adult/child €5/3.50, 30% discount with Luxembourg Card*) If you thought Train 1900 was tiny, wait until you see the Minièresbunn, 200m from Fond-de-Gras station up an obvious track. There's no ticket office: pay on board. Pulled by a diminutive 1897 steam locomotive, this shrunken miner's train (that's miners, not minors, though kids will certainly love this) runs on 4km of 700mm-gauge track to Lasauvage and continues on to Saulnes in France. Along the way it passes through an old iron ore mine, now a 1.4km tunnel. Before you enter this, the steam locomotive is uncoupled and replaced with an electric tender, meaning you won't be asphyxiated by coal smoke or deafened in the enclosed space.

About 1,100m into the dark, the train stops and everyone gets out for a tour of the mine works. It's sobering to think that during the 130 years these tunnels were in operation, 1,477 people died in accidents – more than one per month. If you've already visited the mine in Rumelange this is small scale by comparison, but it's interesting nonetheless, and you get to see some machinery being demonstrated, including compressed-air drills and jackhammers.

Continuing on, the train arrives in the ex-mining village of **Lasauvage**, where you can step off for a quick look around before it returns or moves on to Saulnes. Until 1921 the entire village was privately owned by a French family. Today it's preserved as a reminder of the past.

If you have time to walk 500m into the village proper you'll find the **Lasauvage Museum** (*Espace Muséologique Lasauvage;* ⟍ *26 50 41 24;* ⊕ *May–Sep 14.00–18.00 Sun; adult €1.50, free for children & holders of Minièresbunn or Train 1900 tickets*), a small documentation centre devoted to the history of Lasauvage during World War II. Throughout this time, members of the resistance movement used the mine to hide from the Nazis.

Also in Lasauvage, close by where the train stops, is the **Museum Eugène Pesch** (⟍ *26 50 41 24;* ⊕ *May–Sep 14.00–18.00 Sun; free*). Rather incongruously, it houses a collection of fossil-laden rocks, which ex-miner Pesch picked up on his travels around this region and elsewhere. A small side room features a diorama of the mine and various tools used therein.

ESCH-SUR-ALZETTE

Luxembourg's second city, with a population of 30,000, Esch/Alzette (as it's often abbreviated) is a low-key affair that exists for its own benefit, not for that of tourists. Nevertheless it's worth a second glance for its host of Art-Deco and Art-Nouveau

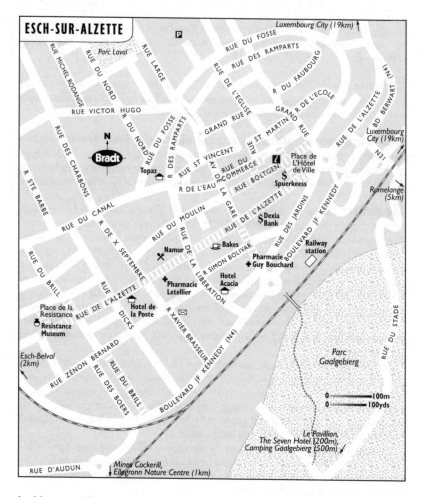

ESCH-SUR-ALZETTE

buildings, and for its small but powerful museum paying tribute to the Luxembourg resistance movement during World War II. Around 15km southwest of the capital and reachable in 20 minutes by direct train (two per hour; €5), you can easily visit on a half-day excursion. Should you wish to linger there are some fine eating choices and several hotels.

HISTORY Esch was settled in the 8th century, and granted city status in 1287. However its time in the spotlight was brief, and by the time iron ore was rediscovered in 1838, it had dwindled in size to a mere village. Its rebirth was dramatic: in 1830, the population was 1,000; a century later that figure had reached 30,000. Local businessmen grew wealthy, and spent their money creating lavish structures in the latest architectural styles. It all came to an abrupt halt in the 1970s, however, with the decline of the steel industry. Like many industrial cities in Europe, Esch was sent reeling and is only now coming to terms with its loss.

GETTING THERE The most convenient way to reach Esch-sur-Alzette from Luxembourg City is by **train**. There are four services every hour throughout the day, taking a little over 20 minutes. **Driving** from Luxembourg City also takes around 20 minutes, depending on traffic.

GETTING AROUND Even Luxembourg's second city isn't huge, and is easy to cover **on foot**. The station is only a two-minute walk from the central shopping area. If you need to take a city **bus**, they cost just €0.50 for a day ticket. For those who need a **taxi**, try Taxi Morgado (☎ 55 77 77).

TOURIST INFORMATION

Esch City Tourist Office pl de l'Hôtel de Ville, 25 rue Boltgen; ☎ 54 16 37; www.esch-city-lu; ⊕ 09.00–17.00 Mon–Fri. The tourist office is a goldmine of advice, information & free leaflets on what to see & do in the region, & can also help with booking accommodation on request.

⌂ WHERE TO STAY

⌂ **Hotel Acacia** (23 rooms) 10 rue de la Libération, L-4005; ☎ 54 10 61; e hacacia@pt.lu; www.hotel-acacia.lu; closed 1 week around Christmas & New Year. In the town centre, the rooms here are spacious & comfortable. Internet access is offered to guests. The restaurant downstairs (⊕ 12.00–14.00 & 19.00–22.00 Mon–Sat; €€€–€€€€) serves reasonable French cuisine. Gastronomic packages are also available. €€€

⌂ **Hotel de la Poste** (20 rooms) 107 rue de l'Alzette, L-4011; ☎ 26 19 00 21; e hoteldelaposte@pt.lu; www.hoteldelaposte.lu. In Esch's central pedestrianised zone, this wonderful Art-Deco hotel was built in 1919. The swish public areas reflect the original design, but the rooms are modern & stylish, with minimalist furniture, parquet flooring & free Wi-Fi. Underground (paid) parking is available for guests. €€€

⌂ **The Seven Hotel** (15 rooms) 50 Gaalgebierg, L-4142; ☎ 54 02 28; e reservation@thesevenhotel.lu; www.thesevenhotel.lu. In a quiet forest on Gaalgebierg hill, overlooking Esch, this has a wooden façade that blends organically with the surrounds. Despite the rural location it is only a 10min walk to the centre, via Gaalgebierg Park & the pedestrian bridge over the railway (coming from town, bear right & up through the park). Although there are only 15 guest rooms, it covers 7 floors, hence the name. Rooms are individually furnished, & have stylish bathrooms, some open-plan. All rooms have free Wi-Fi, minibar & data ports, & 5 rooms have balconies. The roof terrace on the 6th floor has a great view, as does the top-floor '7 Steps to Heaven' suite, with entrance hall & living room below, & a bedroom above with a blue ceiling reflecting the sky, wraparound balcony with stunning views, & an open bathroom with the same view. Top-of-the-range rooms have tea-/coffee-making facilities. The hotel also has a fitness room & *hammam*, massages (for a fee), & the excellent Le Pavillon Restaurant (see below). €€€

⌂ **Topaz** (22 Rooms) 5 rue des Remparts, L-4303; ☎ 53 14 411; e topaz@pt.lu; www.topaz.lu. The Topaz is centrally located, friendly, comfortable & reasonably priced. Rooms have safe, minibar & good bathrooms. Rates drop at w/ends. Parking costs €7 per day. €€

⋀ **Camping Gaalgebierg** (150 pitches) PO Box 20, L-4142; ☎ 54 10 69; e gaalcamp@pt.lu; www.gaalgebierg.lu; ⊕ all year. Close to The Seven Hotel, this campsite enjoys a peaceful woodland location. There's a playground for children & clean shower facilities, some with disabled access. €3.75pp, plus €7 per pitch.

✕ WHERE TO EAT

✕ **Le Pavillon** 50 Gaalgebierg; ☎ 54 02 28 703; www.pavillon.lu; ⊕ 12.00–14.00 & 18.00–23.00 daily, limited menu served all day. If you want fine dining that won't break the bank (although to be honest it might rattle the windows a bit), it's worth coming to The Seven Hotel's restaurant even if you're not staying there. It pre-dates the rooms by a decade, & its reputation for serving good food in relaxed surrounds inspired the building of a hotel around it. The dining room has striking midnight blue & red furnishings, with Art-Nouveau touches hinting at Esch's glory days, & elegantly 'crumpled' tablecloths (red on one side, gold on the other), reminiscent of a tart's boudoir. The large terrace looks out over forest. The menu is French-influenced, including *cassoulette*, stroganoff or *steak tartare*, but with modern touches & using local produce where possible. Unusually for Luxembourg, the mains include at least 2 vegetarian options. €€€–€€€€

✗ **Namur** 64 rue de l'Alzette; ☎ 54 17 78; ⏲ 12.00–18.00 Mon, 08.30–18.00 Tue–Sat. The Namur patisserie & chocolate shop renowned throughout Luxembourg City has found its way to Esch. You can sample all the same mouth-titillating naughties available in the big city, including a changing *menu du jour* at lunchtimes. €–€€

🖵 **Bakes** 57 rue de l'Alzette; ☎ 53 11 28; ⏲ 07.00–18.30 Mon–Sat. Part of a national bakery chain; sandwiches & snacks are sold here at very reasonable prices. €

ENTERTAINMENT AND NIGHTLIFE Just behind the town hall, **place Boltgen** is surrounded by cafés and is a good place to look for an evening drink or a light snack.

Before the **Rockhal** (*5 av du Rock 'n' Roll;* ☎ *24 55 51 (information),* ☎ *24 55 55 55 (tickets); www.rockhal.lu*) opened in 2005, the country was usually overlooked by major music artists on a European tour. Now Luxembourg's largest and newest rock venue has put the country on the radar, having played host to big names such as Muse, Arcade Fire, The Prodigy and many others. Check the website for upcoming events.

The Rockhal is, however, just one part of **Esch-Belval** (*www.belval.lu*), a work-in-progress rejuvenating the site of a former steel mill west of the centre. To date it also includes a hotel, the Belval Plaza shopping mall (see below), and free parking. Some of the huge blast furnaces have been preserved, forming an imposing backdrop to the new commercial centre growing in their shadow. Besides shops, Belval Plaza contains a multi-screen cinema, **Cine Belval** (*7 av du Rock 'n' Roll;* ☎ *57 57 58; www.cinebelval.lu*), and several bars and restaurants, including a sub-branch of a Luxembourg City drinking institution, **Café Urban** (*www.urban.lu;* ⏲ *09.00–01.00 Mon–Fri, 10.00–01.00 Sat, 15.00–22.00 Sun, later on Sun if a concert is on at the Rockhal*).

SHOPPING Rue de l'Alzette in the heart of Esch is the country's longest pedestrianised shopping street. If you can't find what you're looking for down here, it probably isn't worth having.

West of the city, the **Belval Plaza** shopping mall (*av du Rock 'n' Roll; www. belvalplaza.com*) is large enough to have fully grown trees inside. To get there follow the signs to Esch-Belval. As well as the entertainment options above, it contains a growing number of retail outlets selling everything from food to DVDs.

OTHER PRACTICALITIES

Medical

✚ **Pharmacie Guy Bouchard** 15 av de la Gare; ☎ 26 53 54; ⏲ 08.30–18.30 Mon–Fri, 08.30–18.00 Sat

✚ **Pharmacie Letellier** 85 rue de l'Alzette; ☎ 54 92 88; ⏲ 08.30–12.00 & 13.45–18.15 Mon–Fri

Banks

$ **Dexia Bank** 27 rue de l'Alzette; ☎ 54 50 11; ⏲ 08.30–16.30 Mon–Fri

$ **Spuerkeess ('S-Bank')** 3 pl de l'Hôtel de Ville; ☎ 54 37 611; ⏲ 08.15–16.30 Mon–Fri

Post office

✉ **Post office** Corner rue Zénon Bernard; ☎ 54 70 35; ⏲ 07.00–19.00 Mon–Fri, 09.00–18.00 Sat

WHAT TO SEE AND DO

Architectural walking tour (*Information* ☎ *54 16 37*) For those with an interest in Art-Deco or Art-Nouveau architecture, Esch has many fine buildings from the early years of the 20th century, when the south of Luxembourg had one of the most prosperous economies in Europe. A free booklet, available in English from the tourist office, provides a guided route and historical explanations of the most significant sights. It's the beautiful exterior façades, and particularly the upper gables, that make these buildings worthwhile – most of the lower levels have since been transformed into anonymous modern shops and have lost their charm.

The city's main street, rue de l'Alzette, where many of the buildings are located, is also a pedestrian precinct. The purple, angled streetlights that run along its length look like a row of cranes bowing in salute to the past industrial age, and act as a strange contrast to the stone façades.

Resistance Museum (*Musée de la Résistance; pl de la Résistance;* ☎ *54 84 72; www. musee-resistance.lu;* ⏰ *14.00–18.00 Thu, Sat & Sun; free*) At the western end of rue de l'Alzette, this small but moving museum recounts the history of the Luxembourg resistance movement during the Nazi occupation. The story, told in pictures and documents (proclamations, newspaper cuttings, etc), covers the rise of Nazism in 1930s Germany to the liberation of Luxembourg in 1944. Captions are all in French, so ask at the front desk for their English translation.

Numerous resistance movements emerged across the country in response to the 1940 occupation: the LPL (Letzebuerger Patriote-Liga) and the LVL (Letzebuerger Volléks-Legioun) were just two that appeared in the first year alone. To concentrate their efforts, the disparate groups joined together in 1944 as l'UNION – a unified resistance force. More than just an information centre, the museum is also a shrine to honour those who suffered and died. In front of the building is a **Memorial to the Fallen** (Monument aux Morts), inaugurated on the same day as the museum in 1956.

Parks Elsewhere in the city centre, the striking **footbridge** (*passerelle*) over the railway has won awards for its innovative design. The city end is accessed by a lift that takes you up three floors to deck level. The far end leads straight into the hilly and thickly forested **Parc Gaalgebierg**. In contrast, just north of the centre on rue Large, **Parc Laval** is arranged more formally, with flowerbeds and fountains separating the trees. Both parks make a pleasant retreat from the sprawl.

Mine Cockerill (*Off rue Jean-Pierre Bausch, 2km south of Esch;* ☎ *26 54 42 41 or* ▫ *621 22 89 51;* ⏰ *09.30–12.00 Sat, guided tours other days 08.00–12.00 on request*) To reach this hard-to-find museum, head south on rue Jean-Pierre Bausch and after 1km you pass under a railway bridge and you'll see the turning on your right. City bus 12 also passes by. The museum – the red building on the lower level – was the pithead office, and contains mining equipment and changing rooms with helmets and overalls hanging up, looking as though the miners could report for duty tomorrow even though the pit closed in 1967. It's run by volunteers and may not open if they go on holiday, so call ahead.

Ellegronn Nature Centre (*Centre d'acceuil Ellegronn;* ☎ *26 54 42 41;* ⏰ *10.00– 22.00 Tue-Sun; free*) Near Mines Cockerill, the Nature Centre hosts displays of various creatures you probably won't glimpse if you walk around the surrounding nature reserve. Down in the cellar is a 'bat cave' exhibit – the real bats live in the disused mine. If you fancy a walk in the woods, pick up the brochure for the 5km **nature trail** (*Sentier Didactique Natura 2000*). Is the same building is the **An Der Schmedd Café** (☎ 26 54 32 89; *www.anderschmedd.lu*; ① meals 12.00–14.00 & 18.30–20.30 Tue–Sun), if you need a pick-me-up.

RUMELANGE

Rumelange is a small working town with one excellent redeeming feature that makes a visit worthwhile – the National Mining Museum here is one of the most fascinating attractions in the country. Note that there is nowhere to stay here, so you will need to make this a day visit.

GETTING THERE Rumelange can be reached from Luxembourg City in about half an hour by **train** or by taking **bus** 197 (four per hour). If coming by train, the majority of services require a change onto a connecting service in Noertzange. To get to the mine, turn right as you exit the station and head up the main road. It's about 800m to the entrance (about a ten-minute walk). **Driving** from Luxembourg City takes around 20 minutes.

✖ WHERE TO EAT

✖ **Brasserie du Musée** Carreau de la Mine Walert; ☎ 56 70 08; ① when the mine museum is open. The mining museum's brasserie has a wide-ranging menu of tasty local, French & Italian dishes. *The* thing to try is, however, *la gamelle du mineur*. This traditional miner's lunch (served in a metal lunch box, or *gamelle*) is an all-in-one goulash-style stew with beef, carrots, potato, pepper & kidney beans. It's delicious & filling, & will set you up well for a day down the pit. €€

WHAT TO SEE AND DO

National Mining Museum (*Musée National des Mines; Carreau de la Mine Walert;* ☎ 56 56 88; *www.mnm.lu*; ① *Apr–Jun & Sep 14.00–18.00 Thu–Sun; Jul–Aug 14.00–18.00 Tue–Sun, last departure at 16.30, open all year for groups (min 15 people) by prior arrangement; adult/child €8.50/5*) The problem with Luxembourg's iron ore was that it never contained much iron: just 34%. This was fine for the steel industry when higher-quality alternatives were too expensive to import, but in the second half of the 20th century the situation changed, and rock from Sweden, Mauritania and Brazil containing up to 74% iron suddenly became a viable option. It dealt a fatal blow to the region's mines, and the last one closed in 1981.

This mine in Rumelange actually ceased operating long before the industry died. It shut down in 1963, and opened as a museum a decade later. Visits are deliberately not too technical in order to make them fun for kids. One-hour tours start with a 20-minute train ride, taking you around the hillside and underground. You'll then be shown around a number of galleries containing machinery, photographs, and mannequins that add fleshy detail to the stories of sweat, toil and hardship. Tour leaders are usually ex-miners who tend to speak only German, French or Luxembourgish, but if you ask you'll be given an audio tour in English, told by the 'ghost' of a miner. An English-speaking guide can be arranged if you book in advance.

The interior mine temperature is a steady 10°C, so bring something warm to wear even on hot days. It's also humid, which makes it feel even cooler. Individual visitors may have to wait (maximum 30 minutes) for a group to become large enough, but you can look around the museum by the entrance in the meantime.

Working conditions in the mines changed dramatically over the years. Prior to 1930, life was cheap. Miners were paid by the weight of ore they extracted, and as a result voluntarily worked long hours and took huge risks to increase production: cutting corners with vital elements such as blasting, and not bothering to shore up unproductive shafts. Accidents were commonplace and many died.

Things only became safer in 1930 when an hourly wage was introduced. Work was still hard, but the pay was extremely high, which made it a popular job. Miners could expect to earn two or three times the national average salary. They had disposable incomes and cars – a relative rarity in pre-war Europe. All the spare cash they had also explains why so many bars and cafés thrived in mining towns such as Rumelange.

Another unexpected safety development occurred when Polish miners joined the workforce. They brought their own experience and knowledge with them, teaching the locals to use pine posts instead of oak to support tunnel roofs. Oak pillars used to break without warning when the roof caved in – which it often did – burying workers underneath. But pine creaks before it fails, acting as a natural early-warning system, and many lives were saved as a direct result of this change.

As an additional souvenir, the museum sells a sweetish, apple-based liqueur, called *galeriewasser*. Its 'traditional' credentials are a little dubious (it's been on sale only a short time), but it is both palatable and popular.

DUDELANGE

With around 18,000 inhabitants, Dudelange is Luxembourg's third-largest town. Sitting close to the French border and on the edge of the mining district, the town can trace its origins back 2,000 years, but it only grew prosperous on the back of the 19th-century industrial boom. As did other settlements in this area, it took a serious knock with the decline of the mines in the 1970s, but has since regained its self-esteem. It's now a pleasant little town, well away from the beaten tourist path, with some green squares and easy access to the countryside. For more of an unusual diversion, it also hosts the country's largest 'rope garden'.

GETTING THERE AND AROUND Occasional direct **trains** connect Luxembourg City with Dudelange-Ville station in 15 minutes. Otherwise there are twice-hourly connections via Bettembourg (20 minutes total). Sitting beside two motorways, Dudelange is also easily to reach by **car** in 15–20 minutes from the capital. **Bus** 5 runs every 15 minutes between Dudelange and Esch-sur-Alzette (25 minutes), passing through Rumelange (15 minutes) *en route*.

The town is small enough to cover **on foot**, but is also served by a small network of local buses.

TOURIST INFORMATION
Dudelange Tourist Office 21 rue du Commerce; 51 89 47; ⊕ 09.00–12.30 & 13.30–17.00 Mon–Fri. The tourist office will offer advice, information & free leaflets on what to see & do in the region, & can help with booking accommodation on request.

The Industrial South DUDELANGE

5

☖ WHERE TO STAY AND EAT

☖ **Cottage Hotel & Restaurant** (45 rooms) rue Auguste Liech, L-3401 Dudelange; ✆ 52 05 91; e cottage@pt.lu; www.cottage-hotel.lu. 45 bedrooms ranks this city centre hotel as slightly more than just a cottage, but the atmosphere remains friendly, welcoming & low-key. It's 2 blocks from the central place Hôtel de Ville, by the railway (but quiet despite that). The rooms are clean, if simply furnished. The homely restaurant (⊕ 12.00–14.00 & 18.30–21.30 Mon–Fri; €€– €€€) serves a small but tasty selection of fish & meat dishes, plus a good range of pastas. €€

✗ **Restaurant Parc Le'h** rue du Parc; ✆ 51 99 90 90; www.parcleh.lu; ⊕ 12.00–14.00 & 19.00–22.00 Wed–Sun; no lunch Sat. Located in a lovely white villa in wooded parkland, beside the Parc Le'h Adventures rope garden (see *What to see and do,* below), this stylish restaurant dishes up swanky French food in elegant surrounds. €€€€

✗ **Mamma Mia** 27 pl Hôtel de Ville; ✆ 26 51 00 33; www.mammamia.lu; ⊕ 12.00–14.00 & 18.30–23.00 Thu–Tue. Gold tablecloths & emerald-turquoise seats brighten this friendly pizzeria on the main square. The pasta is homemade & the pizzas delicious. The desserts are also worth checking out: any place that can make a decent *zabaglione* – sweet, warm, velvety, & with a kick of *marsala* – is alright in my book. €€–€€€

OTHER PRACTICALITIES

✚ **Pharmacie du Lion** 92 av G-D Charlotte; ✆ 26 52 10 10; ⊕ 08.00–12.30 & 13.30–18.30 Mon–Fri

$ **Spuerkeess ('S-Bank')** 49–51 pl de l'Hôtel de Ville; ✆ 51 16 13; ⊕ 08.15–16.30 Mon–Fri

✉ **Post office** 16–18 rue Jean Jaurès; ✆ 51 15 31 31; ⊕ 08.00–12.00 & 13.30–18.00 Mon–Fri, 09.00–12.00 Sat

WHAT TO SEE AND DO

Mont Saint-Jean Castle (*Château Mont Saint-Jean;* ✆ *51 61 21 269; always open; free*) On a low wooded hill 1km west of the railway station on route de Kayl (the N31, bus 5 also passes close by) are the ruins of a medieval castle. Follow the tarmac path to the hilltop from the roadside car park (about ten–15 minutes' walk). No-one has been able to date it accurately, and today all that remain are the foundations, but you get an idea of the layout from this. It's worth the extra effort to climb the concrete observation tower for a bird's-eye view over the site, not least because this gets you above tree level and you can see further.

Parc Le'h Adventures (*Corner of rue du Parc & rue de la Forêt;* m *621 50 00 02; www.parclehadventures.com;* ⊕ *Jul to mid-Sep 10.00–20.00 daily; Apr–Jun & mid-Sep to Oct 14.00–19.00 Tue, Thu, Sat–Sun & public holidays; adult/child €20/12–18, depending on age*) For the energetic, this large 'rope garden' climbing park has around 90 obstacles that are graded from easy to 'extremely difficult', including aerial runways and rope ladders. The toughest apparatuses have minimum age restrictions, but there are plenty of options for adventurers of all ages. Parents might be more tempted by the adjacent **Restaurant Parc Le'h** (see *Where to stay and eat,* above).

Museum of Forced Conscription (*Musée des Enrôlés de Force;* pl de l'Hôtel de Ville; ✆ *51 41 23;* ⊕ *08.30–11.15 Tue & Thu, Sun & public holidays on request; free*) This small museum in the town centre pays homage to the young men of Luxembourg who were designated as 'German' by the Nazis in 1942, and conscripted against their will to serve in the Wehrmacht.

St Martin's Church (*Eglise St Martin;* ⊕ *08.00–18.00 daily; free*) At the heart of town, this twin-towered neo-Gothic parish church doesn't look special from the outside, but has a surprise waiting within. Adorning the interior walls are some spectacular murals painted in the 1920s by a German monk named Notker Becker.

BETTEMBOURG AND PEPPANGE

Just north of Dudelange and ten minutes south of Luxembourg City, Bettembourg is home to Parc Merveilleux, the country's primary attraction for younger children. Neighbouring Peppange is a farming village (there are as many tractors parked in the driveways of the houses as there are family cars), yet despite its diminutive size it boasts not one, but two interesting rural museums.

GETTING THERE AND AROUND Three or four **trains** each hour make the short hop between Luxembourg City and Bettembourg. To get from Bettembourg centre to Parc Merveilleux, **bus** 304 runs hourly Monday to Saturday, passing the entrance. On Sundays and public holidays, you'll need your own transport – it's a 15-minute drive from the capital. You can **walk** from Bettembourg station to the park in about 15–20 minutes (it's signposted), but it's not a particularly pleasant journey along a busy road.

Getting to Peppange is also straightforward. **Bus** 194 passes through every 20 minutes Monday to Saturday *en route* between Luxembourg City and Bettembourg, taking 20 minutes from the former, five minutes from the latter. Sunday is trickier without your **own transport** as there are only a few buses in each direction. The 15.21 from Luxembourg City (returning at 18.24) is the only realistic choice that fits with the museums' limited opening times.

✕ **WHERE TO EAT**

✕ **Restaurant Parc Merveilleux** route de Mondorf, Bettembourg; ☎ 52 98 90; www.parc-merveilleux.lu; restaurant Apr to mid-Oct ⊕ 12.00–15.00; self-service ⊕ 09.30–19.00. Inside Parc Merveilleux are several dining options. At the upper end of the scale, catering to the Luxembourgers' belief that one should never go without a proper lunch no matter where you are, this restaurant offers sit-down service with fine French cuisine & an accompanying wine list. Elsewhere in the park are several self-service cafeterias, which can provide ravenous hordes with everything from ice cream, sandwiches or a portion of chips, to a substantial hot lunch. *Restaurant €€–€€€; self-service €*

WHAT TO SEE AND DO

Parc Merveilleux (*route de Mondorf, Bettembourg;* ☎ *51 10 481; www.parc-merveilleux.lu;* ⊕ *Apr to mid-Oct 09.30–19.00 daily, last entry 18.00, Madagascar & Amazonia pavilions 11.00–17.00; adult/child €8/5*) Older children may find this zoo-meets-attraction park a little tame – it certainly doesn't have Disneyland's wild rides (or its tackiness come to that) – but pre-teens will find it '*merveilleux*'. And anyone with a love of wildlife will encounter enough here to keep them entertained for several hours.

The park is home to parrots, ibises, lemurs, deer, flamingos, dingoes, and other exotically colourful birds and mammals. Zoophobes shouldn't fret, however, as the enclosures are designed with animal welfare in mind. One excellent new attraction has given the park's substantial lemur population additional space to roam around: 'Madagascar, Home of the Lemurs' is a massive walk-through tropical glasshouse filled with indigenous plants to make the animals feel relaxed, and to allow humans and lemurs to scrutinise each other on equal terms without that depressing barrier of bars. It isn't the rainforests of southern Africa, but is probably the more likely of the two still to be here in 25 years' time.

Meanwhile, in the park's small petting zoo kids can get hands-on and feed the, er, kids (only special goat food purchased in the shop please). Perhaps best of all is the walk-through Amazonian enclosure, built on two levels to allow you to see the fish and crocodiles from above and at eye level, while tropical birds flit around freely.

Away from the animals there's a miniature train and go-karts for youngsters, and an adventure playground with plenty to clamber over. In another corner, a fairy-tale wood features animatronic dioramas of Cinderella et al.

Although clearly aimed at the youngest generation, the park does have a serious conservation message to convey, and educational displays highlight deforestation in the animals' native habitats, particularly in Madagascar and the Philippines. The texts are only in German, but the pictures tell the story well enough.

The park's forest location only enhances its charm, as woodland birds casually fly in and out to join the permanent residents.

Peppange Rural Museum (*Musée Rural de Peppange; 38 rue de Crauthem, Peppange;* \ *51 09 06;* ⊕ *May–Sep 14.00–18.00 Tue–Sun, Oct–Mar 14.00–18.00 Thu & public holidays, all year for groups on request; adult/child €4/2*) This expansive museum sprawls through a large barn and an adjacent farmhouse, and is crammed full of artefacts. Local heritage is the theme here. In the farming room are scythes, threshing machines, ploughs, and that most essential of countryside household items: a pot still for making illegal hooch. The papier-mâché cow in the milking shed, and the worried-looking plastic pig in the abattoir/butcher's shop may be obvious fakes, but this just adds to the overall charm. Out back is a working kitchen garden with real vegetables on the go, a collection of beehives and a blacksmith's forge, plus a metallurgical exhibit showing how ores were smelted in the Middle Ages. Another wing has kitchens and dining rooms laid for dinner and afternoon tea. Things take a turn for the strange in a room that's filled with both priests' vestments and stuffed animals – presumably this juxtaposes the equal importance of religion and hunting in rural life?

This is a fascinating glimpse of 'the way things was', and although the layout is higgledy-piggledy and there's little by way of explanatory signs, it's well worth checking out.

If the museum tour leaves you feeling hungry or thirsty, never fear as it ends in the **Café Am Musée** (⊕ *10.30–22.00 Tue–Sun*), which serves drinks and bar snacks. On a quiet afternoon you might be the only customer and the landlord may spend his time patrolling the bar swatting flies – of which there are many in this part of rural Luxembourg.

Carriage Museum (*Musée des Calèches; 49a rue de Crauthem, Peppange;* \ *51 09 06;* ⊕ *Jul–Sep 14.00–18.00 Sun, or on request by prior arrangement; adult/child €3/1.50*) About 200m further into the village from the rural museum, this barn houses a dusty but interesting collection of horse-drawn buggies, along with some grander carriages that once belonged to the grand ducal court. Some have been lovingly restored; others are showing their age.

6

The Moselle Valley

The wines of Luxembourg are an undiscovered secret, itching to take the world by storm. Few people outside the country are even aware they exist. And still fewer have noticed how good they are. Until now ...

Oft-overlooked by the wider world, Europe's smallest wine-growing region stretches a mere 42km along the west bank of the Moselle River, which briefly grazes the Grand Duchy *en route* between France and Germany – the river also forms the German border, and the water is jointly administered by both nations. The country as a whole has 1,350ha of vines, but the overwhelming majority are here – besides its fertile soil, the location enjoys a microclimate particularly suited to winemaking.

One inescapable fact is that the quality of Luxembourg's wines is steadily improving. Throughout the 20th century, 'good' years were considered rare, but 'bad' years have now become the exception. It's hard not to attribute this to global warming, but standards have also risen as more and more young winegrowers appear, armed with modern winemaking techniques and a determination to concentrate on quality above quantity. Overall output is actually lower than it was 25 years ago, but what is made is far more enjoyable to drink. Quality is governed and denoted by the *Marque Nationale des Vins Luxembourgeois*. The distinction *Appellation Contrôlée* appearing on the little label on the back of the bottle signifies its contents have been given the official thumbs-up, and the better wines are graded as *Vin Classé*, *Premier Cru*, or even *Grand Premier Cru*.

Another effect of global warming is that the wine harvest is getting earlier. Once it took place in October, but mid-September is now the norm. The majority of grapes are used to make white wines, and a few rosés, which most closely resemble those from the Alsace in terms of taste and character. Increasing temperatures have meant red wines are starting to appear, made from Pinot Noir grapes, and though few in number their quality is catching up fast with that of the whites and rosés. The sparkling wines, meanwhile, enjoy an enviable and growing international reputation (see box, page 111). Many of these adhere to strict production criteria and are legally classified as *crémants*.

The export market for Luxembourgish wine is fairly small – domestic demand is high enough to account for the bulk of production, and this has helped keep it under wraps. Some is exported to Belgium and the other neighbours, but very little elsewhere. There are, however, a handful of outlets in Britain – to find a local supplier check the FAQ section of the Luxembourg National Tourist Office's UK website (*www.luxembourg.co.uk*), which has a list of current importers.

A visit to this region is a must for wine enthusiasts. Not only will you be impressed by the quality, the prices may also come as a pleasant surprise, both in the shops and in bars and restaurants. Some wineries are happy for visitors

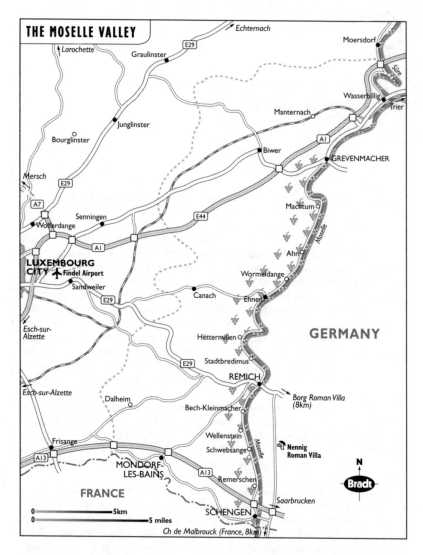

THE MOSELLE VALLEY

just to turn up at the front door, and you may get a free tour and tasting (larger places tend to charge for these privileges). You're generally discouraged from appearing at smaller premises at harvest time, simply because the overworked staff are too busy.

Besides buying wine, there are several wine museums here, and practically every village holds its own festival, with attendant tasting opportunities, naturally. The two biggest events are the Grevenmacher wine festival (see page 134) and the Riesling Open (see page 130).

HISTORY

The precise origins of winemaking in the Luxembourg Moselle are not entirely clear. It is known that the Romans cultivated grapes and made wine here almost 2,000 years ago, but no-one is exactly sure whether they brought the vines with them or found them already in place. Nevertheless, this early knowledge of viniculture went into hibernation in the Dark Ages following the demise of the Roman Empire. It was only revived when monasteries first appeared and the monks began dabbling. For many years these wine estates were either owned by the Church or by wealthy noblemen, but in 1795 Napoleon's forces took control, bringing their revolutionary

FRUITS OF PLEASURE

Like their counterparts in the Alsace, Luxembourg's still wines are made from single grape varieties, always indicated on the label. The vast majority use one of eight types, each of which creates a wine with a distinct character. Without regard to my personal safety, I have selflessly tried them all on your behalf.

ELBLING The region's original grape variety has been cultivated here since Roman days, and during the Middle Ages it was common throughout central and eastern Europe. Ripening early, it produces light, dry and acidic wines, good for cutting through deep-fried and fatty foods.

RIVANER The most common Luxembourg grape variety, accounting for almost 30% of output. A hybrid of Riesling and Sylvaner grapes (and either a close relative of, or the same grape as Müller-Thurgau, depending on which source you believe), it produces a dry and quaffable table wine with a light bouquet, popularly drunk as an aperitif.

RIESLING The so-called 'king of wines' is dry, rounded, distinctive and elegant. It tastes and is a little more expensive than some of the other varieties, and goes very well with fish.

AUXERROIS Well-rounded, medium-dry, and with a very fruity bouquet that makes it decidedly drinkable, this matches most light foods, including salads.

PINOT NOIR Originating from Burgundy, this is the only red wine grape grown in any significant quantity. Also used to make some very fine and improving rosés, it's light, fruity, and goes down a treat with red meats.

PINOT GRIS Produces a full-bodied, spicy and medium-dry wine that's a particular favourite with women (but hey, I like it too). A close cousin of Pinot Noir, from which it has been mutated over time, it's well suited to duck and guineafowl.

PINOT BLANC A further mutation of the Pinot Gris grape has given us Pinot Blanc. Elegant, fresh and smooth, try it with hors d'oeuvres or veal.

GEWÜRZTRAMINER Produces perhaps the most unmistakable of all wines. Dry, spicy and fruity, it divides drinkers: people either worship or shun it. I'm in the former camp. Try it with your cheese as an alternative to red wine or port.

Seven other grape varieties including Chardonnay are also grown here, but you won't find them very often as they are only produced in tiny amounts.

A perfect way to enjoy the scenery without exerting yourself is aboard the **MS *Princesse Marie-Astrid*** (✆ *75 82 75; www.visitmoselle.lu; daily excursions Easter–Sep, check website as schedules & fares vary*). Built in 2010, this fifth incarnation of the region's most prized tourist asset is a 60m boat with the capacity to carry up to 500 passengers. The *Princesse* cruises the waters of the Moselle, covering various routes, usually between Wasserbillig in the north and Schengen in the south. You can sit and enjoy the view as you glide slowly past the vines, or have a meal in its highly regarded restaurant. Some trips go as far as Trier and Bernkastel in Germany, and other options include lunch or dinner. Board at several places along the river, including Remich, Schengen and Grevenmacher. Return fares depend on the distance travelled, and start from €3. On the Sunday of the Riesling Open wine festival (see page 130) you can sail aboard for free. Euro fact collectors may like to note that the Schengen treaty of 1985 was signed aboard this boat's great-grandmother: the second *Marie-Astrid*.

and egalitarian ideals. It meant many peasant winegrowers finally gained ownership of the vineyards they'd previously worked on behalf of others.

In the 20th century, the wine business began getting organised. The first wine producers' co-operative was founded in 1921, and in 1935 the *Marque Nationale* was introduced as a guarantee of quality. The *crémant* designation for sparkling wines arrived in 1991, and since then the business hasn't looked back.

GETTING THERE AND AROUND

To appreciate the region fully you'll need your **own transport**. It isn't that you can't get around by **bus** – you can, quite easily – but something with ample boot space for those bottled purchases enables you to savour a taste of the region's bounty when you get home. Nowhere here is much more than 30 minutes by car from Luxembourg City.

To follow this chapter from south to north along the wine route by public transport, bus 185 travels between Mondorf-les-Bains and Remich twice every hour (less often on Sundays), passing through Schengen, Remerschen and Schwebsingen and Bech-Kleinmacher. Bus 175 (two per hour, hourly on Sundays) takes a shorter route from Mondorf to Remich, calling at Wellenstein and Bech-Kleinmacher. Bus 450 runs hourly between Remich and Grevenmacher, stopping at all points in-between. Bus 485 travels hourly between Grevenmacher and Wasserbillig, before continuing to Echternach in the Müllerthal. Wasserbillig is the only town linked to the railway – **trains** arrive from Luxembourg City twice per hour; the journey takes 30–40 minutes.

Cycling is a relaxing way of getting around – the road by the river is flat, dropping just a few metres in 42km between Schengen and Wasserbillig. Bikes can be rented from RentaBike Miselerland (*main office: 115 route du Vin, L-5416 Ehnen;* ☎ *621 21 78 08; www.rentabike-miselerland.lu*), which has 13 locations along the valley from Schengen to Wasserbillig. See the website for a complete list with opening times. Rentals cost €7 per 24 hours, up to a maximum seven days; each outlet can supply maps. The real beauty is you can drop bikes off at any of the 13 sites so you don't have to return them to your starting point.

For more exercise, the long-distance **Sentier de la Moselle** footpath follows a 55km marked trail along the valley, passing through vineyards and joining the towns and villages between Schengen and Wasserbillig. A free leaflet available from tourist offices has a map and indicates the location of facilities along the way, including eating and sleeping options. The full walk takes anything from two days upward, depending on how often you stop to sample the local nectar.

One small thing to watch out for here: in many towns and villages the main drag is called route du Vin (and is shown thus on maps), but the Luxembourgish name Wäistrooss is used interchangeably. Addresses are prone to switch without warning. We've followed the personal preferences of the establishments concerned.

TOURIST INFORMATION AND LOCAL TOUR OPERATORS

For more information than you can possibly ever absorb on Luxembourg's wines, visit www.vins-cremants.lu, the website of the Commission de Promotion des Vins & Crémants de Luxembourg, the wine industry's marketing arm.

The regional tourist bureau's website is www.visitmoselle.lu.

Two companies operate large pleasure boats offering dinner cruises and a range of other tours on the water. Based in Grevenmacher, the MS *Princesse Marie-Astrid* (see box opposite) is regarded as the region's crown jewel, and is its biggest tourist attraction. Another boat operator, **Navitours**, runs excursions from Remich (see *Remich*, page 124, for details).

From May to September on Sundays and public holidays, a special **Vineyard Tour** bus (*Wäistrooss-Bus*; ✆ 75 82 75) makes the trip between Mondorf-les-Bains and Wasserbillig three times in each direction, stopping everywhere in-between. Audio commentary is available in English, French and German. The bus departs central Mondorf at 10.40, 13.40 and 16.40, returning from Wasserbillig train station at 12.10, 15.10 and 18.10. Normal public transport fares apply: €1.50 for short hops, €4 all day. It's free with a Luxembourg Card.

You can also arrange wine tasting tours via **Wine Tasting with Friends** (✆ 35 65 75 333; *www.winetasting.lu*). They will organise customised visits to the cellars tailored to your requests, including return transport, for up to eight people.

A TOUCH OF SPARKLE

Only appearing for the first time in 1990, Luxembourg's increasing range of sparkling wines is making people sit up and take notice. Time and again local wineries are winning prizes, gold medals and other accolades in international competitions. Unlike their still counterparts, they tend to be made from several grape varieties blended together, in combinations that vary from one winemaker to the next. Provided they adhere to strict rules, wines produced using the so-called *méthode traditionnelle* (whereby secondary fermentation in the bottles is used to create the sparkle), they can be given the name *crémant*. Crémant de Luxembourg tends to be lighter and less acidic than 'real' French champagne, and have more delicate bubbles, which actually makes them more palatable in many people's eyes. They are also considerably cheaper, with good ones available in the shops for around €10 a bottle. Follow the lead of many locals and order it in Luxembourg's restaurants as an aperitif, and you'll be recognised instantly as someone 'in-the-know'. You won't be disappointed with the taste either.

There are two main reasons to come to this little town on the French border. Luxembourg's only casino and the extensive Domaine Thermal spa resort both involve opportunities to relax on a serious scale, but in very different ways: the former is probably bad for your wallet and your stress levels; the latter may also be bad for your wallet, but you'll feel a million dollars when you come out.

Mondorf has been at the centre of the Luxembourg tourist industry since day one, when liquid gold was struck by accident. Taxes on imported salt in the 19th century were making this commodity prohibitively expensive. In the hope of finding a domestic source, a 736m-deep borehole (a European record for many years) was dug in the village in 1841. They didn't hit the vein of rock salt they were hoping for, but by chance they found a mineral-rich spring instead. Word soon got around about the curative waters that gushed out, and people have been flocking here to sample its restorative powers ever since.

GETTING THERE AND AROUND

Bus 175 links Luxembourg City and Mondorf-les-Bains in 30 minutes (two per hour, hourly on Sunday). **Driving** yourself takes around 25 minutes. To reach the Moselle Valley, bus 175 continues on to Remich (20 minutes). Bus 185 also links Mondorf twice hourly with Remich, travelling via Schengen (15 minutes).

Everything in central Mondorf can be easily covered **on foot**, and it's difficult to get lost. If you find yourself crossing the narrow river Gander at any point, you've actually left Luxembourg and are in France.

TOURIST INFORMATION

Tourist office 26 av des Bains; ☎ 23 66 75 75; www.mondorf-info.lu; ⊕ 09.00–12.00 & 13.00–18.00 Tue–Sat, also Apr–Oct 14.30–18.30 Sun. The tourist office offers advice & free leaflets on places of interest in the region, & can help with booking accommodation on request.

WHERE TO STAY

Mondorf Parc Hotel (113 rooms) av des Bains, L-5601; ☎ 23 66 65 49; e domaine@mondorf.lu; www.mondorf.lu; closed 1 week around Christmas/New Year. Don't be fooled by the unassuming concrete egg-box exterior of the Domaine Thermal's main on-site hotel; the interior is very swish. Guests have free access to the Domaine's 'Le Club' spa & wellness centre (see page 115); other treatments cost extra. You can access the baths directly from the hotel, enabling you to take advantage of their luxuriant towelling bathrobes. If you manage to drag yourself away, the modern, comfortable rooms have Wi-Fi, safe, AC, minibar & balconies – those at the back have views of the park. Public areas have been designed to maximise the use of daylight, with large panoramic windows. There are 2 restaurants (see page 114) & a plush bar. €€€–€€€€

Casino 2000 (31 rooms) Rue Théodore Flammang, L-5618; ☎ 23 61 12 13; e info@casino2000.lu; www.casino2000.lu. If you can't bear to be parted from the flashing lights & gaming tables of the casino, you can overnight there. Rooms are stylish & modern, & comfort levels consciously ratcheted up to encourage you to linger. AC, free parking & internet access are all available. €€€

Hotel Beau Sejour (11 rooms) 3 av Dr Klein, L-5630; ☎ 26 67 75; e info@beau-sejour.lu; www.beau-sejour.lu; closed Christmas & New Year. This small, friendly & family-run hotel was renovated in 2011, moving it up a notch in comfort & price. Rooms are sleek with a purple theme, & have squeaky-clean bathrooms. The hotel restaurant, *Le Nid Gourmand* (⊕ 12.00–14.00 & 19.00–21.00 daily; €€) serves decent French food. Out front is a large shady terrace. €€€

Welcome Hotel (21 rooms) av des Bains, L-5601; ☎ 23 66 65 49; e domaine@mondorf.

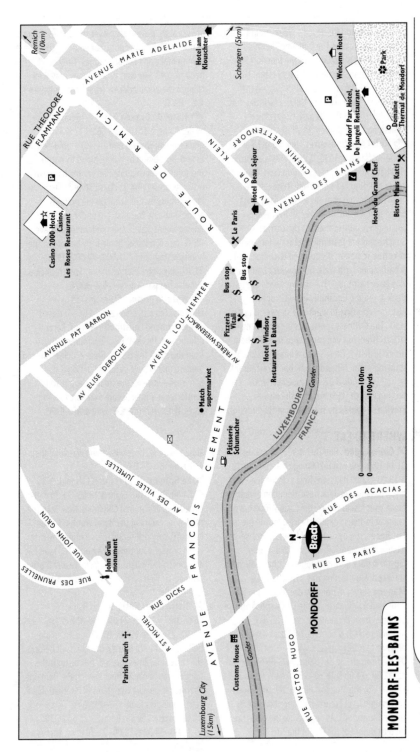

MONDORF-LES-BAINS

MONDORFF

lu; www.mondorf.lu; closed 1 week around Christmas/New Year. The Domaine Thermal's budget option is next door to the Mondorf Parc. Rooms are basic, smallish, but very clean. The reception & b/fast room are 30m away in the Parc. Guests have access to the spa facilities, but you need to cross the car park to get there – something to think about in winter. €€€

🏠 **Hotel Am Klouschter** (60 rooms) 8 av Marie-Adélaïde, L-5635; 📞 26 67 39; e akmo@ elisabeth.lu; www.goeres-group.com. This grand building is a beautifully renovated & nearly converted convent – the 'nearly' part being that 4 resident nuns still live here & you may encounter them in the corridors. Guestrooms are tastefully decorated in shades of 'coffee 'n' cream', & equipped with free Wi-Fi & bathrooms with walk-in showers (2 suites also have bathtubs). The showerheads are sleek & shaped uncannily like microphones, just too tempting to wannabe shower singing stars. The wellness centre has a gym, sauna, & jacuzzi (free, but you can pay to reserve them for exclusivity). There's also a beauty salon, smoking room, billiard room, bar & restaurant (🕐 *12.00–14.00 & 18.00–21.00 daily;* €€€) serving French–Luxembourgish cuisine. Previously owned by the sisters of the order of

St Elisabeth, it was taken over the Goeres Group in mid 2011 & it was not clear whether they plan to make any major changes. They don't need to – it's fine as it is – but they may well change the email address (check the website). €€–€€€

🏠 **Hotel du Grand Chef** (39 rooms) 36 av des Bains, L-5610; 📞 23 66 80 12; e info@ grandchef.lu; www.grandchef.lu; 🕐 mid-Feb to mid-Nov. Grand by name, grand by nature, this former French nobleman's home has been restored, preserving its classic style & décor in an atmosphere of calm. On the grounds of the Domaine Thermal, but under separate management, its elegant modern rooms have Wi-Fi, safe & minibar. Some have balconies. The hotel's restaurant (🕐 *12.00–14.00 & 19.00– 21.30 daily;* €€€) serves mainly French cuisine, but also has pasta dishes. €€–€€€

🏠 **Hotel Windsor** (25 rooms) 58 av François Clement, L-5612; 📞 23 66 51; closed 2 weeks around Christmas/New Year. Recently refurbished, this hotel is a few moments' walk from the spa & the casino. Blue- & beige-themed modern rooms have parquet flooring & mats. Some are a little on the small side, but still comfortable. Discounts are available for long stays. *Without b/fast* €€; *with b/fast* €€€

✗ WHERE TO EAT

✗ **Casino 2000** Rue Théodore Flammang; 📞 23 61 14 10; www.casino2000.lu; 🕐 12.00–14.30 & 19.00–22.00 daily; Les Roses closed Tue–Wed. If you have no need for fresh air or don't want to break your losing streak, the Casino 2000 has a range of in-house dining choices. Top-of-the-pile **Les Roses**, run by head chef Peter Körner, serves gastronomic French delights such as rabbit, lobster & duck in chic surrounds. It has a Michelin star & prices reflecting this. Elsewhere, **Le Manège** serves marginally cheaper fusion food with global influences, while **Le Purple Lounge** produces basic & cheap bar meals all day, including salads & burgers. *Les Roses* €€€€€; *other restaurants* €€–€€€€

✗ **De Jangeli** av des Bains; 📞 23 66 65 25; 🕐 12.00–14.00 & 18.30–22.00 daily (until 22.30 Fri–Sat). In the Mondorf Parc Hotel, De Jangeli serves upmarket French-influenced cuisine in relaxed surrounds. As opposed to the rest-cure dietetic nature of the rest of the site, this is

aimed more at those who aren't watching their waistline. €€€–€€€€€

✗ **Le Bateau** 58 av François Clément; 📞 23 67 64 80; 🕐 11.30–14.00 & 18.00–21.30 daily; closed 2 weeks around Christmas/New Year. The tiled-floor eatery of the Hotel Windsor has an intimate, cosy restaurant, plus a more down-to-earth brasserie for those in a hurry. The food has a distinctly fishy slant, with *fruits de mer* & other seafood, as well as meat dishes, pasta & salads. €€–€€€€

✗ **Bistro Maus Katti** av des Bains; 📞 23 66 65 30; 🕐 10.30–21.00 Mon–Thu & Sat, 10.30–23.00 Fri, 10.30–20.30 Sun. In an old building that once housed the spa itself before the current facilities opened, this bistro is the budget way to eat without leaving the Domaine Thermal. It serves tasty plates of international & Luxembourgish food. €€–€€€

✗ **Le Paris** 3 av des Bains; 📞 23 66 86 30; 🕐 12.00–14.00 & 18.00–21.30 daily. There's a café at the front, & a bar, while the restaurant proper is at the back in a semi-conservatory with panoramic windows & a garden terrace. The chic dining room has a grey laminate floor, red-&-white walls & a white-painted wooden ceiling, completed by glass 'dandelion clock' lampshades. Wooden latticework trellises (with bark) give an organic feel, breaking the room into semi-secluded alcoves. Food is tasty, French–Luxembourgish, & reasonably priced, including classics such as *weinzossis* with creamy mustard sauce & mash. €€–€€€

✗ **Pizzeria Vitali** 39 av François Clement; ✆ 66 80 44; ⊕ 12.00–14.00 & 18.00–22.00 Tue–Sun; closed Wed dinner. This jovial pizzeria is unassuming from the outside, but all-out no-frills Italian within (even though most of the staff are French). If Serie A football was showing on a TV in the corner instead of a fish tank, the image would be complete. No corny gingham tablecloths, no outsized 'compensatory' peppermills, nor walls hung with pictures of the Leaning Tower of Pisa – just honest good eating. Simple wooden furnishings convey an overwhelming sense of 'brown', but the waiters are chirpy, & the pasta & pizzas excellent value. €€

✗ **Pâtisserie Schumacher** 26 av François Clement; ✆ 26 67 09 03; www.schumacher. lu; ⊕ 07.00–18.00 daily. This branch of the Wormeldange-based baking empire serves tasty cakes & snacks for a few euros. €

SHOPPING
Match Supermarket Centre Blériot, av François Clement; ✆ 26 67 69; ⊕ 08.00–19.00 Mon–Thu & Sat, 08.00–20.00 Fri, 08.00–13.00 Sun. In the heart of town.

OTHER PRACTICALITIES
Medical
✚ **Pharmacie de Mondorf** 4 av des Bains; ✆ 26 67 601; ⊕ 08.15–18.15 Mon–Fri, 08.15–12.15 Sat. There are also staff doctors in the Domaine Thermal if you get into trouble.

Banks
$ **BGL BNP Paribas Bank** 43 av François Clement; ✆ 42 42 20 00; ⊕ 09.00–12.00 & 13.30–16.30 Mon–Fri

$ **Dexia Bank** 56 av François Clement; ✆ 23 66 81 35; ⊕ 08.30–12.00 & 13.30–17.00 Mon–Fri
$ **Spuerkeess ('S-Bank')** 62 av François Clement; ✆ 23 66 81 26; ⊕ 08.15–11.45 & 13.30–17.00 Mon–Fri

Post office
✉ **Post office** 15 av Lou Hemmer; ✆ 23 60 62 31; ⊕ 08.00–12.00 & 13.30–17.00 Mon–Fri

WHAT TO SEE AND DO If you want to take in all the outdoor sights, pick up the leaflet for the **Vade Mecum** historical circuit (an easy 8km) from the tourist office. It includes background information giving you the low-down on what you're looking at.

Domaine Thermal de Mondorf (*av des Bains;* ✆ *23 66 69 99; www.mondorf. lu; thermal pool & Le Club* ⊕ *14.00–22.00 Mon, 09.00–22.00 Tue–Thu, 09.00–23.00 Fri, 09.00–20.00 Sat–Sun, other facilities* ⊕ *13.00–19.00 Mon, 10.00–19.00 Tue–Fri, 09.00–19.00 Sat, 09.00–18.00 Sun; Le Club: adult €31.50 (€18.50 after 17.30), thermal pool: adult/child €11.50/8.50*) With its thermal spa and wellness centre, this is a one-stop shop for de-stressing and pampering. The resort's core areas are its **thermal pool** and **Le Club**. The former, filled with mineral-rich 38°C water, is half indoors, half out – you can float between the two, while a range of whirlpools, waterfalls and jets around the sides massage and pummel your body into submission. Owing to the temperature and high salt content, short dips only are recommended. You can also drink the water – there's a fountain in the reception area. It's reputed to have internal cleansing properties and be good for the skin, but drinking too much also has a dramatic 'purgative' effect, so take care. Adjoining the pool, Le Club has a range of masochists' delights, including a dry Nordic sauna, a steam room, a 10°C plunge pool, jacuzzis and an outdoor swimming pool. Bathing suits are optional in this area (hence there's no access to under 16s), but compulsory in the thermal pool, which is open to everyone. Le Club also has a women-only sauna.

Other facilities offered by the Domaine cost extra. A 25-minute massage, for example, is €39. *Rasul* (Turkish mud treatment) costs €35, while 50 minutes being soothed by hot stones is €78.

Besides the relaxation centre, the spa also has a serious medical wing where the elderly and infirm are sent for prescribed rest cures.

Behind the spa is a lovely 50ha wooded **park**. Home to a healthy population of squirrels it's a delightful place for a quiet stroll. Most of it is woodland and lawns, but on the west side are the **Orangerie** pavilion (used for weddings and other receptions), and the ordered box hedges and formal box hedges of the **Jardin Français**. To reach this area you cross a bridge over the river and are technically in France, even though the Luxembourg government owns the land.

Casino 2000 (*rue Flammang;* \ *23 61 11; www.casino2000.lu;* ⊕ *from 10.00 daily; closed Christmas Eve*) Luxembourg's only casino has all the tempting glitz and sparkle you'd expect from an establishment that exists solely with the purpose of separating you from your hard-earned cash. There's lots of low lighting and plush red carpet. Apparently it has the highest number of slot machines (280) for 200km in any direction. Of course there are few clocks to remind you how long you've been gambling, but the adjacent Purple Lounge Bar does have windows, allowing you to keep some track of whether it's day or night – a design flaw, surely? The one-armed bandits are open all day, and the serious gaming begins at 19.00 when the blackjack, roulette and other favourites kick into action.

Parish church If all that gambling has filled you with guilt, you can always pop over to the nearby parish church, sitting on a small mound overlooking the town. It's painted light pink and impossible to miss. The 18th-century building is renowned for its Rococo furnishings and superb frescoes.

GAMES WITHOUT FRONTIERS

The three countries of Benelux had long ago given up on border controls, but the Schengen Treaty was designed to extend this and to abolish checks across a far wider area. The original agreement was signed on 14 June 1985 by the leaders of Belgium, France, Germany, Luxembourg and the Netherlands, and the ceremony took place aboard the MS *Princesse Marie-Astrid*, positioned symbolically astride the tri-nation border between Germany, France and Luxembourg, close to Schengen. Some reports say the excitement of the occasion was too much for the geographically challenged French President Chirac, who is said to have commented at the time how proud he was to be signing the treaty on the 'Dutch Moselle'.

Originally a document about internal borders, Schengen has since been expanded to include a common visa policy, the harmonisation of external border controls, and cross-border co-operation between police forces. Thirty countries have now signed up in one way or another (the Republic of Ireland and the UK only joined the sections covering the synchronising of police activities), but to date just 15 have actually implemented all its conditions.

Jean Grün (1868–1912), born in Mondorf, made his name in the last years of the 19th century as the self-proclaimed 'world's strongest man'. In 1889, a taste for adventure led him to emigrate to the United States, where he toured the country performing feats of strength as John Grün. For a time he also joined fellow strongman Alexander Marx, and they performed together as the Two Marx Brothers. Over the following years, he appeared to great acclaim in circuses, music halls and variety shows across America and Europe.

Despite his size (he weighed around 150kg) Grün was always gentle and well liked, and he made friends everywhere he went. Eventually tiring of showbusiness, he moved to England and worked for a time as a pub landlord, but when he fell mortally ill, he asked to return to Mondorf to die. On his deathbed, doctors and nurses kept him happy by pretending to be hurt by his strength when he touched them, even though he was weakened by age. He died in obscurity, but this good-natured Hercules's lasting legacy was in becoming one of the first Luxembourgers to be recognised and to achieve fame on a global scale.

John Grün Monument On rue John Grün, by the church, this small memorial honours Mondorf's most famous son, professional strongman and performer Jean Grün (see box above). It was erected in 1920, eight years after his death, and was moved three times before settling at its present location.

Customs house Also near the church, south of the main street, is a road that within 10m crosses the river into France (becoming rue de Paris), and the contiguous French village of Mondorff (with two 'f's, just to confuse). It's worth a quick detour, as on the right, just on the Luxembourg side, the walls of the former customs house have been covered with lifelike painted figures, including a gendarme standing around looking important as small boys play around him.

Dalheim Roman Theatre (*Neie Wee, Dalheim; m 621 24 30 01; ⊕ Jun–Sep 15.00–18.00 Sat–Sun; free, guided visits €3*) The otherwise nondescript hamlet of Dalheim, around 4km north of Mondorf, contains one of the Grand Duchy's oldest archaeological sites. Driving northeast from Filsdorf on the N13, just before Dalheim take the turning on the left signposted to the 'Archéoparc'. Park on the left, and the theatre is down the lane on the right. Although opening hours are limited, it's right by the road and you can peer through the fence at any time. It was once part of the Roman town of Ricciacum, founded during the reign of Emperor Augustus. The theatre, once 62.5m across, was built in the early 2nd century AD. The curved stone terraces around the stage could allegedly accommodate an audience of 3,500, although from what remains that claim seems far-fetched to me.

SCHENGEN

Lodged in the extreme southeast of the country, Schengen is a small village whose significance resonates around Europe because of the treaty signed here that bears its name. Even though almost everyone has heard of it, few can point to it on a map. Yet it's been on the tourist trail for centuries: Goethe stayed in Schengen Castle in 1792, and Victor Hugo passed the same way 80 years later. Its origins are far older:

the name derives from the Celtic word *Scen*, meaning 'reed water', and it was first mentioned as Sceidingas in AD877. Today there are few facilities, including no post office, so forget about sending a postcard from the de facto 'centre of Europe'. There is, however, a wonderfully romantic place to stay (see below).

GETTING THERE AND AROUND **Bus** 185 connects Schengen with both Mondorf-les-Bains and Remich, once each hour in either direction. Both journeys take 15 minutes. **Driving** from Luxembourg City takes half an hour. Once in Schengen, everything is within a couple of minutes' walk.

⌂ WHERE TO STAY AND EAT

⌂ **Château de Schengen** (30 rooms)
2 Beim Schlass, L-5444; ☏ 23 66 38; e reception. schengen@goeres-group.com; www.goeres-group.com. A former convent, this magnificent château has been converted by the Goeres Group into a stylish hotel, with 500-year-old Flemish & French tapestries hung on the walls of its grand central staircase. Opulent wooden-floored rooms are individually decorated, & have Wi-Fi. Wine tastings can be arranged in the adjacent 14th-century tower (the kind of round turreted spire that inspires you to shout

'Rapunzel! Rapunzel! Let down your hair!' in a loud voice). The Am Schlass Restaurant (🕑 12.00–14.00 & 18.30–21.00 daily; €€€) serves delicious Luxembourgish classics using local produce, including *truite au Riesling & brochet* (pike). Mirrors on 3 walls make the room feel bigger than it is. The décor is an eclectic mix, with canopied ceilings designed to create a market stall feel – the kitchen was once run by the gardener's wife, & she sold his produce on the market. It's all 'Laura Ashley does Weinstube', or perhaps 'rustic Versailles' – in a fun way. €€€

WHAT TO SEE AND DO
European Monument (*Monument de l'Europe*) The first thing striking visitors to this riverside monument celebrating the unification of Europe, is just how big it isn't. Photographs of the three starry monoliths all manage to avoid including handy humans for scale, and you start believing it stands several storeys high. When you get there, you realise the reason there are no humans in the pictures is they would completely obscure that which you came to look at – it's actually only 2m high and 3m wide. You stop, you take your picture, and you move on. But you probably won't marvel.

Schengen Castle (*Château de Schengen*) The castle first appeared in the 13th century, but has changed dramatically over the years. In 1812, owner Jean-Nicolas Collart decided he wanted something more modern than a medieval lean-to, so he demolished all bar the one round tower you see today (which probably served as his prison). Collart used the stones from the demolished fortress to build a new manor house on the original site. In 1939, this became a house of retreat for nuns belonging to the Order of the Sisters of Saint Elizabeth. Today it's an upmarket hotel (see above), but you can wander around the grounds.

Schengen European Museum (*Musée European Schengen; rue Robert Goebbels;* ☏ *26 66 58 10; www.schengen-tourist.lu;* 🕑 *Easter–Sep 10.00–18.00 Tue–Fri & 11.00–18.00 Sat–Sun, Oct–Easter 10.00–17.00 Tue–Fri, 14.00–17.00 Sat–Sun; free*) This museum covers the building of the EU, and specifically the breaking down of international borders via the Schengen Treaty, including a collection of customs officers' hats you're unlikely to see again at a land border near you. Elsewhere there are sections on the region's Neolithic past, the Moselle's role as a transport route, wine-growing, and of course the Schengen visa. The original 1985 agreement only covered drivers from Benelux, Germany and France, who were given a card with a green dot on it enabling them to pass through borders unhindered. It has since become a slightly more complex beast. If you need statistics on any of the 27 member states, you'll also find those here. Digest them in the adjacent **An Der Aler Schwemm Café** (⊕ *10.30–21.00 Mon–Thu, 10.30–23.00 Fri–Sun*).

Malbrouck Castle (*Château de Malbrouck; Manderen, 57480 France;* ☏ *+33 3 87 35 03 87; www.chateau-malbrouck.com;* ⊕ *Apr–May & Sep–Dec 14.00–17.00 Mon, 10.00–17.00 Tue–Fri, 10.00–18.00 Sat–Sun, Jun–Aug open 1hr later; adult/child €7/5.50*) With one round and three square towers, this imposing hilltop castle is visible for miles. It's 8km from Schengen in the French *département* of Lorraine, and worth a side trip. Crossing from Schengen into Germany, turn right at the roundabout towards France, pass through Apach, then head left towards Manderen (it's signposted from there).

The castle wasn't always in such pristine shape. Before a major restoration project in the 1990s it was a pile of rubble and photographs inside show the transformation. It was built by Arnold VI (1365–1455), a local lord who ruled over a substantial wedge of land between the Saar and Moselle rivers. The interior rooms follow a logical route through each tower and along the parapets, and contain artefacts from the castle's heyday. There are excellent panoramic views from the final (highest) tower, which also contains a stonemasonry exhibit. Malbrouck has a Trier (and thus Luxembourg) connection: Arnold VI's son, Jacques de Sierck, was consecrated Archbishop of Trier here in 1439 (he couldn't go to Trier as there was plague there). He was also Elector of the Holy Roman Empire.

REMERSCHEN

Remerschen is a tiny hamlet in the heart of the vines, a few kilometres north of Schengen. There are two main motives to come here: to sample and buy wine, and to stay in the excellent youth hostel. In summer you can also swim (or if you have the right equipment, sail and windsurf) in the small lakes that lie between the village and the river (€3 entry to the beach, with changing facilities), and the walking trails in the area are popular with birdwatchers.

GETTING THERE **Bus** 185 connects Remerschen with Schengen and Remich, once each hour in either direction. **Driving** from Schengen takes only a couple of minutes. In fact, the distances are so short you could conceivably walk it in less than half an hour.

 WHERE TO STAY AND EAT

🏠 **Youth Hostel** (150 beds) 31 Wäistrooss, L-5440; ☏ 26 66 731; e remerschen@ youthhostels.lu; www.youthhostels.lu. All wood & glass, this swanky hostel is another excellent feather in the national Youth Hostel Association's cap. Book ahead as it's very popular. The hostel has a prime site near a lake. Most rooms have 4–5 beds, but there are a couple of 18-bed dorms & 2 singles. 4-bed rooms can be rented out as doubles for a slightly higher fee. Some rooms have balconies with lake views. The building has full disabled access. Staying here also gets you free entry to the nearby village swimming pool. *€33.50 sgl, €19.50pp in dorms, inc bed, b/fast & bedding. Non-members pay €3 extra.*

✗ **Le Chalet** Breicherwee; ☏ 26 66 51 91; www.lechalet.lu; ⊕ 12.00–14.00 & 18.30–22.00 daily; closed Mon–Tue 'out of season'. This lively bar/restaurant enjoys a fabulous location by Remerschen lake. The interior has wooden decking, giving it an end-of-the-pier feel, with red & wood furnishings, & large windows making the most of the view. The balcony almost overhangs the water. The food is tasty & good value, including *tarte flambée*, pizza, pasta, & *friture de la Moselle*. €€–€€€

WHAT TO SEE AND DO
Caves Sunnen-Hoffmann (6 rue des Prés; ↳ 23 66 40 07; www.caves-sunnen.lu; call ahead to arrange a visit; free) The Sunnen winegrowers, the fifth generation in a family business founded in 1872, are a relatively small outfit: the vineyard contains only 7.5ha of vines and produces 40,000–45,000 litres a year. What sets it apart is it went fully organic in 2000 – the first winery in Luxembourg to do so. This was not a straightforward operation as all its widespread pockets of vines had to be consolidated into one place to protect them from the communal helicopter pesticide spraying that occurs here. You can usually visit just by showing up during working hours Monday to Friday, although as the business is small everyone may be out in the fields. Call ahead to arrange a visit at weekends, and to be sure of a welcome at other times. Not only are their wines organic, they taste good. And the experts agree, judging from the gold medals and awards certificates adorning the walls. As elsewhere, there is an increasing trend towards *crémant* – the first was produced here in 1999.

Caves du Sud (32 route du Vin, L-5440; ↳ 23 66 41 65; www.vinsmoselle.lu; ⊕ May–Oct 10.00–21.00 Tue–Sun; Nov–Apr 10.00–19.00 Tue–Fri, 10.00–21.00 Sat–Sun; cellar tours adult/child €3.50/3) Opened in 1948, this mansion is the southernmost outlet for Domaines de Vinsmoselle, a co-operative created in 1966 to group together many smaller vineyards. Today the estates account for 60% of the country's wine production – Caves du Sud alone has the capacity to store more than 6.5 million litres. You're welcome to come inside and sample some (for a fee), and even more welcome if you buy. There's also a bar and restaurant – the former is in the shape of an old wooden 'wine boat', a craft that once sailed the river, transporting wine barrels.

SCHWEBSINGEN

There's little to Schwebsingen (also called Schwebsange), a further 2km north from Remerschen, but it does have the only sailing harbour in the Luxembourg Moselle, plus a campsite next door. During Schwebsingen's wine festival on the first Sunday in September each year, wine flows from the village fountain in front of the church.

GETTING THERE Bus 185 joins Schwebsingen to Mondorf-les-Bains, Schengen and Remich, travelling once each hour in either direction. **Driving** from Schengen takes only five minutes.

WHERE TO STAY AND EAT Beside the café on the campsite there is nowhere to eat in Schwebsingen. Your best bet is to head south to Remerschen, or for a wider choice, north towards Remich.

Ⓧ **Camping du Port** (160 pitches) RN 10, L-5447; ↳ 23 66 44 60; e info@camping-port. lu; www.wellenstein.lu; ⊕ Mar–Oct. Next to the sailing harbour & the river, this campsite is clean with modern facilities. An on-site café sells snacks. *€3.50pp, plus €5 per pitch.*

WHAT TO SEE AND DO
Mediterranean Garden (Mediterraner Garten; 89 route du Vin; ↳ 26 66 55 37; www.mediterraner-garten.lu; ⊕ May–Sep 15.00–18.00 Tue–Sun; free) We may be 1,000km from the Med, but that didn't stop two private collectors designing and

planting a Mediterranean-style garden. In 2009 it was given to the Luxembourgish nature foundation Hëllef fir d'Natur (*www.hfn.lu*), in return for help in maintaining it. Covering 1,900m², it contains 1,000 varieties of plant, including subtropical and tropical species that have unexpectedly thrived in the mild Moselle microclimate.

WELLENSTEIN

Wellenstein is a cute little village where many houses have shuttered windows and colourful window boxes. Nothing much happens here, but it's quiet, can be a good base for longer stays, and there are a couple of opportunities to sample the regional produce.

GETTING THERE **Bus** 175 connects Wellenstein with Luxembourg City, via Mondorf-les-Bains, and Remich, twice each hour in either direction. **Driving** from Remich takes only five minutes.

TOURIST INFORMATION
Tourist office 4 Heenegässel; 23 69 98 58; www.siw.lu; ⏱ 08.30–11.30 Mon–Wed & Fri. Provides advice & free brochures on regional places of interest, & can help with accommodation reservations.

WHERE TO STAY AND EAT
Winegrowers' houses (3 houses – information & reservations via tourist office). In the village are a number of lovely houses dating from the 18th century. 3 have been luxuriously decked out in period furnishings, fitted with all mod cons, & made available for rent on a weekly basis as self-catering villas sleeping 4–6. All 3 have living room, dining room, kitchen, bathroom & separate toilet. Bedding is provided. €480–510 per house per week.

There are no restaurants in Wellenstein. Head into Remich for a good choice of eateries (for more details, see page 125).

WHAT TO SEE AND DO
Caves des Vignerons de Wellenstein (*13 rue des Caves;* 26 66 141; *www. vinsmoselle.com;* ⏱ *07.30–19.00 Mon–Fri, 10.00–19.00 Sat–Sun, cellar tours May– Oct 09.00–17.00 daily, other times & in groups by appointment; cellar tours adult/ child €3.50/3*) In operation since 1930, this is another outlet of the influential Domaines de Vinsmoselle co-operative. Tastings are available, and guided tours of the cellars – the largest in the country – are possible.

BECH-KLEINMACHER

There's only one reason to come to this tiny village on the wine route, 3km south of Remich. But it's a good one.

GETTING THERE **Bus** 175 connects Bech-Kleinmacher with Luxembourg City, via Mondorf-les-Bains, and Remich, twice each hour in either direction. Bus 185 (once per hour), will get you there from Schengen and the other riverside villages to the south. **Driving** from Remich takes only a few minutes.

WHERE TO STAY AND EAT There is nowhere to stay in Bech-Kleinmacher, but Remich is only a short distance away.

✖ **Waistuff 'A Possen'** 4 Keeseschgässel; ☎ 23 69 82 33; ⏰ 11.00–21.00 daily. Next to the museum, this wooden-floored dining room has tiled tables & stained-glass windows. Out back is a terrace draped in vines. Trying a local wine is a must, obviously, but there's also tasty food, ranging from quiche to pâté, both homemade & served with chips & salad. €–€€

WHAT TO SEE AND DO

'A Possen' Wine and Folklore Museum (*Musée Folklorique et Viticole 'A Possen'; 2 Keeseschgässel;* ☎ *23 69 73 53; www.musee-possen.lu;* ⏰ *Easter–Oct 11.00– 19.00 Tue–Sun (last entry 18.00), Nov–Dec & Mar 11.00–19.00 Fri–Sun (last entry 18.00); adult/child €5/2.50)* This excellent museum is in a restored 1612 house and its neighbours. The collection within is somewhat eclectic, veering from 200-year-old Villeroy & Boch crystal glasses to teddy bears and period rooms – the kitchen with its time- and smoke-blackened walls is particularly atmospheric.

A modern extension has added space to display toys dating from 1860–1960, including dolls, teddies and handmade train sets. One carousel is powered by a 1950s Philips record player, and a miniature rollercoaster is run by the electric motor from a Citroën 2CV.

It's pretty cramped inside the older building, and anyone of normal dimensions will need to stoop now and again to avoid banging their head. The collection there includes old cast-iron stoves and cobblers' equipment. Naturally, considering the location, the emphasis is on winemaking equipment, including two giant wine presses out front that confirm you've come to the right address. The adjacent tasting room has morphed into a restaurant (see *Where to stay and eat,* above).

REMICH

Grevenmacher may be the Moselle's administrative capital, but Remich is its tourist hub. An attractive town stretching along the riverbank, it has the biggest choice of food and accommodation in the region. Almost everything is either on the Esplanade, the main road beside the river, or one block inland. The town's biggest landmark is the road bridge crossing to Germany. As you sit on the café terraces watching the giant cargo barges plough up- and downstream, you'll realise how important the river is as a transport link – and also wonder how the swans that patrol the waters manage not to get annihilated.

GETTING THERE Bus 175 (twice per hour) travels between Luxembourg City and Remich in 40 minutes. **Driving** takes half an hour. For other points along the river bus 185 heads south towards Schengen, while bus 450 travels north to Grevenmacher, both on an hourly basis.

GETTING AROUND While Remich is fairly spread out, most hotels and restaurants are within a few minutes' **walk** of the bridge, as are the boat jetties and the bus station. **Bikes** can be rented (€7 per day) from the Hotel St Nicolas, or from RentaBike Miselerland in the bus station. If you're planning a tour, you can return the latter to any of 12 other participating outlets in the Moselle (see *Getting there and around* at the start of this chapter).

Trips on the **river** are available with Navitours (see page 124) and Remich is also a regular stop on the MS *Princesse Marie-Astrid*'s route. See page 110 for more details.

Landlubbers can ride up and down the Esplanade on the De Jhangeli tourist '**train**' (☎ *26 74 71 14; Easter–Aug daily, Sep–Oct Tue–Sun; check bus station for departure times*).

REMICH

Grevenmacher (15km)

Caves St Martin
Pavillon St Martin ✕

Belle-Rive ↟

ROUTE DE STADTBREDIMUS

RUE DE LA CITÉ

LUXEMBOURG
GERMANY

Moselle
FLOW

Pavillon Desom ✕

RUE DICKS

Caves St Remy-Desom

Bacchus statue

ESPLANADE

Restaurant Fuli ✕

Hotel St Nicolas/
Restaurant Lohengrin ✕

Auberge de Cygnes ✕

Café Romano
Hotel Restaurant
Creperie Esplanade

RUE DAUVELT

RUE DES VERGERS

RUE HIER.
ZIGSBERG

RUE ERNST

PLACE
DU MARCHE

RUE DES PRES

R DES CHAMPS

RUE NEUVE

Bus station
Boat
jetties

Restaurant ✕ ✕ Restaurant
de la Moselle   La Croisette
✕ L'Aventore
✕ ProArte

Camping Mosella
am Rothaus ▲

Mosel-Camping
Dreiländereck Nennig ▲

Borg Roman Villa (10km),
Nennig Roman Villa (2km)

ROUTE DU VIN

RUE DE MACHER

Schengen
(8km)

ROUTE DE L'EUROPE

ROUTE DE
LUXEMBOURGE

RUE DE
MONDORF

ROUTE DE
DES VIGNES

CHEMIN
LAMORT - VELTER

AVENUE DES VIGNES

Hotel de Vignes ↟

Hotel Domaine la Forêt ↟

Luxembourg
City (18km)

N

Bradt

0   300m
0   300yds

123

TOURIST INFORMATION AND LOCAL TOUR OPERATORS

Navitours PO Box 47, L-5501; ✆ 75 84 89, m 621 13 00 54; e info@navitours.lu; www.navitours.lu; adult/child from €7.50/4. Offers excursions on the river departing from the jetty just south of the bridge. 1hr cruises run Mar–Oct 11.00, 15.15, 16.30 & 17.45 Mon–Sat, & 11.00, 14.50, 16.30 & 17.45 Sun & public holidays. Longer cruises depart Mar–Oct 12.15 daily (2hr 45mins, adult/child €14/7; 4hrs, adult/child €17/8.50). Other departures are available for groups on request. On Sun a lunch cruise departs at 12.30 (board at 12.00), returning at 16.00 (adult/child €42.50/20).

🛈 **Tourist office** pl de la Résistance, rue Ernst; ✆ 23 69 84 88; ⊕ mid-Jun to mid-Sep 10.00–12.30 & 13.30–18.00 daily

🏠 WHERE TO STAY

🏠 **Hotel de Vignes** (24 rooms) 29 route de Mondorf, L-5552; ✆ 23 69 91 49; e info@hotel-vignes.lu; www.hotel-vignes.lu; ⊕ mid-Jan to mid-Dec. For those who prefer to stay surrounded by vines rather than by the river, the Hotel de Vignes is further inland on the edge of town in a quiet semi-rustic location. Rooms are spacious & modern, with minibar & free Wi-Fi. Most have balconies; all have valley views. If it's too much trouble to head back into town, the in-house restaurant (⊕ daily 11.45–14.00 & 18.30–21.30; €€€–€€€€) serves good French & regional cuisine, with lobster & (in season) game – the panoramic terrace is a big plus. €€€

🏠 **Hotel Domaine la Forêt** (16 rooms) 36 route de l'Europe, L-5531; ✆ 23 69 99 99; e laforet@pt.lu; www.hotel-la-foret.lu; closed 2 weeks in Jan, 1 week in Jul. Also on the outskirts of town on the road to Luxembourg City, the Domaine bills itself as much as a 'wellness & beauty resort' as a hotel. In addition to the beautiful heated swimming pool, there's a sauna, steam room, solarium & fitness room to keep you out of trouble. Rooms have minibar & safe; some have balconies with forest views. The restaurant produces local seasonal food & has an extensive wine list. A wide terrace looks out over the valley. €€€

🏠 **Hotel St Nicolas** (42 rooms) 31 Esplanade, L-5533; ✆ 26 663; e hotel@pt.lu; www.saint-nicolas.lu. The St Nicolas, founded in 1885, is a traditional & friendly family-run hotel in the centre of Remich. Named after the patron saint of fishermen, the building is an eclectic mix of old & new. Rooms have been refurbished & are modern, with light furnishings, fans, minibar & kettle. Those at the front on the 1st floor have balconies with river views. Some bathrooms have whirlpool baths (perfect for soaking away the guilt of having spent the entire day tasting wine). The extensive wellness area includes (deep breath): indoor & outdoor pools, fitness room, sauna, *hammam*, a 'fresh air court', an 'ice grotto', a silent room, foot therapy, & massage rooms (all free except massages). Free internet access is available from terminals on the ground floor, & there is free Wi-Fi throughout. The old-style foyer/lounge has an open fireplace to keep you toasty in winter, while the Restaurant Lohengrin (see opposite) is one of the better places to eat in town. €€€

🏠 **Hotel Esplanade** (18 rooms) 5 Esplanade, L-5533; ✆ 23 66 91 71; e info@esplanade.lu; www.esplanade.lu; ⊕ Feb–Dec. A central hotel with a fine location opposite the river, rooms here are comfortable, if a little old, & are well appointed for the price. Those at the front with waterside views cost slightly more. No lift. Meals can be served on the terrace at the front. €€

🏠 **Hotel Villa Belle-Rive** (8 rooms) 49 route de Stadtbredimus, L-5570; ✆ 27 07 56 77; e bellerive@pt.lu; www.bellerive.lu. Opened in mid 2011, this small friendly hotel is 1km north of central Remich, between Caves St Martin & Caves St Remy-Desom. Lovely sleek rooms have balconies (those at the front have river views), wood flooring, safe, minibar, free Wi-Fi & fresh flowers (a nice touch). The funky bedside lights are touch-sensitive balls. Bathrooms are spotless. B/fast arrives on 'afternoon tea' trays, brought to your table as there's no space for a buffet. The restaurant (see below) is worth the journey in itself. €

🏕 **Camping** If you want to stay under canvas & experience the Schengen agreement at work, there are 2 convenient campsites just over the river in the German village of Nennig. Both have waterside locations & clean facilities.

Immediately south of the bridge (on the right, coming from Remich) is **Mosel-Camping Dreiländereck Nennig** (*Sinzerstrasse 1, D-66706 Nennig, Germany;* ✆ *+49 6866 322; www.mosel-camping.de*). Just north of the bridge is **Camping Mosella am Rothaus** (*Rothaus 1,*

D-66706, Perl-Nennig; ✆ *+49 6866 510*). From either it's a 5min walk back to Remich, with all its eating & drinking delights. No border controls, naturally. Both are open Apr to mid Oct & charge around €20 for a pitch & 2 people.

✕ WHERE TO EAT

✕ **Pavillon St Martin**   53 route de Stadtbredimus; ✆ 23 66 91 02; ⏱ Feb to mid-Dec 12.00–15.00 & 17.30–21.30 Tue–Sun. 1km north of central Remich, the Caves St Martin's restaurant has a reputation as one of the best places for regional speciality *friture de la Moselle* – a plate of deep-fried local river fish. Eat with your fingers: smaller sprats can be eaten whole; larger beasts require more selective nibbling. In summer there's a peaceful terrace with a beautiful river view. €€€–€€€€

✕ **Restaurant Lohengrin**   31 Esplanade; ✆ 26 663; www.saint-nicolas.lu; ⏱ 12.00–13.45 & 18.30–21.45 daily. The cosy restaurant of the Hotel St Nicolas is an old-style dining room with linen tablecloths & silver-plated cutlery. Head chef Serge Duc turns out excellent French & Mediterranean cuisine, with a few Luxembourg specialities added for good measure. For a more romantic evening in summer, dine alfresco by candlelight on the garden terrace. €€€–€€€€

✕ **Villa Belle-Rive**   49 route de Stadtbredimus; ✆ 27 07 56 77; www.bellerive.lu; ⏱ 11.30–22.00 Wed–Mon, closed 4 weeks in Jan–Feb. A lovely modern dining room in the hotel of the same name, just north of Remich centre, with grey tiled floors, minimalist white walls on 2 sides, & stone bricks on a 3rd (the 4th is glass). There are chic purple-&-mauve table furnishings & an orchid theme spilling over from the guestrooms. The excellent food is refined & French-influenced: *tournedos Rossini*, foie gras, lobster thermidor … The wine list includes offerings by St Remy-Desom, 200m away. €€€–€€€€

✕ **L'Aventore**   14 Quai de la Moselle; ✆ 26 69 95 95; ⏱ 11.00–15.00 & 18.00–22.00 daily. South of the bridge, opposite where the boats dock, is a row of brasserie restaurants all with similar food & prices. All are aimed predominantly at the German tourist market, judging by the regular appearance of *sauerkraut* on their menus. L'Aventore is arguably the best of the bunch. Just to confuse you, it was formerly known as 'Quai 14', & on my visit the old name was more visible than the new. This may change. Dishes include salads & *bouchée à la reine;* vegetarians will need to like lasagne in order not to starve. €€–€€€

✕ **Restaurant La Croisette**   4 Quai de la Moselle; ✆ 26 66 05 05; ⏱ lunch & dinner. Spread over 2 floors with a panoramic terrace overlooking the river. The lower pizzeria serves a fine range of pasta & pizza dishes at very reasonable rates; the meatier fare upstairs has more of a French bias & costs a little more. €€–€€€

✕ **Auberge de Cygnes**   11 Esplanade; ✆ 23 69 88 52; ⏱ 12.00–14.30 & 18.00–22.00 Wed–Mon, 12.00–14.30 Tue, closed Wed in low season. This convivial eatery is decked out in tasteful mauve, & the French–Luxembourgish dishes are mighty tasty & good value. Downstairs, in the low-ceilinged cellar, delicious pizzas are on offer in a charming atmosphere for under €10. Service in both is friendly & attentive. €€

✕ **Restaurant de la Moselle**   2 Quai de la Moselle; ✆ 23 69 86 85; ⏱ 11.30–22.00 daily. This French-inspired outlet has a good selection of salads, plus more carnivore-pleasing mains for those who need more protein in their diet. €€

✕ **ProArte**   55 rue de Macher; ✆ 26 66 07 80; www.proarte.lu; ⏱ 11.45–23.00 Tue–Sun. The high incidence of pizzerias in Remich seems designed to reflect what tourists want. This charming & friendly place, decorated in red & cream shades, is south of the bridge & 1 block inland. Pastas are freshly made & the pizzas cooked in a wood-fired oven. Heftier meaty mains are also available. €–€€€

✕ **Restaurant Brasserie Creperie l'Esplanade**   5 Esplanade; ✆ 23 66 91 71; ⏱ 12.00–14.30 & 18.30–21.30 Thu–Tue. With such a mouthful of a name it's no surprise that the menu here covers every base imaginable within the combined French & Luxembourgish range. House specials include local fare such as *friture de la Moselle & brochet au beurre blanc* (pike in cream sauce). €–€€€

🍴 **Café Romano** 9 Esplanade; ☎ 23 69 71 28; ⊕ 08.00–22.00 daily in season. For lighter meals

this place offers pancakes sweet & savoury, plus ice creams & *other* options such as *tarte flambée* for very little money. €

OTHER PRACTICALITIES

✚ **Pharmacie des Vignerons** 27 rue Foascht; ☎ 23 66 90 31

$ **Dexia Bank** 1 rue Ernst; ☎ 23 69 41; ⊕ 08.30–12.00 & 13.30–17.00 Mon–Fri

$ **Spuerkeess ('S-Bank')** 2 pl du Marché; ☎ 23 66 90 03; ⊕ 08.15–11.45 & 13.30–17.00 Mon–Fri

✉ **Post office** 15 pl du Marché; ☎ 23 60 63 31; ⊕ 08.00–12.00 & 13.30–17.15 Mon–Fri

WHAT TO SEE AND DO

Caves St Martin (*53 route de Stadtbredimus;* ☎ *23 69 97 74; www.cavesstmartin. lu;* ⊕ *shop Apr–Oct 10.00–12.00 & 13.30–17.30 Tue–Sun, guided tours Apr–Oct 10.00–11.30 & 13.30–17.00 Tue–Sun, advance booking for tours recommended; adult/child €4.50/2.50*) At 1km north of central Remich, the caves are cut into cliffs, maintaining both a romantic atmosphere and a practical 13°C storage temperature. The 45-minute tours explain the 80-year history of the cellars, the production processes that go into making the flagship *crémants*, and include a glass of the fizz itself (grape juice for children). The terrace of the Pavillon St Martin (see *Where to eat*, page 125) is a good spot to chill out and absorb everything you've just learned.

Caves St Remy-Desom (*9 rue Dicks;* ☎ *23 60 40; www.desom.lu; summer only, call in advance; tours €3.50/5.50/6.50/8.50 with 1/2/3/4 glasses*) One of the country's largest independent wine producers, accounting for 3% of national output, Desom also promotes its *crémants* above all else. It produces one of Luxembourg's few red wines: a quite palatable Pinot Noir. Desom is 500m north from the centre, by the river. You can taste (and buy) wines without a pre-booked tour in the adjacent Pavillon Desom, which also serves snacks whilst you imbibe.

Bacchus fountain In the middle of town by the river, the town's main fountain is crowned with a statue of Bacchus, god of wine. He sits astride a barrel toasting all and sundry, leaving you in no doubt about the region's *raison d'être*. If the way his cups quite literally overfloweth isn't enough to get you all excited, you'll be delighted to know he revolves as well – until being turned off at 20.00 each evening, that is.

Nennig Roman Villa (*Römische Villa Nennig; Römierstrasse 11, Perl-Nennig, Germany;* ☎ *+49 6866 1329;* ⊕ *Apr–Sep 08.30–12.00 & 13.00–18.00 Tue–Sun, Mar & Oct–Nov 13.00–16.30 Tue–Sun; adult/child €1.50/0.75*) One of two Roman villas across the border in Germany (see also below), this is the smaller one but both make interesting side trips from Remich. Roughly 2km away (follow the signs), little remains of the original building, so perhaps telling you it once had a 140m façade is a meaningless statistic. What you can see is a huge, beautifully preserved 3rd century AD mosaic, rediscovered by a farmer in 1852 whilst out digging his fields. The 160m² masterpiece, in a purpose-built pavilion erected after it was uncovered, is one of very few large Roman mosaics still displayed in their original location. A multi-media show points out features of interest, and provides a virtual glimpse of the villa in its prime.

Borg Roman Villa (*Römische Villa Borg; Perl-Borg, Germany;* ✆ *+49 6865 91170; www.villa-borg.de;* ⊕ *Tue–Sun & Feb–Mar 11.00–16.00, Apr–Oct 11.00–18.00, Nov–Dec 11.00–16.00; adult/child €4/2*) About 10km into Germany (head over the bridge from Remich, continue east on the main road for 8km, then turn right to Borg and follow the signs to the villa), this huge Roman villa has been reconstructed to how it may have looked in its heyday, when owned by an ex-soldier granted land for his services to Rome. Wander around the 7.5ha estate, tour the villa itself, or try some ancient specialities in the tavern, based on recipes recorded by the Roman epicurist Apicius. The villa's baths can be rented for special events.

EHNEN

The big draw in little Ehnen is its excellent wine museum, but there are also some nice places to stay overnight and/or enjoy a meal. The local wine festival takes place in mid-September.

GETTING THERE AND AROUND Bus 450 passes through Ehnen on its way between Grevenmacher and Remich, hourly in either direction. Wormeldange is only a couple of kilometres further north, and you can walk between the two villages in under half an hour.

WHERE TO STAY AND EAT

🏠 **Bamberg's Hotel** (12 rooms) 131 route du Vin, L-5416; ✆ 76 00 22; e bamberg@pt.lu; ⊕ mid-Jan to Nov. A small, friendly, family-run establishment in a restored old white building 100m from the museum. Facilities are somewhat basic & old, but adequate for the price. The French–Luxembourgish restaurant (⊕ 12.00–14.00 & 18.30–21.00 Wed–Mon; €€€) is more upmarket, & does a fine *friture de la Moselle*. €€

🏠 **Hotel Simmer** (15 rooms) 117 route du Vin, L-5416; ✆ 76 00 30; e info@hotel-simmer.lu; www.hotel-simmer.lu; ⊕ Feb–Dec. Originally opened in 1863, the Simmer has been run by the same family since 1955. The strangely roofed building beside the wine museum looks like a reject from a *Munsters* TV show. It's a tad old fashioned (the furniture appears unchanged in half a century), but is atmospheric & homely. Rooms have sturdy wooden beds, & creaky wooden floors. Some cheaper ones have shared bathrooms. No lift. The lounge is wood-panelled neo-Gothic, with intricate carvings & a large

hearth – if you need Play Stations & flatscreen TVs this probably isn't for you. The restaurant's (⊕ 12.00–14.00 & 19.00–21.00 Wed–Sun; €€€–€€€€) cosy dining room also has a large stone fireplace. The menu is refined French–Luxembourgish, with an autumn mushroom menu offered when the fungi are up. The front room is an open conservatory with river views, & there's a large terrace. €€

✘ **Taverne Am Keller** 119 route du Vin; ✆ 26 74 75 63; ⊕ 10.30–01.00 Tue–Sun. At the cheap & cheerful end of the scale, this small cellar bar/restaurant (the 'cellar' is actually only 50cm below street level) can rustle up a decent *menu du jour* (⊕ Tue–Fri) for under €10. Otherwise it serves standard Luxembourgish dishes. For Sun lunch indulge yourself with the €20 all-you-can-eat buffet. Although technically open all day, whether you can get fed between accepted mealtimes depends on whether the chef is there. Credit cards not accepted. €–€€

OTHER PRACTICALITIES For a pharmacy, bank or post office, head for Wormeldange, 1km north.

WHAT TO SEE AND DO

Ehnen Wine Museum (*Musée du Vin Ehnen; 115 route du Vin;* ✆ *76 00 26;* ⊕ *Apr–Oct 09.30–11.30 & 14.00–17.00 Tue–Sun; adult/child €3.50/1.50*) This excellent museum occupies a beautiful 18th-century house, which was itself a winery until the early 1900s. The slightly eccentric miscellany of winemaking equipment forming the bulk of the collection has been donated over the years by local viticulturists as they've progressively upgraded their kit. Galleries follow the

A STOP ALONG THE WAY

Between Remich and Grevenmacher, in addition to the somewhat larger villages of Ehnen and Wormeldange covered in the main text, there are several other tiny hamlets, each no more than a speck on the map. But here too you will find some good dining options, as well as yet more opportunities to sup great wines. All the places mentioned below can be reached via bus 450, which runs hourly in each direction between Remich and Grevenmacher.

Two kilometres north of Remich, **Stadtbredimus** traces its roots back to the Celts. Today the village is mainly notable for being the headquarters of the Domaines de Vinsmoselle wine co-operative (*www.vinsmoselle.lu*). Their restaurant and tasting room is An der Tourelle (*12 route du Vin;* \ *23 698 511; www.tourelle.lu;* ⊕ *11.30–14.00 & 18.00–21.30 Thu–Tue;* €€€€), which occupies the 15th-century round tower of Stadtbredimus Castle. This is where chef Jean-Marie Hemmen, who served his apprenticeship under Lea Linster, Luxembourg's top celebrity chef, produces excellent regional specialities with classic French finesse. The circular high-ceilinged dining room is light, airy and elegant, and the wine list, of course, promotes the Domaines's produce.

A kilometre north again, blink-and-you-miss-it **Hëttermillen** offers a further chance for tasting. Domaine Viticole Cep D'Or (*15 route du Vin;* \ *76 83 83; www.cepdor.lu;* ⊕ *Easter–end of Dec 08.00–12.00 & 14.00–19.00 Mon–Fri, 15.00–19.00 Sat–Sun; end of Dec–Easter 08.00–12.00 & 14.00–19.00 Mon–Fri, 17.00–19.00 Sat*) is a large winery across the road from the river, with a shop and a bar. Tastings are available in both, but the latter has a large terrace with river views

Ahn is a pretty riverside hamlet between Wormeldange and Grevenmacher, but besides the Riesling Open wine festival (see page 130), there's not a lot here demanding your attention. With one notable exception: Restaurant Mathes (*37 route du Vin;* \ *76 01 06; www.restaurant-mathes.lu;* ⊕ *12.00–14.00 & 19.00–21.30 Wed–Sun; closed 2 weeks in Nov;* €€€€–€€€€€) is a large, modern establishment over the road from the river, with a panoramic terrace taking in the view. The French–Luxembourgish food is excellent, if not cheap, and includes local fish classics such as *friture de la Moselle* and *brochet au Riesling*.

And if you think nothing much happens in Ahn, wait until you see **Machtum**. Again however, there are exceptions. Besides the Riesling Open in September, there is Wäistuff Deisermillen – Caves Jean Schlink-Hoffeld (*85 route du Vin;* \ *26 72 91 40;* ⊕ *Nov–Apr 15.00–21.00 Fri–Sat, 12.00–21.00 Sun, May–Oct 15.00–22.00 Fri–Sat, 12.00–22.00 Sun, closed 3 weeks around Christmas/New Year*). The tasting room just north of Machtum run by Caves Jean Schlink-Hoffeld is a modern building overlooking the Moselle. Snacks (€) to wash the wine down here include local hams and cheeses. When the Deisermillen is closed, you can also taste and purchase wines at the winery itself in the village (*1 rue de l'Eglise;* \ *75 84 68;* ⊕ *08.00–12.00 & 13.00–18.00 Mon–Fri, 08.00–12.00 & 13.00–17.00 Sat; closed 3 weeks around Christmas/New Year*). Their range includes some of Luxembourg's finest reds.

top   The Golden Lady (Gëlle Frau) in Luxembourg City is a national monument to freedom (TS) page 74

Rows of graves [above] (RLH/LTOL) page 82 and a memorial to fallen soldiers at the American Military Cemetery, Hamm [right] (RLH/LTOL) page 82

below   A recreation of the Battle of the Ardennes in the National Museum of Military History, Diekirch (TS) page 191

above   Sizzling *mettwurst* sausages, a perennial Luxembourg festival favourite (TS) page 30

below   An array of nuts and nut-based foods and liqueurs go on sale at Vianden's annual nut market (TS) page 181

right — **Try before you buy at the local *caves* (literally cellars) in Remich**
(LTO) page 122

below — **Dray horses bring in the brews, ahead of the National Day Festival in Luxembourg City**
(TS) page 34

bottom — **While away an afternoon in the rolling Moselle Valley vineyards**
(LTO) page 107

above Enjoy the peace and quiet of nature in the picturesque forests of the Ardennes (LTO) page 171

below The market town of Larochette lies in the heart of Little Switzerland (WP/A) page 166

above   Hikers get some fresh air with a walk in the wilds of Little Switzerland (WT/A) page 166

right   Place du Marché in Echternach; Luxembourg's oldest town (DR) page 152

below   Hot-air balloons drift above the forests and streams of Little Switzerland (SS) page 141

above The 10th-century Bourglinster Castle is home to two wonderful restaurants (SS) page 92

below Clervaux Castle is home to 'The Family of Man', the most culturally important photographic exhibition in the world (SS) page 211

above   Hitting the high notes at Luxembourg City's charming Christmas Market (TS) page 68

A chance for enthusiasts to get into character at the annual Vianden Medieval Festival parade, [bottom left] (TS) page 181 while local merchants bring ancient crafts to life [bottom right] (TS) page 181

above   Luxembourg's largest body of water, the Upper Sûre Lake, provides half of the country's drinking water (C/D) page 202

below   The tiny town of Esch-sur-Sûre; a village so attractive it just begs to grace the cover of 1,000 jigsaws (DR) page 198

winemaking process in logical order from growing the vines through to bottling. Dioramas also show how people lived 100 years ago – if they're to be believed, every home had its own still for making grape brandy (life was clearly never dull in the villages). Ask for an English translation of the display texts, or if a member of staff is available they're often happy to show you around. Guided or not, visits always end with a chance to try some wine.

There's a plan to introduce interactive touch-screen displays when funding becomes available, which will make the museum more appealing to children. For now, it's a little old-fashioned, but fascinating nonetheless.

At the back is a small vineyard where each national grape variety is grown, and labelled to help you tell them apart. Like other grapes grown on government land they're turned into wine, but this isn't sold commercially. Instead it's used to represent Luxembourg, and served up at official functions in foreign embassies. The museum forms the focal point of the Riesling Open wine festival in September (see box, page 130).

Viticole Kohll-Reuland (*5 Am Stach/12 Hohlgaass;* \ *76 00 18;* ⊕ *by appointment only*) On a hillside on the edge of the vines, this small craft winery has a terrace at the back overlooking Ehnen. It produces some decidedly above-average fermented grape products, not least an excellent Riesling. Call ahead as they may be out in the fields.

Caves Jean Leuck-Thull (*23 Neie Wee;* \ *76 81 25;* ⊕ *by appointment only*). Another of Ehnen's finer wineries, this is notable for a rare wine type: Gris de Gris, made with Pinot Gris grapes, but the skins are left in the mix initially to impart a yellow-pink colour and an extra layer of complexity in the flavour. Worth seeking out.

Dolizy et Guillon (*5 rue Kiirchegaessel;* \ *45 67 06,* m *691 48 49 55; www.distillerie. lu;* ⊕ *by appointment only*). As a change from wine, this small distillery in the heart of Ehnen produces around 20 different liqueurs and *eaux de vie*. Their Marc de Gewürztraminer is particularly good.

Walking For fresh air and exercise, try the **walking route** around Ehnen (5km; 1½ hours; maps available from the museum and hotels). Starting beside the museum, follow the 'blue flag' arrows with '1' on them. Although short, the path takes you through a variety of landscapes: open vineyards, deciduous forest, the backstreets of Ehnen, along the banks of babbling brooks, and even through a 'micro-gorge' (don't get too excited – 'micro' is the keyword here). A much shorter **historical walk** through the town is also possible and there's an accompanying multi-lingual booklet that provides historical information on the days when Ehnen was owned by the Bishops of Trier. It won't detain you longer than half an hour at a slow pace.

WORMELDANGE

Wormeldange's narrow streets are lined with colourful painted houses. The village consists effectively of just two parallel roads: route du Vin by the river, and rue Principale, 50m inland. Most facilities are in the latter. This area is particularly known for its Riesling wines, and in September the Riesling Open wine festival celebrates the fact (see box, below). There's little to see at other times, but it's pretty and makes for a relaxing place to stay.

GETTING THERE AND AROUND Bus 450 passes through Wormeldange on its way between Grevenmacher and Remich, hourly in either direction. **Driving** from Luxembourg City takes little more than half an hour. Wormeldange is only a few hundred metres across, thus getting around on foot is a simple matter.

WHERE TO STAY AND EAT

Auberge Koeppchen (5 rooms) 9 Berreggaass, L-5485 Wormeldange-Haut; 76 00 461; ⊕ Feb–Dec. Just above the main village in Wormeldange-Haut, getting to the Koeppchen can be a shock to the system whether arriving by car, bike or on foot. It's a short, steep climb up the valley, but the tremendous views over the vines, river &

rooftops of Wormeldange from its terrace (& some rooms' balconies) do compensate. The restaurant (⊕ *12.00–13.30 & 18.00–21.00 Wed–Sun;* €€–€€€) here is renowned for producing some of the best *friture de la Moselle* in the area. And no, nothing fell on my keyboard when I was typing that address – it really does contain all those double letters. €€

THE RIESLING OPEN

The third weekend each September is the time when many smaller wineries not normally set up for visitors throw open their doors. The Riesling Open (*www.rieslingopen.com*) centres on four villages: Ehnen, Wormeldange, Ahn and Machtum. On Friday evening things officially get under way in Wormeldange with the crowning of the year's Queen of the Riesling. And from a wine-lover's perspective, things start getting interesting on Saturday afternoon, with tastings (15.00–20.00) at participating wineries.

The place to start is at the Wine Museum in Ehnen at 15.00 (see page 127). Once Ehnen's mayor has made a short welcome speech, he, the Queen of the Riesling in all her finery (and her attendant princesses), and various local luminaries, take a tasting glass each and – accompanied by a band – amble off for a crawl of the village's wineries, stopping for a chilled Riesling at each. You are welcome to take a glass and tag along behind the official procession, and you will also be offered a free wine, or three. Away from the procession, tastings cost a few euros each.

Sunday is the main day, with street parties and stalls everywhere from 11.00, and tasting opportunities aplenty (not free). To get between each locality, a free shuttle bus runs half-hourly between 11.00 and 21.30 in each direction between the southernmost (the Wine Museum) and northernmost (Caves Schlink-Hoffeld in Machtum) points. More fun (if slower) is sailing aboard the MS *Princess Marie-Astrid* (see page 110), which makes the same round trip a couple of times on Sunday afternoon (see the website for a timetable). This is also free for one day only, and of course there's a bar on board dispensing yet more Riesling.

The Sunday packs four different party atmospheres into one festival. In Ehnen, everyone, including the winery owners, relocates to the museum and there's reverential tasting with discreet background music. Machtum is livelier, but only in two distinct locations. In the picturesque hamlet of Ahn there's little to do for 364 days a year, but in September it comes alive as it's home to eight wineries – to visit these at other times you need to call ahead. Wormeldange, the largest village, is party central. It has a carnival atmosphere with bands playing on the street, and waffles, sausages and other snacks available. Rue Principale is heaving with revellers by early evening.

🏠 **Relais du Postillon** (14 rooms) 113 rue Principale, L-5480; ✆ 76 84 85; 📧 relais@pt.lu; www.relaisdupostillon.lu; closed 2 weeks around Christmas/New Year. In an old building in the heart of Wormeldange, the very pleasant Postillon's basic but clean rooms have a decidedly pink theme running throughout (walls, bedding, carpet, bathroom) – someone here clearly likes the colour. No lift, but there's a fitness room instead to get you in shape for the stairs, & bikes can also be rented here (€7.50/12.50 for a half/full day). If you arrive mid afternoon the front door may be locked. If it is, ask next door in the Patisserie Schumacher & someone there will check you in. €€

✗ **Carrozza Pizzeria** Around the back of the Relais de Postillon; ⊕ 12.00–14.00 & 18.00–23.00 daily. Bright & breezy, this pizzeria is in a conservatory comprising perspex pyramidal roofs, which maximise the daylight & bring summer inside even when it's cold & wet outside. A terrace at the back sits beneath the vine-covered slopes. The interior vines draped over the beams are 100% plastic, but help to heighten the sense of place. Take your time over your meal as there's not much else to do of an evening. For something apart from pizza & pasta, try the excellent *flames* (called *tartes flambées* elsewhere). An Alsace speciality, these are pizza bases with cream & egg on top in place of tomato & cheese. They're delicious, but incredibly rich – don't have a starter unless you're enormously hungry &/or greedy. They come in 4 different varieties, but if your arteries are up to the task, the *Flames du Vigneron* is the house special: topped with bacon, onions, grapes, tomato, mangetout & parsley, it comes with a free glass of wine. €€

ENTERTAINMENT AND NIGHTLIFE There's no nightlife as such in Wormeldange. Community life in the evening revolves around the **Wormer Stuff** (*156 rue Principale;* ✆ *76 00 35*), an old wooden-panelled pub with brown everywhere, and a row of locals ensconced at the bar at all times.

On the third weekend of September, Wormeldange hosts the annual **Riesling Open** wine festival (see box opposite).

OTHER PRACTICALITIES

➕ **Pharmacie de Wormeldange** 35 route du Vin; ✆ 76 00 20; ⊕ 08.30–12.15 & 13.30–18.15 Mon–Fri; 09.00–12.00 Sat

$ **Caisse Raiffeisen Bank** 123 rue Principale; ✆ 76 03 37; ⊕ 08.30–11.45 & 13.30–16.45 Mon–Fri

$ **Spuerkeess ('S-Bank')** 67 rue Principale; ✆ 76 00 84; ⊕ 08.15–11.45 & 13.30–17.00 Mon–Fri

✉ **Post office** 86 rue Principale; ✆ 76 01 20; ⊕ 14.00–17.00 Mon–Fri

WHAT TO SEE AND DO

Crémants Poll-Fabaire (*115 route du Vin;* ✆ *76 82 11; www.vinsmoselle.lu, www. pollfabaire.lu; shop* ⊕ *07.00–17.00 Mon–Fri, 10.30–20.00 Sat, 10.30–12.30 & 15.00–20.00 Sun, tours May–Aug 09.00–17.00 or by appointment; cellar tour adult/child €3.50/3*) The Wormeldange outlet for the Domaines de Vinsmoselle co-operative is located in a grand mansion on the north edge of town. Step in to taste, buy, or tour the cellars.

Domaine Mathes (*73 rue Principale;* ✆ *76 93 93;* 📧 *mathes@pt.lu; www.mathes.lu; shop* ⊕ *09.00–12.00 & 14.00–17.00 Mon–Fri*) J P Mathes were founded in 1907, and have won numerous awards. You can drop by the shop any time to taste and buy. To arrange a guided visit of the *domaine*, call ahead or email.

GREVENMACHER

Back in the 13th century Grevenmacher was surrounded by high walls with four gates and 28 towers – indeed, the town name itself means 'the count's walls'.

Although they were pulled down in 1688 on the orders of Louis XIV, the Moselle region's official capital has retained some Old-World charm in its twisting streets and houses adorned with flowery window boxes. Even without the lure of wine, it has another star attraction in the form of the lovely Butterfly Garden. It's also the home port of the MS *Princesse Marie-Astrid*. On the Friday after Easter a wine market takes place, featuring 40 local winemakers, and the mid-September wine festival is the region's largest (see box, page 134).

Despite this, Grevenmacher seems less geared up to deal with the demands of the tourist industry than elsewhere. It's a bustling town, but if you don't want to camp there's nowhere to stay in the centre – the nearest hotel is on the outskirts beside the motorway.

GETTING THERE AND AROUND Buses 130 and 135 link Grevenmacher directly with Luxembourg City, several times each hour. In the city they leave from the 'Royal' stop just north of the Centre Hamilius bus station, and take around 45 minutes. Buses 475 and 485 connect Grevenmacher to Echternach on a regular basis, while bus 450 plies the route south to Remich, hourly in each direction. **Driving** from Luxembourg City takes little more than half an hour. Although Grevenmacher is the largest town in the Luxembourg Moselle, it is still compact and getting around on foot is easy.

TOURIST INFORMATION
Tourist office 10 route du Vin; 75 82 75; ⏱ 08.00–12.00 & 13.00–17.00 Mon–Fri, 10.00–15.00 Sat

WHERE TO STAY
Hotel Simon's Plaza (36 rooms) 7 Potaschberg, L-6776; 26 74 44; e info@ simons-plaza.com; www.simons-plaza.com. This large, new hotel is just outside town by the motorway. Fortunately it's a bit flashier than your standard motel. Rooms are bright & stylish with laminate floors. Internet access & a fitness room are provided. There's also a restaurant (French–Luxembourgish) if you can't face the trek back into town. €€–€€€

Camping Route du Vin (135 pitches) route du Vin, L-6794; 75 82 75; e sitg@pt.lu; www. grevenmacher.lu; ⏱ Apr–Sep. A popular & clean campsite by the river, right in the heart of town, although space is limited as many pitches are permanently occupied. Has everything for holidaymakers, from an open-air swimming pool to tennis courts & a kids' playground – or at least that's what they tell you: the pool & tennis courts are next door & run by the municipality. €4.20pp, plus €4.50 per pitch.

WHERE TO EAT
Les Bateliers 10 route du Vin; 26 74 58 80; ⏱ 11.30–14.00 & 18.00–22.00 Wed–Sun, 11.30–14.00 Tue. On the ground floor of an apartment building by the tourist office, this doesn't inspire from the outside, but things improve as you walk through the door & find the interior tastefully decked out in pastel shades. The service is friendly, & the French–Luxembourgish menu both tasty & excellent value. Needless to say there's a terrace out front with a river view. The menu also includes Luxembourg classics such as *judd mat gaardebounen*, *bouchée à la reine*, & *jambon frites*. Vegetarians, however, should seek out the pizzerias around the corner. €€–€€€

Saison Art 15 route de Thionville; 26 72 90 66; www.saisonart.lu; ⏱ 12.00–14.00 & 18.30–22.00 daily; closed 2 weeks in Jul. A few blocks back from the river, this sleek new restaurant has wooden floors & chic décor. French cuisine is the order of the day, from lamb & *poussin* to *escargots*. €€–€€€

ENTERTAINMENT AND NIGHTLIFE Held over the second weekend in September, Grevenmacher's **wine festival** (see box, page 134) is the biggest such event in the Luxembourg Moselle.

OTHER PRACTICALITIES

✚ **Pharmacie de Grevenmacher** 19 route de Trèves; 🕾 75 00 28; ⏱ 08.30–12.00 & 13.30–18.30 Mon–Fri, 08.30–12.00 Sat

$ **Dexia Bank** 2 pl du Marché; 🕾 75 00 261; ⏱ 08.30–12.00 & 13.30–17.00 Mon–Fri. There are also several other banks in the vicinity.

✉ **Post office** 1 Schiltzenplatz; 🕾 75 02 06 31; ⏱ 08.00–12.00 & 13.30–17.15 Mon–Fri

WHAT TO SEE AND DO Pick up a leaflet of the official **Grevenmacher walking tour** from the tourist office. Individually the landmarks it highlights aren't that scintillating, but taken as a whole it's an interesting walk through history that gets you intimate with the town's past, leading you down some quaint little side streets you may not otherwise have found.

Butterfly Garden (*Jardin des Papillons; route de Trèves;* 🕾 *75 85 39; www.butterfly. lu;* ⏱ *Apr to mid-Oct 09.30–17.00 daily; adult/child €6.50/3.50, combi-tickets available inc a visit to Caves Bernard-Massard €10/12/13 for 1, 2 or 3 glasses, child €6*) The wondrous Butterfly Garden is a little treasure owned by the Bernard-Massard winery – this gets 50% more visitors than the main estate, and it's not surprising. Established by an Englishman in 1870, it's been delighting visitors ever since. The 600m² hothouse is kept at 28°C and 95% humidity to keep the resident butterflies happy, so be prepared to sweat and for your camera lens to steam up. Stroll through the enclosure as 500 tropical beauties flutter past your eyes – the front desk has colourful charts to help you identify the key species. Pride of place in this lepidopterous cavalcade is a massive atlas moth from south Asia. With a wingspan of around 20cm it dwarfs even the giant blue morphos from South America. Do keep half an eye on where you put your feet as there's also a colony of ground-dwelling Chinese quails here, which patrol the paths looking for titbits. The garden is about 500m north of the centre – just follow the butterfly pictograms on the signs.

Kulturhuef (*54 rue de Trèves;* 🕾 *26 74 641; www.kulturhuef.lu;* ⏱ *14.00–18.00 Tue–Sun; free*) Near the Butterfly Garden this cultural centre is home to two small museums. The **Printing Museum** (*Musée de l'Imprimerie*) explains the history of printing in Luxembourg, primarily in the years 1850–1950. The ancient printing presses are still used by schools and local artists. Beside it is the **Jean Dieudonné Playing Cards Museum** (*Musée du Jeu de Cartes Jean Dieudonné*) – you can probably guess what you'll find in there. Apparently the Dieudonné family worked in Grevenmacher, and were one of Europe's leading playing cards manufacturers from 1754 to 1880. The displays show you how the cards were made.

Caves Bernard-Massard (*22 route du Vin;* 🕾 *75 05 451; www.bernard-massard. lu; cellars* ⏱ *Apr–Oct 09.30–18.00 Tue–Sun, other times by appointment; adult €4.50/6.50/7.50 for 1, 2 or 3 glasses, child €2.50*) Here is where the wine industry and mass tourism meet head-on. Established in 1921, it's the largest independent winery in Luxembourg, and set up to cater for both coach parties and individuals. Most of their output is *crémant* or sparkling wine (the flagship *brut* and *demi sec* can't be called *crémant* because they contain Chardonnay grapes imported from France). The cellars here contain six million bottles of fizz, and four million are sold per year – half of those to Belgium. A tour of the facilities shows how the big boys do it. Tours can be done in English, and include a tasting of one, two or three glasses (choose when you buy the ticket). If you're in a small group (space restrictions prevent it being included on larger visits), ask to see the final plant, where – if the automated production line is operating – you can follow the labelling and corking process from the freezing of the bottle's neck and removal of the frozen yeast plug, to corking, labelling and boxing. It's a remarkable gizmo that resembles something off the set of *Edward Scissorhands*. Up to 3,500 bottles per hour can roll into the shops this way – older hand-bottling production lines once restricted output to 1,000 bottles per day.

Caves des Vignerons (*12 rue des Caves;* ✆ *75 01 75; www.vinsmoselle.com;* ◷ *07.00–12.00 & 13.00–18.00 Mon–Fri, 10.00–12.00 & 13.00–18.00 Sat; tours adult/ child €3.50/3*) This is the northernmost estate of the Domaines de Vinsmoselle co-operative. As elsewhere, you can taste, buy, or tour the cellars. Or do all three.

WASSERBILLIG

At the north end of the route du Vin, Wasserbillig sits at the confluence of the Moselle and Sûre rivers. The border here heads northwest with the former, while the latter bids the country farewell and veers east into Germany. If you're passing it's worth stopping off to look at the small aquarium. Beyond that, however, most visitors to this frontier town are German drivers looking to tank up cheaply, and the southern approaches are an ugly string of petrol stations with a queue of BMWs and Audis outside each.

GETTING THERE AND AROUND Wasserbillig is the only town in the region connected to the outside world by **rail**, and is on the main line between Luxembourg City (two per hour) and Trier in Germany. **Bus** 485 also passes through once an hour on its way between Grevenmacher and Echternach.

The aquarium is five minutes' **walk** northwest of the bus and train station (if heading in the direction of Echternach by bus, continue one stop past the station).

 WHERE TO STAY AND EAT There is nowhere to stay in Wasserbillig. For eating, besides the café above the aquarium, there is a cheap-and-cheerful Chinese, an Italian, and even (if you must) a Burger King, but none of these offer much to write home about. There are far better dining options in Echternach to the west, and along the Moselle to the south.

WHAT TO SEE AND DO
Aquarium (*Rue des Pépinières/Promenade de la Sûre;* \ *26 74 02 37; www. wasserbillig.lu;* ☉ *Easter–Sep 10.00–18.00 Tue–Sun, Oct–Easter 10.00–18.00 Fri–Sun; adult/child €3/1.50*) Anyone spoiled by the scale of the London Aquarium and similar giants may find this little collection slightly old-fashioned, but it has a quaint charm and is a good way to check out some local aquatic fauna. Larger tanks are home to Moselle species including barbel and carp, and also sturgeon, while smaller ones have the usual motley crew of tropical guppies and angelfish. One South American tank is stocked with piranha, and three seawater tanks have surgeonfish, angelfish, a moray eel and corals. The two largest tanks (40,000 and 30,000 litres) are open to the elements, allowing sunlight to stream in. Above the aquarium is a small café (€–€€) with a terrace overlooking the gently flowing river Sûre.

TRIER

Trier is in the German state of Rhineland-Palatinate, not in Luxembourg at all, but its historical connections – the Bishops of Trier ruled much of Luxembourg for many years – make it an interesting side trip. It also has some of the most important Roman remains outside Italy. With regular train connections to Luxembourg City, it can easily be visited on a day trip from the capital, or tagged onto the end of a tour of the Moselle: it is just 12km from Wasserbillig and also sits on the river (called the Mosel here), which is why we include it in this chapter.

HISTORY Trier's roots go back some way. It was a Celtic settlement occupied by the Treveri tribe, until falling under Roman rule around 50BC when Julius Caesar occupied and annexed Gaul (to which Trier belonged at the time, as did Luxembourg). It became a city (Augusta Terverorum) in 16BC, making it one of the oldest in Germany. This was pillaged and destroyed by rampaging Germanic tribes in the late 3rd century AD, but was rebuilt from the rubble, renamed Treveris, and became a thriving centre of commerce and culture. In the 4th century it was the most important Roman city north of the Alps and at its peak may have had as many as 70,000 inhabitants.

When the Roman administration moved out in the early 5th century, Trier fell into decline. Many grand buildings crumbled and streets reverted to fields as farmers moved in to graze their herds. In 870 the Franks made the city part of Eastern Francia, which later became the Holy Roman Empire. When a relic of St Matthias was brought here its religious significance soared. The Bishops of Trier suddenly had power, and the region became an important Germanic state.

Nearby France also had designs on the city, and it made several attempts to gain control, beginning with the Thirty Years War (1618–48), before Napoleon finally succeeded in 1794, around the same time Luxembourg also fell under French influence. After the fall of Napoleon in 1815 it was handed to Prussia. Trier was heavily bombed during World War II, but like many German cities it was rebuilt in a style sympathetic with how it looked beforehand. The six existing Roman sites, plus the two main churches and the out-of-town Igel Column, are inscribed on the UNESCO World Heritage List.

GETTING THERE AND AROUND Trains from Luxembourg City (45 minutes) run to Trier via Wasserbillig (14 minutes) every hour throughout the day. Trains every second hour also stop at Igel (see page 140). If you're **driving**, it's 12km from the Wasserbillig border.

With a population around 105,000 Trier is larger than Luxembourg City, and yet like the latter, most sites are in a relatively compact old town and can be visited **on foot**.

If you plan to move around a lot, the **Trier Card** (€9 per person or €19 for two adults and three children) can save you a great deal. It gives you access to free public transport in the city, 25% off at most sights and museums, and other freebies and discounts. Alternatively, if you plan to delve deep into Trier's Roman past, purchase an **AntikenCard**, covering the museums and the four main Roman sites (two baths, the amphitheatre and the Porta Nigra). Tickets can be bought at participating sites and the tourist office. The Basic card (€9) gets you into the Landesmuseum and two Roman sites free; the Premium card (€14) gets you into all four Roman sites, the Landesmuseum and secures discounted entry at other museums and attractions.

Like everywhere it seems these days, you can tour the city by **miniature train**. The **Römer Express** (☏ *+49 651 99 35 95 25; www.roemer-express.de; May–Oct every 25mins daily 10.00–18.00, Nov–Dec & Mar hourly Mon–Fri, 10.00–17.00 every 30mins Sat–Sun; adult/child €7/4*) leaves from the Porta Nigra, and trips last 35 minutes.

TOURIST INFORMATION

ⓘ Tourist office An der Porta Nigra; ☏+49 651 978 080; www.trier-info.de ⊕ Jan–Feb 10.00–17.00 Mon–Sat, 10.00–13.00 Sun, Mar–Apr & Nov–Dec 09.00–18.00 Mon–Sat, 10.00–15.00 Sun, May–Oct 09.00–18.00 Mon–Sat, 10.00–17.00 Sun & public holidays, 24 & 31 Dec 10.00–13.00, closed 25 & 26 Dec & 1 Jan. Sells brochures (few are free) & souvenirs, dispenses information & can help with reservations. You can book various city tours in the company of Roman noblemen in togas or gladiators, but only the standard walking tour & coach tour are available in English. See the website for more information.

 WHERE TO STAY Of course there are hotels in Trier, but this guide is about Luxembourg. Thus we recommend you stay there and make this a day trip!

✖ WHERE TO EAT

✖ Blesius Garten Olewiger Strasse 135; ☏+49 651 36060; www.blesius-garten.de; ⊕ restaurant 12.00–14.15 & 18.00–22.15 daily, bar 11.30–01.00 Sun–Thu, 11.30–02.00 Fri–Sat. A little out of town in the eastern suburb of Olewig (1km past the amphitheatre), this craft brewery – literally so, because their beers are called 'Kraft' – has a winter garden, a beer garden, & good German food, including meats cooked on a charcoal grill (the latter available evenings only). €€

✖ Zum Domstein Hauptmarkt 5; ☏+49 651 74490; www.domstein.de; ⊕ 08.30–midnight, kitchen 11.30–22.00. A sprawling pub-restaurant with tiled floors & wood panelling. It has 1 terrace on Trier's main square, a courtyard in the middle, & yet another terrace at the back by the cathedral. It serves classic German food, plus 'Roman' dishes. To sample the German version of Mosel(le) wines, ask for the *Weinproben* (wine tasting), where you'll be served 3 100ml or 6 50ml tasting glasses. B/fasts are served 08.30–11.00. €€

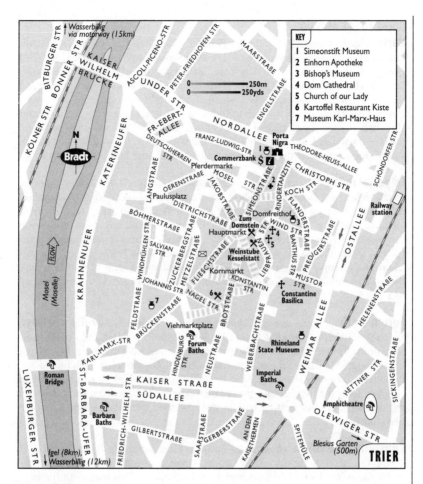

✕ Kartoffel Restaurant Kiste Fahrstrasse
13–14; +49 651 979 0066; www.kiste-trier.
de; ⏲ 11.00–midnight, kitchen 11.30–22.00. As
the name hints (*Kartoffel* is potato), carbohydrates
& starch are high on the agenda: baked, fried, as
potato salad with sausage, with a Schnitzel …
You name it, you can get it with spuds here, either
in the large dining room or on the expansive terrace
beside an unusual fountain sculpture. €–€€

✕ Weinstube Kesselstatt Liebfrauenstrasse
10; +49 651 41178; www.weinstube-

kesselstatt.de; ⏲ 10.00–midnight daily, hot food
11.30–14.30 & 18.00–22.00. The interior of this
bar/café is dominated by a large wine press, &
the terrace out front is a secluded spot for a glass
& a snack in the shadow of the Liebfrauenkirche.
Reasonably priced food features cheeses,
baguettes, salads, & daily specials. Cold dishes
are available all day. The wine list is from the
Weinstube's own winery. There's no table service
(except for bringing food), so order at the bar
'pub-style'. €–€€

OTHER PRACTICALITIES
✚ Einhorn Apotheke Simeonstrasse 9; +49
651 97563, ext 0; www.einhorn-apotheke-trier.
de; ⏲ 08.30–18.30 Mon–Fri, 09.00–16.00 Sat
$ Commerzbank Simeonstrasse 58; +49 651
71690; www.commerzbank.de; ⏲ 09.00–13.00

& 14.00–16.00 Mon & Wed, 09.00–13.00 &
14.00–18.00 Tue & Thu, 09.00–14.00 Fri
✉ Post office (counter in McPaper
newsagent) Fleischstrasse 62, Schiltzenplatz;
+49 1802 3333; ⏲ 09.30–20.00 Mon–Sat

WHAT TO SEE AND DO

Porta Nigra (*Porta Nigra Platz;* ☎ *+49 651 75424;* ⊕ *Apr–Sep 09.00–18.00 daily, Oct & Mar 09.00–17.00 daily, Nov–Feb 09.00–16.00 daily; adult/child €3/1.50*) Everyone's first port(a) of call, the huge 'Black Gate' is, well, a black gate – with stone blackened by time, not because it was designed that way. It's one of the largest surviving Roman monuments, yes, 'north of the Alps'. Climb to the top for a view across the old town. From the 11th to 18th centuries it was part of the St Simeonstift church, hence the appearance of a few Catholic saints and bishops as bas reliefs on the interior walls of an ostensibly Roman monument. On the west façade you can still see the scars where the church tower (long gone) once butted up against it.

Imperial Baths (*Kaiserthermen; Im Palastgarten;* ☎ *+49 651 436 2550;* ⊕ *Apr–Sep 09.00–18.00 daily, Oct & Mar 09.00–17.00 daily, Nov–Feb 09.00–16.00 daily; adult/child €3/1.50*) Going to the baths was central to Roman life in Trier, and these, built in the 4th century AD, were some of the largest ever built anywhere. Today you can wander over and under the site. Only a few walls remain above ground – signs tell you where the *caldarium, tepidarium* et al once were. Below ground is a vast labyrinth of (dank) passages and rooms, once used by the army of staff to service the bathers without getting in their way, and also as boiler rooms to heat water up to a 'just right' 40°C.

Forum Baths (*Thermen am Viehmarkt; Viehmarktplatz;* ☎ *+49 651 994 1057;* ⊕ *09.00–17.00 Tue–Sun; adult/child €3/1.50*) Originally built around AD100, these were probably Trier's earliest baths. They once covered 8,000m². After the collapse of the empire the baths fell into ruin, and later building work left them buried and forgotten – they were rediscovered in 1987 during excavations for an underground car park. Only the part beneath the square has been unearthed, but two *caldaria*, a *frigidarium*, and some heating systems can be viewed, preserved within a modern glass museum.

Constantine Basilica (*Konstantin Basilika; Konstantinplatz;* ☎ *+49 651 42570;* ⊕ *Apr–Oct 10.00–18.00 Mon–Sat, 12.00–18.00 Sun, Nov–Mar 11.00–12.00 & 15.00–16.00 Tue–Sat, 12.00–13.00 Sun; free*) Built by Emperor Constantine in the early 4th century as part of a palace complex, this is either the largest or second-largest single room building surviving from Roman times, depending on which source you believe. Either way, its only rival is the Pantheon in Rome. At 67m long, 27m wide and 33m high it really is impressive. The upper walls have been embellished and added to over the centuries, but the lower walls are incredibly thick and have stood the test of time, including during intense Allied bombing in 1944 (photos on the walls show how it looked before and after the raid). Originally the imperial throne room, in the Middle Ages it was the residence of the Bishops of Trier. Then in 1856 it became (and still is) a Protestant church, the first in otherwise Catholic Trier.

Barbara Baths (*Barbarathermen; Südallee; not open to the public*) The city's third baths were built in the 2nd century AD. Because of ongoing building work they are closed indefinitely, but you can peer over the low wall for free: there's a viewing platform to give you a general impression.

Amphitheatre (*Olewigerstrasse 25;* ☎ *+49 651 73010;* ⊕ *Apr–Sep 09.00–18.00 daily, Oct & Mar 09.00–17.00 daily, Nov–Feb 09.00–16.00 daily; adult/child €3/1.50*) Nestled in a grassy bowl, this arena, built in the 2nd century AD for bloodthirsty spectacles featuring gladiators and wild beasts, once accommodated crowds of 20,000. It sits on the edge of Trier, overlooking the city and overlooked by vineyards. It formed part of the city walls, although little remains of those. In the Middle Ages it was used as a quarry, but fortunately not all the stones were carted away and there's plenty left. The central 'stage' looks solid, until you walk down the steps and realise the dirt and gravel conceal a wooden floor. The cellar below sits on bedrock, and the water down here is the water table. In Roman times, condemned prisoners were kept here alongside the lions, tigers and other exotic fauna destined to carry out the sentence.

Rhineland State Museum (*Rheinische Landesmuseum; Weimarer Allee 1;* ✆ *+49 651 97740; www.landesmuseum-trier.de;* ⏰ *10.00–17.00 Tue–Sun; adult/child €6/3*) Trier's history from the last Ice Age to the Romans via the Celts is told here. A bronze headdress that was once the decoration for a Celtic horse is particularly noteworthy, as is a Roman sandstone sculpture of a bear subduing a wild boar, dating from AD200, symbolising the struggle between life and death. There's also a 'wine ship' burial monument, and a large collection of mosaics. A model of the city shows how it looked in Roman days, while a replica of Igel Column (see page 140) is in the central courtyard.

Simeonstift Museum (*Stadtmuseum Simeonstift Trier; Simeonstrasse 60;* ✆ *+49 651 718 1459; www.museum-trier.de;* ⏰ *10.00–18.00 Tue–Sun; adult/child under 10 €5/free*) The 11th-century Simeonstift (Simeon's College) is beside the Porta Nigra. It was once home to the priests who held services in the two St Simeon churches. It now houses a collection of (mainly local) art from medieval to late 19th century. The oak floor of the upper level of the cloister is original, dating from 1060. There are also pieces from further afield, including Coptic textiles from Egypt and east Asian statues.

Cathedral (*Dom; Domfreihof 6;* ✆ *+49 651 979 0790; www.dominformation.de;* ⏰ *Apr–Oct 06.30–18.00 daily, Nov–Mar 06.30–17.30 daily; free*) Formerly the site of a Roman temple dedicated to Helen, the newly converted Emperor Constantine tore that down and replaced it with a Christian church in the 4th century, one of the earliest in northern Europe. The current Gothic building dates from the 11th century. Up the steps on the right at the far end is the cathedral's prized possession: the **Holy Robe** (*Heilig Rock*), allegedly a tunic worn by Christ, and brought to Trier by the Empress Dowager Helena. The earliest mention of it only dates from the 11th century however, so it depends on your level of belief as to whether you accept its authenticity. In contrast to the crowds of eager pilgrims queuing to shuffle past this, the cloister, shared with the adjacent Liebfrauenkirche, is a haven of calm. Also inside the church is a **Treasury** (*Domschatzkamer; €1.50*), containing the usual array of shiny religious treasures.

Church of our Lady (*Liebfrauenkirche; Liebfrauenstrasse 2;* ✆ *+49 651 978 080;* ⏰ *Apr–Oct 06.30–18.00 daily, Nov–Mar 06.30–17.30 daily; free*) With only a cloister separating it from the Dom, this is almost two churches in one. Although it too stands on Roman foundations, the bulk of this Gothic building dates from the 13th century. It is mainly notable for its unusual cruciform shape with a central tower.

Bishop's Museum (*Bischoeflisches Museum; Windstrasse 6;* ✆ *+49 651 710 5255; www.bistum-trier.de;* ⏰ *09.00–17.00 Tue–Sat, 13.00–17.00 Sun; adult/child €3.50/2*)

Behind the cathedral, this has a collection of Roman artefacts, plus early examples of Christian art, including some well-preserved 9th-century frescoes depicting the crucifixion.

Museum Karl-Marx-Haus (*Brückenstrasse 10;* \ *+49 651 970 680;* ⊕ *Apr–Oct 10.00–18.00 daily, until 20.00 on 1st and 3rd Fri of month, Nov–Mar 14.00–17.00 Mon, 11.00–17.00 Tue–Sun; adult/child €3/2*) Contrary to his image, Karl Marx (1818–83) wasn't born in some urban dystopia populated by a downtrodden proletariat, but in this well-appointed Baroque townhouse in genteel Trier. The house, built in 1727, contains displays on the history of communism and socialism, and early copies of Marx's writings, including first editions of the *Communist Manifesto* (1848) and *Das Kapital* (1867). Other photos and manuscripts cover Marx's life and work, from birth to his eventual exile and death in London.

Roman Bridge (*always open; free*) With foundations dug in 16BC, this bridge spanning the Mosel was the largest in the northern empire. It is included on the UNESCO list for that reason, but the Roman deck has long gone, replaced by a modern roadway. Only parts of columns are original, so there isn't a lot to see.

Igel Column (*always open; free*) If driving from Trier to Luxembourg, take the N49 rather than the motorway, as this passes through the village of Igel (8km from Trier and 4km from Wasserbillig). In the centre is a 23m stone column, a decorated tomb, erected in the 3rd century AD as one of the largest Roman funerary monuments in Europe. It's on the main road (on the right coming from Trier), but you'll need to keep your eyes peeled as it sits in a narrow gap between two buildings.

7

The Müllerthal

One of the smallest and certainly the most dramatic of Luxembourg's regions, the Müllerthal is a must-see on any tour. Thanks to the early Dutch tourists' tendency to over-exaggerate, it's also known as Little Switzerland, and people have long been drawn to its pretty towns and unusual topography.

To add confusion to the mix, not only is the whole region technically known as the Müllerthal ('Valley of the Mills'), there's also a valley at its heart sharing the same title, and an eponymous village at one end, the address of which could feasibly be written: 'Müllerthal, Müllerthal, Müllerthal'. It'll keep you on your toes if anyone asks you for directions.

Whatever you call it, it packs a lot into a small space. First there's Echternach, the regional capital and the nation's oldest city. A wealth of ancient sights and arguably the prettiest town square in Luxembourg make this a thoroughly agreeable place. Meanwhile, the castles of Larochette and Beaufort both rate highly on the European scale of grand old ruins, and have been partially restored to hint at the power they once wielded.

From manmade piles of stones to those created by nature, the countryside between the castles and towns is a veritable wonderland of ravines, dense forest and cliffs. Crossed by an extensive network of hiking trails, it's paradise for walkers and guaranteed to entertain everyone, whether you're looking for a testing cross-country yomp or a casual Sunday afternoon stroll.

Pinning the tail on the regional donkey is one of Luxembourg's quirkiest events, which takes place each year on Whit Tuesday. If you always believed that grown-ups prancing around waving handkerchiefs was the exclusive preserve of English morris men, the world's only 'Dancing Procession' will make you think again.

LITTLE SWITZERLAND

When Dutch tourists first arrived in this area a century ago, they took one look at the rugged rocky landscape and immediately dubbed it '*Klein Zwitserland*' ('Little Switzerland'). Compared with the flat farmlands of the Netherlands it may indeed seem like the Alps, but we should put things in a little perspective. Don't be fooled into expecting extensive snow-capped vistas because you'll leave disappointed – the highest point is, after all, only 414m above sea level.

What you will find is a maze of spectacular craggy outcrops, pathways, gorges and valleys. Situated between Beaufort and Echternach, and completely encompassing Berdorf, it has some of the best walking routes and the most sublimely beautiful scenery in the country.

Like many of nature's greatest creations, Little Switzerland owes its existence to water. It formed over a million-year period as the Ernz Noire and Hallerbach rivers

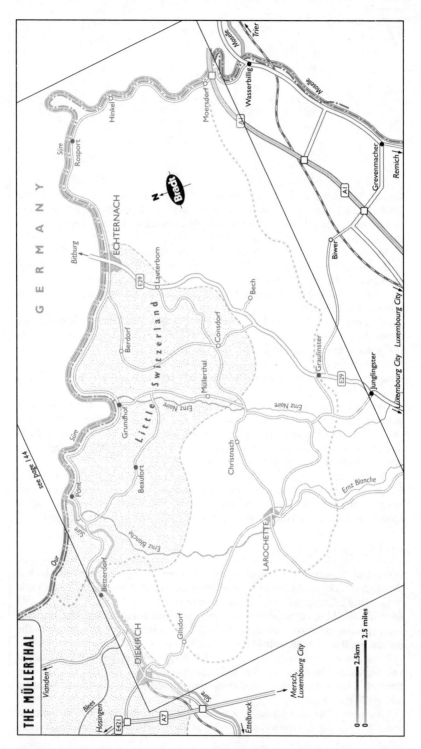

THE MÜLLERTHAL

GERMANY

Moselle
Trier
Moselle
Wasserbillig
Grevenmacher
Remich
A1
Biwer
A1
Luxembourg City
Luxembourg City
Junglinster
Graulinster
E29
Hinkel
Moersdorf
Süre
Rosport
Bitburg
ECHTERNACH
E29
Lauterborn
Bech
Consdorf
Berdorf
Müllerthal
little Switzerland
Ernz Noire
Ernz Noire
Grundhof
Pont
Süre
Beaufort
Christnach
Ernz Blanche
LAROCHETTE
Ernz Blanche
Betterdorf
Gilsdorf
DIEKIRCH
Vianden
Blees
Hosingen
E421
A7
Süre
Mersch,
Luxembourg City
Ettelbruck

see page 144

N
Bradt

0 ___ 2.5km
0 ___ 2.5 miles

gouged away at the sandstone plateau, a former seabed that had covered the area for 20 million years. When the sea receded, time and weathering, particularly of limestone deposits accumulated in cracks in the sandstone, eventually carved the exposed rock into gnarled and twisted formations.

This isn't just a land of breathtaking beauty; it's also tranquil and very peaceful. Beyond the clomping footsteps of fellow hikers the air is filled with birdsong and gently trickling water. Best of all, it's easily accessible for hikes of almost any length, with well-maintained trails and clear signposting. Many of the best start and finish right by the bus station in Echternach. Visit the information offices in Echternach, Beaufort or Berdorf to pick up maps.

GETTING THERE AND AROUND For getting to and between the main towns in the region see the relevant sections. **Bus** 108 makes occasional forays between the villages of Little Switzerland, and number 416 passes through on its way between Larochette and Echternach, but between them they run no more than ten services at irregular times through the day. Realistically if you want to see a lot of the countryside you'll need your **own transport**, or good **hiking** legs.

WHERE TO STAY AND EAT To explore the region you could base yourself in one of the main tourist centres such as Echternach, Beaufort, Berdorf or Larochette. For an even quieter stay (if such a thing were possible), there are also hotel options in several smaller villages.

Hotel Brimer (25 rooms) 1 route de Beaufort, L-6360 Grundhof; `26 87 871; e info@ hotel-brimer.lu; www.hotel-brimer.lu; ⏰ Feb to mid-Nov. Family run for 4 generations, the rooms here are large, comfortable & pleasantly decorated. Balconies have woodland views. When you're tired of walking, the hotel has a newer wing with a swimming pool, sauna, solarium & steam room. The restaurant (⏰ 12.00–13.45 & 18.30–20.30 daily; €€€€) is known for its gastronomic excellence – the food has French influences. A lighter menu is served all day. €€€

Hotel Restaurant Le Cigalon (13 rooms) 1 rue de l'Ernz Noir, L-6245 Müllerthal; `74 94 95; e lecigalon@internet.lu; www.lecigalon. lu; ⏰ mid-Feb to Dec. Exuding elegance & charm, this small hotel in the heart of Little Switzerland is surrounded by forest. Some rooms have balconies. The restaurant (⏰ 12.00–13.45 & 19.00–20.30 Wed–Mon; €€–€€€), which serves French *haute cuisine* in a refined atmosphere, enjoys a good reputation & is very popular (reservations recommended at w/ends). Seasonal ingredients are used wherever possible. The cheaper Taverne (⏰ same hours as restaurant; daily; €€–€€€) is more laid-back with wicker & bamboo décor, & serves excellent salads, *tartes flambées* and heartier fare. Large

windows make this more of a conservatory, looking out onto the summer terrace, but there's a fire for chilly evenings. €€–€€€

Hotel Au Vieux Moulin (13 rooms) Maison 6, L-6562 Lauterborn; `72 00 681; e info@hotel-au-vieux-moulin.lu; www.hotel-au-vieux-moulin.lu; ⏰ Feb–Dec. As the name implies, this is a former mill, which enjoys a beautiful secluded location in the hamlet of Lauterborn, near Echternach. It's close to the main road, but a gushing stream & birdsong do their best to mask traffic noise. There's no lift. The large rooms have Wi-Fi & offer 4-star comforts, but represent excellent value. 6 newer rooms have balconies, & you can dangle your feet in the stream running alongside, a couple of steps away down a grassy bank. The restaurant (⏰ Tue–Sun; closed Tue lunch; €€€–€€€€) serves French–Luxembourgish cuisine – gastronomic arrangements are available. €€

Hotel Restaurant Dimmer (29 rooms) 4 Grenzwee, L-9392 Wallendorf-Pont; `83 62 20; e hdimmer@pt.lu; www.hoteldimmer.lu; ⏰ mid-Feb to Nov. As the clue in the hamlet's name suggests, this is by a bridge opposite the German village of Wallendorf (once part of Luxembourg until the river was made the border). The 1871 building was the railway

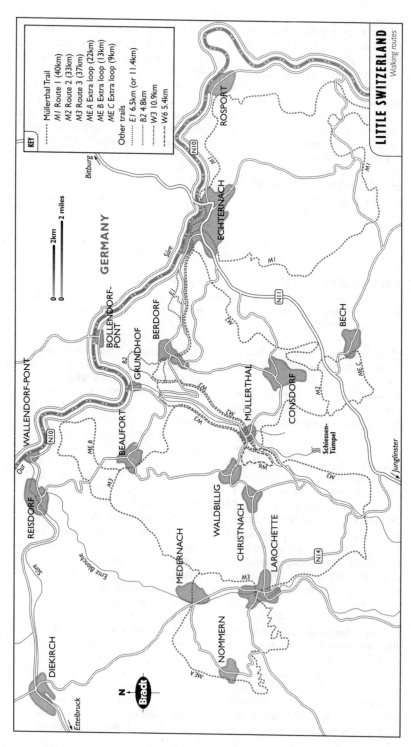

LITTLE SWITZERLAND
Walking routes

KEY

Müllerthal Trail
M1 Route 1 (40km)
M2 Route 2 (33km)
M3 Route 3 (37km)
ME A Extra loop (22km)
ME B Extra loop (13km)
ME C Extra loop (9km)

Other trails
E1 6.5km (or 11.4km)
B2 4.8km
W3 10.9km
W6 5.4km

GERMANY

0   2km
0   2 miles

N

Bradt

ROSPORT

ECHTERNACH

Bitburg

Süre

BOLLENDORF-
PONT

WALLENDORF-PONT

Our

Süre

BERDORF

GRUNDHOF

BEAUFORT

REISDORF

DIEKIRCH

Ettelbruck

Ernz Blanche

MEDERNACH

NOMMERN

WALDBILLIG

CHRISTNACH

LAROCHETTE

MÜLLERTHAL

CONSDORF

Schiessen-
Tümpel

BECH

Junglinster

N10

N11

N14

144

hotel (the tracks are long gone), & has been in the Dimmer family ever since. Clean rooms (some with balconies) have linoleum floors, wood furnishings, & safes. Some bathrooms have bathtubs; others showers. The lobby's free Wi-Fi signal just about reaches the rooms. A wellness centre on the 2nd floor has a Turkish bath, 'rain showers', & a *caldarium*. The basement has a place for hikers to clean muddy boots, & a fitness room. There's a lively bar, & a French–Luxembourgish restaurant (⊕ 12.00–14.00 & 18.00–21.00; €€–€€€) with 2 sections. The old part with tiled floors, wooden furnishings & an open hearth is 'Weinstube chic'; the newer extension has laminate floors & a lighter décor. **€€**

🏠 **Hotel Restaurant L'Ernz Noire** (11 rooms) 2 route de Beaufort, L-6360 Grundhof; 📞 83 60 40; e lernznoire@pt.lu; www.lernznoire. lu; ⊕ mid-Feb to Dec. Opposite the Brimer, past the rather incongruous wooden crocodile – no, I don't know either – the Ernz Noire offers similar standards & services. The restaurant's head chef, David Albert, has a growing international reputation, uses regional organic products, & tries to stay seasonal when he can. A wild mushroom menu is offered in autumn, & there are other good vegetarian choices (⊕ 12.00–14.00 & 19.00–21.00 Wed–Mon; closed Tue, & Wed lunch except in peak season; €€€–€€€€). Part of the restaurant is a conservatory. A lighter menu with salads is available exclusively on the terrace. **€€**

⚊ **Camping du Rivage** (50 pitches) 7 route de Echternach, L-9392 Wallendorf-Pont; 📞 83 65 16; e voogt@pt.lu; www.wallendorf-kajaks.de;

⊕ mid-Apr to Sep. Owned by the neighbouring Hotel Dimmer (you can use its wellness centre), this has good, clean facilities. You can make a campfire by the river here – ask the management where to light up. Ronn's Kajaks is based on site (see page 149) if you want to paddle all the way to Echternach. If you're camping & prefer to potter about, borrowing a kayak is free. €6.25pp, plus €7.80 per pitch; small tents €7.50 pp, no pitch fee.

⚊ **Camping Cascade** (100 pitches) 3a rue des Moulins, L-6245 Müllerthal; m 621 27 30 43; info@campingcascade.com; www. campingcascade.com. 500m below the Schiessentümpel falls, this quiet campsite has basic facilities in a fabulous location beside a gushing stream. €3pp, plus €3.50 per pitch.

⚊ **Camping Buchholz** (40 pitches) Bech Gare, L-6230 Bech; 📞 26 78 48 40; ⊕ Mar–Oct. This small campsite is right on the Echternach–Luxembourg City long-distance cycling route – even if you're not staying here you'll pass through it on your bike. Diminutive former Bech railway station is now the camp office. It's in the middle of nowhere, simple, clean & wonderfully quiet. €2.80pp, plus €3 per pitch.

✗ **Brasserie Heringer Millen** 1 rue des Moulins, Müllerthal; 📞 26 78 47 17; ⊕ 12.00–14.00 & 19.00–21.00 daily. The brasserie in the Heringer Millen information centre is modern, on 2 levels, & surrounded by large windows & a terrace. The stylish décor features red linen on wooden tables. The tasty food is modern Luxembourgish, even if the house speciality is Alsace *tarte flambée*. **€€**

WHAT TO SEE AND DO

Hiking The best way to appreciate the region's grandeur is to take up thy daypack and walk. There's a maze of paths and trails to follow covering hundreds of kilometres. Most routes are over well-drained sandy soil, so even if the weather becomes inclement you're unlikely to get bogged down. Routes vary from an easy couple of clicks, to a 100km slog that takes in pretty much everything. The tourist offices in the region (see pages 149, 150, 153, 164 and 166) are well clued-up and can provide you with maps and advice on the best routes to suit your requirements. Each route is clearly marked, and there are signposts at key intersections to point you in the right direction, leaving little chance of getting lost. This wasn't always the case however: members of the Luxembourg resistance were able to hide out here for much of World War II without being found by the Nazis.

The land on either side of the paths is thickly forested – the natural plant cover on the sandstone is beech, while oaks have colonised the marl and limestone. Any conifers you see (except the pines on the high plateau) were introduced by man. This is a strange lost world: fallen giants are left where they drop, unless they land on one of the trails. The valley floors have their own microclimate as the tall trees and high cliffs trap moisture and allow little sunlight to penetrate. This keeps the daytime temperature in many places at a cool 12°C no matter what's going on in the wider world, and the air is thick with humidity, making it a haven for mosses, plants and mosquitoes. Slugs abound here too, and I can personally vouch for the presence of voracious horseflies – you may want to consider insect repellent. The valleys are also a refuge for birdlife. Don't be surprised to encounter woodpeckers or treecreepers, and there are plentiful chaffinches, wagtails and buzzards. You may even catch sight of a kingfisher. Eagle owls and peregrine falcons also nest on the rock walls, but are somewhat shyer and harder to spot.

Nearly all the region's hotels are used to hikers, and many will make you a packed lunch, possibly provide a shuttle service to/from trailheads, and may even arrange for your bags to be taken to your next destination. See www.trailhotels.lu for information on which hotels participate in the latter scheme. See also www.hiking-in-luxembourg.co.uk for more general information.

The majority of trails are slow going, even if they don't look far on the map. There's usually a lot of up and down involved as you negotiate past giant boulders, meaning averaging 3km/h is good going. Note that our map only shows the selected trails mentioned below. There are dozens of others, far too many to display here – pick up large-scale maps from any local tourist office.

Müllerthal Trail Those looking for a serious workout may want to attempt this trail. It is divided into three separate looping routes, which look on a map as if they are holding hands at the points where they join up. You can tackle them individually, or for a real challenge do all three and the three 'extra' add-on options, a round trip of 150km. That will take you past almost everything there is to see in this region. Without the add-ons, the three main routes still total 110km. **Route 1** (40km) in the east around Echternach, and **Route 3** (37km) in the west around Waldbillig, Beaufort and Larochette, are both through relatively rolling countryside and classified as 'moderate/average'. **Route 2** (33km), around Consdorf and Berdorf, may be shorter, but is over the most challenging terrain and classified as 'difficult'. Either way, only the super-fit and the foolish would consider tackling one of the routes in a single day. Taking two days over each, or a week to do the lot, is a more sensible option. All the trails are marked by prominent wooden signposts. For information, advice and printable pdf trail maps, see www.mullerthal-trail.lu.

B2 Shorter trails all have an alphanumeric designation. B2 (4.8km) is a popular looping route starting in the centre of Berdorf that takes in the best of the rocky outcrops. **Casselt** (also on route B8) is a stunning rocky bluff with a 100m vertical drop and a view extending across the Sûre River to Germany. This point is also on the 2,500km transcontinental GR5 path (*Grande Randonnée 5*), extending from Hook of Holland on the Dutch North Sea coast to Nice on the French Riviera. You may encounter serious long-distance walkers here (it takes three months to cover the lot).

Further along B2 is the **Seven Gorges** (Siewenschlüff). This rocky area contains seven tiny gorges, more like fissures in the rock. They are numbered one to seven, enabling you to walk through them in logical sequence. But beware: some of the gorges really are narrow and it's best to leave large packs at the entrance – walls are barely more than shoulder width apart at best, and anyone of above-average girth may struggle. No 3 is a tight fit and the side walls slope, making it a bit of a scramble. No 6 warns you in advance that it shrinks to just 30cm wide at one point – and they do mean it. I consider myself average build, and I barely squeezed through after some creative jimmying. The final descent back to your starting point via No 7 involves negotiating a short metal ladder. Despite the effort, the area is worth checking out and is a highlight of the region. The Luxembourg fire brigade comes here to practice extracting injured people from tight situations.

W3 Route W3 (10.9km) takes you partly through more pastoral scenery on a loop of the Müllerthal Valley from Grundhof to Müllerthal and back. The west side, heading south from Grundhof, passes along the edge of managed conifer forest, heading gently up the valley floor. The return winds uphill first through old deciduous woodland, which looks like it should be occupied by hobbits, and then you're back on the rocky terrain on the side of the plateau, and can detour into more narrow gorges. Stop at the **Devil's Isle** (Île du Diable), another rocky bluff with great views, or climb the **Pulpit** (Predigtstuhl), a giant rock overhanging the main road where the trail crosses it – steep steps around the back lead to the top.

E1 One of the best paths to follow is **E1**, linking Echternach and Berdorf. It's around 6.5km, so allow at least two hours one-way for time to stop and admire the scenery. If you only plan to follow the route in one direction, consider the easy option by taking bus 111 (hourly) from Echternach to Berdorf and starting from there. That leaves you with a slightly downhill trek – Berdorf is 200m higher than Echternach. The trail passes through every rock feature imaginable as it twists and turns between chimneys, crevices, caves, cliffs and narrow gorges. Many have been named over the years: one extraordinary rock stack is **Malakoff Tower** (Tour Malakoff), while a narrow chasm through which the path squeezes has become the **Labyrinth**. The **Wolf Gorge** (Gorge du Loup) does have a genuine claim to its name, as wolves once sheltered in this tiny canyon. Don't go expecting to spot one, however – none have been seen since 1885. Signs of human intervention are also plainly visible. Look closely at the roofs of the several caves beside the path and you'll see gouge marks left where grindstones were quarried out and removed for use in the many mills that give the region its name. Quite why they took the risk of chipping large rocks off the cave roofs while standing underneath them is beyond me. Perhaps it provided a better-quality stone, or maybe it just made them easier to transport once they were through with cutting.

If you don't want to finish in Echternach, the E1 can be extended on a loop back up to Berdorf, making a total walk of around 11.4km.

WHERE ARE ALL THE CANOES?

Considering how much water there is in Luxembourg, there aren't many places where you can legally get into it and paddle about. The Upper Sûre Lake is one obvious exception (see page 202), as long as you stay upstream from its pontoon bridge. Elsewhere most rivers are either off-limits, or access is restricted throughout much of the year. The problem is that many stretches of water are privately owned, and boats passing through are seen as a threat to the lucrative fishing business. Other oft-used reasons for limiting access are that the water is too shallow, and that the wielding of paddles poses a danger to ducklings along the riverbanks. Happily, one of the few places accessible during the summer months is along the Sûre River in the Müllerthal.

W6 The most photographed and popular location of all is **Schiessentümpel**, a small cascading waterfall by the road just south of Müllerthal village, on the road to Christnach. You'll pass it on the W6 (5.4km) circuit starting in Müllerthal. There are hundreds of similar cascades in the region, and the water doesn't drop more than a metre or two, but what makes this stand out is the attractive stone bridge crossing the stream just above the falls. It turns the scene into an impossibly photogenic spot that teems with visitors on summer weekends, as people paddle, and clamber over the rocks in search of the perfect holiday snap. Although it's right by the road, you can't stop there if driving. Instead, there's a car park 500m further up – when you see the size of it you'll get an idea of just how overrun it can get at peak times. Arrive on a weekday morning to have the place to yourself. To get from the car park to the falls, follow the signs onto a trail above the Ernz Noire River. It takes just ten minutes each way at a gentle pace, but wear sturdy shoes to avoid turning an ankle as the path is rocky and uneven. Don't forget to admire the many other cascades along the way. They may not have bridges framing them, but they're just as appealing as the star attraction. The car park here is also a jumping-off point for more walking trails: the 9km (three hour) route in the direction of Consdorf and beyond is particularly scenic.

Combining walking trails Since the shorter trails cross over one another at regular intersections, you can combine routes to create longer ones. **B2** and **W3** link together well to create a round route of 15km taking in the craggy terrain of the upper Müllerthal and the gentler lower river valley. For a longer day hike start on the B2 from Berdorf, via Casselt and the Seven Gorges, then veer off downhill on the W3 when you cross it, for a loop of the Müllerthal Valley as far as the Predigtstuhl. Then veer off onto the **B13**, which will carry you back to your start point. The whole trip is around 18km and takes between seven and nine hours with stops.

Other short walks There is a 4km trail (allow one to 1½ hours) linking Müllerthal and Consdorf; a 5km (1½ hour) trek down the beautiful Müllerthal Valley itself, starting from the eponymous village and finishing in Berdorf; and a 5km (1½ hour) path between Hallerbach and Beaufort Castle that follows the routes of small rivers most of the way. For a more challenging workout, serious hikers may want to tackle the **Fred Welter Path**. Marked by yellow crosses, it follows a 23km circuit (passing close to Berdorf, Consdorf and Müllerthal, which all provide convenient refreshment opportunities). Allow a full day for this.

Nordic walking For those who prefer to stride along wielding two sticks, three routes have been laid out in the region, with lengths of 6km, 9km and 11km. Two of these start in Consdorf; the other in Müllerthal. For information and route maps visit one of the regional tourist offices.

Mountain biking In addition to the walking trails, Little Switzerland has (at the last count) four cross-country circuits suitable for mountain bikers, ranging in length from 13km to 36km. Pick up leaflets from any tourist office. **Ronn's Bikes and Kajaks** (*7 route de Echternach, Wallendorf-Pont;* \ *83 65 16; www.wallendorf-kajaks.de*) based at the Camping du Rivage in Wallendorf-Pont (see *Where to stay and eat,* page 148), rents mountain bikes for €15 per day.

Canoeing and kayaking The stretch of the Sûre separating Little Switzerland from Germany is open to paddling enthusiasts between April and September.

Rent canoes, kayaks and rafts from **Outdoor Freizeit** (*10 rue de la Sûre, L-6350 Dillingen;* ✆ *86 9139;* ✉ *info@outdoorfreizeit.lu; www.outdoorfreizeit.lu; Apr–Sep, departures 09.00–16.00 daily*) for one-way trips downstream as far as Echternach (18km). **Ronn's Bikes and Kajaks** (*7 route de Echternach, Wallendorf-Pont;* ✆ *83 65 16; www.wallendorf-kajaks.de*) also rents kayaks from April to October. The standard route from April to mid-July (€12.50 per person) is 12km long: allow 2½ hours. A longer 16km route (€17.50 per person; 3½ hours) is also possible. Canadian canoes capable of carrying two adults and one child are available for €30/35 for the short/long route respectively. In peak season (mid-July to September), a 14km route in a kayak costs €15 per person and €40 in a Canadian canoe. High-season rentals are limited to 200 kayaks per day, so advance reservation (only available for pre-noon departures) is highly recommended. Be warned that while you won't have to bring the kayaks back yourself, there's no return transport laid on. You'll have to make your own way back by bus or make other arrangements. Bus 500 leaves Echternach hourly at 46 minutes past each hour (past odd-numbered hours on Sundays) and zips you back to Dillingen in 12 minutes. Alternatively, rent a mountain bike to get you home (€25 per person in combination with kayak rental – road map and helmets provided). Inflatable rafts are also available for €25 per person (minimum six people), but only when water levels are high enough. Cars can be parked on the grounds.

Places of interest Tourist Center Heringer Millen (*1 rue des Moulins, Müllerthal;* ✆ *26 78 47 17;* ⊕ *10.00–17.00 Mon–Sat, 11.00–16.00 Sun; free*) is a renovated water mill, with a shop, an information centre and a brasserie (see page 145). The shop sells local produce such as liqueurs, beeswax candles, honey, goats' cheese, and of course, home-milled flour. There's also an exhibit of milling equipment. The mill workings themselves are visible through a glass panel in the shop floor – head through the door at the back and down the steps, and you'll see them close up. Plastic duck races are occasionally held in the mill race, and if you happen to be there at the right time, you can purchase an entrant in the shop. A short distance away is a large wooden sculpture, the Mikado de crayons de bois, a pile of giant 'pencils' that looks at first glance rather like – would you believe it – a pile of wood. But a board around the back reveals a different story. It's an orientation point, and each pencil is aimed somewhere. So if you needed to know you were 0.6km from Schiessentümpel, this will tell you. It will also tell you that you're 0.1km from the mill – but you could probably work that out for yourself.

Christnach is a picturesque hamlet in the middle of Little Switzerland. The village has protected status, and any new houses must adhere to strict controls and be constructed using traditional methods and materials that blend with the local style.

The tiny village of **Waldbillig** is mainly notable for being the birthplace of Michel Rodange, the Luxembourg literary world's official 'number-one son'. His house is a white building near the centre, marked with a plaque by the door.

You'll pass through **Bech** if cycling the cross-country route between Echternach and Luxembourg City. It'll certainly stick in your mind as you pass through an old railway tunnel here. It may only be a few hundred metres long, but makes an unusual treat. Don't be put off by how dark it looks: motion sensors prompt the lighting of the way as you enter, a bit like a cyclist's version of the parting of the Red Sea. It's bizarre and surreal, especially as you'll more than likely find yourself alone – the tourist brochure publicity shots of reams of happy families pedalling through don't give an accurate picture. On the other hand, it's also occasionally used for discos. You can also reach the tunnel by road, arriving in Bech (10km southwest of Echternach), and then following the signs to Buchholz campsite. The tunnel is 100m from the parking area and easy to spot.

BERDORF

There isn't much to the village of **Berdorf** other than hotels, but its location right at the heart of Little Switzerland makes it an ideal place to overnight for those who don't fancy the relative bustle of Echternach. A great many paths head out from the village in all directions into the rocky ravines and valleys. It's quiet here – very quiet. Once you're done with walking, the only entertainment is dining or drinking in your hotel. If you want anything more exciting you'll have to head into Echternach itself.

You can go rock climbing in Berdorf, but you need to have experience, and also to get hold of a climber's licence before you start. Contact one of the local tourist offices for more details.

GETTING THERE AND AROUND Bus 111 passes through Berdorf hourly in each direction *en route* between Echternach (seven minutes) and Luxembourg City (50 minutes). If **driving** it's just five minutes from Echternach, 40 minutes from Luxembourg City. Alternatively, enjoy the scenery and **walk** between Berdorf and Echternach. It's about two hours along the incredibly beautiful E1 trail. As for getting around, well, you came here to walk didn't you?

TOURIST INFORMATION

Tourist office 7 An der Laach; 79 06 43; www.berdorf.net; ⊕ mid-Sep to Jun 12.00–18.30 Mon–Sat, Jul to mid-Sep 09.00–18.00 Mon–Sat, 10.00–12.30 Sun. The tourist office offers advice & free brochures on what to see & do in the region, including walking maps, & can help with booking accommodation. It's also the reception for the campsite, & offers guided walks, usually 1 a week at 10.15 Tue (it can vary). Costs are €12/8 per adult/child.

WHERE TO STAY AND EAT Despite its place at the heart of the Müllerthal, all Berdorf's hotels seem to share a soporific, 'back in time' feel. Besides the odd incursion by Wi-Fi, the 21st century seems to have passed everyone here by.

Hotel Restaurant Le Bisdorff (26 rooms) 39 rue Heisbich, L-6551; 79 02 08; e hotelbisdorff@pt.lu; www.hotel-bisdorff.lu; ⊕ Easter to mid-Nov. A friendly 4th-generation family hotel, Le Bisdorff has a charming location surrounded by greenery, plus a large & restful garden across a quiet lane. Flower boxes brighten up the exterior. Tastefully decorated, comfortable rooms are a tad old-fashioned, but have minibar & safe. Half have balconies. The 1st-floor landing hosts a dresser with pewter plates, while antique furnishings fill other public areas. There's free Wi-Fi in the lounge, and elsewhere there's an indoor swimming pool, sauna, solarium & steam room. Owner & restaurateur Sylvie Bisdorff is one of Luxembourg's most renowned chefs, & wrote the recipes in the *Luxembourg Culinaire* book (see *Appendix 2, Further Information*, page 229). Her wonderful creations also end up on the menu here (⊕ 12.00–13.30 & 18.30–20.30 Wed–Sun; €€€€–€€€€€), bringing in diners from far & wide. The dining room has a vague lobsterish theme, running from paintings to live examples on 'death row' in the fish tank. A host of gastronomic packages are available. €€€

Hotel-Restaurant Herber (20 rooms) 53 route d'Echternach, L-6550; 79 01 88; e gillenro@pt.lu; www.hotel-herber.lu; ⊕ Apr to mid-Nov. Another long-running family establishment, some rooms here have balconies. All have safe, minibar & Wi-Fi, & there's a solarium for guests. Special rates are available

On Whit Tuesday morning, 50 days after Easter, medieval fever hits Echternach as the annual Dancing Procession pays homage to its founding father St Willibrord. The origins of this bizarre ritual are somewhat obscure. First recorded in the 15th century, some historians believe it may be older, possibly 11th century. There are those that suggest pagan beginnings, others that it was an embellishment to yearly tithe processions, when people from the parishes under the jurisdiction of the abbey came to Echternach bringing offerings. Legend has it that pilgrims from the nearby village of Waxweiler simply began performing a 'hopping dance' as they marched, and it caught on. Another theory stems from pilgrims coming to visit St Willibrord's grave, often to pray for healing from the epidemics of plague and epilepsy that blighted Europe in the Middle Ages. People may have thought that by imitating the movements of the latter disease, they would be protected against or recover from it. There are even suggestions the idea originated in Cornwall, but there is no consensus about this. Alternatively, it may have come to Luxembourg with Willibrord himself. In short, there are as many theories as there are historians studying it.

Whether the dance's roots are pagan or Christian, it has now been thoroughly absorbed by the Church. And despite occasional attempts to ban it, it's a popular local custom in which everyone gets involved. In 2010 it was inscribed on the UNESCO List of the Intangible Cultural Heritage of Humanity, an honour that has put it on the map and will likely raise its profile in future.

It all kicks off with Mass, followed at 09.15 by the arrival of guest bishops in the square by the abbey, accompanied by a golden statue and relic of Willibrord. The Bishop of Echternach makes a speech from the abbey steps, then the first dancers set off at 09.30, weaving their way around the streets before arriving at St Willibrord's tomb in the basilica's crypt. Participants cover the route hopping slowly from one foot to the other, in time to an endlessly repeated ancient melody performed by dozens of groups of musicians. The simple tune, based on a traditional folk song, goes round and round for hours and if you listen to its relentless routine for too long there's a fair chance you risk insanity. At the very least you won't get the infernal thing out of your head for weeks.

It will be 13.30 by the time the last group completes the 2km route. Some start out from Prüm (in Germany) and Waxweiler the evening before, marching their way through the night to Echternach.

Although called a Dancing Procession, it could equally be termed the 'hop, skip and shuffle' procession as the step isn't complicated and anyone can master it. Participants dress in white shirts and – ahem – 'dance' their way forward in rows, linked together by white hankies (which have no symbolic meaning – they merely serve the practical purpose of keeping everyone in line). It's a joyful spectacle, both to participate in and to watch. Around 12,000 pilgrims take part, either dancing or in one of the 50 or so bands that serenade them by playing 'that' tune, and thousands more line the streets to see the medieval equivalent of 'The Timewarp' from *The Rocky Horror Show*: a hopping step to the left, followed by a hopping step to the right ...

for long stays, & gastronomic w/ends can be arranged. The restaurant (⏰ *12.30–13.15 & 19.00–20.30 daily;* €€€) serves good French cuisine, but the opening hours are somewhat limited, so you need to turn up on time. €€

⌂ **Hotel-Restaurant Kinnen** (25 rooms) 2 route d'Echternach, L-6550; ☎ 79 01 83; e hotelkinnen@pt.lu; www.hotelkinnen. lu; ⏰ Apr to mid-Nov. In the middle of the village, the white façade of this large building is conspicuously losing its battle with invading creepers – but in the most attractive way. The public areas of the sprawling interior have retained their traditional wooden beams & whitewashed walls. There's a sun lounge at the back & a front terrace. Rooms are clean, comfortable & stylish, & the marble & tile en suites are spotless. The French & regional food in the restaurant (⏰ *12.30–13.30 & 19.00–20.30 daily;* €€€) is tasty too. To burn off the fat, major walking routes begin just a few steps away. €€

⌂ **Hotel-Restaurant Pérékop** (20 rooms) 89 rue d'Echternach, L-6550; ☎ 79 93 29; e perekop@pt.lu; www.hotel-perekop.com; ⏰ Apr to mid-Nov. Run by the Schuster family, the clean & welcoming Pérékop, just outside Berdorf on the road to Echternach, has a peaceful

setting almost entirely surrounded by fields, & close to the walking trails. Rooms are simply furnished, some with balconies overlooking the countryside. Each has its own parking garage (free). The bright, airy restaurant (⏰ *12.30– 13.15 & 19.00–20.30 daily;* €€–€€€) serves a blend of traditional & modern regional cuisine. HB & FB arrangements include soft drinks, beer & open wines. €€

⌂ **Hotel-Restaurant Scharff** (21 rooms) 1 rue de Consdorf, L-6551; ☎ 79 02 20; e hscharff@pt.lu; www.hotel-scharff.lu; ⏰ Apr to mid-Nov. The Scharff has been run by a family of that name since 1897. The modern façade may hide this fact, but the older furnishings in its interior public areas betray its long history. Guest rooms have been refurbished to bring them up to scratch, & have modern clean bathrooms. The restaurant serves lunch at 12.00, dinner at 19.00 (€€€). €€

Å **Camping Bon Repos** 39 rue de Consdorf, L-6551; ☎ 79 06 31; e info@bonrepos.lu; www. bonrepos.lu; ⏰ Apr–Oct. This neat, well-organised campsite is close to the village centre, & has washing machines, free Wi-Fi, a small shop & clean showers. *€6pp, plus €6 per pitch.*

WHAT TO SEE AND DO The small parish church, **Eglise St Jean**, opposite the Hotel Kinnen in the centre of Berdorf, is noteworthy for the fact its altar sits on an old Roman stone, featuring carvings of gods and goddesses. This tiny church also seems to require eight confessionals, which leaves you wondering what really goes on here after dark.

ECHTERNACH

When I first saw Echternach I was immediately smitten. On the German border, by the banks of the river Sûre, it's a simply lovely place, which anyone with a soft spot for old European architecture will enjoy. With its arched shop frontages and wrought-iron shop signs, from some angles and with a favourable wind you may blink and think you've been transported to Salzburg, but in miniature. Yet even with a population of just 4,900, Echternach still evokes a cosmopolitan city feel that belies its stature. And with a great choice of hotels, restaurants and bars it also makes an ideal base for a day or three whilst exploring.

The town is dominated by its medieval abbey, founded in AD698 by St Willibrord – a Northumbrian monk – whose body lies in the crypt of the basilica. Around that, some of the old city walls remain intact, and five of its original watchtowers have been restored, fitted with all mod cons, and made available as holiday apartments (see *Where to stay*, page 156). In May and June, music fills the air as the Echternach International Music Festival comes to town. And on Whit Tuesday, thousands participate in the annual Dancing Procession (see box, page 151).

On the edges of town, paths head into the heart of Little Switzerland (see page 141). A large white board by the bus station marks the start of many trails, and lists the choices available – the tourist office can also furnish you with maps and offer advice on the best options. Meanwhile, three long-distance biking routes radiate out from Echternach, taking you as far afield as Luxembourg City if your legs are up to the challenge.

HISTORY This area was originally settled by Merovingians in the late Roman period, and subsequently became part of the Holy See of Trier in Germany. But it was only when the English monk Willibrord arrived in AD698 that a town appeared and began to prosper. Willibrord received the land from Irmina, daughter of Dagobert II, King of the Franks, and he immediately founded the abbey that became his home. Despite some major setbacks, such as a fire that burned down most of the abbey in 1016, the town continued to grow, and it's had city status since 1236. Although badly damaged during World War II, it has since been thoroughly restored, and is prospering again now that tourists have rediscovered its charms.

GETTING THERE Echternach is 35km northeast of Luxembourg City, and can be reached in half an hour by **car**. The railway line that once brought tourists into town has become a long-distance cycle path, but the former station – Echternach Gare – is now the bus depot. Between them, **buses** 110 and 111 leave Luxembourg City for Echternach every 30 minutes (€5), taking under an hour to complete the journey. Bus 111 travels via Berdorf through the heart of Little Switzerland. From elsewhere, bus 500 links Echternach hourly, via Diekirch, with Ettelbruck and its onward **train** connections. Several routes, including buses 474, 475 and 485, link Echternach with Grevenmacher in the Moselle Valley, two or three times every hour.

Buses on most routes are less frequent on Sundays. Check timetables in advance or you may find yourself with a long wait.

GETTING AROUND Echternach is compact, flat and easily manageable **on foot**. A walk from the abbey to the lake at the opposite end of town takes 15 minutes. Rue de la Gare, linking the bus station with the town centre, and part of the main market square have been pedestrianised, making strolling about a pleasure.

You'll know you're in a tourist town when you spot the little 'train', Voyages Bollig (⬎ 72 86 38; *May to mid-Sep, Apr–Nov on request for groups (min 20); adult/ child €6.50/4.50*), which plies an hourly route taking children and the lazy between the town and the lake. It leaves place du Marché on the hour between 11.00 and 17.00, and returns on the half hour between 11.30 and 16.30.

There are three long-distance **biking routes** you can follow from Echternach – pick up maps from the tourist office (see below). The 37km route to Luxembourg City is a straightforward cycle path following a conveniently flat former railway much of the way, even passing through an old tunnel (see page 149). Bikes can be rented from the youth hostel.

TOURIST INFORMATION
🄸 **Echternach Tourist Office** 9–10 Parvis de la Basilique; ⬎ 72 02 30; e info@echternach-tourist.lu; www.echternach-tourist.lu; ⊕ 10.00– 13.00 & 14.00–17.30 Mon–Fri, also open mid-Jul to mid-Sep 10.00–16.00 Sat, 10.00–12.00 Sun. The office has a wealth of leaflets & local knowledge, & arranges guided tours of the city & the surrounding countryside.

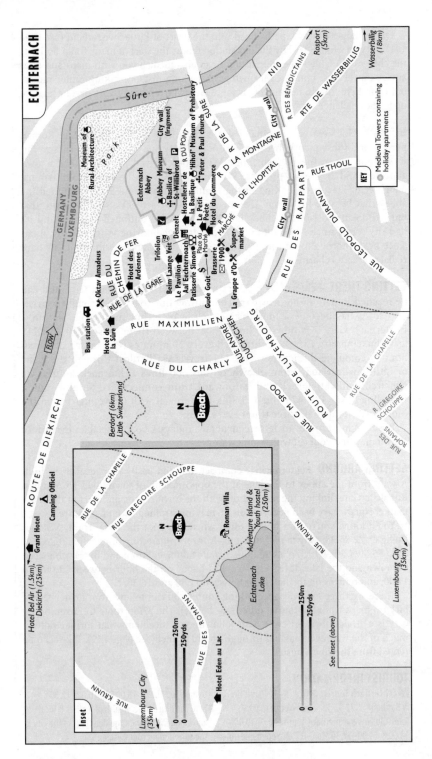

Müllerthal regional tourist bureau 9–10 Parvis de la Basilique, in the same builing as the Echternach Tourist Office; ☎ *72 04 57;* e info@ mullerthal.lu; www.mullerthal.lu, www. echternach-tourist.lu

WHERE TO STAY

🏠 **Hotel Eden au Lac** (60 rooms) Oam Nonneseess, L-6474; ☎ *72 82 83;* e hotel@ edenaulac.lu; www.edenaulac.lu; ⏰ mid-Mar to Nov. Designed to resemble a giant Swiss chalet, with wooden balustrades & window boxes bursting with geraniums, the Eden au Lac prides itself on being the only 5-star hotel in the Grand Duchy aimed at families & relaxation rather than the business trade. On the side of a small hill it enjoys a beautiful setting in 8ha of landscaped grounds, looking down over Echternach Lake. As you'd expect, no stone is left unturned in the quest for customer service. There's an indoor & outdoor pool, a squash court, a sauna, solarium, fitness & wellness centre, plus massages (for a fee). If you venture out & get tired, a free shuttle service will bring you home. Even the smallest rooms are spacious, & while they & the bathrooms are on the old side, they contain all modern comforts, including minibar, Wi-Fi, safe & whirlpool bath. Most have private balconies. There's an open hearth in winter, & a huge terrace. Compared with the cost of similar luxury in Luxembourg City, even the bill is a relative snip. Emphasis on the 'relative', mind. The upmarket restaurant serves refined French cuisine. €€€–€€€€€

🏠 **Hotel Bel Air** (39 rooms) 1 route de Berdorf, L-6409; ☎ *72 93 83;* e belair@pt.lu; www.belair-hotel.lu; closed 1 week in early Jan. If you want coddling & indulgence without breaking the piggy bank, this luxury retreat is a couple of kilometres west of town on the road to Berdorf. Located in the heart of the woods, some hiking trails virtually graze the front door. The quietly genteel lounge bar, with panelled walls hung with reproductions of old masters, & sumptuous sofas & armchairs you can sink into & never escape from, has the feel of an Edwardian country house. There's a fair smattering of chandeliers in other public areas. The in-house wellness centre features a sauna, Turkish bath, fitness room & an indoor swimming pool like something from a Greco-Roman villa. Rooms have minibar, safe, Wi-Fi & AC. Those at the back have balconies overlooking private gardens & the forested hills beyond. Some rooms at the front also have balconies. €€€

🏠 **Grand Hotel** (36 rooms) 27 route de Diekirch, L-6401; ☎ *72 96 72;* e grandhot@pt.lu; www.grandhotel.lu; ⏰ mid-Mar to mid-Nov. The imposing & indeed 'grand' Grand first opened its doors in 1935. On the road to Diekirch, with forested slopes behind & a river out front, this feels like the countryside, but is just a few metres west of the bus station. Comfortable modern rooms with a light touch in furnishings have minibar & internet access. Some larger suites in the new wing have balconies. To keep you busy downstairs, besides the terrace bar & chandelier-bedecked restaurant there's also an indoor swimming pool with massaging water jets, a sauna, solarium & Turkish bath. €€€

🏠 **Hostellerie de la Basilique** (14 rooms) 7–8 pl du Marché, L-6460; ☎ *72 94 83;* e info@ hotel-basilique.lu; www.hotel-basilique.lu; ⏰mid-Mar to mid-Nov. Tucked in a corner of the market square by the town fountain, this is a slice of home comfort dropped into the heart of the city. Elegant marble & pale wood interiors exude a sense of calm. All rooms are equipped with minibar, safe & marble-clad bathrooms. Alternatively, sit & relax on the hotel's flower-laden terrace & soak up the romantic views. The restaurant is also well worth checking out. €€€

🏠 **Hotel de la Sûre** (28 rooms) 49 rue de la Gare, L-6401; ☎ *72 94 40;* e restknep@ pt.lu; www.hoteldelasure.lu. Close to the bus station, this friendly hotel has been recently renovated. Rooms are decorated in light shades & pine, with laminate floors & satellite TV. Some have whirlpool baths. The hotel's Steak House Restaurant (⏰ *12.00–14.00 & 18.00–22.00 Tue–Sun;* €€–€€€) serves … well, you can probably guess. But they also have seasonal dishes, not all of which contain cow. €€–€€€

🏠 **Hotel des Ardennes** (30 rooms) 38 rue de la Gare, L-6440; ☎ *72 01 08;* e ardennes@ pt.lu; www.hotel-ardennes.lu. A mere stone's throw from the bus station, yet only 5mins' walk from the centre, this family-run establishment offers modern comforts in a lovely old building garlanded with window boxes. The hotel bar has photos taken when the Sûre flooded in 1993, and again in 2003. Simple but pleasant rooms come with either bath or shower. The hotel sauna & fitness rooms are free for guests. There's a secluded covered terrace & garden at the back & secure parking for motorbikes. €€

🏠 **Hotel du Commerce** (44 rooms) 16 pl du Marché, L-6460; ✆72 03 01; e chactour@pt.lu; www.hotelcommerce-echternach.lu; ⊕ mid-Feb to mid-Nov. The largest of the city-centre hotels, the Commerce looks a little drab from the outside, but is perfectly fine within. It offers simple, clean & comfortable rooms. Each has a coffee table & armchairs, although some of the furniture is starting to show its age. Guests can make use of the fitness centre & sauna. The quiet rear garden has a climbing frame & a slide to keep younger kids entertained. There are no fewer than 3 restaurants, plus a terrace on the main square. €€

🏠 **Hotel Le Pavillon** (11 rooms) 2 rue de la Gare, L-6440; ✆72 98 09; e lepavillon@ internet.lu; www.lepavillon.lu. In the thick of the action, on the junction of the main square & rue de la Gare, this warm friendly place has neatly decorated rooms with laminate floors & ultra-thick duvets, Wi-Fi & minibar. The covered terrace out front is heated when necessary. No lift. Parking is available at the rear. €€

🏠 **Le Petit Poète** (12 rooms) 13 pl du Marché, L-6460; ✆72 00 721; e petitpo@pt.lu; www.lepetitpoete.lu; ⊕ mid-Jan to Nov. In the centre of the old town, this small friendly hotel occupies the perfect spot on the main square, directly opposite the ancient 'Dënzelt' Building. The biggest selling point is that front rooms look out onto this timeless scene. Clean, newly decorated guest rooms are spacious & comfortable, but offer little beyond standard facilities. Bathrooms are very clean, if on the small side. No lift. All in all, the combination of unbeatable price & location makes this arguably the best value for money in town. The restaurant downstairs (see opposite) is another plus. €€

🏠 **Medieval Towers** (4 apts) Information & bookings c/o Echternach Tourist Office; 9–10 Parvis de la Basilique, L-6486; ✆72 02 30 or 72 02 72; e info@echternach-tourist.lu; www. echternach-tourist.lu. Want to know what it's like to live inside an ancient city wall? Try this, then. 20 watchtowers once ringed the city, keeping it safe from marauding invaders, & 8 survive today. 5 of these, along a stretch of wall on the southern flank of town, have been lovingly restored, luxuriously refurbished, & 4 are available to rent on a weekly basis as self-catering apts (the 5th is permanently booked). Towers sleep 4–6. €400–660 per week per apt, plus €50–60 cleaning fee.

🏠 **Youth Hostel** (118 beds) Chemin vers Rodenhof, L-6479; ✆72 01 58; e echternach@ youthhostels.lu; www.youthhostels.lu. Another of Luxembourg's spotless hostels, this occupies a prime semi-rural location by the lakeshore. Friendly, quiet & clean; rooms have 2–6 beds, & each has a bathroom. 2-bed rooms have special access, with priority given to disabled guests. You can rent mountain bikes for guided or unguided tours (€15/8 per day/half-day) – the bike path circling the lake passes right through the middle of the building. Nordic walking is also organised. The hostel is a 15min walk from the city centre, & has free Wi-Fi. Another big attraction is the 14m indoor climbing wall, also open to non-guests, & the kids' trampolining area (€2 for 10mins). €19.50pp inc bed, b/fast & bedding. Non-members pay €3 extra.

⛺ **Camping Officiel** (300 pitches) 5 route de Diekirch; ✆72 02 72; e info@camping-echternach.lu; www.camping-echternach. lu; ⊕mid-Mar to Oct. Echternach's official campsite really is called the Camping Officiel, leaving you in no doubt as to its status. It's a few hundred metres along the main road to Diekirch, close to the river. The large site has an outdoor swimming pool, tennis courts & every conceivable convenience, but there's also space for 150 stand-alone tents in addition to the 150 wired-up pitches for the inevitable flurry of Dutch caravans. €5.30pp, plus €6.50 per pitch.

✕ WHERE TO EAT

✕ **Les Jardins Gourmands** 1 route de Berdorf; ✆72 93 83; www.belair-hotel.lu; ⊕ 12.00–14.00 & 19.00–21.00 daily; closed 1 week in Jan. The

Hotel Bel Air's elegant French restaurant has a hushed quiet about it. That slight whooshing sound you hear may be a vehicle passing outside, or it may be a sharp intake of breath as another unsuspecting customer sees the prices on the extensive wine list. It's best not to study that part too hard & instead to admire the view from the panoramic windows on 2 sides of the spacious dining area: looking out onto a swathe of trees, they bring a sense of nature's serenity indoors. This is a bit of restrained decadence, but worth it as the food is lovingly prepared, & the service top-notch. Vegetarians, however, should perhaps look away now. Reservations are recommended at w/ends. €€€€–€€€€€

✗ Brasserie Hostellerie de la Basilique 7–8 pl du Marché; ☎72 94 83; www.hotel-basilique.lu; ⊕ Apr to mid-Nov 12.00–14.00 & 18.00–21.00 daily. The restaurant of the Hostellerie de la Basilique has a terrace almost entirely hemmed in by flowers, offering scenic outdoor dining opposite the town hall & beside a pretty fountain. The interior brings calm sophistication in elegant surrounds. The menu ranges from good-value Luxembourgish classics to slightly more expensive German- & French-tinged specials. Food reflects the seasons & includes locally caught game in autumn. €€–€€€€

✗ Restaurant La Grappe d'Or 7 route de Luxembourg; ☎26 72 16 33; www.lagrappedor.lu; ⊕ 12.00–14.00 & 19.00–22.00 Wed–Mon; closed Tue, Sat lunch, Sun & Mon dinner. Although on the surface just another of those slightly upmarket French-inspired meat & fish places that you can't help falling over in Luxembourg, this distinguishes itself by also displaying Portuguese influence (a rare find despite the large Portuguese population), & to prove it there's a shop next door selling imported wines & ports. There's also a 4-course gastronomic menu with specially matched wines. The restaurant is very popular at w/ends, so book in advance. €€€

✗ Brasserie 1900 19 pl du Marché; ☎26 72 12 65; ⊕ 12.00–14.00 & 19.00–22.00 daily. Split in two by a series of lattice screens, the bar side of this popular restaurant is a locals' meeting point. Serving the usual mixture of French, Luxembourgish, & veal-based tourist pleasers, the interior is a contradiction in terms: somehow it simultaneously achieves both a modern & retro look. The dining area is a long line of tables with a continuous dark-green banquette down 1

side. Over in the bar, you can eat from the same menu whilst sitting on high stools at even higher tables. The dishes sound a little last year, but are presented with modern panache. Oh, & they taste good too. €€–€€€

✗ Oktav Amadeus 56 rue de la Gare; ☎27 21 15 15; ⊕ 11.00–23.00 daily. Pizzeria/trattoria beside Echternach bus station, with a terrace at the front. There are 2 dining rooms – 1 a chic modern space with a purple/mauve theme, right down to the chandelier in the entrance hall. The other side is more informal, but the same menu is offered in both: including pastas, good salads, & the house speciality, veal. The pizzas are both excellent &, at first glance, colossal – the size of an old dustbin lid – but the crust is wafer thin, so consuming one is less daunting than you expect. You'll still need to be hungry though. There's also a take-away service. €€–€€€

✗ Restaurant Le Jardin des Ardennes 38 rue de la Gare; ☎72 01 08; www.hotel-ardennes.lu; ⊕ Mar to mid-Jan 12.00–14.00 & 19.00–21.00 Fri–Wed; closed Thu & Sun evening. Head around the back of this hotel restaurant to find its cobbled terrace & garden (also accessible through the building). You'll be jostling for space with a model railway, but you sit below trellised kiwi fruit & grape vines. The menu is a mix of Luxembourgish, French & tourist standards, & the salads are particularly good. *Salads* €€; *other mains* €€€

✗ Restaurant Le Petit Poète 13 pl du Marché; ☎72 00 721; www.lepetitpoete.lu; ⊕ 11.30–14.00 & 18.30–21.00 Tue–Sun; closed Tue in low season. This cheerful & friendly restaurant has a large terrace occupying a prime spot on the main square. The 3-course *menu du jour* (lunchtimes only) represents outstanding value for money. Elsewhere the menu is mainly French, with dishes varying each week according to the chef's whims. A limited choice of simple dishes (*croque monsieur*, spaghetti, etc) is available throughout the day until 22.00. €€

✗ Youth Hostel Chemin vers Rodenhof; ☎72 01 58; www.youthhostels.lu; ⊕ daily. The youth hostel's cafeteria offers exceptional value, & you don't have to stay there to dine. The terrace is by the lake. Evening meals cost €10 for 3 courses (€9 for YHA members), with Luxembourgish specialities & vegetarian meals available on request. A simpler menu is served at lunchtime. €

♀ **Patisserie Simon** 31 pl du Marché; ✆ 72 93 47; ⊕ Wed–Mon. For an indulgent nibble, the Simon bakery does an excellent line in cakes & pastries. One local speciality is *macarons mous*, sweet & moreish marble-sized almond cookies that are best described as half macaroon, half marzipan. At €5 per 100g bag they make a great souvenir or a fattening afternoon treat. Be warned though: once opened, a bag won't last long. Simon also has a reputation as the best of the several ice-cream parlours dotted along rue de la Gare. €

ENTERTAINMENT AND NIGHTLIFE The **Café Aal Eechternoach** (*38 pl du Marché;* ✆ *26 72 08 80;* ⊕ *11.00–01.00 Fri–Wed*), the liveliest, loudest place in town, is actually a pleasant little café with half-timbered ceilings and stone walls, which fits appropriately with Echternach's 'olde worlde' ambiance. Nevertheless the café isn't rooted in the past. On the contrary it attracts a young crowd, who cram the bar's music-filled interior on weekend evenings while tourists frequent the picturesque terrace. They also serve, for a Luxembourg pub, an unusually good selection of Belgian beers.

If you're in Echternach on Whit Tuesday, you'll have a tough job avoiding the legendary **Dancing Procession**, which takes place all over town (see box, page 151).

With slightly more modern origins, the **Echternach International Festival** (*PO Box 30, L-6401 Echternach;* ✆ *72 83 47;* e *musique@internet.lu; www. echternachfestival.lu*) has been turning the city into a global music arena since 1975. Over a six-week period from mid-May to the end of June, major stars flock here to perform. The programme is largely classical, but also includes jazz works – the King's Singers and the Royal Liverpool Philharmonic Orchestra were among those who appeared in 2011. See the website for the programme and ticket details.

Opposite the abbey, the **Trifolion** (*2 Porte Saint Willibrord; tickets* ✆ *26 72 39 500; www.trifolion.lu;* ⊕ *13.00–17.00 Mon–Fri*) opened in 2010, and is a cultural, touristic and congress centre with a 650-seater auditorium. It hosts musical performances and other events – ticket prices and performance times vary so check the website.

SHOPPING Unusually for Luxembourg, most shops open for business on Sunday afternoons. If you run out of supplies there's a **Match** supermarket opposite the post office (*1 route de Luxembourg;* ⊕ *08.00–19.00 Mon–Sat, 09.00–13.00 Sun*). A **market** is held on the main square on the second Wednesday of each month.

Gudde Goût (*21 pl du Marché;* ✆ *27 76 26 64;* ⊕ *09.00–18.00 Tue–Sat, 13.00–18.00 Sun*) is a global delicatessen, but its USP is the selection of local '*Echternoach*' products, including mustards, liqueurs and a host of other things.

OTHER PRACTICALITIES

Medical
✚ **Pharmacie du Lion** 32 pl du Marché; ✆ 72 00 27. Hours similar to Pharmacie Thiry.
✚ **Pharmacie Thiry** 12 pl du Marché; ✆ 72 03 09; ⊕ 08.30–12.00 & 13.30–18.00 Mon–Fri

Banks
$ **BGL BNP Paribas Bank** 25 pl du Marché; ✆ 42 42 20 00; ⊕ 09.00–16.30 Mon–Fri
$ **Dexia Bank** 11 rue de la Gare; ✆ 24 59 69 00; ⊕ 08.30–12.00 & 13.30–16.45 Mon–Fri

$ **ING Bank** 10 pl du Marché; ✆ 72 87 75; ⊕ 09.00–12.00 & 13.00–17.00 Mon, Wed & Fri, 09.00–12.00 & 13.00–18.00 Tue & Thu
$ **Spuerkeess ('S-Bank')** 20 pl du Marché; ✆ 72 00 351; ⊕ 08.15–16.30 Mon–Fri

Post office
✉ **Post office** 2 route de Luxembourg; ✆ 72 94 90 32; ⊕ 08.00–12.00 & 13.30–17.15 Mon–Fri

WHAT TO SEE AND DO To join the historical dots in a single walk, follow the **Via Epternacensis**. This trail is marked by a series of bronze plaques embedded in the

To the left of the Dënzelt, take a look at the decorative metalwork on the front of the **Café Beim Laange Veit** (*39 pl du Marché*), showing a fiddler hanging from the gallows. There are several folk tales about how he came to be in that predicament. One suggests a local musician named Veit went on a pilgrimage to the Holy Land, taking his wife for company. Unfortunately, she fell ill and died on the trip, and on Veit's return to Echternach his mother-in-law accused him of murdering her daughter. He was quickly found guilty and sentenced to hang.

Another legend claims Veit was merely a local horse thief who got caught, but he wound up on the gallows just the same. Before the sentence was carried out he was offered a last request, as was the custom. He chose to play the violin one more time, and the tune he played was so beautiful and catchy that everyone joined in, and the town square was filled with dancing. The music was also so delightful it allegedly lifted Veit up and carried him away to Heaven, never to be seen again. Alternatively, he just ran off when everyone was distracted and having fun. You decide. Either way, it's all completely true, of course.

streets, linking all sites of significance, starting at the tourist office and ending at the Roman villa. The accompanying leaflet, available from the tourist office, has a map and gives background information about each of the 15 stopping-off points.

The beating heart of Echternach is **place du Marché**. Surrounded by picturesque buildings, the central market square is a gathering point for tourists and locals alike. In summer, free outdoor musical performances are held here. On other occasions it offers bikers and classic car enthusiasts a chance to converge and mutually admire each other's polished chrome before revving up and heading out for a countryside tour.

Forming the square's stunning centrepiece, the magnificent **Dënzelt** Building was formerly the local seat of justice. It was built in the 14th century, and then rebuilt in Gothic style in 1444 following a fire. It has passed through several subsequent incarnations, becoming Renaissance in 1520, Baroque during the 18th century and neo-Gothic in 1895. A final restoration was made necessary after it was damaged during the liberation of Echternach in 1944. The statues on the front, created by Lambert Piedboeuf, date from the neo-Gothic makeover. The four in the corners represent the cardinal virtues – temperance, justice, prudence and fortitude – while the Virgin Mary and King Solomon preside over the centre. Standing alone and off to the right is Robert of Monreal, Abbot of Echternach during the 16th century. Today, wedding services are performed in the first-floor hall. Getting invited to one is your best chance of looking inside.

One of the best free sights in town is available each evening in spring and early summer, simply by looking up. Swifts and house martins gather in the skies in huge numbers, swooping around as they dine on the abundant insects, attracted by warm air rising off the paved square. There always seem to be a few circling above, but at peak feeding times numbers swell into the hundreds and beyond. Anyone interested in birds can't help but be charmed by the spectacle.

The vast Benedictine **Echternach Abbey** was founded in AD698 by St Willibrord (see box, page 160), and it grew rapidly in influence to become the most powerful institution in Luxembourg. The third abbot, Beornrad, was a favourite of Emperor

Though a national hero in Luxembourg, and the nation's only saint, Willibrord was actually Northumbrian. Born in AD658, as a child his father sent him to study at the monastery in Ripon. He grew up under the influence of Wilfrid, Bishop of York, who preferred Roman Catholicism to the Celtic Christianity that was dominant in the area. At the age of 20 he moved to Ireland, where ten years later he was ordained as a priest. Vowing to preach the gospel to non-believing heathens, he crossed to mainland Europe along with 11 companions in 690, charged with the task of bringing Christianity to the stubborn Frisians whether they wanted it or not. He subsequently made two pilgrimages to Rome, and became Archbishop of Utrecht in 695. Befriending the Frankish nobility, he was lavished with gifts of land, allowing him to build a string of churches and monasteries. In 698, he received what is now Echternach, and founded the monastery that became his base.

He died in November 739, aged 81. According to his wishes he was buried in Echternach, and soon after was venerated as a saint. Biographies written at the time preached effusively about the 'miracles' he allegedly performed, bringing a string of pilgrims to his tomb. So many came that by AD800 the small church where he lay had to make room for a larger, three-aisled version to cope with demand. Even today, thousands still turn out for the annual Dancing Procession to his tomb: a lasting testament to the Briton who achieved eternal fame far from home.

Charlemagne, and when he died in 797, Charlemagne himself took direct control for a year. Over time the buildings have seen their fair share of trauma. A great fire levelled almost everything in 1016. In 1794, Napoleonic troops arrived and set about deconsecrating the abbey. The monks left at this time, and most of the treasures were auctioned off. For the following century the buildings were used as a porcelain factory – early photographs of Echternach show thick black smoke billowing from its chimneys, yet you can be certain no pope was being elected. Then as recently as 1944, the retreating Nazis took their turn and destroyed the basilica as a parting gesture. The current buildings, dating from between 1727 and 1736, are today used as a boys' boarding school. Only a few parts are open to the public.

The **Abbey Museum** (*Musée de l'Abbaye; 11 Parvis de la Basilique;* \ *72 74 72;* ⊕ *Easter–Jun, Sep–Oct 10.00–12.00 & 14.00–17.00 daily, Jul–Aug 10.00–12.00 & 14.00–18.00 daily; adult/child €3/1.50*) is located in the main building's vaulted cellars. One of Willibrord's most important acts in Echternach was to found a scriptorium, in which teams of monks set about making brilliantly illuminated copies of important religious texts. Their work reached its glorious zenith sometime during the 11th century. The books were intended primarily for religious study, but were also occasionally commissioned by various Germanic emperors. The originals were long ago moved to Spain and elsewhere for safekeeping when the abbey closed, but faithful copies of many are on display here. Top draw is the gleaming golden *Codex Aureus* – copy or not, it remains an extraordinary example of medieval craftsmanship. The museum also has exhibits on the life of Willibrord and the history of the abbey.

The **Basilica of St Willibrord** (*Basilique St Willibrord; Parvis de la Basilique;* \ *72 02 30; free*), together with its crypt, remains the most important religious building in Luxembourg. Having been gutted by fire in 1016, ransacked by the French in 1794 and blown up by the Nazis in 1944, the building has undergone drastic and involuntary remodelling on several occasions. Rebuilding work following the last atrocity was only completed in 1953. Look out for the 'Echternach system' windows that line the walls: two narrow arches nestled below a larger one – a similar style is also seen in parts of the German Rhineland, but is thought to have originated here. The stained-glass picture windows are relatively modern, and tell the story of Echternach from its founding until the French occupation. On the left wall are the remains of a 3m wooden crucifix. The original was shattered in the pounding of 1944, and rather than restore it this fragment was left as a poignant reminder.

Fortunately, the basilica's **crypt** escaped virtually unscathed by the successive ravages. As a result, many of the frescoes on the ceiling are 11th- and 12th-century originals. But pride of place down below goes to the **tomb of St Willibrord**, in beautifully carved Carrara marble. This is where the Dancing Procession culminates. Behind the tomb are alleged to be the remains of the earliest church that Willibrord founded on the site, although you can't actually get around the back to see anything.

A new side wing in the basilica (the entrance is at the far end on the left) houses an **information centre** (⊕ *09.00–12.00 & 14.00–17.00 Mon–Sat, 14.00–17.00 Sun & holidays; free*) with explanations about the Dancing Procession and its UNESCO status. It has videos so you can see what the procession looks like on the 364 days of the year when it isn't happening.

Museums and other places of interest

'Hihof' Museum of Prehistory (*Musée de Préhistoire; 4a rue du Pont;* ✆ *72 02 96;* ⊕ *Apr–Sep 10.00–12.00 & 14.00–17.00 Tue–Sun; adult/child €2/1*) In the so-called Hihof, a former poorhouse beside the Peter and Paul Church, this museum concentrates on the manufacture and use of prehistoric tools. Artefacts from all over the world are displayed on the first floor, including a large collection of flint, and other stone and bone implements, plus arrowheads from around Europe. Most date from the Mesolithic Period (9500–5500BC) or earlier – some primitive stone axes from Africa are thought to be one million years old. Modern-day equivalents – penknives, lighters, etc – displayed alongside their ancient counterparts demonstrate visually what the occasionally abstract lumps of rock were intended for. An exhibition of porcelain on the ground floor stems from the time the abbey served as a factory, while photos on the walls show the devastation in Echternach during the winter of 1944–45.

Museum of Rural Architecture (*Musée de l'Architecture Rurale; Municipal Park;* ⊕ *Easter–Oct 13.00–17.00 Tue–Sun; free*) The Rococo pavilion housing this exhibition was built in the municipal park in 1765. The small display on the first floor contains a number of model buildings showing the architectural influence of the abbey on farms in the region. The leafy **park** itself is a pleasant place for a stroll, especially by the river.

Peter and Paul Church (*Eglise SS Pierre et Paul; rue de la Montagne; free*) Built in the 11th century and expanded in the 18th, the current church on a small mound in the centre of town is a mix of Romanesque and Gothic styles. The Romans were the first to build here, and excavations on the site have revealed fortifications dating back to AD275. Since then, successive occupants have restyled and rebuilt. There was also a small convent here at the time Willibrord arrived in 698, supporting the church's claim to be the oldest surviving Christian monument in the country. The highlight of a visit today is seeing the beautiful blue floral frescoes covering the vaulted ceiling.

7

Echternach Lake (*Lac d'Echternach*) The 60ha lake is a relatively recent creation, having only been dug during the 1970s. It's 2km long and ringed by paths – you can easily walk around it in an hour without breaking sweat. The lakeshore is largely a managed environment, but some areas have been set aside and left to their own devices as habitats for nature. In other areas fishing is allowed (ask about permits in the town hall). Alternatively, take to the water in a **pedalo** (*adult/child €5/3 for 30mins*), tickets are available from the Pavilion du Lac Café near the car park. The café also dispenses cold drinks, snacks and ice creams. The lake is a pleasant 15-minute walk southwest of the centre, beside a babbling stream for most of the way.

Adventure Island (*Echternach Lake;* ✆ *72 01 58; www.adventure-island.lu; min 6 people, advance reservation only, contact the youth hostel; fees vary*) On an island in the lake by the youth hostel (see *Where to stay*, page 156), this rope garden is an adventure park for all ages (from 11 years). Note there's a minimum height requirement of 1.5m. The rope course is laid out 10m above the ground, with aerial runways and giant swings. You can choose from various programmes, such as the 90-minute Action Run or the three-hour Mammut Run (*adult/child €40/35pp*). Activities are suspended in bad weather.

Roman Villa (*Villa Romaine; 47a rue des Romains, L-6478;* ✆ *26 72 09 74;* ⏱ *Easter–Sep 10.00–12.00 & 13.00–17.00 Tue–Sun; adult/child €1.50/free*) Whilst digging Echternach Lake in 1975, construction workers unearthed the remnants of a large Roman villa. After recording their precise layout, the foundations were removed and reconstructed at a new location a few metres away. There isn't a whole heap left of the house – just an outline of the walls and a few columns – and little is known about its occupants, but what is impressive is the sheer scale of the place: covering an area of 120m by 60m, it's one of the largest private Roman dwellings known to have existed in northern Europe, and was clearly owned by a wealthy family. Information displays fill in the blanks and give an idea of how life would have looked when the villa was in its heyday, between AD60 and the 5th century.

Alfred Toepfer Bridge Four kilometres northwest of Echternach on the N10 is Weilerbach (take bus 500). This is where you'll find the Alfred Toepfer Bridge, named after the creator of the Luxembourg–Germany Nature Park, of which the Our Natural Park (see page 185) forms the Luxembourg half. It's a picturesque covered wooden footbridge on stone pillars, straddling the Sûre at one of its prettiest points. By the bridge is a **memorial** to those in the US 5th Infantry who gave their lives crossing the river into Germany at this point on 7 February 1945. If you venture to the other side you too will be in Germany, although there's no sign. On the far side is a footpath taking you 3km to the next bridge upriver in Bollendorf, from where you can return to the Luxembourg side.

Henri Tudor Museum, Rosport (*Musée Henri Tudor; 9 rue Henri Tudor;* ✆ *73 00 66 206; musee-tudor.lu;* ⏱ *Sep–Jun 14.00–18.00 Wed–Sun, Jul–Aug 14.00–18.00 daily; adult/child €4/free*) The village of Rosport, 5km east of Echternach, is where most of Luxembourg's bottled water originates. I would suggest you visit the bottling plant, but it can only be done on group tours by special arrangement. Rosport was also, however, the home of one of the country's most famous sons, Henri Tudor, and this museum honours him and his achievements. It deals with the

Depending on your viewpoint in the 'petrolhead' versus environmentalist debate, Henri Owen Tudor (1859–1928), the son of an Englishman who came to Luxembourg looking for adventure, was either the greatest scientist on the planet, or an evil engineer whose dabbling irrevocably changed the course of history. Born in Rosport, it was Tudor's development of the world's first functioning accumulator battery in 1881 that eventually enabled cars to run as they do. He was still a student at the time, albeit one who corresponded with American scientific guru Thomas Edison. His first battery continued working uninterrupted for 16 years, powered by a homemade dynamo connected to a watermill. By 1884, Tudor had developed a smaller mobile unit, which he patented – becoming the official inventor of the lead-acid battery. All right, if he hadn't been successful – and all he really did was tinker with an earlier failed design created by French physicist Gaston Plante – someone else may have been, and we probably wouldn't be riding around on carthorses today. But who can say in what direction the transport revolution might have headed?

The battery wasn't Henri's only claim to fame. He also built the world's first electric car – the 'Energy-Car' – which was unveiled at a 1905 exhibition in Liège. It was made and sold in unknown numbers in Rosport, and at the family's other factory in Brussels. But it could never compete with the internal combustion engine, which had already become the market standard. In a sadly ironic twist, when Tudor died in 1928, aged 69, it was from lead poisoning, contracted during his tireless research. Doubly ironic, the lessons learned from studying the effects of lead on workers in his factories later became enshrined in German health and safety laws.

life and work of the inventor and industrialist who developed the lead accumulator battery, the world's first electric car, and was one of the first to bring electric lighting to western Europe.

Heading uphill from the river, it's on the left after the church, and shares Tudor's former family home with the town hall. Visits begin on the third floor with the story of his life (see box, above) and hands-on demonstrations of various bits of equipment, showing how electricity is generated by friction, static, magnetism, etc. You are given a battery with your ticket to activate certain exhibits. Explanations are in French and German only, but it's fascinating for adults, and has enough buttons and knobs to keep even world-weary children amused.

This house was one of the first in the country to get electric lighting, thanks to Henri's efforts, not long after the royal palace. His company also supplied Echternach with electricity, illuminating it for the first time in 1886 and the original plans and contracts for this are displayed here. The Tudor Accumulator Company also played a role in Britain's industrial heritage, providing power to, among other places, the Dukinfield cotton mill near Manchester. Nansen even took Tudor's accumulator batteries with him on his early Arctic expeditions in 1893–96.

Once you've completed the tour take a moment to enjoy the peaceful surrounds of the large gardens in which the museum is located. Müllerthal Trail No 1 (see page 146) passes right through here if you feel the urge to just keep on walking. The stream running through the gardens was, appropriately enough, once used to generate electricity.

BEAUFORT

With a population of just 1,800, Beaufort is very manageable. Also known locally as Befort, it lies on the edge of Little Switzerland and can be used as a base for walking. The primary reason to come here, however, is to marvel at the ruins of the medieval castle, just below the town proper.

GETTING THERE Reaching Beaufort from Echternach takes a mere 20 minutes on **bus** 414 during the week, but it only runs once every two hours. It doesn't run at all on Sundays, when you need to take the equally rare bus 500 as far as Reisdorf, and then switch to the 502, with a 45-minute wait in-between for the connection. The total trip, including waiting time, takes almost 1½ hours, which is a test of patience. The two towns are less than 10km apart. Bring your own vehicle or travel on another day if you're starting from Echternach.

Between Beaufort and Luxembourg City the situation is much better. Bus 107 makes the direct trip in each direction in one hour (once every other hour). Incredibly, it also operates on Sunday.

Beaufort is fairly compact and it only takes a matter of minutes to walk from one end to the other.

TOURIST INFORMATION

🛈 **Tourist office** 87 Grand Rue; ✆ 83 60 81 301; www.beaufort.lu; ⏰ 10.00–19.00 daily (varies slightly with seasons). The tourist office offers advice & free brochures, including walking maps, & can help with booking accommodation.

🏠 WHERE TO STAY AND EAT

🏠 **Hotel Meyer** (33 rooms) 120 Grand Rue, L-6310; ✆ 26 87 61 23; e hotelmeyer@pt.lu; www.hotelmeyer.lu; ⏰ Easter–Dec. Beaufort's upmarket option is a modern, stylish hotel in the centre of town. The attractive large garden has sunbeds for relaxation, if you're lucky enough to be visited by the great golden orb in the sky. Spacious comfortable rooms have minibar & hairdryers. An indoor swimming pool, sauna, solarium & fitness centre are available for guests' use. The restaurant (⏰ 12.00–13.30 Sun & holidays, & 19.00–20.30 daily; €€€–€€€€) serves posh Luxembourgish & French cuisine, while a separate brasserie (⏰ 12.00–14.00 & 18.00–21.00 daily; €€) dishes up simpler fare. €€€

🏠 **Auberge Rustique** (8 rooms) 55 rue du Château, L-6313; ✆ 83 60 86; e info@aubergerustique.lu; www.aubergerustique.lu. A hotel since 1790, this little auberge is on the road between the village & the castle, about halfway between both. Simple, happy rooms have floral décor & spotless bathrooms. No lift. The restaurant (⏰ 12.00–20.45 daily; €–€€) & bar area is 'bijou', shall we say, but there's a sunny terrace outside for claustrophobic guests. The food – Luxembourgish, French or bar snacks – is hearty & unpretentious, but the bill should be as tiny as the dining room. €€

🏠 **Youth Hostel** (80 beds) 6 rue de l'Auberge, L-6315; ✆ 83 60 75; e beaufort@youthhostels.lu; www.youthhostels.lu; ⏰ mid-Jan to mid-Dec. In the heart of Beaufort, the hostel has a kitchen, TV room, internet access, a barbecue area & a common room. Rooms contain 2–12 beds. The canteen (€) serves cheap lunches & dinners, with vegetarian meals available on request. €17.50pp inc bed, b/fast & bedding. Non-members pay €3 extra.

🏕 **Camping Plage** (312 pitches) 87 Grand Rue, L-6310; ✆ 83 60 99 300; e camplage@pt.lu; www.campingplage.lu; ⏰ all year. Come here if you want tennis courts & swimming pools with waterslides in your campsite. Located near the woods, this is the complete opposite of the Beau Site (see next), with every distraction laid on for bored children: bingo, discos, you name it. The reception is the local tourist office. You can also rent bikes (€7.50/15 per half/full day). €5.50pp, plus €6.50 per pitch.

⚑ Camping Beau Site (56 pitches) 3 route d'Eppeldorf, L-6312; ☏ 83 68 23; e beausite@ pt.lu; ⊕ mid-Apr to mid-Oct. A small, quiet campsite with no frills, no restaurant & no swimming pools swarming with happy holidaymakers. No nothing in fact, except a clean shower block. How refreshing. But your kids might find it dull. *€4.50pp, plus €4.50 per pitch.*

✗ Pizzeria Um Bierg 110 Grand Rue; ☏ 83 60 70; ⊕ 12.00–13.30 & 18.00–21.30 Wed–Mon; ⊕ Mar to mid-Dec. The name tells you what you need to know: this place serves up good-value pizzas to those who've grown tired of their hotel restaurant. *€–€€*

SHOPPING Beaufort's number-one local produce is *cassero*, the tasty blackcurrant liqueur made and sold by the castle. It is available elsewhere in the country, but the big advantage of buying it *in situ* is you get to try it as well (see *What to see and do*, page 166). There's also a bakery in the village with a small tearoom attached, and a mini supermarket.

OTHER PRACTICALITIES
✚ Pharmacie de Beaufort 84 Grand Rue; ☏ 26 87 66 60
$ Spuerkeess ('S-Bank') 1 rue Kummel; ☏ 83 63 95; ⊕ 08.15–11.45 & 13.30–17.00 Mon, Tue & Fri

✉ Post office 37 Grand Rue; ☏ 83 60 68; ⊕ 13.45–17.00 Mon–Fri

WHAT TO SEE AND DO
Beaufort Castle (*Château de Beaufort; 9 rue de l'Eglise;* ☏ *83 60 02; www.beaufort. lu;* ⊕ *Apr–Oct 09.00–18.00 daily (last entry at 17.30); adult/child €3/1, audio guide €3*) For a major defensive stronghold, Beaufort Castle's location at first seems somewhat unwise, as it sits in a small hollow below the level of the town it allegedly guards. But when you see how protected it is from behind by a curtain of sheer stone cliffs, the situation doesn't seem quite so crazy. The exposed front areas were also once graced by a wide deep moat, although this has long since disappeared and been replaced by rather less daunting grass.

The oldest parts of the current ruin date from around 1150, when a simple fortress was built on the rocky outcrop here. Its origins are thought to go back further, possibly to Roman times, but its first written mention doesn't occur until 1194, when a certain Walter de Wiltz was named the first Lord of Befort. The modest building was extended over the following centuries into a magnificent home.

This growth ended abruptly in 1639, however, when the lords of Beaufort, bankrupted by the Thirty Years War, were forced to sell. The new owner, Baron de Beck, governed Luxembourg on behalf of the Spanish king. He built a new Renaissance-style château directly behind it and left the original building to crumble – it was even used as a quarry at one point. Such wilful neglect only halted in 1850 when the government declared it a protected monument. It was later bought by the Linkels family, and during the 1920s and 1930s, one Edmond Linkels made it his life's work to restore the castle and open it to the public – he's also widely credited with kick-starting the tourist industry in the whole region. His wife Madame Linkels moved into the **new château** (*not open to the public*) in 1935, and she lives there to this day. Well into her nineties at the time of writing, the sprightly and elegant old lady still oversees the running of the castle, which is now owned by the state.

In the old castle, children in particular will enjoy the **torture chamber**, which has been restocked with some painful-looking machinery clearly designed for extracting maximum confessions from unruly serfs. The 20-minute audiovisual presentation (every hour, on the hour) on the castle and medieval life is in German, but an explanatory leaflet is available from the ticket desk. Only a few rooms have roofs, so watch out in inclement weather.

Rain or not, be sure to try some *cassero*, the castle's homemade blackcurrant liqueur – the fruit used was once grown on the estate, but is now imported from Dijon in France. The drink is delicious and packs in more fresh blackcurrant flavour than I've ever encountered in mass-produced French *cassis*. It also makes an excellent aperitif when blended with *crémant* and drunk as *kir royal*. Besides *cassero*, the castle also sells a raspberry liqueur (*framboise des bois*), a punchier *cassero-kirsch* blend, and several fiery *eaux de vie*.

Starting across the road from the castle entrance, behind the car park, is a short (4km) **nature trail** that leads past a small swan-encrusted lake (the latter forming a scenic foreground for photos even if you're not up for the hike). The walk takes around one and 1½ hours depending on how many stops you make to appreciate the joys of nature. The looping path ends up in the town proper, from where it's a short stroll downhill back to the castle.

LAROCHETTE

One of the Grand Duchy's undiscovered gems, the old market town of Larochette largely escaped the appalling devastation of World War II that laid waste to many of its neighbours. As it nestles below craggy bluffs in the narrow White Ernz Valley, the opposing forces took up positions on hilltops on either side. Most of their shells passed over the heads of the townspeople, leaving them unscathed.

Like several Luxembourg towns, it's the castle that grabs your attention, sitting romantically on a rock above the houses. With a population of just 2,000, Larochette is small and compact. If there's a drawback, it's that one of the main north–south cross-country highways passes straight through the middle. The speed restrictions and narrow streets cause a bottleneck and make the roads busy from morning till evening. Despite this, traffic does die away at night and you're more likely to be kept awake by incessant cock crowing than by trucks rumbling through in the early hours.

GETTING THERE **Bus** 100 travels between Luxembourg City (one hour) and Diekirch (20 minutes), passing through Larochette in each direction every hour. For Echternach (45 minutes), you'll need bus 414, which runs ten times a day, Monday to Saturday only.

TOURIST INFORMATION
🚶 **Tourist office** 33 Chemin J-A Zinnen; 📞83 76 76; www.larochette.eu; ⊕ Sep–Jun 08.00–12.00 & 14.00–17.00 Mon–Fri, Jul–Aug 08.00–12.00 & 14.00–17.00 daily. Located in a 1725 manor house, 1 block back from the main street, the tourist office has a useful free booklet of 14 short walks in the vicinity. These range in length from 1hr to 4hrs, & all are circular, starting & finishing in the town centre.

🏠 WHERE TO STAY
🏠 **Auberge Op der Bleech** (9 rooms) 4 pl Bleech, L-7610; 📞87 80 58; e bleech@vo.lu; www.opderbleech.lu; closed for 2 weeks in Sep. The rooms in this small hotel are individually decorated, some have shared bathrooms & most offer ADSL internet access. A solarium & sauna are available for guest use, & there's the obligatory terrace at the front with castle view. €€
🏠 **Hotel de la Poste** (25 rooms) 11 pl Bleech, L-7610; 📞87 81 78; e hotelposte@pt.lu; www.

hotelposte.lu; ⊕ mid-Mar to mid-Nov. The friendly de la Poste has cosy rooms with basic facilities. The front terrace has a grand view up to the castle & across the main square. Wi-Fi access is available. No lift. There's free parking for cars & a garage for motorbikes. €€

🏠 **Youth Hostel** (77 beds) 45 Osterbour, L-7622; ☎ 83 70 81; e larochette@youthhostels. lu; www.youthhostels.lu. The youth hostel is in a modern building in a small park on the northern edge of town. All 14 rooms in the main building have just 2 beds. 7, 5-bed bungalows suitable for families & 1, 14-bed chalet are also available. There's internet access, & the cafeteria serves cheap meals, with packed lunches & vegetarian meals on request. *€19.50pp inc bed, b/fast & bedding. Non-members pay €3 extra.*

⋏ **Camping Birkelt** (424 pitches) 1 Um Birkelt, L-7619; ☎ 87 90 41; e info@camping-birkelt.lu; www.birkelt.lu; ⊕ Mar–Oct. In a rural spot just west of Larochette is this large, clean & popular family campsite. All mod cons are provided, including a heated swimming pool & a cybercafé. *€19.50–38 per pitch (varies throughout the season).*

⋏ **Camping Auf Kengert** (180 pitches) L-7633 Larochette/Medernach; ☎ 83 71 86; e info@kengert.lu; www.kengert.lu; ⊕ Mar–Oct. A few kilometres west of Larochette, this large but restful campsite (there's no disco & no entertainments programme) has been in business for 40 years. If you're energetically inclined, it's within an easy hike of Larochette, although it is uphill on the way home. As well as full facilities for family campers, complete with electrical hook-ups (€2 per day extra), on-site shop, swimming pool, etc, there's also a quiet side field for basic camping if you just want to pitch a tent under the trees. They can provide walking maps that begin & end at the campsite, & handy laminated cycling guides, which attach to the front of your bike & feature photographs of major points along the way, so you don't have to keep leaping off to consult a map. The campsite's website has a route description of how to find it. *€10-15pp (varies throughout season).*

✖ WHERE TO EAT

✖ **Op der Bleech** 4 pl Bleech; ☎ 87 80 58; www.opderbleech.lu; ⊕ 12.00–14.30 & 18.00–21.00 Thu–Mon, closed Christmas/mid-Jan & 2 weeks in Sep. The restaurant of the eponymous auberge has tasty French–Luxembourgish dishes that will satisfy appetites & taste buds without breaking the bank. Unusually, the w/day *menu du jour* is available in the evenings as well as the

---

THE VILLAGE THAT ISN'T

Meysembourg, a tiny hamlet just west of Larochette, occupies a unique page in Luxembourg's history. There was a time when it was a small yet prosperous place, but things turned sour in 1846. Out of personal greed, the local lord of the manor, Franz Reuter de Heddesdorf, engineered a situation whereby all the local farmers owed him money at exorbitant rates of interest. He then foreclosed, forcing them to sell their land and property. Out of protest, the entire population – 12 families totalling 68 people – upped sticks and left as one, taking their remaining possessions with them to Antwerp and emigrating *en masse* via the Red Star Line to America. They all finished up in the town of New Riegel, Ohio.

With the landlord abandoned, the village fell into neglect and all but disappeared. All that remains is the current manor house (*not open to the public*), which is impressive enough, but only dates from the 1880s, and a few other buildings to serve as a reminder of the past. The population of today's Meysembourg can best be described as 'a few'. Even the pot-holed road leading from nearby Angelsbourg is testament to a century of neglect – if you think a 30km/h speed limit on a deserted and straight country lane is overkill, just wait till you see how your car bounces around if you decide to exceed it!

normal lunchtime-only deal. There's unobtrusive background music, & garish tartan curtains (all right, so you can't win 'em all), along with the traditional tiled floors & wood-beamed ceiling. The meat dishes are heavily biased towards veal, which is apparently what the (mainly Dutch) clientele want. Service is friendly though, & there's a floral theme throughout, with paintings of flowers on the walls & real ones in the windows. €€–€€€

✗ **Op der Millen** 50 rue de Larochette, Medernach; ✆ 26 87 37 40; ◷ 12.00–14.00 & 18.00–21.30 Tue–Sun. On the main road 1km north of Larochette, this restaurant is in an imposing old building. Wood-beamed ceilings & glossy tiled floors dominate the décor. Half the menu covers the usual French–Luxembourgish fare, but other dishes reflect the owner's

Portuguese roots, including grilled squid & *bacalhau* (salt cod). The riverside terrace has great views, although the proximity of the main road takes the edge off the idyll. €€–€€€

✗ **Hua Ting** 23 pl Bleech; ✆ 83 76 92; ◷ 12.00–14.00 & 18.00–22.00 daily. For those craving variety from the standard European menus found in most Larochette restaurants, this is your means of escape. It serves fairly standard Cantonese food, but can nonetheless be a relief from all that very rich (however delicious) local fare. €€

⊑ **Café de la Place** 5 pl Bleech; ✆ 87 91 69; ◷ until late. This cheap & cheerful café offers simple snacks such as *croque monsieur* for just a few euros, & fuller meals for not a great deal more. The square is a pleasant place to sit outside should the weather behave. €–€€€

SHOPPING For cheap snacks and stocking up for picnics, try the **Fischer bakery** (*6 pl Bleech;* ✆ *87 92 77*). For other basic supplies there's a small grocery, the **Epicerie Self-Service** (*16 rue de Mersch;* ✆ *87 91 68*).

OTHER PRACTICALITIES
Medical
✚ **Pharmacie de Larochette** 7 rue de Medernach; ✆ 83 70 18; ◷ 08.30–12.00 & 14.00–18.30 Mon–Fri, 08.30–12.00 Sat

Banks
$ **BGL BNP Paribas Bank** 14 pl Bleech; ✆ 42 42 20 00; ◷ 09.00–12.00 & 13.30–16.30 Mon–Fri

$ **Spuerkeess ('S-Bank')** 1 pl de la Gare; ✆ 83 70 33; ◷ 08.15–11.45 & 13.30–17.00 Mon–Fri

Post office
✉ **Post office** 8 rue de Medernach; ✆ 83 71 36 31; ◷ 08.30–12.00 & 13.30–17.00 Mon–Fri

WHAT TO SEE AND DO
Larochette Castle (*Château de Larochette;* ✆ *83 74 97; www.larochette.lu;* ◷ *Easter–31 Oct 10.00–18.00 daily; adult/child €3/1*) One of the country's more impressive medieval piles, Larochette Castle has been partially restored. Built in the 11th century, it was expanded gradually, and by the end of the 14th century there were no fewer than five manor houses within its walls. One of these, the Créhange house (dating from 1385), was restored during the 1980s and is the giant building on the sandstone promontory that looms impressively over Larochette today. Pictures in its various rooms offer an artist's impression of what life was like in the days of yore, without the need for wordy captions. Some rooms are also used for temporary exhibitions. The castle as a whole was destroyed by fire in the 15th century, and besides the Créhange house and some emergency work to shore up the neighbouring Hombourg house, most of it remains a crumbling ruin. You can drive up to the front door (follow the signs), but a better alternative is to walk along rue de Mersch and after 100m head up the path on the right (signposted). This loops around through the woods and emerges by the castle entrance in a matter of minutes.

The castle has a great view over Larochette, but for an even better **panorama** that includes the castle, turn left past the town map at the bottom of rue de Mersch, then take the steps heading up and to the right after 100m. Cross the car park and follow the path, then a steep wooden staircase, up through the rocks to an old stone house guarding the entrance to the valley opposite the castle.

It's possible to continue along the paths leading into the woods away from the watchtower, which link up with the spidery web of trails lacing across the country. Ask in the tourist office and they'll furnish you with a map.

INDUSTRIAL MUSEUM (*Musée de l'Industrie*) At the lower end of rue de Mersch, the museum has a small collection of old sewing machines and industrial looms retrieved from woollen and textile mills in the regions as they closed down. There's no entrance fee and more to the point, there's no entrance, nor any opening times – instead you can view the displays at any time of day or night by peering through the windows: one on rue de Mersch itself, the other around the corner on Chemin J-A Zinnen. It's located in the centre of Larochette, by that most trusty of reference points, the town map.

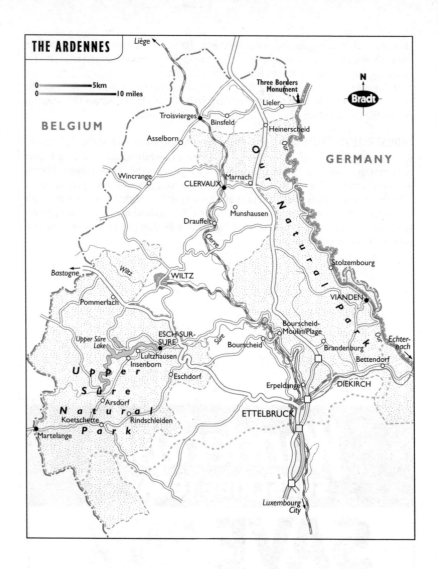

THE ARDENNES

0 _____ 5km
0 _____ 10 miles

N

Bradt

Liège

Three Borders
Monument

BELGIUM

Lieler

Troisvierges

Binsfeld

Heinerscheid

Our

GERMANY

Asselborn

Wincrange

Marnach

CLERVAUX

Munshausen

Drauffelt

Clerve

N a t u r a l   P a r k

Stolzembourg

Bastogne

Wiltz

WILTZ

VIANDEN

Pommerlach

Bourscheid-
Moulin/Plage

*Upper Sûre
Lake*

ESCH-SUR-
SURE

Sûre

Bourscheid

Brandenburg

*Echter-
nach*

Lultzhausen

Insenborn

Bettendorf

U p p e r

Eschdorf

Erpeldange

DIEKIRCH

S û r e

ETTELBRUCK

N a t u r a l

Arsdorf

Koetschette

Rindschleiden

P a r k

Martelange

*Luxembourg
City*

8

The Ardennes

You'll kick yourself if you miss northern Luxembourg. Compact Clervaux, home to the world's most important photographic exhibition, and beautiful Vianden with its jaw-dropping castle, are already reason enough to visit. But there's also Esch-sur-Sûre, a village so attractive it just begs to grace the cover of 1,000 jigsaws; and Bourscheid Castle, which dominates the local landscape. Not forgetting all the museums commemorating the Battle of the Ardennes, the undoubted star of which is in Diekirch. Add to that mix the breathtaking scenery and a string of fascinating rural museums and you could spend weeks exploring.

The Luxembourg Ardennes, known locally as the 'Eisléck' or 'Oesling', covers the northern third of the country. It's a rural world of gently rolling plateaux covered in farmland, cut by deep valleys where the often narrow floors are mainly pastoral, and the sheer slopes on either side are covered with dense forest. Most of the upper plateau is around 500m above sea level, making the highest point in the country, at 580m, barely noticeable above the rest.

Many towns are located low in the valleys, and are often invisible from the major roads that follow the flatter world across the high plateau. Someone driving through this landscape of fields, trees, and only the odd village could be forgiven for thinking hardly anyone lived here at all. It's only when you descend to the lower level you realise there's a whole string of thriving urban centres, albeit tiny by any scale other than Luxembourg's.

One other thing you'll notice is how wonderfully quiet most of the rural highways are. Even though it covers an area the size of Greater London, this region is practically deserted by comparison, and it makes getting around an absolute joy. The winding roads that zigzag up and down between successive river valleys are great for mountain biking, and especially popular with touring motorcyclists (as is the scarcity of traffic police, although I could never responsibly endorse that as a reason to go) – many hotels here actively welcome bikers.

In a country full of walking routes, this region is particularly well set up for hikers. Practically every commune (local district) and village produces its own trail maps. There are even two circuits for those who want a long-distance point-to-point walk with a baggage-carrying service thrown in. There are also 15 marked mountain-biking trails, covering a total distance of 300km. This isn't the sort of terrain I'd recommend for normal bikes, however, as there's a little too much steep up and down for casual pedalling. A book of bike routes, titled *Mountain Bike Tour: Luxembourg Ardennes* (see *Appendix 2, Further Information*, page 229), is produced by local publisher Editions Guy Binsfeld and is available in local bookshops for €12. Maps are also available for €5.

Finally, a personal observation: I've visited the Ardennes on many occasions and am yet to enjoy a visit when it stayed dry throughout. There appears to be a local microclimate at work, presumably as a result of it being the first major area of upland that North Sea weather systems encounter after passing over low-lying Belgium and the Netherlands. Indeed, the statistics show it receives some 100–200mm more rain and is one or two degrees colder than the southern half of the country. Take waterproofs and/or an umbrella, and don't say I didn't warn you!

HISTORY

That the Ardennes was always much fought over is evidenced by the plethora of heavily fortified castles that dot the landscape. But the events of medieval times pale in comparison with what occurred during the mid 20th century. While all of Luxembourg was occupied by the Nazis during World War II, it was this region that suffered most, especially during the ultimately fruitless German counterattack of December 1944 and January 1945 (see box, page 174). When you look at photographs taken in the immediate aftermath of the Ardennes offensive, it's hard to imagine how anyone could have survived the experience. But survive they did, and they also rebuilt and prospered.

There's a lingering sense of gratitude throughout Luxembourg towards the American liberators, but in the north, which had to be liberated twice, the bonds are especially strong. Across the Ardennes you'll see old anti-tank guns and other war memorabilia standing by the roadside, and memorials to the tragic events of a not-so-distant past. American visitors are often surprised to see the Stars and Stripes fluttering happily alongside the Luxembourg flag at many of these sites.

Nevertheless, the services are being toned down as the memory fades. While it will never be forgotten, there's a sense that the 60th anniversary in 2004–05 drew a line under the past, and now is the time to move on. The focus today is on recording and documenting the events accurately for future generations, recognising that *everyone* suffered. That's seen as the best way to rebuild ties and ensure the mistakes made back then are never repeated.

HOLLYWOOD'S WAR

Several major American films have depicted the Battle of the Ardennes. The most famous is probably *Battle of the Bulge* (1965), a big-budget all-star epic starring Henry Fonda and Robert Shaw. However, as well meaning as it might be, it does bend reality in search of spectacle. Not least of all, most of the big tank battle sequences take place on what appears to be the wide-open spaces and arid plains of central Spain, an area that looks nothing remotely like the moist hilly forests of the Ardennes. There isn't a great deal of snow in it either. The epic 1970 biopic *Patton* with George C Scott also mentions the campaign briefly, but barely more convincingly, as part of a wider canvas. Arguably the best portrayal is the 1949 offering, *Battleground*, which focuses mainly on General McAuliffe's stirring defence of the Belgian town of Bastogne (see page 217), during which he made the most famous and succinct refusal to surrender speech in history, simply saying 'Nuts!' Although this movie was largely filmed in a studio, they did at least make the effort to put some trees and fake snow on the ground. Moreover, since it was made just four years after the actual events, veterans of the battle appear as extras and worked as advisors on the set. But it is a tad annoying that they keep referring to the town they are defending as 'Bass-tone' (it's 'Bass-tonyuh').

The north is relatively sparsely populated, and public transport connections tend to reflect this. Wiltz, Clervaux, Ettelbruck and Diekirch all have **train** stations. To reach Vianden on public transport you'll need to catch a **bus** from Ettelbruck, Diekirch or Clervaux. Esch-sur-Sûre is connected to Ettelbruck by bus, but few other places. If you plan to do a lot of exploring, and I heartily recommend that you do, then unless you have time, patience and dedication, **driving** yourself is the most realistic option. **Taxi** companies are often single-person, single-vehicle operations, so your chances of finding one depends on their availability.

VIANDEN

Nestled in a steep valley on the banks of the Our River, Vianden's setting alone would make it worth visiting. But the addition of one of Europe's most impressive medieval castles, perched on a rock gazing imperiously down over the small town, sends its tourism credentials rocketing skyward. When you add the museums, churches, views, and an adventure rope garden for the restless, it becomes somewhere no-one should miss. It may not cover a huge area, but it packs an awful lot into a tiny space, and in-between are at least a dozen hotels and an even greater choice of eateries.

One thing you may notice is that the vast majority of your fellow visitors are Dutch. They clearly know what the rest of the world is just waking up to. Many signs and menus are designed in response to this, and aimed to appeal to Dutch tastes. You're as likely to be greeted with a '*goedemiddag*' as you enter a restaurant here as you are a '*Bonjour*' or '*Moïen*'.

The local population certainly enjoy throwing a party and dressing up. All manner of special rituals, festivals and markets are held throughout the year, and if your arrival coincides with one of these it'll add an extra dimension to your visit – see *Entertainment and festivals*, page 180.

Walking around Vianden presents the visitor with something of an enigma. It's one of Luxembourg's most-visited spots, and deservedly so. The main streets in the centre are lined with bars, hotels, cafés and restaurants. There are places modelled on Swiss chalets, with eateries serving cheese fondue to perpetuate the illusion, and a chairlift to carry you up to a lofty viewpoint. On that one hand this is full-on Touristville. Yet take two steps down practically any side street and it's as if you've been transported to another world: into a quiet rural village with cobbled streets, where the smell of wood smoke lingers in the air even in summer, and where you feel that to breathe too heavily would disturb the sleeping dogs. The two conflicting halves together are what make Vianden such a vital and enjoyable place to be.

HISTORY Vianden's history inevitably revolves around that of its castle, and the rock on which it stands – its original name, Viennensis (or Vienna), is even thought to derive from *vien*, the Celtic word for 'rock'. While the Romans had left their mark and established a small fort, the town really took off when the Counts of Vianden built a castle here between the 11th and 14th centuries.

It didn't take long for trouble to brew. In 1248, Count Henry I of Vianden invited the Trinitarians to celebrate Mass in the castle chapel, as a gesture of thanks for brokering the release of his father Frederic II, who'd been taken prisoner whilst on a crusade. This act greatly offended the local Templars, who'd previously been authorised to hold services there, and they petitioned the pope to have Henry excommunicated. Seeking a compromise, the Archbishop of Trier split Vianden into two parishes. The Templars retained the lower town on the left bank of the river, where they founded the St Nicholas Church. Meanwhile, the castle chapel became the parish church of the upper town, until a new Trinitarian church was completed several years later.

Somehow the two disparate halves got along, and Vianden's town charter was granted in 1308, giving its citizens the same status as those in Trier, then the most powerful city in the region. Already protected by the castle, the town was now enclosed by ramparts with 24 guard towers and five city gates. Throughout the Middle Ages Vianden county covered an area as large as today's Luxembourg, and stretched as far as Bitburg in modern Germany. At its peak in the 15th century the town was thriving thanks to its craftsmen. Seven guilds were formed: the coopers, drapers, goldsmiths, locksmiths, masons, tailors and tanners. The tanners were the most powerful, and turned leather production into a major local industry, which survived until the 1950s.

But the good times didn't last. When the Nassau family inherited the county in the late 15th century, they considered it a minor plaything, moved out of the castle and ruled by proxy through bailiffs. The French, who occupied Luxembourg in 1794, dealt a further blow by abolishing the county altogether. Then a final

A WASTE OF LIFE

The Battle of the Ardennes, or Battle of the Bulge as it's popularly known, was a desperate final throw of the dice by an already defeated regime. The Nazi goal was to split the Allied line in half, capturing Antwerp, and forcing the Allies to negotiate a peace treaty in German favour. After their breakout from Normandy in 1944, the Allies had advanced faster than anticipated. This created enormous supply problems, slowing them down, and the Nazis seized on this weakness. Their assault began on 16 December 1944, achieving near total surprise. At the time, snowstorms in the area were keeping Allied aircraft grounded, but they also proved troublesome for the Nazis because poor road conditions hampered their movements.

The Allies were quick to respond, and within a week 250,000 reinforcement troops had arrived, halting the advance just short of the Meuse River in Belgium on Christmas Eve. Led by General Patton, the counter-attack came in early January, with the aim of cutting off the Germans and trapping them in a pocket. The temperature was unseasonably low, and trucks had to be run every half hour otherwise their oil would freeze, and weapons would jam. But the battle went on, and late in the month the objectives were realised.

The exact number of casualties may never be known. At least 8,500 Americans perished, with another 21,000 missing, presumed dead. Around 20,000 Germans died, not counting the 32,000 recorded as 'missing'. There were also 1,000 British victims, as well as almost 4,000 Belgian and Luxembourgish civilians who were caught in the middle. It was the bloodiest battle that US forces experienced in World War II. And as a result of artillery bombardments, countless villages and towns in Luxembourg and eastern Belgium were virtually wiped off the map. All because a select few in the Nazi high command had refused to accept defeat as inevitable. And what did it achieve? Nothing. In the end it served little purpose other than to prolong the war, and cause untold suffering on both sides.

insult was served in 1820 when the castle's owner, William I, first Grand Duke of Luxembourg, sold it on the cheap to a local merchant, who in turn went about zealously asset-stripping the building, literally selling it stone by stone and reducing it to a ruin. In the end, the slide was only halted when then Grand Duke Jean gave the castle to the state in 1977, and a major restoration project got under way.

GETTING THERE The quickest way to reach Vianden from Luxembourg City – the whole journey takes less than an hour – is to catch the **train** to Ettelbruck, followed by **bus** 570 (two every hour). The bus also passes through Diekirch. There are a handful of direct connections to other parts of the country from Vianden: for example bus 663 runs to Clervaux four times a day.

GETTING AROUND Since it consists of no more than a handful of partly cobbled streets, you won't get lost in Vianden. Getting around **on foot** is simple, although the slog up to the castle can be heavy going after a long Luxembourg lunch. It's easy to figure out where you are: if walking on the flat you're probably on rue de la Gare or rue Victor Hugo; if walking on a slope you're almost certainly on Grand Rue. The old stone bridge across the Our forms the centrepiece of the town. If you do somehow lose your bearings just look up, as the castle dominates the skyline from virtually everywhere.

If you feel the need to let someone else transport you, there's always '*Benni*', the miniature **tourist 'train'** (m *621 26 71 41; www.benni-vianden.lu*). Round trips lasting 30 minutes depart from beside the Our Bridge (*May–Sep from 11.00 Tue–Sun; adult/child €6/3, 20% discount with Luxembourg Card*).

Guided **walking tours** can be arranged through Guides Touristiques des Ardennes (\ *84 93 25 27*; e *guides.ardennes@vo.lu*). Costs vary according to length and number of people.

To venture further afield, you can rent a **bike** from the Hotel Petry (\ *83 41 42*) or from the bus station (*Location de Vélos*; \ *26 87 41 57*).

TOURIST INFORMATION
🛈 Tourist office Right by the bridge in the town centre, 1a rue du Vieux Marché; \ 83 42 57; www.tourist-info-vianden.lu; ⏱ 08.00–12.00 & 13.00–17.00 Mon–Fri, 10.00–14.00 Sat–Sun & public holidays

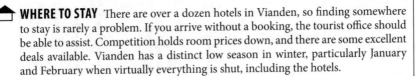

WHERE TO STAY There are over a dozen hotels in Vianden, so finding somewhere to stay is rarely a problem. If you arrive without a booking, the tourist office should be able to assist. Competition holds room prices down, and there are some excellent deals available. Vianden has a distinct low season in winter, particularly January and February when virtually everything is shut, including the hotels.

🏠 **Hotel Belle-Vue** (59 rooms) 3 rue de la Gare, L-9420; \ 83 41 27; e info@hotelbv.com; www.hotelbv.com; ⏱ Apr–Dec. Owned by the Petry family, who also run the Hotel Petry (see page 177), the bulk of this large hotel has been extensively renovated along environmental lines. Heating is provided by solar energy where possible, & also by wood-burning stoves in winter. Waste heat from cooling & refrigeration systems is used for water heating. The entire hotel is wheelchair-accessible, & rooms are light, modern & equipped with 'ergonomic' beds (their word), & have free Wi-Fi, safe & refrigerators. Balconies at the back have castle views. There are walk-in showers, bathrooms in the new wing & some have whirlpool baths. They are also equipped with motions sensors, which may plunge you into darkness if you linger. The hotel has an indoor pool, a jacuzzi with changing facilities, 2 saunas & massage rooms. The huge

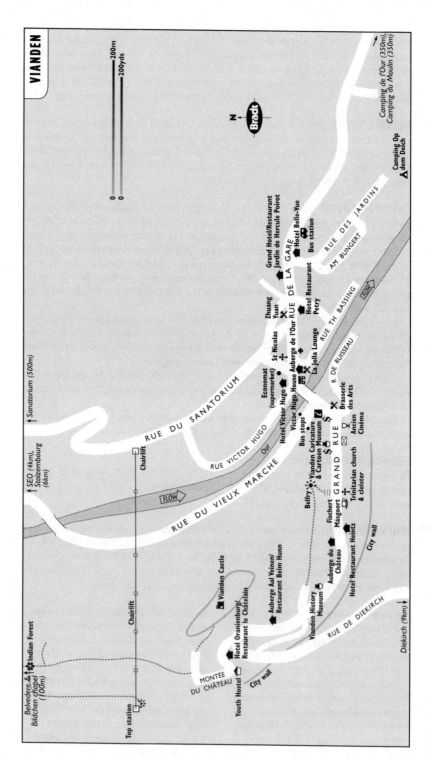

VIANDEN

200m
200yds

Belvedere &
Indian Forest

Bildchen chapel
(100m)

SEO (4km),
Stolzembourg
(6km)

Sanatorium (500m)

Top station

Chairlift

Chairlift

RUE DU SANATORIUM

RUE DU VIEUX MARCHE

RUE VICTOR HUGO

Our

FLOW

Economat
(supermarket)

St Nicolas

Hotel Victor Hugo

Auberge de l'Our

Zhuang
Yuan

RUE DE LA GARE

La Jolla Lounge

Grand Hotel/Restaurant
Jardin de Hercule Poirot

Hotel Belle-Vue

Bus station

RUE DES JARDINS

AM BUNGERT

Hotel Restaurant
Petry

RUE TH BASSING

EOW

R. DE RUISSEAU

Brasserie
des Arts

Ancien
Cinéma

Bus stops

Vianden Caricature
& Cartoon Museum

GRAND RUE

Trinitarian church
& cloister

Belfry

Fischert

Masgoort

Vianden History
Museum

Auberge du
Château

Hotel Restaurant Heintz

City wall

RUE DE DIEKIRCH

Diekirch (9km)

Vianden Castle

Auberge Aal Veinen/
Restaurant Beim Hunn

Hotel Oranienburg/
Restaurant le Châtelain

Youth Hostel

MONTÉE
DU CHÂTEAU

City wall

Camping de l'Our (350m),
Camping du Moulin (350m)

Camping Op
dem Deich

N

Bradt

176

terrace can seat 160 & still has space to squeeze in a giant ornamental fountain at its centre. €

🏠 **Auberge Aal Veinen** (9 rooms) 114 Grand Rue, L-9411; 🗞 83 43 68; e ahahn@pt.lu; www.hotel-aal-veinen.lu. The smell of wood smoke may permeate up from the grill restaurant below this lovely little auberge, on the long street leading up to the castle. The building dates from 1683, & it shows in the charmingly authentic interior – rooms on the top floor have sloping ceilings, wooden roof beams, black tiled floors & half-timbered walls. The furnishings are more modern & comfortable, but blend well with the old setting. The bathrooms are also top notch. The auberge bills itself as 'biker-friendly', offering a secure garage for motorbikes & a drying room with tumble dryer. No lift. Free Wi-Fi is available. €€

🏠 **Grand Hotel du Vianden** (57 rooms) 6 rue de la Gare, L-9420; 🗞 83 41 70; e hotviand@ pt.lu; www.grandhotelvianden.com. The second of Vianden's 'big' hotels. Standard rooms are fairly basic, but better options have balconies, whirlpool baths, jacuzzis, minibar, internet & castle views, in a variety of combinations. Guests can make use of the sauna, solarium & whirlpool bath. Private parking (free) is available. €€

🏠 **Hotel Auberge du Château** (42 rooms) 74–80 Grand Rue, L-9401; 🗞 83 45 74; e chateau@pt.lu; www.auberge-du-chateau. lu; ⏰ mid-Feb to Nov. The auberge has been run by the Nelissen family for 35 years. Tastefully decorated rooms abound with light colours & abstract art on the walls. The terrace at the back has fine views. The hotel seeks to appeal to cycling & mountain-biking groups by offering a laundry service, plus a storeroom with bike-washing facilities. A secure garage is available for cycles & motorbikes. Dogs are allowed in the rooms (1 per room, €5 per night). €€

🏠 **Hotel Oranienburg** (26 rooms) 126 Grand Rue, L-9411; 🗞 83 41 531; e info@ hoteloranienburg.com; www.hoteloranienburg. com; ⏰ Apr to mid-Nov. Run by the Hoffman family for 3 generations, the Oranienburg occupies a fabulous site just below the castle entrance. Needless to say the view is stunning. Rooms are comfortable & brightly decorated. HB & FB packages are available, which are worth considering as the hotel's restaurant is one of the best in town. Other facilities include a solarium, garden & bar with terrace. €€

🏠 **Hotel Petry** (26 rooms) 15 rue de la Gare, L-9420; 🗞 83 41 22; e hotel.petry@pt.lu; www. hotel-petry.com; ⏰ Mar–Dec. Rooms in this friendly, family-run hotel are spacious & lightly furnished with vinyl floors. The bathrooms are spotless. The best room has a jacuzzi. The Petry prides itself on its green credentials & besides the usual imploring of guests not to want the towels changed every day, the toilets are flushed from an environmentally sound 20,000-litre rainwater tank. Staff are helpful & knowledgeable, & the hotel is fully wheelchair-accessible. You can rent bikes here, or try out the sauna, steam bath, solarium or fitness centre. Between the hotel's 2 good restaurants (see *Where to eat*, page 179) is a snug little bar – the perfect place for a nightcap, with a wood-burning stove. €€

🏠 **Hotel Restaurant Heintz** (30 rooms) 55 Grand Rue, L-9410; 🗞 83 41 55; e hoheintz@ pt.lu; www.hotel-heintz.lu; ⏰ May–Oct. Another cosy, family-run outfit, next to the Trinitarian church. Clean, large, quiet rooms have laminate or carpet floors & are decorated in light shades. The bright modern duvets in the rooms help to balance some of the stuffier period furniture in the public areas. Rooms at the back have balconies with window boxes. The leafy garden terrace would be an escape from the traffic, if Vianden had any. Parking is behind the hotel, with a garage for motorbikes. €€

🏠 **Hotel Victor Hugo** (20 rooms) 1 rue Victor Hugo, L-9414; 🗞 83 41 601; e info@ hotelvictorhugo.lu; www.hotel-victor-hugo.lu; ⏰ mid-Mar to Dec. Bright, friendly & right in the heart of Vianden. Rooms are decorated in warm, cheerful shades of peach. Bathrooms are very clean, but could perhaps do with a 21st-century makeover. Other facilities include a sauna & solarium. The lively bar downstairs, also popular with locals, has a rather-too-large-for-the-room tree in its centre. You may have to wrestle with the foliage to reach a table. A secluded garden terrace at the back has a fabulous view of the castle. The enormous b/fast room doubles as the restaurant at lunch & dinner. Some rooms have balconies. €€

🏠 **Auberge de l'Our** (9 rooms) 35 rue de la Gare, L-9420; 🗞 83 46 75; e info@ aubergevianden.lu; www.aubergevianden.lu; ⏰ mid-Feb to Dec. At the cheaper end of the scale, this 2-star place offers basic accommodation in a great spot by the bridge at the very heart of the town. Rooms are comfortable, but you may want to pack a pair of sunglasses to deal with glare from those dazzlingly bright blue & yellow duvets. No lift. *With shared bathroom €; with en suite €€*

🏠 **Vianden Youth Hostel** (66 beds) 3 Montée du Château, L-9408; 83 41 77; e vianden@youthhostels.lu; www.youthhostels. lu; closed 2 weeks around Christmas/New Year, & 1 week in Feb. Backpackers & budget-minded travellers will be happy to note Vianden has another of Luxembourg's 'hostels in tremendous locations'; this one a few metres from the castle. In a traditional old house, it has been completely renovated & is suitable for individuals, families & groups. Rooms have 2–12 beds & are spread over 2 floors, with bathrooms on each level. The canteen provides packed lunches & vegetarian meals on request. *€17.50pp, inc bed, b/fast & bedding. Non-members pay €3 extra.*

🏕 **Camping de l'Our** (120 pitches) 3 route de Bettel, L-9401; 83 45 05; e campingour@ pt.lu; www.camping-our-vianden.lu; ⊕ Apr–Oct. About 1km out of town, by the Our River. Pitch your tent by the water & hear it gurgling past the flysheet as you slumber. On-site facilities include clean showers, washing machines & a café/ restaurant. *€5pp, plus €5 per pitch; electricity €2.20.*

🏕 **Camping du Moulin** (160 pitches) route de Bettel, L-9401; 83 45 01; e info@ campingdumoulin.lu; www.campingdumoulin. lu; ⊕ May–Sep. Next door to the Camping de l'Our, this also enjoys a riverside location around a 10min walk from the action. Laundry facilities, clean showers & a bar are all available. *€6pp, plus €5 per pitch.*

🏕 **Camping Op dem Deich** (200 pitches) 3 route de Bettel, L-9401; 83 45 75; e campingour@pt.lu; www. campingopdemdeich.lu; ⊕ Apr–Sep. Completing Vianden's trilogy of campsites, this has laundry facilities & clean shower blocks, but little else. No matter, as the northernmost pitches are only a few steps from the town centre, where you'll find everything you need. Like its neighbours, this is also on the riverbank. *€6pp, plus €5 per pitch.*

Cottages & chalets Contact Famille Petry, 7 An der Gaessel, L-9452 Bettel; 83 41 87; e petryjac@pt.lu; www.chaletpetry.com. If you plan to stay awhile & want an even quieter location close to Vianden, there is good *gîte*-style accommodation in the little village of Bettel, 2km away in the direction of Echternach. Chalets & cottages sleep 2–8. *€230–275 w/ end, €280–495 per week, excluding €40 cleaning costs.*

✖ **WHERE TO EAT** Many restaurants here are associated with hotels and may also close in winter.

Expensive

✖ **Restaurant le Châtelain** 126 Grand Rue; 83 41 531; www.hoteloranienburg.com; ⊕ Apr to mid-Nov 11.30–15.00 & 17.00–21.00 daily. The Hotel Oranienburg's restaurant is the top eating spot in town – quite literally, as it also sits at the upper end of Grand Rue. Chef-hotelier Jean-Paul Hoffmann creates delightful menus with a decidedly French tinge that reflect the seasons. The gastronomic menu is on the pricey side, but if your budget stretches that far it's a foodie's delight, & the service is impeccable. If not, there are plenty of à la carte alternatives to suit all tastes. The wine list has some good-value choices. The hotel's bar/brasserie menu (also served on the terrace; €€–€€€) is simpler & cheaper. *€€€€–€€€€€*

Upmarket

✖ **Beim Hunn** 114 Grand Rue; 83 43 68; www.hotel-aal-veinen.lu; ⊕ 12.00–15.00 & 18.00–22.00 daily, closed Tue out of season. You'll smell the charcoal wood smoke emerging from the kitchen of the auberge Aal Veinen well before you get here. The pretty bar & restaurant area, dimly lit by candles & sprawling over 2 floors, is an enjoyable place to eat, & service is brisk & friendly. Blackened oak beams & pillars are everywhere, as is the cockerel motif, whether embroidered, engraved, sculpted or stuffed. The house special is spare ribs cooked over a charcoal grill. Other fare includes fondues: cheese overdoses can be ordered individually, but the meat-laden *fondue bourguignonne* requires a min of 2 people. The steaks are also good. If you've still got room after tackling one

Mid range

✕ **Au Jardin de Hercule Poirot** 6 rue de la Gare; ☎ 83 41 70; www.grandhotelvianden.com; ⏰ 12.00–14.00 & 18.00–21.00 daily. Located in the Grand Hotel, 'In Hercule Poirot's Garden' (no, I don't get the connection either) serves up the usual mixture of French & Luxembourgish meat & fish dishes, including Ardennes ham. The hotel café serves lighter snacks (€–€€€) & has a large terrace. €€€

✕ **Belle-Vue** 3 rue de la Gare; ☎ 83 41 27; www.hotelbv.lu; ⏰ Apr–Dec 12.00–14.30 & 18.00–21.30 daily. Another of those tiled floor, curtained, beige tablecloth joints that quickly become familiar in the Ardennes. The French–Luxembourgish fare includes Ardennes pâté, plus local trout. Bring an appetite. Mains include a free trip to the salad bar, adorned with sporting trophies won by the local fishing club. A simpler menu is available all day in the bar & on the terrace. €€€

✕ **Petry Restaurant & Pizzeria** 15 rue de la Gare; ☎ 83 41 22; www.hotel-petry.com; ⏰ mid-Feb to Dec 12.00–14.30 & 18.00–21.00 Wed–Mon. The Hotel Petry runs 2 separate restaurants. The more down-to-earth pizzeria is an excellent economical choice with friendly service, offering a large range of tasty pasta & pizza dishes for under €10. The interior designers seem to be going for log-cabin chic here, with false wooden walls & ceilings, although the slate tile floors are a nice touch. The more upmarket traditional restaurant a few metres away has old-style décor with undressed stone walls,

Cheap and cheerful

✕ **Heintz** 55 Grand Rue; ☎ 83 41 55; www.hotel-heintz.lu; ⏰ Apr–Oct 11.30–14.00 & 17.30–20.30 Thu–Tue, closed Thu lunch out of season. Adding to Vianden's somewhat surreal Swiss-wannabe charms, the Heintz is another place where the house speciality is cheese fondue. Other choices bring diners a little closer to home, by including such Ardennes classics as ham, chips & salad, & locally caught trout. There's also a healthy selection of vegetarian options. €€

of the carnivorous onslaughts, there's a fine selection of single-malt Scotches behind the bar. €€€–€€€€

half-timbered walls & wooden ceilings. Quietly unobtrusive background music helps create a restrained air while the service is friendly & efficient. Outside is an expansive terrace. The menu is a mixture of middle-European tourist fare (veal), French dishes (steak & fish), a good choice of filling salads & Luxembourgish specialities including Ardennes ham, trout & *paschtéitchen*. There are even a few vegetarian options. Like the hotel bar, the restaurant also has a wood-burning stove. *Restaurant* €€–€€€; *pizzeria* €–€€

✕ **Victor Hugo** 1 rue Victor Hugo; ☎ 83 41 601; www.hotel-victor-hugo.lu; ⏰ mid-Mar to Jan 12.00–14.30 & 18.00–21.00 daily. '*Régale si tu peux, et mange si tu l'oses*' – 'Treat if you can, eat if you dare,' wrote Victor Hugo. Unsurprisingly, the restaurant that bears his name, just across from where he lodged, contains mementoes everywhere, from quotations on the walls to portraits. The large dining room (it can seat 150 if you fancy bringing friends & throwing a banquet) is comfortably opulent, with linen tablecloths, candelabras & creaky floorboards adding to the ambiance; plus a large open fireplace for autumn evenings. A massive painting covering one entire end wall evokes a Parisian street of the 1870s. Service is brisk & efficient, & the menu a good choice of hearty & filling French & Luxembourgish dishes, including Ardennes ham & *judd mat gaardebounen*. Bar meals are served all day. €€–€€€

✕ **La Jolla Lounge** 35 rue de la Gare; ☎ 52 56 55; www.lajollalounge.com; ⏰ 10.00–22.00 daily. Technically this riverside eatery-cum-café is really just the downstairs of the Restaurant de l'Our, but its ambiance & menu make it completely different. While the upstairs appeals to an older, more traditional clientele, the La Jolla goes for the younger, trendier set. With no indoor area, it consists of a covered upper stone terrace, & a lower level down by the river (umbrella protection only when the elements conspire against you). The view up to the castle is awesome, & candles at dusk add to the scene. Happily the food, while only simple fare including mixed grills, chicken & chips, & pastas & salads, doesn't disappoint either, & the service is cheerfully efficient. The mighty *salade campagnarde* (farmer's salad) is a hefty challenge even for hungry diners. You can also order the charcoal-grilled meats cooked upstairs in the main restaurant (restaurant hours only). €€

✗ **Zhuang Yuan** 8 rue de la Gare; ☎26 87 41 27; ⏱ 11.30–14.00 & 17.30–22.00 daily; closed Mon in low season. Serves filling Cantonese dishes at reasonable rates. It's more or less the same as every other Chinese restaurant you've ever seen in Europe, but is an alternative to all the hotel-based eateries. €€

✗ **Restaurant de l'Our** 35 rue de la Gare; ☎83 46 75; www.aubergevianden.lu; ⏱ 11.30–21.00 daily; closed Thu in low season. A slightly old-fashioned, but undeniably good-value place offering Luxembourgish & tourist fare. The biggest selling points, besides the price, are the panoramic windows looking out over the castle & the river. The menu, available all day in the brasserie, or 12.00–15.00 & 18.00–21.00 in the restaurant, runs the full gamut from hamburgers, through to salads, steaks & Ardennes ham. The house speciality is meats cooked over a charcoal grill (restaurant hours only). You can also buy meats in the adjoining shop (see *Shopping*, opposite). €–€€

Rock bottom

✗ **Brasserie des Arts** 3 Grand Rue; ☎26 87 44 50; ⏱ 10.00–22.00 daily. Come here to satisfy your ice-cream & pancake cravings. Pancakes with sweet fillings start at around €5, & even the more substantial savoury choices will leave your wallet smiling. €

🍽 **Fischer Mäsgoort** 43 Grand Rue; ☎83 41 61; www.fischer.lu; ⏱ 07.00–18.00 daily. By the Trinitarian church, this bakery sells excellent pastries & snacks. The café operates on a self-service basis, & there's a terrace outside where you can devour your purchases. €

ENTERTAINMENT AND FESTIVALS If all the quaint medievalness of Vianden gets too much, take a break in the 21st century at the **Ancien Cinéma** (*23 Grand Rue;* ☎ *26 87 45 32; www.anciencinema.lu;* ⏱ *from 15.00 Tue–Sat, from 11.00 Sun*), an all-in-one arthouse cinema, bar, jazz club and café. The front area has the laid-back feel of a blues/jazz café furnished with eclectic jumble sale cast-off chairs and tables. The back room – the old cinema – still has a screen, and during the day when there are no other events on, it shows silent movies and cartoons. More serious films are shown some evenings. There's occasional live music.

The good burghers of Vianden just love to dust off their finest medieval threads and dress up. And to give themselves every excuse to climb into those pantaloons and suits of armour they've devised all manner of festivals and celebrations throughout the year. Some have ancient origins and are played out to keep old traditions alive; others were cooked up recently to draw in the tourists. All are worth a look if you're in town at the right time.

One unique event is **Jaudes**. On Good Friday each year local children decorate a dog rose bush – also called a Judas tree – with bright ribbons, and then carry it through the streets to commemorate Judas's suicide. Other Catholic celebrations that you'll also find elsewhere in the country include the annual pre-Lent **Carnival**, known here as Fuasicht, and a religious procession in late May or June to mark **Corpus Christi**.

The annual **Medieval Festival** (*Festival Médiéval; www.castle-vianden.lu*) in August is when the gloves really come off. Although a recent invention despite its name, it has grown into Vianden's biggest moneyspinner (see box opposite).

The **Sound and Light Event** (*www.soundandlight.info*) takes place in mid-August, on the Saturday following the Medieval Festival, when the castle is bathed in coloured lights and tickled by lasers to the tune of decidedly un-medieval rock music. The fun kicks off at 22.30, and culminates in a massive firework display.

Held on a Sunday in mid-October (usually the second, but it may move if it clashes with elections), the **Nëssmoort** (*www.nessmoort.lu*), or Nut Market, really does date back centuries, although it only became an established feature on the calendar after World War II. There are 2,000 walnut trees in the surrounding valley, and the harvest from these is sold here, not just as bags of whole nuts (though there are certainly plenty of those), but also as various nut-related food items and intoxicating liqueurs. Other stalls sell sausages and beer, and it's basically one big excuse to eat, drink and be merry. (Warning: this festival may contain nuts.)

Come mid-November things are getting a little chilly in Vianden, but the locals have a special way of warming up. To celebrate **St Martin's Day** (Miertchen) people enjoy walking through the streets in a procession whirling giant flaming balls (made from oil-soaked rags wrapped in chicken wire) around their heads. Embers seem to fly everywhere, and how they don't all end up in the burns unit is a mystery. Or maybe they do, but no-one's letting on so as not to frighten off the tourist trade.

Over the middle weekend in December, the knave and damsel costumes get dusted off for a second outing at the annual **Medieval Christmas Market**.

SHOPPING Vianden's speciality is a sweet walnut liqueur (*nösslikör*), sold and consumed in quantity during the Nut Festival (see above), and available in the shops at other times.

Economat supermarket 1 rue du Sanatorium; ⊕ 09.00–12.00 & 14.00–18.00 Mon, 08.00–12.00 & 14.00–18.00 Tue–Fri, 08.00–12.00 & 14.00–17.00 Sat, 09.00–12.00 Sun. This small supermarket is near the bridge.

Les Saveurs des Ardennes Auberge de l'Our, see *Where to stay*, page 177; ⊕ 09.00–12.00 & 13.00–18.00 daily. A *charcuterie* selling locally produced Ardennes hams, pâtés & sausage, as well as liqueurs & spirits.

MEDIEVAL FESTIVAL

For ten days in early August, folk from all around converge on Vianden and slip into character to recreate an ancient fair as, well, it *might* have been (if you ignore the camera-toting tourists). The town centre is closed to traffic at this time and it gets busy. Clustered around the bridge and lining Grand Rue are stalls selling trinkets, leatherwear, woollens, hats, wooden toy swords, plus sausages and other hot snacks. The swords in particular are always a huge hit (literally) with younger kids. An even bigger hit with everyone is the fine gentleman who can usually be found wandering the streets with a great horned owl (*Bubo virginianus*) perched proudly on one arm. As you enter the castle grounds (normal entry fees apply), things step up a gear. Inside are demonstrations of woodturning, weaving, and a smithy. Better still, if you've ever wanted to know what it's like to wield a lethal weapon (those concerned about health and safety should skip to the next paragraph), for a few euros you can launch a many-pointed sharpened metal axe towards a distant target, or hone your crossbow skills. Within the castle itself are yet more stalls, and regular demonstrations of belly dancing, musicianship, whip cracking, axe wielding and of course, sword fighting by angry young men clad in armour.

OTHER PRACTICALITIES
Medical
✚ **Pharmacie Luc Manderscheid** 27 rue de la Gare; ↘83 46 14; ⊕ 08.30–12.00 Mon–Sat & 13.30–18.00 Mon–Tue & Thu–Fri

Banks
$ **BGL BNP Paribas Bank** 4 Grand Rue; ↘42 42 20 00; ⊕ 09.00–12.00 & 13.30–16.30 Mon–Fri
$ **Dexia Bank ATM** 3 Grand Rue, next to the Brasserie des Arts

$ **Spuerkeess ('S-Bank')** 18 Grand Rue; ↘50 14 78 80; ⊕ 08.15–11.45 & 13.30–17.00 Mon–Fri

Post office
✉ **Post office** 27 Grand Rue; ↘83 41 31; ⊕ 08.00–12.00 & 13.30–17.00 Mon–Fri

WHAT TO SEE AND DO
Vianden Castle (*Château de Vianden;* ↘ *83 41 081 or 84 92 91; www.castle-vianden.lu;* ⊕ *Apr–Sep 10.00–18.00 daily, Mar & Oct 10.00–17.00 daily, Nov–Feb 10.00–16.00 daily, closed 1 Nov, 25 Dec & 1 Jan; adult/child €6/2*) This is a 'can't miss' sight on several levels. For one thing it's visible for miles and you'll spot it long before you arrive in Vianden. More importantly, however, you shouldn't miss it as it's one of northern Europe's largest and most impressive medieval monuments. It also rates among Luxembourg's most popular attractions, with some 200,000 visitors annually.

Building work began in the 11th century and continued for more than 300 years – by the 15th century the castle rivalled almost any in Europe. Unfortunately the Nassau family, who inherited Vianden at this time, didn't really care much for it. They never lived here and governed from afar. But at least it remained intact for 400 years.

A bigger slap in the grand old building's face came in 1820. William I of Orange-Nassau was handed Vianden by the Congress of Vienna in 1815. He promptly cashed in by selling his prize to the highest bidder: a local merchant named Wenceslas Coster. Coster dismantled the castle and sold it, window by door by brick. Too late, William I was forced by public outrage to buy it back – or what remained of it. He reconstructed the chapel in 1851, but most remained a desolate wreck for over a century. Fortunately, a ten-year restoration programme carried out by the government when it acquired the property in 1977 has returned it to something akin to its former glory.

One of the most interesting rooms is the Salle Jemmy Koltz (room 10), which contains photos taken before, during and after the restoration work, clearly showing the transformation and rebirth the building has undergone in the last 30 years. Three models of the castle show it intact in 1643, as it would have appeared to Victor Hugo in 1871 – ie: in its most pitiful state of disrepair – and again as it looks today.

Also of particular note is the unusual split-level chapel. Dedicated to St Anthony, it was not only the castle chapel, but also a church for the local townspeople. Counts and other nobles worshipped on the elaborately painted upper tier, safe and secure in the knowledge they wouldn't be disturbed by the town's oiks and peasants. The latter could access the plain stone lower level directly from the outside, without having to enter the castle and pose a security risk to the resident nobs.

Belfry (*Beffroi; always open; free*) All alone on the end of a rock promontory, below the castle and above the main town, the four-storey belfry or Hockelstour was erected in 1603 as a watchtower. The building itself isn't much to look at, but the panoramic views from outside make the short climb worthwhile. To get there (on foot only) take Montée du Beffroi leading off Grand Rue, then follow the somewhat overgrown gravel path to the end. Alternatively, climb the steps leading up between numbers 58 and 60 Grand Rue, opposite the Trinitarian church (there's no sign).

Vianden History Museum (*Musée d'Histoire de la Ville de Vianden – Musée Veiner; 96–98 Grand Rue;* \ *83 45 81;* ⊕ *Easter–Oct 11.00–17.00 daily; adult/child €3/1.50*) Sprawling over the labyrinthine rooms of two adjacent houses with endearingly creaky floors, this is an eclectic collection linked only by a common Vianden theme. The first section, Beim Becker, is a bakery museum, with waffle irons, bread slicers, and ovens dating from 1950 (the building was once a bakery). A history section follows, beginning in Celtic days and continuing to the present day, via the Counts of Vianden. The final part is devoted to Edmond de la Fontaine (1823–91), who wrote operettas and other light-hearted songs under the pseudonym 'Dicks'. His father was the first Luxembourgish governor of the Grand Duchy, when it was ruled from the Netherlands by Willem II. Dicks himself moved to this house in 1881 and died here ten years later. His songs were written in Luxembourgish and celebrate local life, including tunes about hunting and fishing. He was so celebrated after his death that in 1948 he got to feature on a set of stamps. The museum contrasts period furniture with tableaux and songs from his more famous operettas. The museum courtyard also has mock-up of a blacksmith and a tannery. Explanations are in German, but you can borrow an English translation.

Vianden Caricature and Cartoon Museum (*Musée de la Caricature et du Cartoon de Vianden; 48 Grand Rue;* m *621 283790; www.caricature.eu;* ⊕ *Jun–Aug 13.00–17.00 Tue–Sun; adult/child (under 10) €4/free*) This small museum pretty much does what you expect from the name, displaying the artworks of leading satirists, not just from Luxembourg, but from around the world.

Victor Hugo House (*Maison de Victor Hugo, 37 rue de la Gare;* \ *26 87 40 88; www. victor-hugo.lu;* ⊕ *11.00–17.00 Tue–Sun; adult/youth (13–25)/child €4/3.50/2.50, inc audio guide*) Victor Hugo obviously knew a thing or two about location. The house where he lived for three months in 1871, during his exile from France as a political refugee, has the best view in town. While sitting at a desk by the window, he was inspired by the sight of the then ruined castle to pen a string of poems. The study where he worked has been restored to how it looked in his day. The rest of the

The Ardennes VIANDEN 8

house tells his life story, and contains original manuscripts and documents. One far-sighted letter sent from here in June 1871 talks of the 'United States of Europe', some 85 years before the EU became a reality.

Trinitarian church *(Eglise des Trinitaires; Grand Rue; ⊕ 09.00–18.00 daily; free)*
The church and its adjacent cloister were once the centre of a monastery, founded in 1248. Damaged by fire on several occasions, it closed in 1793 and the building became the parish church. Still one of the country's most significant religious monuments, check out the interior twin-aisled nave with its spectacularly vaulted roof, and the fabulously ornate Rococo altar, dating from 1758. The French organ was installed in 1693 – if you're lucky enough to catch it during a recital, or when the organist is practising, the sound fills the room to haunting effect.

The **cloister** was partially destroyed during the suppression of the monastery in 1793, and only restored in the 1950s. Today it's a place for quiet reflection away from the not-exactly heaving streets, with a small garden and a stone well at its centre. Embedded in the walls are sculptures and tombstones from the churchyard and around the town. In spring and early summer you may find the peace shattered by chattering swallows, which nest in the shelter of the roof beams.

St Nicolas Church *(Eglise St Nicolas; corner of rue du Constitution & rue de la Gare; ⊕ 09.00–18.00 daily; free)* This tiny church is mainly notable today for being very photogenic. It was founded in 1252 by the Templars, as the parish church of the left bank when the town split in two. In the spirit of many old Luxembourgish buildings, this one also had to be rebuilt (in 1724) following a fire. The interior is very simply decorated, and rather cramped.

Chairlift *(Télésiege; 39 rue du Sanatorium; ☎ 83 43 23; ⊕ 10.00–18.30 daily, last descent at 19.00; adult/child €3.50/2 single, €4.80/2.50 return)* For an unbeatable panoramic vista, or simply a cheat's route to higher walking paths through the forest, the alpine-style chairlift whisks you 220m up a near-vertical hillside in five to ten minutes, depending on how many stops are made for younger children to be slipped into safety harnesses. From the top station there's a superb view down over the castle and across miles of Germany and Luxembourg. This lofty perch gives a real sense of how heavily forested the region has somehow managed to remain. A small café at the top sells drinks and snacks if you require refreshment or feel the need for a scenic beer before descending. To get back to river level, either take the easy option and ride the chairlift back the way you came, or walk down one of the (sometimes muddy) trails through the woods. The latter option also allows you to detour via the Indian Forest (see below) or the castle. Of course, if you're feeling particularly masochistic you could always walk up and ride down, but if considering this option do bear in mind there's no ticket office at the top.

Indian Forest *(☎ 83 42 571; m 691 90 12 23; www.vianden-info.lu; ⊕ Apr–Oct 10.00–18.00 daily; adult/child from €16/11, reservation essential, 30% discount with Luxembourg Card, combi tickets with chairlift available)* The Indian Forest 'rope garden' consists of 45 challenges including aerial runways, ropewalks and climbs. They range on the adrenalin scale from tame (to anyone over the age of eight) to mildly hair-raising for adults, but younger visitors will enjoy it most. All elements are fully supervised, and safety harnesses are used throughout, so there's no danger involved (which may limit the excitement for some, but it's better than risking accidents). To get there, it's a ten-minute walk along a forested path from

the castle car park. The route is slightly uphill, but that's as close as cars are allowed. If you prefer walking downhill, take the chairlift to the top and then follow the signposted trail (also ten minutes). You can choose different packages with varying levels of skill and difficulty – a complete circuit takes around two hours. You can also arrange horseriding and kids' quad biking here.

Even if you don't want to visit the Indian Forest, follow the same trails to reach a small **belvedere** just beyond its entrance. From it is a great view down over the lake created by the damming of the Our. A little way along the path to the left is the picturesque woodland **Bildchen Chapel**, and behind it another panoramic lookout.

OUR VALLEY

The steep and beautiful Our Valley (that's 'oor', not 'hour', by the way) picks up the mantle from where the Sûre and the Moselle leave off, forming the northern section of Luxembourg's border with Germany. Besides Vianden – the only urban centre of any significance – the valley is an almost deserted green world where nature still reigns. To reflect this the land here has been given partially protected status and designated as the natural park of the Our, which covers an area of 300km^2 in northeast Luxembourg and also includes areas around Clervaux.

Salmon were once common in the rivers here and were a staple in the diet of the townsfolk of Vianden, but the damming of the rivers with barrages and weirs to harness the water has meant the fish can no longer reach their traditional spawning grounds. Local dietary preferences have had to move on as a result.

GETTING THERE AND AROUND An absence of people means a scarcity of public transport. If you want to see the region by **bus**, route 663 makes the 45-minute journey between Clervaux and Vianden on an occasional basis (€5), following a scenic route along the Our Valley for much of the way.

Getting between Vianden and Stolzembourg is slightly easier as number 570 makes the 6km trip (€1.50) every half-hour throughout the day.

TOURIST INFORMATION For information visit the tourist office in Vianden, or the natural park's website (French or German only) at www.naturpark-our.lu.

 WHERE TO STAY AND EAT Few places in the Our Valley north of Vianden have facilities, other than a smattering of cafés aimed at local customers. It's more convenient to stay in Vianden and make side trips.

OTHER PRACTICALITIES Likewise, for your shopping and banking needs Vianden is where to head for.

WHAT TO SEE AND DO
SEO (*Centrale de Vianden; N10, 4km north of Vianden;* \ *84 90 311; www.seo.lu;* ⊕ *Easter–Sep 10.00–20.00 daily, Oct–Easter 10.00–16.00 daily; free*) Around 4km upriver from Vianden is the huge SEO hydro-electric project. If you believe the space it occupies in the official Vianden guide, this should be as fascinating as everything else in the area combined. It isn't, but it is worth a second glance if you're in the area and/or into ridiculously large feats of engineering. To reach the SEO, drive north from Vianden beside the river Our. Or take bus 570 in the direction of Stolzembourg (twice each hour). The SEO buildings are spread out and the visitors' entrance isn't immediately obvious, so ask the driver to tell you when to get off.

Besides its copper mine, Stolzembourg also booked its place in history for another totally different reason. It was here on 11 September 1944, around 16.30 and some 96 days after the D-Day landings, that Allied troops walked onto German soil for the first time. A small reconnaissance squadron, led by Sergeant Warner W Holzinger of the US Fifth Armoured Division, crossed the Our Bridge to reach the German village of Keppeshausen on the far side. They spent some time reconnoitring pillboxes along the Siegfried Line, then returned to base in Luxembourg. Their initial foray lasted less than two hours, but was hugely significant, making headline news around the world and representing a massive morale boost to the Allies. Today a small **plaque** by the bridge in Stolzembourg provides a somewhat low-key memorial to the momentous occasion.

The SEO was designed solely to cope with peak daytime demands, and works on the same principles as Dinorwig power station in Snowdonia. Water drops 280m from an upper storage lake into a lower one, and the force this creates is harnessed to drive turbines. The same water is then pumped back up at night when demand is lower.

At full whack, the ten turbines process 437m³ of water every second, generating one gigawatt of electrical power. Unfortunately this can only be sustained for 4½ hours before the upper lake is empty. It then takes another 7½ hours to reverse the process and pump all 6.8 million m³ back to the top, ready to repeat the cycle. Raising the water uses more electricity from thermal power stations than the SEO generates, which doesn't seem to make a whole lot of sense from an environmental perspective. The argument is that the thermal power stations would be churning out their excess power at night anyway, as it's more efficient than shutting them down.

The turbine hall and the workings of the power station are hidden deep inside a hill. The visitors' entrance brings you into a 100m tunnel lined with displays explaining the history of hydropower and other forms of green energy. At the far end is a viewing gallery looking out onto the turbine hall: a vast manmade chamber containing nine of the 11 huge turbines (the tenth was added later and is in a second hall, not open to the public; the 11th, a 220MW whopper, was under construction in 2011). Behind you, a second glass window allows you to peek into the control room, with more dials, monitors and flashing lights than you'll find on the bridge of Captain Kirk's *Enterprise*.

Upper basin (*Bassin Supérieur; always open; free*) The basin stores water for the SEO and can also be visited, but don't bother unless you enjoy staring at reservoirs. If you could actually see the water level falling when the turbines are in use, it would have some surrealist appeal, but since you can't the experience is akin to watching wood warp. It's fresh air I suppose, and the steps you need to climb will give your legs a workout. You'll find it a couple of kilometres from Vianden, on the road west out of town. On the plus side there's a café by the car park, to give you a reason to be there.

Stolzembourg Copper Mine (*Mine de Cuivre; meet in the museum (Musée Koffergrouf) at 5a rue Principal, Stolzembourg, at the southern end of the village; www.stolzembourg.lu;* ⊕ *mid-Jul/Aug at 14.00 daily; May/Jun & Sep/Oct 14.00 Sun*

& public holidays only; adult/child €6/3, 30% discount with Luxembourg Card; entry by guided tour only) Copper was mined in Stolzembourg in fits and starts between 1717 and 1943, but was hardly a continuous industry – this mine sometimes closed for decades when it became unprofitable, and only restarted when new technology made it viable once more. Over the centuries it was gradually expanded, and new levels and shafts dug. In the years since it closed for the last time the lower nine levels have flooded, and are deliberately left that way to maintain stability. After sustained heavy rain the water level also rises in the public galleries, and tours may be cancelled – call ahead to confirm if in doubt. Stolzembourg is 6km north of Vianden, and can be reached by car or via bus 570 (twice hourly).

To visit the mine you must join a tour. Don't turn up too early, as there's little else to do in Stolzembourg and the museum building where tours commence may be locked until 15 minutes beforehand. Visits are usually given in German or Dutch, sometimes in French or Luxembourgish – the website has details of which will be used. There's little information in English, but guides can usually add a few comments if you ask. Don't worry though: words become irrelevant once you're inside the mine – this experience requires no subtitles.

You first get to look round the museum (containing ore-bearing rocks and pieces of mining equipment), then watch an introductory DVD explaining the regional geology and the history of the mine. It's then a 20-minute scenic walk up a cutesy valley to reach a small office near the shaft entrance. Here you'll be kitted out with wellies, hard hat and plastic waterproof coat. You may look daft and feel stupid, but trust me: all three are utterly essential.

Finally you enter the mine proper. If it hasn't rained for a long time you may get to walk through a dry rock passage, but this is unlikely. More often than not you'll part wade, part negotiate a plankwalk along an extremely narrow, low-ceilinged tunnel in which the Vietcong would feel at home. The rocky roof is rough-hewn and uneven, and if you are of average height you will need to stoop most of the way to minimise the number of times you bang your head. But no matter how much care you take, collisions are inevitable and you'll soon be grateful for that hat. There are also points where water gushes down in torrents and you have to walk through a curtain of moisture – that's when the raincoat earns its keep, although you may still get wet.

No, really. This is fun. Honestly.

At the end of the 200m entrance tunnel the mine expands and provides a welcome chance to stand up. Here you can see mineral-bearing rock seams and peer down into the flooded access shaft leading to the lower levels. When you look at the water, remember that the flooded world extends another 100m beneath your feet. Finally you'll have to negotiate a series of seven steep stepladders to reach the surface – you may have been walking horizontally since you entered, but I'm afraid the land above you wasn't flat.

So, to recap: hydrophilic vertically challenged troglodytes will relish the experience. Those who suffer from severe claustrophobia may wish to avoid it, and this is one attraction that is sadly, but most definitely, not wheelchair-accessible. But anyone in-between who is fit enough to climb seven ladders, enjoys an adventure, and doesn't mind feeling slightly damp and cramped will have a blast. This may be as close as you get to pot-holing without signing up for a course.

Walking trails Dozens of trails lace up, down and across the Our Valley. Most are relatively short and can be covered in an hour or three. A bigger challenge is the 58km **Our Path**, which starts in Weiswampach in the far north near the

Belgian border, then follows the Our through Stolzembourg and Vianden, finally heading inland and ending in Diekirch. The trail map – available from regional tourist offices, as are maps for shorter walks – shows what facilities are available *en route*. The full walk takes around two days, depending on how often you break the journey to admire the view from a café terrace.

DIEKIRCH

Along the southern edge of the Ardennes, Diekirch lacks the chocolate-box charm of somewhere like Vianden, and doesn't have a stunning castle as a compelling focal point, but instead has a host of good museums. One of these – the National Museum of Military History (see *What to see and do*, page 191) – ranks among the best in the Grand Duchy, and you could easily spend a day looking round them all.

Initial impressions don't always tell the full story. If you arrive by car your first taste of Diekirch is likely to be the scruffy one-way system encircling the centre, and if you don't stay in the right lane you could easily find yourself catapulted in every which direction. Nevertheless, once you've found your way into the safe haven of the old town within, things improve. The streets here are pleasantly quiet and pedestrianised, lined with good restaurants, and have a genteel square in the centre where you can sit and relax with a beer.

Take care if using a map to navigate your way in Diekirch. The town's planners have chosen to ignore the accepted practice of placing French street names above and more prominently than their Luxembourgish alternatives on the signs (thus making them consistent with the maps). Hence you may look at your map and see Grand Rue, then look at the sign and see Grussgaass (sometimes the German Grossestrasse is also used, just to confuse the matter further). Or you may be aiming for place de la Libération, only to find yourself on Maartplaz and not realise these are actually one and the same. It'll keep you on your toes, but there's one saving grace: the centre is the size of a postage stamp and you'll have a tough job getting lost.

Another quick warning: avoid Diekirch on a Monday. The entire town appears to take a 24-hour siesta and trying to achieve anything can get frustrating. Most restaurants are closed, as are the bulk of the museums. You may even find the front door of your hotel is locked if you arrive without a booking. In fact, I can vouch from personal experience that the front door of your hotel may be bolted even if you *have* a reservation. Just come on a different day and be spared the heartache.

GETTING THERE Diekirch railway station is 400m west of the centre. Hourly **trains** from Luxembourg City take 35 minutes (€5), with a change in Ettelbruck. **Bus** 570 travels between Diekirch and Vianden every 30 minutes, taking a quarter of an hour. Bus 500 (hourly) gets you from Echternach in 40 minutes.

By **car** it takes around half an hour from Luxembourg City.

GETTING AROUND Despite Diekirch being one of the Ardennes's largest towns, everything you need is in a small central area that can easily be covered **on foot**. Most of this is pedestrianised anyway, so you'll have to walk.

One block west of the centre, you can hire both city and mountain **bikes** from Rentabike Dikrich (*27 rue Jean l'Aveugle;* ✆ *26 80 33 76; www.rentabike.lu;* ⏰ *Apr–Sep 10.00–17.00 daily*). The former cost €7.50 per day, the latter €15.

The nearest **taxi** service, Eurotaxi Lux (*58 rue Jean Antoine Zinnen, Ettelbruck;* m *621 22 39 47*), is 5km away.

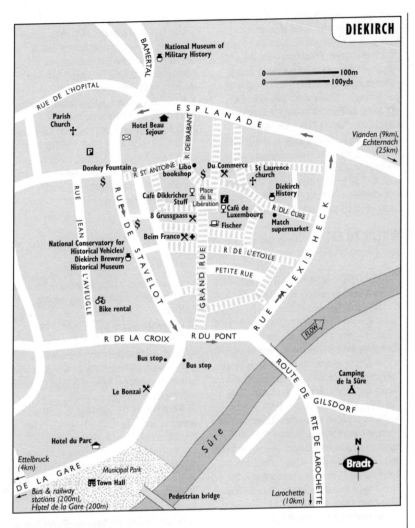

DIEKIRCH

National Museum of Military History

Vianden (9km), Echternach (25km)

RUE DE L'HOPITAL

ESPLANADE

BAMERTAL

Parish Church

Hotel Beau Séjour

R DE BRABANT

Donkey Fountain

R ST ANTOINE

Libo bookshop

Du Commerce

St Laurence church

Diekirch History

Place de la Libération

Café de Luxembourg

R DU CURE

Café Dikkricher Stuff

8 Grussgaass

Fischer

Match supermarket

RUE JEAN L'AVEUGLE

RUE DE STAVELOT

Beim Franco

National Conservatory for Historical Vehicles/ Diekirch Brewery Historical Museum

R DE L'ETOILE

GRAND RUE

PETITE RUE

RUE ALEXIS HECK

Bike rental

R DE LA CROIX

R DU PONT

FLOW

Bus stop

Bus stop

Camping de la Sûre

ROUTE DE GILSDORF

Le Bonzai

Sûre

RTE DE LAROCHETTE

Hotel du Parc

N

Bradt

Ettelbruck (4km)

DE LA GARE

Municipal Park

Town Hall

Bus & railway stations (200m), Hotel de la Gare (200m)

Pedestrian bridge

Larochette (10km)

TOURIST INFORMATION

Tourist office 3 pl de la Libération; 80 30 23; www.diekirch.lu; ⊕ 10.00–17.00 Mon–Fri, 11.00–16.00 Sat. Provides advice & free brochures on what to see & do in Diekirch & the surrounding region, & can help with hotel bookings on request.

WHERE TO STAY

Hotel Beau Séjour (10 rooms) 12 rue Esplanade, L-9227; 26 80 47 15; e bsejour@ pt.lu; www.hotel-beausejour.lu. A lick of paint has worked wonders for this small central hotel, turning it into the best choice in town. Rooms, decorated in tasteful pale yellow, have been given a modern makeover & are very comfortable, with minibars & sumptuous thick duvets on the beds. Service is friendly & welcoming. The hotel's location right on the ring road means parking can be a problem, but it does quieten down at night. €€–€€€

Hotel de la Gare (5 rooms) 73 av de la Gare, L-9233; 80 33 05; e restgare@pt.lu; closed 2 weeks around Christmas/New Year. First opened as a hotel in 1863, & run by the Infalt family since 1918, this hotel's small stature keeps it friendly & intimate. Rooms are simple &

somewhat old-fashioned, but pleasant enough & the bathrooms are very clean. No lift. Located close to the station, 5mins from town. The restaurant offers a range of reasonably priced Luxembourgish food, & lays claim to having the only terrace in Diekirch with a river view. €€

🏠 **Hotel du Parc** (40 rooms) 28 av de la Gare, L-9233; ☎ 80 34 721; e info@hotel-du-parc.lu; www.hotel-du-parc.lu; ⏰ mid-Jan to mid-Dec. Opposite the small municipal park, this comfortable choice just outside the centre is on the road to the station. Rooms are clean & well maintained, with free Wi-Fi. Don't be fooled by the photos in the brochures & on the hotel website that show it located in an idyllic park-like setting. The park *is* opposite the front door, & the front rooms do have an excellent view of its dancing fountains & the river. But in-between is the main road to Ettelbruck. On the plus side the traffic quietens down significantly in the evening. Free parking is available at the back. €€

⛺ **Camping de la Sûre** (196 pitches) route de Gilsdorf, L-9234; ☎ 80 94 25; ⏰ Apr–Sep. A clean campsite with standard facilities, on the banks of the river, but only a few hundred metres from the centre. There's a playground for kids & a café. *€6pp, plus €5 per pitch, & €1 'eco-tax'.*

✖ **WHERE TO EAT** If eating out on a Monday you may find choices are limited, as many restaurants pick this as their weekly rest day.

✖ **Beau Sejour** 12 rue Esplanade; ☎ 26 80 47 15; www.hotel-beausejour.lu; ⏰ 12.00–15.00 & 18.00–22.00 Tue–Sun. The French–Luxembourgish food served here is prepared with sufficient lightness of touch you can forgive them the horrific Richard Clayderman-esque piped muzak coming through the loudspeakers. Despite the latter there's an intimate atmosphere, with service that's attentive but falls short of clingy. The dining area, warmly decorated in tasteful yellow hues & hung with copies of Impressionist works, makes lingering a pleasure. The hotel's brasserie serves a limited menu all day. The house speciality is the (in their words) 'formidable bouillabaisse'. I believe this term is used in its French sense (wonderful), rather than the English (daunting). €€€–€€€€

✖ **Restaurant du Commerce** 1 rue du Marché; ☎ 26 80 37 74; ⏰ 10.00–14.00 & 18.00–22.00 Tue–Sun. This restaurant bills itself as an Argentinian steakhouse, & the succulent steaks are certainly there in force, but other dishes show French influence. Vegetarians may struggle. €€€–€€€€

✖ **Le Bonzai** 6 av de la Gare; ☎ 80 21 19; ⏰ 12.00–14.30 & 18.00–23.00 Tue–Sun. Good-value pan-Asian cuisine from various sources – Vietnamese, Chinese, Malay & Thai – is served here amid a swathe of bamboo décor. It's popular with the locals. €€–€€€

✖ **Beim Franco** 14 Grand Rue; ☎ 26 80 48 58; www.beimfranco.lu; ⏰ 11.30–14.30 Tue–Sat & 18.00–22.30 Mon–Sat, closed 4 weeks in summer. Friendly no-frills pizzeria with simple furnishings, tiled floors, & photos all over the walls of former diners having a good time. €€

✖ **Fischer** 1 Grand Rue; ☎ 26 80 05 61; www.fischer.lu; ⏰ 07.00–18.00 Mon–Sat, 07.00–12.00 Sun. The Diekirch branch of the nationwide bakery chain serves snacks & light meals, & has a dining room with a pleasant terrace. €

ENTERTAINMENT AND NIGHTLIFE Bars. Er, that's it. There are several cafés on the central place de la Libération (aka Maartplaz). None wins any awards for stylish interiors, but in summer they have terraces on the square. Most serve reasonable light snacks for a few euros if you need a quick *croque*.

♀ **Café de Luxembourg** (aka Café 'Beim Fränk') 5 pl de la Libération; ☎ 26 80 39 15; ⏰ daily until late. Beside the tourist office provides free Wi-Fi access for clients & serves light meals.

♀ **Café Dikkricher Stuff** 10 pl de la Libération; ☎ 80 85 24; ⏰ daily until late. On the opposite side of the square, this place offers similar no-frills snacks & drinks.

♀ **8 Grussgaass** 8 Grand Rue; ☎ 26 80 39 73; ⏰ daily until late. During the day this is a restaurant serving French food, but it also has good coffee & a reasonable selection of beers.

SHOPPING

Libo 2–4 rue de Brabant; `80 41 811;
⊕ 09.00–18.00 Mon–Fri, 09.00–17.00 Sat. Has a small selection of English-language books.

Match Supermarket 8 rue du Curé, aka Béiergaass; `80 43 42; ⊕ 08.00–20.00 Mon–Fri, 08.00–19.00 Sat, 09.00–13.00 Sun

OTHER PRACTICALITIES
Medical
✚ **Pharmacie St Laurent** 11 Grand Rue; `80 35 651; ⊕ 08.00–12.00 & 13.30–18.30 Mon–Fri, 13.30–17.00 Sat

$ Dexia Bank 2 pl de la Libération; `80 40 401; ⊕ 08.30–16.30 Mon–Fri
$ Spuerkeess ('S-Bank') 4 rue de Stavelot; `80 42 80 200; ⊕ 08.15–16.30 Mon–Fri

Banks
$ BGL BNP Paribas Bank 5 rue de Stavelot; `42 42 20 00; ⊕ 09.00–16.30 Mon–Fri

Post office
✉ **Post office** pl Guillaume; `80 32 31; ⊕ 08.00–12.00 & 13.30–17.15 Mon–Fri, 09.00–12.00 Sat

WHAT TO SEE AND DO
National Museum of Military History (*Musée National d'Histoire Militaire;* 10 Bamertal; ` 80 89 08; www.nat-military-museum.lu; ⊕ Apr–Oct 10.00–18.00 daily, Nov–Mar 14.00–18.00 daily; adult/child €5/3*) Diekirch's crowning glory, this is one of the best museums in the country. It may bill itself as a repository of general military history, but it focuses very much on one event, and is all the more fascinating for that. It's not just an education for visitors, but also a centre of learning for military historians attempting to catalogue the precise history of the Battle of the Ardennes. The museum is huge and you'll need at least half a day to explore. Its many rooms are filled with life-size dioramas faithfully recreating photographs taken during the battle. The story is told even-handedly from both sides, so that comparison and juxtaposition allow the true story to shine through. Tales are also recounted objectively on a human level, reminding us it was real people who took part, and real lives that were shattered. Many of the items on display were donated by veterans of the conflict or their families, giving the photos names as well as faces.

The main exhibition hall is a vast warehouse stacked to the rafters with armoured military vehicles, troop carriers and motorbikes. Another gallery stands apart from the others by *not* dealing exclusively with World War II. Instead it highlights the Luxembourg army's contribution, albeit small, to international events as part of UN missions. The English-language audio guide (€2.50), narrated by knowledgeable museum curator Roland Gaul, is an excellent investment bringing the dioramas to life. There are more tanks and artillery in the grounds outside.

National Conservatory for Historical Vehicles (*Conservatoire National de Véhicules Historiques;* 20–22 rue de Stavelot; ` 26 80 04 68; www.cnvh.lu; ⊕ 10.00– 18.00 Tue–Sun; adult/child €5/3, inc entry to Diekirch Brewery Historical Museum*) Luxembourg's primary exhibition of motor vehicles is located in an old garage where, in the 19th century, Jean Wagner become the country's premier builder of horse-drawn carriages. In the large main hall are five thematic 'islands' charting the history of motorised transport since the first car arrived in the country in 1904. The stars, naturally, are the restored vehicles themselves, most of which are on loan from private collectors – one was once the personal transport of the grand duke. One side room outlines the history of the garage where Mr Wagner worked; another was his actual workshop, now full of cutaway models inherited from university engineering departments showing how engines work. A third space houses changing exhibitions with a transport theme, reminding us, for example, that without the efforts of one particular Luxembourger, Henri Tudor (see box, page 163), none of this may have happened.

Diekirch Brewery Historical Museum (Musée d'Histoire de la Brasserie de Diekirch; 20–22 rue de Stavelot; ⍝ 26 80 04 68; ⊕ 10.00–18.00 Tue–Sun; adult/child €5/3, inc entry to National Conservatory for Historical Vehicles) Just what you'd expect to find in the same building as a museum about driving: a museum devoted to alcohol. Someone clearly had a masterstroke when they combined these two – although when you delve further, the concept of combining Diekirch's industrial past and present makes more sense, slightly. Sponsored by the brewery that shares the town's name, this small exhibition chronicles the history of the largest local employer through a chronological collection of glasses, bottles and beer mats dating back to 1930. You can sample some of the wares downstairs in the car museum's café, which is a definite point of redemption.

St Laurence Church (Eglise St Laurent; rue du Curé; ⊕ 10.00–12.00 & 14.00–18.00 daily; free) By far the oldest church in Diekirch, and one of the most ancient Christian monuments in the country. An original Roman hall on the site, built in the 3rd century AD, was converted into a Christian shrine sometime around the 6th century. The current building was erected in stages over the remains of this. The belfry appeared in the 12th century, while further expansion was carried out in 1467, creating a mix of Gothic and Romanesque styles – you can still see frescoes on the ceiling dating from this time showing the life of St Laurence. Some original Roman foundations are visible in the crypt which is normally accessible through a separate side entrance, but until building work next door (see below) is completed, visitors must content themselves with peering through a glass panel in the church aisle.

Diekirch History Museum (Musée de l'Histoire de la Ville de Diekirch; rue du Curé; reopening 2012) Bearing witness to Diekirch's long history, a number of well-preserved Roman mosaic floors, most dating from the 3rd century, have been unearthed during excavations around the town. The largest measures 9m by 4m. At the time of writing the museum was closed and awaiting relocation to a brand-new purpose-built site by the St Laurence Church. It should be up and running by the time you read this.

Donkey Fountain (Fontaine des Ânes; rue St Antoine) This little delight, created by Bonifatius Stirnberg, certainly ain't big, but it is clever. And witty, and fun, and it's been a firm local favourite since it was erected in 1980. The four metal donkeys that adorn it articulate in all directions, and passers-by are free to mould their ears, jaws, tails and legs into any positions taking their fancy, where they remain until the next person gives them a whole new look. And the connection with Diekirch? The town mascot is a donkey.

Municipal Park (Parc Municipal; always open; free) Diekirch's town park, stretching along the banks of the Sûre, is a relaxing place to sit or stroll, day or night. Other paths head off further along the river. Forming the centrepiece is a walk-though fountain you can use to cool off on a hot day (yes, they do happen). At dusk the water is tastefully lit from below, changing colours in random patterns.

ETTELBRUCK

With a population of 7,500, Ettelbruck is the largest urban area in the north of the country. It's also a busy junction town where the nation's road and rail links all seem to converge. But it isn't a bad place, once you get away from the one-way system in the station area, and the centre is pedestrianised. The main reason to stop by is to visit the excellent General Patton Memorial Museum (see *What to see and do*, page 194), and perhaps pause to admire his actual memorial on the eastern edge of town.

Legend has it Attila the Hun himself passed through on his way to Trier in AD452, and some say the town's name is a corruption of 'Attila's Bridge' (*Brücke* in German). Nice as that story sounds however, there is no concrete evidence he was actually here. More recently, the town was laid waste by fire in 1778, and again in 1814. The former blaze left only eight houses untouched in the centre, and destroyed almost 500 buildings. There's a small monument to this fact on rue de la Colline, at the end of Grand Rue. The fighting in 1944–45 did just as much damage, if not more.

GETTING THERE If moving around Luxembourg on public transport, the chances are you will pass through Ettelbruck at least once. As the country's biggest transport hub outside Luxembourg City, **buses** head out from here all over the north. The main north–south **railway** line also comes this way – Luxembourg City is 15 minutes to the south with regular connections. **Driving** from Luxembourg City takes about 20 minutes.

GETTING AROUND Ettelbruck is small enough to negotiate **on foot** but if you do need a **taxi**, contact Eurotaxi Lux (*58 rue Jean Antoine Zinnen*; m 621 22 39 47).

One very interesting and picturesque full day trip for **cyclists** is to follow the Sûre River from here to Wasserbillig, where it flows into the Moselle. If you are staying in Luxembourg City, the railway stations in both Ettelbruck and Wasserbillig allow you to set out in the morning and return to the capital in late afternoon.

TOURIST INFORMATION
[i] **Tourist office** 5 rue Abbé Muller; \81 20 68; www.ettelbruck-info.lu; ⊕ 10.00–12.00 & 13.00–17.00 Mon & Wed–Sat. The tourist office offers advice & free brochures on the local region, & can help with booking accommodation on request. It also sells local produce.

WHERE TO STAY AND EAT
⌂ **Hotel Restaurant Dahm** (25 rooms) 57 Porte des Ardennes, L-9514 Erpeldange; \81 62 551; e dahm@pt.lu; www.hotel-dahm. com; ⊕ mid-Jan to Christmas. In the village of Erpeldange, 2km north of Ettelbruck & 4km west of Diekirch, this is an excellent option for exploring both towns. It's in a class above the other choices in the area, although this isn't reflected in the prices. You may need to book ahead during the week as it often fills up with business clientele using the conference facilities. All rooms have minibar, free Wi-Fi & safe; luxury rooms have balconies. 2 restaurants (⊕ *12.00–14.00 & 18.00–21.30*; €€–€€€ *(Luxembourgish)*, €€€€ *(gastronomic)*) offer a choice of gastronomic French or cheaper Luxembourgish dishes – wherever you sit you can mix 'n' match courses from both menus. There's a terrace with decking out the back. Private fishing is also available to guests. €€

⌂ **Hotel Herckmans** (11 rooms) 3 pl de la Résistance (aka Bottermaart), L-9070; \81 74 28; e traiteur@pt.lu; www.steakhouse.lu. On the edge of a pedestrianised zone, this central hotel is quieter than the station area, & has an unusual claim to fame. During the 1848 revolutions that caused upheaval across much of continental Europe, there were disturbances in Luxembourg City. Fearing for its safety, the national parliament relocated to Ettelbruck & stayed here: for one week only it became Luxembourg's official seat of government. The rooms are reasonable, & have satellite TV, minibar & free Wi-Fi. If you get peckish there's a steakhouse (⊕ *12.00–14.00 & 18.30–22.00 daily except 24 Dec;* €€€) downstairs. B/fast €7; without bath €; with bath €€

Å Camping Kalkesdelt (136 pitches) 88 Chemin de Camping, L-9022; ☎ 81 21 85; e site@ pt.lu; ⊕ Apr–Oct. Just outside Ettelbruck, this small campsite has a quiet location & modern clean facilities. There are washing machines, a snack bar & bathrooms with disabled access. The campsite has had the Luxembourg eco-label since 2000, recognising its environmental sensitivity. €6.20pp, plus €8.25 per pitch.

✘ Le Resto 7 rue Abbé Henri Muller; ☎ 81 02 80; ⊕ 11.30–13.45 Thu–Tue & 18.30–21.00 Thu–Mon. aka 'Chez Fred', this friendly diner beside the tourist office has simple red, white & black furnishings. 4 'international' clocks on the wall tell you the current time in, er, Ettelbruck, Mersch, Diekirch & Vianden. The menu is Luxembourgish, featuring *jambon frites* & *bouchée à la reine*, but with a lighter touch than most. The salads are good too, & everything is served briskly & with a smile by the relentlessly cheerful owner. The terrace out front is in the shadow of the St Sebastian Church. €€–€€€

OTHER PRACTICALITIES

✚ Pharmacie Petry 15 Grand Rue; ☎ 81 21 481; ⊕ 08.00–12.30 & 13.30 18.30 Mon–Fri, 08.00–12.00 & 13.30–17.30 Sat. Even if you're not ill, check out this lovely old yellow building with green shutters – arguably the prettiest in town.

✚ Pharmacie Thilges 39 Grand Rue; ☎ 81 21 51; ⊕ 09.00–12.00 & 13.30–17.30 Mon–Fri, 09.00–12.00 Sat
$ Dexia Bank 58 Grand Rue; ☎ 81 62 261; ⊕ 08.30–16.30 Mon–Fri
✉ Post office 2c av Lucien Salentiny; ☎ 81 88 88; ⊕ 08.00–18.00 Mon–Fri, 09.00–12.00 Sat

WHAT TO SEE AND DO

General Patton Memorial Museum (*5 rue Dr Klein;* ☎ *81 03 22; www.patton. lu;* ⊕ *Jun to mid-Sep 10.00–17.00 daily, mid-Sep to May 14.00–17.00 Sun; adult/child* €5/3) More than just paying homage to the American general who led the liberation of Luxembourg, this impressive museum relates the effect of the war on the country as a whole. One room tells the story of the Nazi occupation from May 1940 until the initial liberation of September 1944, covering areas such as forced conscription, and the 791 men and women of the Luxembourg resistance who died in Nazi prisons and concentration camps. Another room contains memorabilia donated by American veterans of the Ardennes campaign, while the top floor has a large diorama depicting an outdoor military hospital from that time. Predictably, one room is devoted to Patton. Photos and other documents show the last months of the general, who survived the war but was killed in a road accident in Mannheim, Germany, in December 1945. He now lies buried with his men in the American Military Cemetery in Hamm, close to Luxembourg City (see page 82).

Historical Urban Trail (*Sentier Urbain; free leaflet available from tourist office; guided tours on request*) This self-guided 2.2km walking circuit takes you around the town centre, stopping at 15 sites of historical or cultural significance. Information boards located at each site fill in the details.

The most noteworthy sight along the trail is the neoclassical **St Sebastian Church** (*pl de l'Eglise; free*). Built in 1841, and consecrated in 1864, it was so badly damaged during the war that most of what you see today dates only from 1948.

At the eastern approaches to Ettelbruck on the main road to Diekirch is the **General Patton Memorial**. He stands guard looking out over the Sûre River. They could have picked a quieter spot for this, but the leafy surrounds help slightly to offset the sound of the traffic whizzing past.

Brandenburg There is little to Brandenburg, but its site alone is worth a swift detour if you're driving north of Ettelbruck or Diekirch – take the signposted side road on the right (heading north) on the N7, about 6km from both towns. The village sits in a narrow valley, and the road down is steep and windy. There's nothing to do but admire the view, which becomes impressive when you round a bend and see the ruins of **Brandenburg Castle** (*not open to the public*) perched on a hillock above the houses at the end of the street.

BOURSCHEID

Bourscheid is not so much one place as a collection of places clustered close to one another. The Sûre Valley here is spectacular and sheer-sided, verging on a gorge. Teetering on a high ridge is Bourscheid village, with a grand view and a good hotel. Down in the valley 250m below (as the dead crow plummets – it's much longer by road) are Bourscheid-Plage and Bourscheid-Moulin, with a range of accommodation choices and even grander views. On the far side of the valley is the village of Lipperscheid. And sitting on a rocky outcrop in-between is what everyone's looking at: Bourscheid Castle.

GETTING THERE AND AROUND Bourscheid is 9km northwest of Ettelbruck. **Bus** 545 runs from there to the upper village every half an hour. Bus 550 travels between Ettelbruck and Bourscheid-Moulin every hour. These two buses run via different routes, and as a result there is no direct public transport link between the upper and lower areas – and consequently no way of reaching the castle by bus.

 WHERE TO STAY AND EAT Choose between the quiet upper village or the riverside locations below. Most visitors go for the latter, which is reflected in the greater choice down there.

Village
🏠 **Hotel Restaurant St-Fiacre** (20 rooms) 4 Groussgaass, L-9140; 📞 99 00 23; e info@st-fiacre.lu; www.bourscheid.com, www.st-fiacre.lu; ⏰ mid-Mar to Dec. If you want to stay in the village & look down on the castle, this traditional inn is the place to come. Rooms are squeaky clean with light pine furniture & free Wi-Fi. Biker & hiker friendly, they can transport your bags to your next stop (for a fee) if you want to travel light. The terrace at the back looks over the valley, while the restaurant (⏰ 12.00–14.00 & 18.30–20.30 Thu–Mon; €€–€€€) serves Luxembourgish & French classics. €€–€€€

Riverside
🏠 **Hotel Restaurant du Moulin** (12 rooms) 1 Buurschtermillen, L-9164 Bourscheid-Moulin; 📞 99 00 15; e hotel@moulin.info; www.moulin.

lu; ⏰ Feb–Nov. In an old watermill, the hotel sits by the water in a picturesque spot by an old stone bridge & has good clean rooms. The terrace at the back overlooks the river, & the heated swimming pool has panoramic windows to bring the countryside indoors as you bob. The sauna & solarium cost extra. The restaurant (⏰ 12.00–13.30 & 19.00–20.30 daily; €€€) offers gastronomic French–Luxembourgish cuisine. **€€€**

🏠 **Cocoon Hotel Belair** (32 rooms) L-9164 Bourscheid-Plage; 📞 26 30 351; e belair@cocoonhotels.com; www.cocoonhotels.com. In a tranquil location by the river, rooms here are large, new & fresh with 4-star comforts, & they have safe, minibar, balconies & free Wi-Fi (officially only in the lobby, but there is a signal). Bathrooms have whirlpool baths & separate showers. The magnificent terrace opens onto an expanse of greenery. The hotel restaurant (⏱ *12.00–14.30 & 18.00–22.00 daily; €€–€€€*) serves a blend of French & Luxembourgish cuisine. The airy dining room is in a domed space bedecked with moss balls hanging from the beams that look like giant Christmas baubles, or weaverbird nests. An alcove bar to 1 side doubles as the wine cellar. As it's run by the same management, guests can use the facilities at La Rive (below) & it all goes on 1 bill. **€€–€€€**

🏠 **Cocoon Hotel La Rive** (21 rooms) L-9164 Bourscheid-Plage; 📞 26 30 351; e rive@cocoonhotels.com; www.cocoonhotels.com. Now swallowed up by the Belgian hotel group that owns the neighbouring Belair, these are effectively 2 parts of 1 thing. Guests can use the facilities at either. A row of 14 chalets/suites between the 2 is run jointly. By a small weir in the river, the sound of gushing water here adds to the idyllic scenery. Some rooms are a bit too stuffed with furniture, making them feel more cramped than they actually are. Cheaper rooms come without river view; those at the upper end have balconies. The stylish wellness centre has a steam room, sauna, fitness room & solarium. There's free Wi-Fi & an internet terminal in the lobby. You can even go fishing for trout here, for a fee. The restaurant (⏱ *12.00–14.00 & 19.00–21.00 Fri–Tue; €€–€€€*) serves French & international dishes (& trout). The fish in the tank are for looking at however, not eating. **€€–€€€**

🏕 **Camping du Moulin** (145 pitches) L-9164 Bourscheid-Moulin; 📞 99 03 31; e moulin@camp.lu; moulin.camp.lu; ⏱ mid-Apr to mid-Oct. Next door to the Um Gritt (below), with the same views, facilities & prices. They even share a website. The only difference is the Moulin closes a week earlier in autumn. Part of this campsite is on the far side of the river, which vehicles reach via a rare sight in Luxembourg: a

ford. Pedestrians keep their feet dry by using the footbridge. *€5pp, plus €10 per pitch.*

🏕 **Camping Um Gritt** (199 pitches) L-9164 Bourscheid-Moulin; 📞 99 04 49; e gritt@camp.lu; gritt.camp.lu; ⏱ mid-Apr to Oct. Spread out along the river, this campsite has clean facilities & a magnificent view. *€5pp, plus €10 per pitch.*

✗ **Brasserie du Vieux Moulin** 7 Buurschtermillen; 📞 90 80 88; www.amkeller.lu; ⏱ 11.00–01.00 daily in season. For simple food in Bourscheid-Plage, this snack bar/café between the Moulin Hotel & neighbouring Moulin campsite offers snacks such as *croque monsieur* for very little money. Even the more substantial pasta dishes are under €10. It has whitewashed vaulted ceilings within, & the inevitably scenic terrace without. The cellar restaurant contains artefacts from the old mill, including millstones, & a well in 1 corner. **€–€€**

Lipperscheid

🏠 **Sport Hotel Leweck** (51 rooms) route de Clervaux (N7), L-9378; 📞 99 00 22; e info@sporthotel.lu; www.sporthotel.lu. On a hilltop on the east side of the valley, this large family-owned hotel has a Germanic-style lobby with wood panels, plus a terrace with tremendous views. Some rooms are modern with laminate floors; others more traditional with carpet. Those at the back have balconies. The wellness centre has an indoor & outdoor pool, sauna, Turkish bath, solarium, fitness room & a 'beauty farm' offering various treatments. There's even a clothing shop, plus a sports hall for guests (hence the name), but most people come here to relax, not exert themselves. Some of that relaxing can be done in the large bar & restaurant – the latter (⏱ *12.00–14.00 & 18.30–21.30 daily; €€€€*) serves French fare including *chateaubriand*. **€€€–€€€€**

OTHER PRACTICALITIES For banks, pharmacies and a post office, head for Ettelbruck (see page 194) or Diekirch (see page 191).

WHAT TO SEE AND DO

Bourscheid Castle (*Château de Bourscheid; Schlasswee, Bourscheid;* 📞 *99 05 70; www.bourscheid.lu;* ⏱ *Apr to mid-Oct 09.30–18.00 daily, mid-Oct to Mar 11.00–16.00 daily; adult/child €5/3*) This grand old castle's commanding position on a rocky spur completely dominates the Sûre Valley in every direction. One look at its strategic location leaves one in no doubt as to why the local lord chose to build his defensive stronghold here. You'd have to be a fool, or have wings, to attack it.

The first stone keep appeared around AD1000, replacing an older wooden construction, and archaeological digs have uncovered evidence that the Romans – no slouches in military terms – were here too. The major fortifications were built in the 14th century, but the glory days didn't last long. By 1512, the ruling Bourscheid dynasty had died out, leaving the castle divided into two. One half was never occupied; the other was abandoned in 1626. Despite centuries of neglect, the setting and sheer scale make this an exhilarating place to visit, arguably number two (after Vianden) in the unofficial national castle league. Ringed by a great stone wall with 11 watchtowers, the site covers an area of 150m by 50m. Clamber over the ruins and explore at your leisure, but don't miss the quite wonderful views from the top of the tallest tower (No 14 on the plan you'll be given with your entry ticket). The restored 'Stolzembourg' house is a multi-level mansion that hosts exhibitions, as well as models of the castle as it would have looked through the ages. For more detail than you could ever absorb, take the informative audio guide tour (included in ticket price). One day each July (usually the second Sunday) the castle hosts its own medieval festival, on a similar theme, but smaller in scale to the one in Vianden.

Walking The area around Bourscheid is thick with walking trails, and the hotels will happily sell you a map. Two moderately easy routes taking in Bourscheid-Plage, Moulin and the castle are marked **AK1** (1½ hours) and **AK2** (two hours). From the bridge in Moulin, both take you first through the Camping du Moulin, along the left riverbank heading upstream, then cross the railway to pass through woodland for 500m until you come to a junction. The shorter AK1 swings up and left through the woods, emerging on the main road by a viewpoint. AK2 takes a more circuitous and loftier route to the same point, passing the castle. Both then re-combine and descend back to river level. There they follow the water back through Camping Um Gritt to the bridge.

Grenglay viewpoint For the best view in the area – if not in Luxembourg – park at the top of the hill above Lipperscheid (use the Hotel Leweck's car park), or take bus 555 from Ettelbruck (hourly Monday to Saturday, three services on Sunday). Look for the street to the right of the small green (looking uphill) called Gringleeswee, where there's a sign to the viewpoint. After 150m, at a junction, take the farm track leading across the fields diagonally to the right, then keep walking for ten minutes. You'll know you've reached the correct spot when you look to your right after some trees and go 'Wow!' Alternatively, a picnic table and stone wall mark the spot. The hillside drops vertiginously down to the river, with the two campsites and three hotels of Bourscheid-Plage and Moulin stretched along its banks. Halfway up the opposite side the tarmac road snakes up to the castle, and in the distance is Bourscheid village, 2km away as the crow flies, but a good 7km by road. Everything is enveloped by an ocean of green. In theory there's nothing to stop you driving up here – the paragliders who come here to leap off the edge do just that – but the track is rough dirt and gravel and not recommended for sensitive suspensions.

Verbegsbierg viewpoint There's another spectacular viewpoint on the Bourscheid side of the valley, between the castle and the village. Bizarrely, it's in the middle of the municipal campsite (permanent trailer residents only). Park by the sign saying 'Camping du SIT Bourscheid'. The viewpoint is beside a trailer to the left of the bar/reception, and looks spectacularly down over a precipice to the nearby castle and valley floor beyond.

ESCH-SUR-SÛRE

Before you even reach Esch you know something special is happening. Turning off the main road between Bastogne and Ettelbruck, the first thing you do is pass through a rock tunnel. It already feels like entering a secret world. And then you round the last bend and see the village proper, and it just gets better.

Make no mistake: Esch is gorgeous, displaying a near-fairytale quality. It clings to the sides of a giant rock that's been marooned by a sharp meander in the Sûre River. Looking down from above are romantically crumbling castle ruins. At the southern end of town is a second tunnel (rather prosaically, both were actually bored in the 1950s to allow construction traffic to access the Upper Sûre barrage). The river bends so severely it turns the land into a virtual island, connected to the 'mainland' only by a narrow isthmus. If you were so inclined you could use the 80m tunnel to bypass the entire place in under five seconds – but why would you want to do that?

Esch has few actual distractions to keep you entertained, but the big draw is the village itself. It's just a fine place to be. Go walking in the surrounding region by day, and enjoy hanging out in Esch by night. Or just sit and enjoy the view. You won't be alone though: while the official population is no more than 250, the numbers swell many-fold on sunny weekends.

GETTING THERE Bus 535 covers the ground between Ettelbruck and Esch in 30 minutes, twice per hour, then continues to Lultzhausen and Insenborn in the Upper Sûre Park. Buses from nearby Wiltz are few and far between, with the timetable designed to benefit the school run. **Driving** from Luxembourg City takes 45 minutes.

GETTING AROUND Esch is tiny. Even **on foot** it only takes a couple of minutes to get from one side to the other.

TOURIST INFORMATION

i Tourist office 15 rue de l'Eglise; ☎ 83 91 121; ⊕ 09.00–11.30 & 14.00–16.00 Tue & Thu, 09.00–11.30 & 14.00–19.00 Wed, 09.00–11.30 Fri. At other times visit the Upper Sûre Park headquarters (see page 201).

WHERE TO STAY

Hotel Beau Site (14 rooms) 2 rue de Kaundorf, L-9650; ☎ 83 91 34 or 89 90 21; e beau-site@beau-site.lu; www.beau-site.lu; closed 2 weeks in Feb. Just across the river from the main village, the Beau Site has the grandest of views from its riverside suntrap terrace. Run by the same family since 1949, rooms are simple, but very pleasant. Long-stay discounts are available. €€–€€€

Hotel de la Sûre (38 rooms) 1 rue du Pont, L-9650; ☎ 83 91 10; e info@hotel-de-la-sure. lu; www.hotel-de-la-sure.lu; ⊕ Jan to mid-Dec. If forced to name 1 hotel in the Ardennes more clued-up to the needs & desires of visitors than any other, I'd have a job looking beyond this place. You can buy the produce of the Upper Sûre Park, rent a bike, eat in its great restaurant, or go point-to-point hiking with a baggage transport service. Or just chill in the highly convivial bar. The massive multi-lingual file left in every room is an information office in itself, & if the file can't answer your question, then Ronald – head chef & son of the hotel owners – probably can. The de la Sûre is a rabbit warren of a place sprawling down a maze of twisting corridors & up & down stairs, filling several neighbouring buildings & an annex down the street. Once inside & assuming you've somehow managed to locate your room, take careful note of the route you followed otherwise you may have a job getting out again. Thanks to

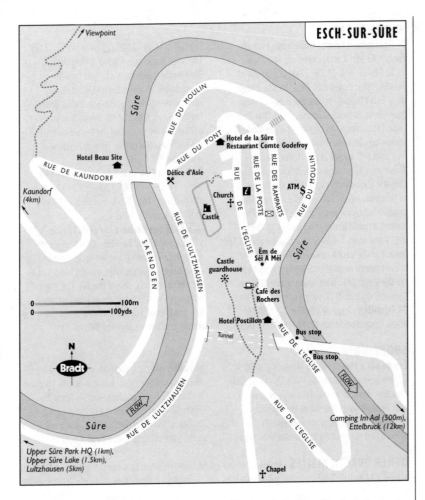

Viewpoint

Sûre

RUE DU MOULIN

RUE DU PONT

Hotel Beau Site

RUE DE KAUNDORF

Kaundorf
(4km)

Délice d'Asie

Hotel de la Sûre
Restaurant Comte Godefroy

RUE DE LA POSTE

RUE DES RAMPARTS

RUE DU MOULIN

ATM

i

Church

Castle

RUE DE L'ÉGLISE

RUE DE LUTZHAUSEN

SAENDGEN

Castle
guardhouse

Ëm de
Séi A Méi

Sûre

Café des
Rochers

0   100m
0   100yds

N

Bradt

Hotel Postillon

Tunnel

Bus stop

Bus stop

FLOW

RUE DE L'ÉGLISE

FLOW

RUE DE LUTZHAUSEN

Sûre

Upper Sûre Park HQ (1km),
Upper Sûre Lake (1.5km),
Lutzhausen (5km)

Camping Im Aal (500m),
Ettelbruck (12km)

RUE DE L'ÉGLISE

Chapel

its quirky layout, the one thing this place doesn't have is a lift. Every room is individually themed & stylishly decorated. If you get bored with sightseeing or walking there's also a sauna, fitness room, steam room & a games area. Free Wi-Fi is available in the bar. The cheapest rooms have shared bathrooms; top-end bathrooms come with steam or whirlpool baths. Some new studio rooms in a separate annex have steam baths, microwave & minibar. The hotel also runs the snack bar across the street, & brands itself as a 'book hotel'. You can borrow books from its growing library, or take one away provided you leave 2 others as payment. The hotel is in the cramped upper village & parking space is limited. €€–€€€

Hotel Postillon (24 rooms) 1 rue de L'Eglise, L-9650; 89 90 33; e conrad@

lepostillon.lu; www.lepostillon.lu. At the entrance to Esch by the tunnel, the Postillon's terrace occupies a prime spot below the castle rock, looking out over the river. Service is friendly & the rooms comfortable with minibars. The hotel also has a sauna. €€

Camping Im Aal (200 pitches) On N27, 500m east of Esch-sur-Sûre, L-9650; 83 95 14; e info@camping-im-aal.lu; www.camping-im-aal.lu; ⊕ Feb–Dec. By the road & the river. Showers here are clean, there's a small shop for supplies, & a riverside café. You can also get a fishing permit here (from €13 for 2 days), or rent mountain bikes (€8–10/15–17 for half/full day). Esch is only a short walk away. €6pp, plus €6.50 per pitch.

8

✗ WHERE TO EAT

✗ Restaurant Comte Godefroy 1 rue du Pont; ☏ 83 91 10; www.hotel-de-la-sure.lu; ⏱ 12.00–15.00 & 18.30–22.00 (21.00 out of season) daily; closed mid-Dec/Jan. The Hotel de la Sûre's friendly restaurant is one of those marvellous forward-thinking places that doesn't regard vegetarians as carriers of some kind of contagious disease. Those who prefer the meat-free path will rejoice at the choice available. Those who do want meat or fish will also find they are abundantly catered for, in a range of Luxembourgish–French dishes using local produce wherever possible. The main dining room is a grand banqueting hall, with the bar area a few steps below & a mezzanine above. The terrace at the back has views over the village's moss-covered roofs. If your budget is up to it try the Menu de la Sûre, using seasonal local produce, with spelt playing a central role. €€€

✗ Postillon 1 rue de L'Eglise; ☏ 89 90 33; www.lepostillon.lu; ⏱ 12.00–14.00 (15.00 in season) & 18.30–21.00 (22.00 in season) daily. The hotel restaurant offers 2 dining choices. Dine inside & pick from a largely French–Luxembourgish menu in an elegant dining room with wooden furnishings & tiled floors. Lighter meals & tourist staples such as spaghetti bolognaise are served on the terrace outside, & in the bar/brasserie below. *Terrace/brasseries* €€; *restaurant* €€€

✗ Délice d'Asie 9 rue du Pont; ☏ 26 88 98 09; ⏱ 11.30–14.30 & 17.30–23.30 daily. As an alternative to hotel food, reasonable Chinese fodder is available here. €€

☕ Café des Rochers 3 rue de l'Eglise; ☏ 83 91 28; ⏱ until late Tue–Sun. Down-to-earth no-frills café serving simple snacks including sandwiches & hamburgers, usually bolstered by a more substantial dish of the day. The interior is nothing to speak of, but the covered terrace is a fine place to sit. For those with a sweet tooth, ice cream sundaes are also on offer. €

SHOPPING

Ëm de Séi a Méi 1 rue du Moulin; ☏ 26 88 90 03; www.emdeseiamei.lu; ⏱ 08.30–18.00 daily; closed Wed out of season. This large emporium sells local products. The wines are available elsewhere, but for other small producers this offers a rare opportunity to promote their wares to a wider audience. There are candles, toiletries, cosmetics, wooden toys, & bric-a-brac in 1 section; & a food area with produce Vum Séi (from the Upper Sûre Park), including a range of herbal infusions. Spelt is at the fore here, & you will find it in the form of pasta, bread, flour & beer.

OTHER PRACTICALITIES There are no banks, but there is a stand-alone **ATM** on rue du Moulin. The nearest **pharmacies** are in Wiltz or Ettelbruck, both 10km away.

✉ Post office 11 rue de la Poste; ☏ 83 91 37; ⏱ 14.00–16.00 Mon–Fri

WHAT TO SEE AND DO

Castle (☏ 83 91 121; *always open; free*) The earliest written mention of Esch has been dated to AD774, but it's likely the Romans were the first to build on this rock. Of the current remains, the little keep is around 1,000 years old, the rest a mere 800. You can clamber over the ruins to your heart's content – but wear good shoes for walking over the stony ground. To reach the castle, take the steps to the left by the Café du Château (a bikers' and locals' hangout).

The castle's southern **guardhouse** is slightly apart from the main ruins, and reached via a long stone staircase leading up between the Café des Rochers and Hotel Postillon. Be careful after rain as the steps can become slippery (there's a handrail). The panoramic view is worth the effort.

Walks For an even more outstanding bird's-eye **view** over Esch, cross the bridge by the Hotel Beau Site, head 100m up the road, then take the track on the right when the main drag swings left. Look for a narrow rocky trail leading up and to the right: the blue/yellow signpost points the way to 'Kaundorf, Liefrange and Martelange'. As you follow the zigzag path up the vertiginous hillside the views become increasingly dramatic, until it finally levels out and heads into the woods. Wear good shoes or walking boots as the path is uneven.

Several **themed walks** can be followed around Esch – pick up brochures from the tourist office or the Upper Sûre Park headquarters. The most popular is **Mysteries of Esch-sur-Sûre**, which comes with an audio guide (*adult/child* €4/2.50, *plus a deposit of ID or* €50). It takes you on a two-hour trail around the village with 21 stops recounting some of its spookier myths and legends. Who cares if most of these were made up for the tour? It's still fun, especially for kids.

UPPER SÛRE NATURAL PARK

Created in 1999 to protect the waters of the Upper Sûre Lake – a major source of Luxembourg's drinking water – this region has been designated as a 'natural park', rather than being given more restricting 'national park' status. The intention is not to freeze all local development and prevent expansion, but rather to encourage responsible use of the land. Farmers can continue making and selling local produce, but under strict supervision and with controls over what pesticides and chemicals are used. The park covers an area of 184km², of which 50% is forested.

Watersports (including scuba diving) are allowed on the lake (though motorboats are banned), and there are hiking and nature trails all over – walking maps are available from local tourist offices.

GETTING THERE AND AROUND Getting to Insenborn and Lultzhausen by the lakeshore is simple as **bus** 535 makes the trip from Ettelbruck, via Esch, twice per hour (40 minutes). Bus 620 links Wiltz and Arsdorf hourly (50 minutes). Moving around within the park is only realistic using your own wheels (motorised or otherwise), or feet.

TOURIST INFORMATION
 Upper Sûre Park headquarters (Maison du Parc) 15 route de Lultzhausen, Esch-sur-Sûre; ☎89 93 311; www.naturpark-sure.lu; ⊕ May–Oct 10.00–12.00 & 14.00–18.00 Mon–Tue & Thu–Fri, 10.00–12.00 & 14.00–17.00 Wed, 14.00–18.00 Sat–Sun, Nov–Apr 10.00–12.00 Mon–Fri & 14.00–17.00 daily. A 1-stop shop for walking maps, general information, & local products.

WHERE TO STAY AND EAT Many people prefer to stay in Esch-sur-Sûre, but there are options within the park itself.

🏠 **Café-Restaurant-Hotel Peiffer** (15 rooms) Maison 36, Insenborn; ☎83 98 97; e jacques.bruyere@alt.lu; www.peiffer.lu. Close to the lake, the Peiffer doubles as a dive centre, offering a tank refill service. The café/restaurant (⊕ *until late Fri–Wed*; €–€€) is cheap & cheerful. Come in for a drink or a simple meal. When I ordered Ardennes ham with salad & chips, the landlord replied with a cheery, 'Good, because that's all we have.' To be fair, he was expecting a wedding party & was saving his best for them, but you get the idea. A few small, basic rooms (just a bed & a washbasin) are available for overnight guests – bathrooms are down the hall. €€

🏠 **Hotel Restaurant Diligence** (11 rooms) 17 rue du Lac, L-8808 Arsdorf; ☎23 64 95 55; e info@ladiligence.lu; www.ladiligence.lu. Located in the sleepy hamlet of (titter ye not) Arsdorf, a few kilometres from the southwest corner of the lake. The hotel is clean, friendly & charming, with window boxes that explode with colour in summer. Rooms are simply furnished, but comfortable. The restaurant (⏱ *12.00–13.45 & 18.00–20.45 Wed–Sun;* €€–€€€) menu has a good selection of wholesome Luxembourgish & French dishes, prepared by the landlord's wife using local produce. The Diligence is on the 'walking with a baggage service' circuit. In the evenings the TV in the bar *is* the centre of village nightlife. The hotel bakes its own bread – the smell wafting up from below will be enough to lure you out of bed in the morning. €€

⌂ **Lultzhausen Youth Hostel** (112 beds) rue du village, L-9666 Lultzhausen; ☏ 26 88 92 01; e lultzhausen@youthhostels.lu; www.youthhostels.lu; ⏱ mid-Jan to mid-Dec. A few steps from the water, this lakeside hostel makes a great budget base. Peace & quiet is guaranteed as no cars are allowed into Lultzhausen. Rooms have 2–12 beds. The restaurant has a terrace with lake view, & can provide packed lunches & veggie options by prior arrangement. The ground floor & all public areas are wheelchair-accessible, & disabled toilets are available. You can rent mountain bikes & canoes. *€19.50pp inc bed, b/fast & bedding. Non-members pay €3 extra.*

SHOPPING Local produce is sold under the label Vum Séi ('From the Lake District') – it's a guarantee of good animal husbandry and respect for the land. Buy from the park headquarters, or from the Hotel de la Sûre's shop in Esch. Spelt – an ancient grain similar to wheat – is a local speciality.

WHAT TO SEE AND DO

Weaving Museum (*Musée de la Draperie; 15 route de Lultzhausen, Esch-sur-Sûre;* ☏ *89 93 311;* ⏱ *May–Oct 10.00–12.00 & 14.00–18.00 Mon–Tue & Thu–Fri, 10.00–12.00 & 14.00–17.00 Wed, 14.00–18.00 Sat–Sun, Nov–Apr 10.00–12.00 Mon–Fri & 14.00–17.00 daily; adult/child €2.50/1.25*) Sharing the same building as the park headquarters, the weaving museum contains a collection of industrial wool-spinning equipment and looms. The building itself is an old textile mill. The machines are driven by giant rubber drive belts and still work, but are no longer used commercially. They can be set in motion on request. Once powered by river water, the giant dam upstream means they now have to use electricity, part of which comes from solar panels on the roof.

Upper Sûre Lake At 19km long and covering an area of 380ha, Luxembourg's largest body of water only came into being when the 50m-high **dam** (barrage) at its eastern end was constructed in 1955. The lake was created to produce hydro-electricity and reduce national reliance on foreign imports, but its contribution to the national grid today is minimal, and it's only used occasionally to meet peak demands. Instead it's now the source of more than 50% of the country's drinking water, and 70% of the population rely on it to at least some extent.

The lake is a popular recreation spot. Artificial beaches along the south shore sometimes fill with as many as 10,000 visitors on warmer summer weekends. To keep the water clean and unpolluted, no human activity is allowed within 5km of the outlet (by the dam). Besides one security launch that patrols the lake, no diesel motorboats are permitted anywhere, while sailing boats and kayaks are allowed on the upriver side of the pontoon bridge. That bridge, linking Lultzhausen on the south shore with Liefrange on the north, was added as an afterthought after the two villages were cut off from one another. It is also possible to go scuba diving in the lake. Tanks can be refilled at the Hotel Peiffer in Insenborn (see page 201). Visit www.scuba.lu for more information.

A **solar-powered boat** (*Solarboot; reserve at least 22hrs in advance with the park headquarters;* ☏ *89 93 31 555;* e *info@naturpark-sure.lu; departures mid-Jun to mid-*

Sep 10.00, 13.45 & 16.00 Tue–Sun, May to mid-Jun & mid-Sep to mid-Oct 15.00 Tue, Thu, Sat & Sun; adult/child €8/4, 30% discount with Luxembourg Card) makes two-hour tours of the lake, departing from the jetty in Insenborn. It can take up to 23 passengers, and it does fill up in summer.

Rindschleiden Parish Church (*⊕ until 18.00 daily; free*) Blink and you may miss it, for Rindschleiden – 5km south of the lake – has the distinction of being Luxembourg's smallest village, consisting of no more than two or three houses and a tiny church. It's the latter that makes it worth the battering your car suspension will get (there's no bus) as it negotiates the narrow pot-holed lanes connecting the hamlet with the outside world. Unassuming from the outside, step inside the 10th-century building (the Romanesque tower was added in the 12th century, despite the date '1750' on the front), to marvel at the stunning 15th-century frescoes covering the vaulted ceiling. These were rediscovered in 1952 during restoration work; the oldest date from around 1435. They depict saints and scenes from the New Testament (the Last Supper is above the door as you enter), and form the largest and best-preserved collection of paintings from this period in Luxembourg. You can still see the original 10th-century foundations (unearthed during the same restoration that revealed the frescoes) by peering underneath the carpet in front of the Baroque altar. Although entry is free, feed a coin into the slot by the door (€0.50 for a generous 'five' minutes) to turn on the interior lights and see the frescoes in greater detail. A free audio explanation recounts the church's long history – press the button on top of the wooden cabinet to the right of the altar. At the entrance you can also pick up a leaflet for the 'Randschleider Pad', a short (1.5km) nature walk in the area.

Walks There are endless **hiking** opportunities in the park. As in other regions, short walks are waymarked with letters; medium-length routes with numbers; and longer national paths with symbols. One very scenic short trek is the **Chemin de la Sculpture**, which rewards minimal effort with great views. It follows a 4.5km 'frying pan' route through the forests and cornfields, in a loop taking you around the **Lultzhausen Sculpture Park**: a series of stone carvings dotted across the hillside. The walk begins and ends in the car park between Lultzhausen and the bridge to Insenborn – follow the 'S' markings. In summer the cornfields are ablaze with flowering poppies and the air fills with butterflies. In winter you can reliably substitute these delights with mud and persistent rain. A full circuit takes about an hour.

For a longer workout, try a 42km circuit of the lake by following the blue wavy line markings denoting the **Upper Sûre Lake Path**. In theory it's possible to cover this in one *very* long day, but you'll have a lot more fun if you break the journey halfway (in Arsdorf, if starting from Esch). Better still, take several days to explore properly.

WILTZ

Every other town in northern Luxembourg either goes for a valley-floor location or sits on a hilltop. Wiltz likes to confound visitors by doing both – the first thing you'll notice is that it's anything but flat. The station and some hotels are in the lower town, sometimes referred to as Niederwiltz. Most of the sights in this bustling town of 4,500 souls are a stiff climb uphill – remind yourself you'll appreciate the castle and its museums all the more for the effort you've put in to reach them.

GETTING THERE AND AROUND Wiltz has a railway station, and direct **trains** travel to and from Luxembourg City every hour, taking an hour (€5). **Driving** takes the same time. An hourly city **bus** schedules its departures with train arrivals, making an ascent to the upper town possible without pain for €1.50. If you're after a **taxi**, call ☎ 95 70 08.

If you have legs of steel, you can rent mountain **bikes** from the tourist office for €10/17 for a half/full day, with a 20% discount for groups of four or more – good luck!

TOURIST INFORMATION

🗐 **Tourist office** Inside the castle, Château de Wiltz; ☎ 95 74 44; www.touristinfowiltz.lu; ⏰ Sep–Jun 09.00–12.00 & 14.00–17.00 Mon–Fri, 10.00–12.00 Sat, Jul–Aug 10.00–18.00 daily

🏠 WHERE TO STAY

🏠 **Aux Anciennes Tanneries** (16 rooms) 42a rue Jos Simon, L-9550; ☎ 95 75 99; e tannerie@ pt.lu; www.auxanciennestanneries.com. The site of a former tannery, this white hotel occupies a tranquil spot in the lower town. You know you're arriving somewhere different if you come on foot, as you cross an old wooden footbridge to get there. Sit on the terrace overlooking the river & enjoy the peace & quiet. Beautifully decorated rooms with elegant flowery furnishings & parquet floors have large comfortable beds & minibar. Bathrooms in more expensive rooms have whirlpool baths &/or jacuzzis. Guests can use the sauna & solarium. €€–€€€

🏠 **Hotel Vieux Château** (8 Rooms) 1–3 Grand Rue, L-9530; ☎ 95 80 18; e vchateau@ pt.lu; www.hotelvchateau.com; closed 2 weeks around New Year, 3 weeks in Aug. Small, friendly hotel in a lovely old building next to the castle, with elegantly furnished rooms & spotless bathrooms. When you sink into the ultra-comfy bed you may never want to get up again. 1 room at the top has a large panoramic rooftop terrace overlooking Grand Rue in 1 direction, the town hall in another, & the castle in a 3rd. No lift. At the back of the hotel is a secluded garden terrace shaded by horse chestnut trees. During the Wiltz Festival, virtuoso performers sometimes stay here. If you're lucky you may be serenaded by beautiful music drifting down the hallway as they limber up for the evening show. For a splash-out meal, try the hotel's exceptional restaurant (see *Where to eat*, below). €€–€€€

🏠 **Beau Sejour** (70 rooms) 21 rue du X Septembre, L-9560; ☎ 95 82 50; e hotel. beausejour@internet.lu; www.hotel-beau-sejour. lu. Large family-run hotel on a noisy street in the lower town, but there's a peaceful garden at the back. Rooms are clean & simple. Some have balconies. Facilities include a sauna, solarium & fitness room, & 2 restaurants. €€

🏠 **Youth Hostel** (109 beds) 6 rue de la Montagne, L-9538; ☎ 95 80 39; e wiltz@ youthhostels.lu; www.youthhostels.lu; ⏰ Apr–Oct. High in the upper town, the youth hostel is in an ancient brewery. Newer rooms in a separate building are wheelchair-accessible. Rooms have 2–12 beds. The canteen provides packed lunches & vegetarian food on request. *€17.50pp, inc bed, b/fast & bedding. Non-members pay €3 extra.*

✕ WHERE TO EAT

As part of a street-long facelift, all bars and restaurants on Grand Rue now have terraces.

✕ **Vieux Château** 1–3 Grand Rue; ☎ 95 80 18; www.hotelvchateau.com; ⏰ 12.00–14.00 & 19.00–21.00 Wed–Sun. The ultra-stylish restaurant of the eponymous hotel is as swish as they come. Exquisite French cuisine is beautifully refined, & presented in a relaxed & friendly setting with attentive service. Dishes featuring lobster or turbot certainly don't come cheap, but are worth every cent. €€€€–€€€€€

✕ **L'Hostellerie des Ardennes** 61 Grand Rue; ☎ 95 81 52; ⏰ 18.00–22.00 Sun–Fri; closed 3 weeks in Aug. The restaurant here has been serving customers since 1929. Its traditionally furnished interior has heavy wooden furniture everywhere & sturdy décor. The French–Luxembourgish food is certainly hearty & tasty, but I can't help wondering if the high prices reflect the reputation rather than the quality. Mind you, the tables at the back do have an excellent view through the windows. €€€–€€€€

✗ Arancio Nero 68 rue de la Fontaine; ☏ 26 95 41 40; ⏲ 10.00–14.00 & 18.00–22.00 Tue–Sun. The 'Black Orange', needless to say, has a black & orange theme running throughout. Food is predominantly Italian, with a good range of pizzas, pastas & salads, along with pricier meat & fish dishes. €€–€€€

✗ Auberge Michel Rodange 11 rue Michel Rodange; ☏ 95 06 69; ⏲ 12.00–14.00 & 18.00–21.00 Wed–Sat. The airy dining room here has warming 'Mediterranean' shades of yellow & ochre, highlighted by a burgundy-coloured ceiling. There's also a terrace. Service is friendly & the French–Luxembourgish menu includes steaks & delicious hearty salads. The auberge also has rooms (€€). €€–€€€

✗ Aux Anciennes Tanneries 42a rue Jos Simon; ☏ 95 75 99; www.auxanciennestanneries. com; ⏲ 11.30–14.00 Sun–Fri & 18.30–21.00 daily. In a quaint old room with whitewashed walls & a vaulted ceiling, the good vibes are in place before you even sit down. This is fine dining with an excellent reputation. Specialities include

local Luxembourgish dishes such as trout & *judd mat gaardebounen*. €€–€€€

✗ Le Panis 29 Grand Rue; ☏ 26 95 07 95; ⏲ 11.30–14.00 & 18.30–21.30 Mon–Thu, 11.30–14.00 & 18.30–22.00 Fri–Sat. Informal Italian joint with uncluttered modern styling & reliably good food. The menu has a wide range of pastas & pizzas, plus more substantial dishes. €€–€€€

✗ Brasserie Moartplatz 2 Hannelanst; ☏ 26 95 08 17; ⏲ 08.00–21.00 Mon–Sat. On a new square close to the castle, this simple self-service restaurant offers reasonably priced if unspectacular dishes such as salads & pasta. There's a sunny terrace outside. Well, I say sunny … €–€€

✗ Prabbeli 8 rue de la Montagne; ☏ 95 92 05 52; ⏲ 10.00–18.00 Mon–Fri. Between the youth hostel & the Jardin de Wiltz, this bright w/day lunch-only diner is fairtrade-accredited, & part of the Prabbeli Centre Cultural, which also has a small cinema. It serves salads, meat dishes & vegetarian options. €–€€

ENTERTAINMENT The otherwise unremarkable **Café de la Bourse** (*41 Grand Rue;* ☏ *26 95 05 24;* ⏲ *11.00–midnight daily*) is a local's hangout & snack bar (selling cheap-as-chips burgers, *croques* and, yes, chips), and a bit rough around the edges, but noteworthy because their beer list runs to almost 50 choices, the best I'm aware of in the Grand Duchy (I would love to be corrected on this point).

Every July the **Festival de Wiltz** (see box, page 208) becomes the focal point of the town.

SHOPPING

Match Supermarket Just by the castle, Centre Commercial Îlot du Château; ☏ 95 94 30;

⏲ 08.00–20.00 Mon–Fri, 08.00–19.00 Sat, 08.00–12.30 Sun

OTHER PRACTICALITIES

✚ **Pharmacie Grotenrath** 25 rue de Tondeurs; ☏ 95 70 76; ⏲ 08.30–12.30 & 13.30–18.00 Mon–Fri, 08.30–12.00 Sat

$ **BGL BNP Paribas Bank** 53–55 Grand Rue; ☏ 42 42 20 00; ⏲ 09.00–16.00 Mon–Fri

$ **Spuerkeess ('S-Bank')** Upper town: 8–10 Grand Rue; ☏ 95 81 831; ⏲ 08.15–16.30 Mon–Fri; Lower town: 23–25 av de la Gare; ☏ 95 06 671; ⏲ 08.15–16.30 Mon–Fri

✉ **Post office** 7 route de Kautenbach; ☏ 95 82 26 32; ⏲ 09.00–12.00 & 13.30–17.15 Mon–Fri

WHAT TO SEE AND DO

Wiltz Castle The castle today lives a multiple life as the tourist office and the location for several museums. The former residence of the Counts of Wiltz has been destroyed and rebuilt several times. The present building with its impressive whitewashed walls was begun in 1631, but not completed until 1720 thanks to small distractions such as the Thirty Years War. The last count fled the invading French in 1793.

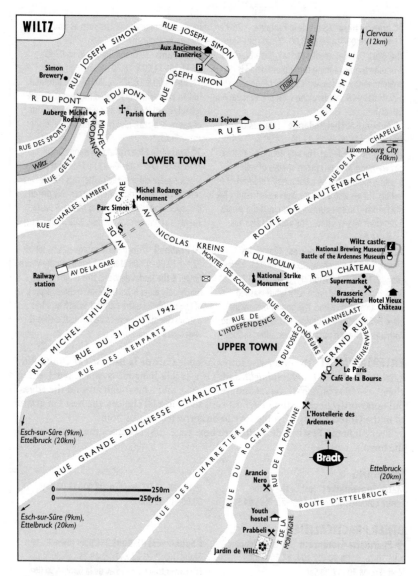

National Brewing Museum (*Musée National d'Art Brassicole; Château de Wiltz;* ✆ 95 74 44; *www.wiltz.lu;* ⊕ *Aug–Jun 09.00–12.00 & 14.00–17.00 Mon–Fri, 10.00–12.00 Sat, Jul–Aug 10.00–18.00 daily;* €3.50 *with audio guide*) and **Battle of the Ardennes Museum** (*Musée de la Bataille des Ardennes;* ⊕ *as above; admission inc with brewing museum ticket*). Accessible via the tourist information desk in the castle, the small National Brewing Museum charts the history of beer, and everything you needed to know about the brewing process. The audio tour is recommended as the displays have few labels, and without it you'll see little more than rooms full of empty bottles. With it you learn about the history of brewing from its origins in Egypt 6,000 years ago to the present. Disappointingly, however, there is no tasting room to complete the full 'surround-sound' experience.

On Saturdays, brewing seminars are led by a representative from the local Simon brewery – the last independent brewery in the country. These give you a chance to create your very own beer in the on-site microbrewery. Courses are often booked out months in advance so plan ahead – contact the tourist office for details, or visit www.brasseriesimon.lu (in French only).

Formerly a separate entity to the brewing museum, some walls have been knocked through giving you direct access to the Battle of the Ardennes Museum, one of the many memorials to the traumatic recent past. It contains the usual plethora of rusty bullet cartridges, 60-year-old tins of luncheon meat, and photos. What sets this one apart is its collection of sombre oil paintings by J Meyers depicting scenes of village destruction in the immediate aftermath of the fighting. There are also some unusual examples of 'swords to ploughshares' where salvaged items have been recycled into saleable trinkets, such as an old grenade used to decorate a letter rack.

National Strike Monument (*Monument National de la Grève*) Midway between the lower and upper town, this monument is impossible to miss. Resembling a stone lighthouse, the giant tower was erected in 1956 to honour the victims of a general strike, called on 31 August 1942, in protest against the Nazi occupation. The strike originated in Wiltz, and earned it the title 'Town of Martyrs'. The reliefs at the bottom are the work of Luxembourg's premier sculptor, Lucien Wercollier. Climb the 100-or-so steps to the top for a sweeping panoramic view.

Wiltz Garden (*Jardin de Wiltz; Rue de la Montagne;* \ *95 92 051; always open; free*) Up the hill beyond the youth hostel (just when you thought you didn't have to walk up any more), Wiltz Garden is a carefully sculpted haven that's part formal bedding, part maze. It's a community project, created and maintained by people with disabilities and the long-term unemployed, who work alongside established local artists and craftsmen. The 2.5ha site contains plants, sculptures, earthworks, water features and fields of stone, all connected by labyrinthine pathways (to move 5m in one direction you may have to detour 50m in another). It's a restful secluded spot, with private seating areas hidden in shady alcoves for 'quiet contemplation' (well, what else did you have in mind?).

CLERVAUX

Approaching Clervaux by road, you may have little idea it's there at all until you stumble upon it. Hidden in a valley and surrounded by plateaux, the only clue indicating human habitation is the tower of Clervaux Abbey peeking above the horizon. The main approach road from the east drops dramatically off a ridge via a series of hairpins, offering great views of the charming little town with its pretty church, and the strikingly white castle at its centre – the whole area feels hemmed in by the sheer wooded slopes all around. The castle is home to the 'Family of Man': the world's greatest photographic exhibition, recognised by UNESCO for its cultural importance (albeit closed at the time of writing for vital restoration work).

GETTING THERE AND AROUND Clervaux is on the picturesque northern railway. **Trains** travel to and from Luxembourg City every hour (one hour; €5), and the station is a ten-minute walk from the centre. **Driving** from the capital takes the same amount of time. Once in the centre, everything else with the notable exception of the abbey is no more than a few paces away.

FESTIVAL DE WILTZ

Held every summer since 1953, the Wiltz Festival is Luxembourg's largest annual musical celebration. The first occasion – a production of Rossini's *William Tell* staged by a German opera company – was a bridge-building exercise to restore cultural ties after World War II. It has since grown into a major event, attracting global stars of the music and dance worlds from Duke Ellington to Riverdance. Everything from opera and classical to jazz is represented. One of the biggest selling points is the fabulous location: most performances are staged in a large open-air bowl theatre beside the castle. The castle wall forms a floodlit backdrop, and with foliage on the other sides it literally becomes a theatre of trees. Instead of gentle coughing and the crunching of snack packets, quieter moments of 'silence' are punctuated by birdsong and the delicate sound of wind rustling the leaves. An occasional motorbike may roar past in the distance, but that never detracts from the experience – in fact it makes the show feel all the more real.

A large awning has kept audiences dry since 1991, alleviating bad weather problems that once plagued the festival. For longer performances you may want to emulate the locals by bringing a cushion or pillow to sit on. A coat or sweater (or a blanket) is also useful as it gets chilly after dark on all but the balmiest of summer days.

Visit the festival website (*www.festivalwiltz.lu*) or ask the tourist office for a complete agenda. Bigger performances sell out in advance, but tickets for smaller and lesser-known acts are usually available on the day.

TOURIST INFORMATION

Tourist office 2 pl de la Libération; 92 00 72; www.tourisme-clervaux.lu; ☺ 10.00–18.00 daily. The tourist office will provide advice & free brochures on what to see & do in Clervaux & the surrounding region, & can help with accommodation reservations on request. An internet terminal is available inside (€1 per 30 mins). They will also rent you a GPS (€5 per day 10.00–18.00, €2.50 per half-day 14.00–18.00), for guided tours with a difference around Clervaux. There are 6 routes to choose from; see webgis.naturpark-our.lu for more information.

WHERE TO STAY

Le Clervaux (22 rooms) 9 Grand Rue, L-9710; 92 11 05; e info@le-clervaux.com; www.le-clervaux.com. This self-styled 'Boutique & Design Hotel' opened in late 2011. As the epithet hints, this is stylish & tasteful, with comfortable rooms & ultra-modern bathrooms. Facilities include the top-floor Sky Lounge, a sauna, fitness centre & pool. The hotel is under the same management as the International across the street, & an enclosed bridge linking the two allows guests to access the facilities in both without venturing outdoors. €€€
Manoir Kasselslay (6 rooms) Maison 21, L-9769 Clervaux-Roder; 95 84 71; e contact@kasselslay.lu; www.kasselslay.lu; closed Christmas, 2 weeks in Feb, & 3 weeks in Sep. In the microscopic village of Roder, 5km east of Clervaux, the Manoir Kasselslay likes to think of itself not as a hotel, but as a 'restaurant with rooms'. There's as much attention to detail in the latter as there is in the former. Traffic noise is hardly a problem as the Kasselslay sits at the end of a country lane – the only people who come this way are headed specifically for it. Super-sleek rooms are individually furnished, have parquet floors & are named after herbs. Bathrooms are shiny & spotless. Combined overnight stay & meal arrangements are available. €€€
Hotel International (52 rooms) 10 Grand Rue, L-9710; 92 93 91; e mail@interclervaux. lu; www.interclervaux.lu; closed 24 & 25 Dec.

The International is Clervaux's top-end offering – the Executive Suite resembles a half-timbered cottage, with a lounge below & a bedroom on the mezzanine. If that seems a little OTT, the standard rooms offer all the international 4-star comforts you'd expect from a hotel with that name, with safe, minibar & Wi-Fi. There's also an upmarket French restaurant, Les Arcades (⏲ *daily 11.30–14.30 & 18.30–21.30;* €€€€), a somewhat more affordable bar/brasserie, & an expansive wellness area featuring a Finnish sauna & a 'salt grotto'. They welcome hikers & can provide packed lunches. €€–€€€€

🏠 **Château d'Urspelt** (30 rooms) Am Schlass, L-9774 Urspelt; ☎ 26 90 56 10; e info@chateau-urspelt.lu; www.chateau-urspelt.lu. In the village of Urspelt, 2km east of Clervaux. As soon as you walk in & see the well in the reception area (which used to be the kitchen), you know you're in for a treat. This lovingly restored 18th-century château has plenty of antiques on show, & each public room has a photo on the wall showing how it looked before restoration (the term 'Lazarus' springs to mind). There's also a spa & wellness centre (reserve in advance for privacy). Exquisitely furnished rooms in milky coffee shades have wooden floorboards & period stylings, but manage to include satellite TV, internet connections & modern bathrooms. The beds are so comfortable you won't want to leave them. Not surprisingly, this is a popular wedding venue & often booked out at w/ends. Across the central courtyard, the Victoria Restaurant (☎ *26 90 56 56 (reservations essential);* ⏲ *18.00–22.00 daily & 12.00–14.00 Sun,* €€€–€€€€) hints at the past whilst keeping one foot in the contemporary: uplighters cast a warm glow over the vaulted ceiling. The menu is French-inspired. But considering the surroundings the prices won't shock – too much. €€–€€€

🏠 **Hotel des Nations** (28 rooms) 29 rue de la Gare, L-9707; ☎ 92 10 18; e info@hoteldesnations.lu; www.hoteldesnations.lu. By the station, 500m north of the centre, the back of this friendly family-run hotel looks out onto greenery. Rooms, in pastel yellow shades, are smallish but very clean & have free Wi-Fi, good bathrooms & separate WCs. Massages & other spa treatments are available, & the wellness centre has a solarium & jacuzzi (⏲ *15.00–20.00 daily;* €8 for 20 mins). The b/fast room is on the 4th floor to take maximum advantage of the fact the valley is narrow here, meaning the trees are little more than 10m away. €€–€€€

🏠 **Hotel du Commerce** (48 rooms) 2 rue de Marnach, L-9709; ☎ 92 91 81; e info@hotelducommerce.lu; www.hotelducommerce.lu; ⏲ mid-Mar to Nov. Right in the centre within metres of the castle, the Commerce is friendly, family run & an institution that's been at the heart of local tourism for decades. The swimming pool is free for guests, but other available wellness treatments cost extra. Some rooms have balconies; all have free Wi-Fi. Bathrooms

FOX ON THE RUN

Michel Rodange (1827–76), the nation's greatest poet, is best known as the author of the epic work *De Renert* (*The Fox*), an adaptation of a traditional German tale, set in Luxembourg. Rodange was a schoolteacher who travelled widely throughout the Grand Duchy, and was an astute observer of regional dialects. He used these to bring his poem to life. *De Renert* is a thinly veiled swipe at the political turmoil of the day – Renert himself is said to represent hypocrisy and deception.

Although Rodange lived and worked in many places, nowhere seems to have taken his presence to heart as much as Wiltz, where he stayed for seven years from 1866 to 1873. You'll find an auberge named after him, and a café (the latter in the house where he resided), not forgetting various monuments and statues. In Parc Simon in the lower town, you can even follow the **Rodange-Reenert Cultural Walk**, a short trail past a collection of sculptures all based on the foxy theme. The random spelling of 'Renert/Reenert' is their idea, not mine, by the way.

are small but very clean. The restaurant is also recommended. €€–€€€

🏠 **Hotel Koener** (48 rooms) 14 Grand Rue, L-9701; 📞 92 10 02; e mail@koenerclervaux.lu; www.koenerclervaux.lu; ⏱ Feb–Dec. Rooms in this city-centre hotel are large & tidy, but the bathrooms, however clean, are a little small – unless you go for the pricier options, in which case you'll have a whirlpool bath. There's a parking garage, a large terrace out front, a restaurant & bar, & a wellness centre with a swimming pool, Turkish bath & relaxation room. €€–€€€

⚑ **Camping Officiel** (125 pitches) 33 Klatzewee, L-9714; 📞 92 00 42; e campingclervaux@internet.lu; www.camping-clervaux.lu; ⏱ Apr–Oct. Located by the river, just 400m from town, the municipal campsite has a swimming pool & snack bar to keep everyone occupied. The shower blocks have been recently renovated, & there's a launderette. *€5.30pp, plus €5.50 per pitch.*

🍴 WHERE TO EAT

🍴 **Manoir Kasselslay** Maison 21, Clervaux-Roder; 📞 95 84 71; www.kasselslay.lu; ⏱ 12.00–14.00 & 18.00–22.00 Wed–Sun. This award-winning establishment is a class apart – if you can afford it. Owners Hans – also the chef – & Maryse Popelaars create a friendly & welcoming dining experience that's elegant without being stuffy. The smells of fresh cooking greet you as you enter. There's a terrace at the back, & behind the main dining area a communal wooden table offering an informal alternative with a view of the kitchen & the wine cellar. The Manoir prides itself on using local seasonal produce, & sources organically wherever possible. Its French menu also sports a refreshingly wide range of vegetarian mains. Several set menus are available with or without wine. For a bargain it's hard to look past the 3-course lunch for €35. Service is attentive but never as relentless as some higher-class establishments can be. The emphasis is on personal service rather than grovelling, & it represents excellent value for money. €€€€–€€€€€

🍴 **Le Bouche à l'Oreille** 29 rue de la Gare; 📞 92 10 18; www.restaurant-leboucheaoreille.lu; ⏱ 12.00–14.00 & 18.30–20.00 daily. The Hotel des Nations's restaurant serves refined French-influenced cuisine with a light touch. The view from the tastefully decorated restaurant (just hints of red & grey contrasting with the white), is so overwhelmingly filled with the trees on the far side of the valley, it's easy to forget you have to cross a main road & railway to get there. The adjacent Brasserie (⏱ *17.00–midnight Mon, 11.00–midnight Tue–Sun*) serves snacks all day, plus main Luxembourgish fare during restaurant hours. *Brasserie €€; Restaurant €€€–€€€€*

🍴 **Da Lonati** 9 Grand Rue; 📞 92 11 051; www.da-lonati.com; ⏱ 11.00–22.00 daily. Part of the new Le Clervaux complex, this restaurant opened in 2011, & serves good Italian food in chic surroundings. €€€

🍴 **Du Commerce** 2 rue de Marnach; 📞 92 91 81; www.hotelducommerce.lu; ⏱ 12.00–14.00 Thu–Tue & 19.00–20.30 daily. The restaurant of the eponymous hotel somehow manages to give an impression of calm & peace even when it's overflowing with customers & the staff are pushed to the limit. Whether you opt to stay here or not, this is a fine choice for an evening meal, with good food & prompt efficient service. Meals are French-influenced & traditional Luxembourgish – fresh game from the Ardennes is served during autumn's hunting season, & there's a reasonable selection for vegetarians. €€€

🍴 **Les Ecuries du Parc** 4 rue du Parc; 📞 92 03 64; www.staell.lu; ⏱ 12.00–14.00 & 18.00–22.00 Tue–Fri, 12.00–14.00 & 18.00–22.30 Sat–Sun. This French–Italian restaurant's rustic location makes it feel like the countryside even though it's just 200m from town up a narrow lane. The building looks like an abandoned station from the outside, but is actually the former stables of the Earl of Clervaux, giving rise to its alternative name (*Pärdsställ*, meaning 'stables'). The interior is homely, with stone walls, brick & wood beam ceilings & tiled floors, & an open fire in winter. You can enjoy a drink in the bar or on the terrace, which has fine views across Clervaux. Choose from pastas & pizzas, fondues, raclettes, or a fuller menu comprising largely French dishes. Pizzas are available all day. *Pizzas €–€€; other mains €€–€€€*

🍴 **La Porte d'Orient** 22 Grand Rue; 📞 26 91 271; ⏱ 11.50–15.00 & 18.00–23.00 Wed–Mon. This Cantonese outlet sticks to the prevailing wisdom that all such places should contain an overwhelming quantity of red furnishings, but yellow & paper screens contrast well to add a lighter touch. Alongside good-value Chinese dishes are more expensive Japanese items including sushi & sashimi. €€

ENTERTAINMENT AND NIGHTLIFE Just out of town, at the top of the hill in Marnach (on the N18 southbound), is the dramatically shaped theatre/concert hall, **CUBE 521** (*1–3 Driicht, L-9764;* \ *52 15 21; www.cube521.lu; performance prices & times vary*). It hosts plays as well as musical and dance performances of various genres. The numerical part of the name derives from the fact Marnach is 521m above sea level.

OTHER PRACTICALITIES
Medical
+ Pharmacie de Clervaux 20 Grand Rue; \ 92 10 15; ⏱ 08.30–12.30 & 13.30–18.00 Mon–Fri, 08.30–12.00 Sat. This building was once a hotel – Victor Hugo stayed in it in 1863, says the plaque in the wall.

Banks
$ BGL BNP Paribas Bank 34 Grand Rue; \ 42 42 20 00; ⏱ 09.00–16.30 Mon–Fri

$ Dexia Bank 2 Grand Rue; \ 24 59 65 00; ⏱ 08.30–16.30 Mon–Fri
$ Spuerkeess ('S-Bank') 18 Grand Rue; \ 92 11 21; ⏱ 08.15–11.45 & 13.30–17.00 Mon–Fri

Post office
✉ **Post office** 54 rue de la Gare; \ 92 11 49 31; ⏱ 08.00–12.00 & 13.30–17.00 Mon–Fri

WHAT TO SEE AND DO
Clervaux Castle (*Château de Clervaux;* \ *92 10 481;* ⏱ *see individual museums following for opening times*) This impressive castle dates back to the 12th century, when the first Lord of Clervaux was Gerhard von Sponheim, brother of the Count of Vianden. It managed to keep its head below the parapet throughout much of its history, but a fire in December 1944 sparked by a Nazi bombardment severely damaged the building. It has since been completely restored. Its most notable features – the bright white walls – are believed to be how the castle looked in its early days, although there probably wasn't an old American tank parked outside as there is now. As well as being the town hall and the tourist office, the castle is home to three museums – a combi-ticket (adult/student €7/3.50) is available giving access to all of them.

The Family of Man (*Château de Clervaux;* \ *92 96 57; www.cna.lu;* ⏱ *Mar–Dec 10.00–18.00 Tue–Sun; adult/child €4.50/2.50*) At the time of writing, The Family of Man was closed for essential renovation work, and will remain shut until 2013. Check with the tourist office for the latest news. When it reopens, what you will find is without a doubt the world's most important permanent photographic collection. This was the brainchild of Luxembourg-born American photographer Edward J Steichen, who created it in 1955 for New York's Museum of Modern Art. He commissioned a team of prominent contemporary photographers to capture the world of the 1950s on film. No fewer than 273 individuals from 68 different countries were involved – of the 503 photos, only four were taken by Steichen himself. The exhibit caused a great stir, and was seen by nine million people when it went on a world tour during the late 1950s and early 1960s. In 1964, it was given to Luxembourg by the American government, honouring Steichen's wish that his baby find a permanent home in his land of birth (his family had emigrated when he was 18 months old, but when he returned he was greeted as a home-coming hero). It's been in Clervaux Castle since 1994.

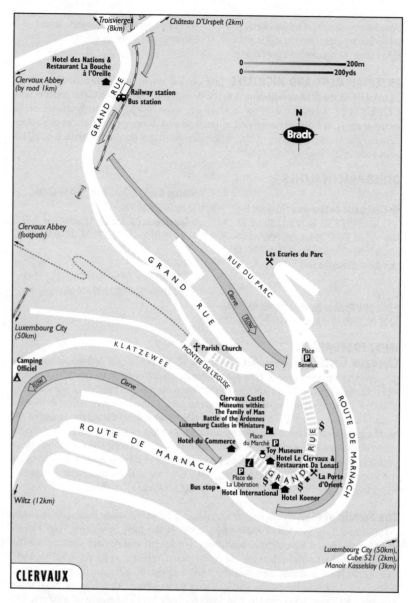

Clervaux map with the following labels:

Troisvierges (8km)
Château D'Urspelt (2km)
Hotel des Nations & Restaurant La Bouche à l'Oreille
Clervaux Abbey (by road 1km)
GRAND RUE
Railway station
Bus station
0 — 200m
0 — 200yds
N
Bradt
Clervaux Abbey (footpath)
GRAND RUE
RUE DU PARC
Clerve
FLOW
Les Ecuries du Parc
Luxembourg City (50km)
KLATZEWEE
MONTEE DE L'EGLISE
† Parish Church
Place Benelux
Camping Officiel
FLOW
Clerve
ROUTE DE MARNACH
Clervaux Castle
Museums within:
The Family of Man
Battle of the Ardennes
Luxemburg Castles in Miniature
Hotel du Commerce
Place du Marché
Toy Museum
Hotel Le Clervaux & Restaurant Da Lonati
GRAND RUE
ROUTE DE MARNACH
Place de La Libération
Bus stop
Hotel International
Hotel Koener
La Porte d'Orient
Wiltz (12km)
Luxembourg City (50km), Cube 521 (2km), Manoir Kasselslay (3km)

CLERVAUX

The cultural significance of this fascinating glimpse into the 1950s was recognised in 2003 when it was added to the UNESCO Register of the Memory of the World. Thematic rooms take you on a trail telling the story of man, covering subjects from love and birth to work and war. Thirty-five sections arc through a tale of hope, despair, and back to hope again. The exhibition isn't just great because of the subject matter – it's thoughtfully presented too. Playful subjects are treated playfully (photos of people on swings hang from the ceiling and actually swing), while serious subjects are static and straight-faced. It also provides an honest account of the age – early photographs show man's excitement at harnessing the atom and looking towards a golden future, then a shot of an atomic explosion brings everyone crashing back to reality.

What you get from the story is up to you. Many pictures are open to interpretation and yours may be different from everyone else's – it was Steichen's intention that no answer be more or less valid than any other. This is one exhibition you should pass through twice. Make the journey on your own to see how the images impact you; then go round again in the company of an audio guide (€2.50) to hear the 'official' version. It may surprise, and will certainly open your eyes to things you missed.

Battle of the Ardennes Museum (*Musée de la Bataille des Ardennes; Château de Clervaux;* \ *92 00 72;* ⊕ *May–Sep 11.00–18.00 daily, Mar–Apr & Oct–Dec 11.00–18.00 Sat–Sun; adult/student (13–25)/child (6–12) €2.50/1.25/0.50*) In one wing of the castle, the display cases here are stuffed to overflowing with memorabilia from weapons to unopened cola bottles. As elsewhere, the exhibits have either been found in the vicinity or donated by veterans and their families on both sides. Upper floors are marginally less cramped and contain German and Allied uniforms, while maps of the offensive highlight the moves and strategies involved.

Luxembourg Castles in Miniature Museum (*Châteaux Forts Luxembourgois en Maquettes;* \ *92 96 86;* ⊕ *May–Sep 11.00–18.00 daily; Mar–Apr & Oct–Dec 11.00–18.00 Sat–Sun; adult/student (13–25)/child (6–12) €2.50/1.25/0.50*) This museum contains exactly what its name suggests. A series of more than 20 of Luxembourg's more significant castles are recreated as 1:100 scale models. Depending on where you are on your travels, you can admire them and go 'been there', identify ones you need to check out, or get an overview of what you're missing. There's a potted history of each and a map showing where they can be found.

Clervaux Abbey (*Abbaye de Clervaux; L-9737;* \ *92 10 27;* ⊕ *09.00–19.00 daily; free*) Built in 1910, the large Benedictine abbey perches on a wooded ridge above Clervaux. From the town only the church tower is visible above the trees, so you get little idea of what awaits. Largely destroyed in World War II, it has been fully restored, although like many historical buildings a continuous cycle of repair ensures builders' scaffolding may always be in evidence. Only the abbey church and crypt are open to the public, as monks still live in the main buildings. The **church** is austere in the extreme, with little ornamentation. The bare concrete walls with nothing to distract you come as quite a shock after the usual displays of glitz and chintz found in most of Luxembourg's Catholic churches. The **crypt** has a photo exhibition detailing daily monastic life. Unlike their counterparts elsewhere the monks here don't devote their time to brewing beer or distilling sticky liqueurs, allowing more time to concentrate on a fully ascetic lifestyle. Nor do they make cheese for sale. Instead, they prefer to stay private and focus on study and worship. The abbey can be reached by car, or head here on foot from the town in about 15–20 minutes – walk behind the parish church to the left and take the steps heading up and to the right at the rear.

Clervaux Parish Church Dominating the lower town alongside the castle, the parish church was also built in 1910. On the inside the style is only marginally less minimalist than in the abbey. The notable exceptions are the beautiful stained-glass windows and the golden decoration of the ceiling behind the altar.

Toy Museum (*Musée du Jouet; 9 Grand Rue;* \ *92 02 28;* ⊕ *Easter–Dec 10.00–12.00 & 14.00–17.00 daily, Jan–Mar 10.00–12.00 & 14.00–17.00 Sat–Sun; adult/child €3/2*)

This playful museum on the main street will appeal to children or those still young at heart. It houses a large collection of metal toys, dolls, model cars and trains, doll's houses, and much else besides. The museum has now been swallowed up by the Le Clervaux Hotel (see page 208).

Cité de l'Image (*Various sites*) The 'City of Images' is an outdoor photographic exhibit designed to add sparkle to Clervaux. At various locations throughout town (including just north of the railway station, and between the station and the centre) you'll see a series of bright 'Warhol-esque' images – sometimes abstract, sometimes with obvious meaning – that dab a splash of colour onto the streets. They're particularly pleasing when lit up in the evening.

From time to time the otherwise empty former **Hotel du Parc** (on the hillside above place Benelux) is used to house temporary exhibitions. Check for posters around town to see if there's anything worth heading up there for.

THE 'FAR NORTH'

Although barely 60km from the capital, the extreme north of the Grand Duchy seems a remote, rural world stuck somewhere else in time. Many people from the south freely admit they seldom venture this way, considering it just a bit 'too far'. Nevertheless, there are several interesting places to visit, including two very good countryside museums, and some lovely hotels, one with possibly the quaintest setting in the country.

GETTING THERE AND AROUND Besides Clervaux and the mildly dull town of Troisvierges, both of which have railway stations connected to Luxembourg City, few people live up here, and there's a corresponding lack of public transport. There are a few irregular **buses**, but to do the area justice you need a **car**.

WHERE TO STAY AND EAT With several notable exceptions you may prefer to base yourself in Clervaux and make side trips.

Auberge du Relais Postal (9 rooms) Maison 164, L-9940 Asselborn; 99 86 16 or 27 80 961; e mouilinas@pt.lu or info@relaispostal.lu; www.relaispostal.lu. Asselborn is no more than a cluster of houses, but it boasts 2 fabulous hotels. This one in the village centre positively reeks of history. Built in 1512, the breathtakingly restored stone building was for 2 centuries the only stop in Luxembourg on the postal coach routes from Antwerp to Rome, & from Mechelen to Innsbruck, both important when the region was under Habsburg rule. Reminding you of its past is a full-size replica of a horse-drawn carriage in the bar, & a museum of communication (of sorts) in the restaurant, with among other things a transatlantic telegraph dating from 1878. Guest rooms are beautifully & individually styled in a luxuriant mix of classic & modern, with parquet flooring.

There's free Wi-Fi throughout. The restaurant (⏲ May–Sep 12.00–14.00 & 18.00–21.00 Wed–Fri, 12.00–21.00 Sat–Sun, Oct–Apr 18.00–21.00 Wed–Fri, 12.00–21.00 Sat–Sun; €€€), with a 7m-deep well visible beneath a glass panel in the stone floor, uses local seasonal produce where possible. Specialities are meats & fish cooked on a charcoal grill, served with chargrilled vegetables & jacket spuds. The kitchen is open, meaning the aromas from the grill waft tantalisingly through the dining room. The Relais also houses a small writing & classroom museum (see *What to see and do*, page 216). €€€

Cornelyshaff (9 rooms) 83 Haaptstrooss, L-9753 Heinerscheid; 92 17 451; e info@touristcenter.lu; www.touristcenter.lu, www.cornelyshaff.info. On the edge of fields, this large building serves a variety of purposes, two of which are hotel & restaurant. Rooms are simply furnished, with tiled floors & wood in abundance, but they are large, comfortable & quiet. Wi-Fi is only available in public areas. The informal restaurant (⏰ *12.00–14.00 & 18.30–21.00 daily*; €–€€), with more wood & tiles, & bright tablecloths, is exceptional value. It has a fireplace for winters & a terrace for summer. Food is traditional Luxembourgish with French hints, & uses locally sourced products in substantial amounts. The best way to wash them down is with the most local product of all, the draught beers created in the microbrewery below your feet. €€

🏠 **Domaine du Moulin d'Asselborn** (15 rooms) Maison 158, L-9940 Asselborn; ☏ 99 86 16; ✉ moulinas@pt.lu; www.hotelvieuxmoulin. lu; closed 3 weeks in Feb & 3 weeks in Nov. The old watermill in Asselborn covers all bases: it's a museum & art gallery, a café & a fine restaurant. If you want to enjoy the last to the full, it also has a good-value hotel. To get here by car (no public transport), head for Asselborn just south of Troisvierges, then follow the signs. It's in a secluded valley down a narrow country lane, around 1km from the village, & totally rustic: the road goes nowhere else so there's no traffic & nothing beyond the sound of a gushing stream to disturb the peace. Simply furnished guest rooms have part-wood-lined walls, giving them a log-cabin feel. Downstairs are several eating options (restaurants ⏰ *12.00–14.00 Wed–Fri & Sun–Mon, 18.30–21.00 Wed–Mon*; €–€€€€): the 'Vieux Moulin' offers gastronomic French cuisine; 'The Mill Inn' serves grills & steaks (⏰ *dinner only Thu–Sat*); while the 'Brasserie Mille Stuff' cooks up Luxembourgish dishes & bar snacks all day long. The seasonal game menu in the main restaurant is excellent, while some of the trout is so fresh you may, as I did, see it being removed from the adjacent stream as you dine. If you're into birdwatching, there's a hide about 100m up the dirt track opposite the mill. Whether a guest or not, you can still visit the mill workings. €€

WHAT TO SEE AND DO
Ardennes Draught Horse and Tourist Centre 'A Robbesscheier' (*Musée Rural du Cheval de Trait Ardennais 'A Robbesscheier'; Frummeschgaas, Munshausen;* ☏ *92 17 451; www.touristcenter.lu;* ⏰ *08.30–18.00 Mon–Fri, 10.00–17.00 Sat–Sun; adult/child €2–10, depending on programme*) Besides having a mouthful of a name, this living museum is designed to preserve knowledge about traditional farming methods and will appeal particularly to children. It's very much a hands-on experience, where you can ride on donkeys or in horse-drawn wagons, learn about herb gardens, feed the sheep or try your hand at beekeeping or baking bread. Fourteen 'workshops' are available, each lasting around 30–45 minutes, and entry packages usually include a choice of six – sign up in the museum office. It's free if you just want to wander around the grounds. You could easily spend a day here. The café-restaurant next door is a cosy little tavern that'll keep mums and dads as amused as the kids are on the farm. Set lunches go for around €10.

Munshausen is around three minutes by bus 670 (one per hour, €1.50) from Drauffelt station, which is on the main line between Clervaux (five minutes, €2.50) and Luxembourg City (one hour, €5). Trains run hourly in each direction.

'A Schiewesch' Museum of Rural Life (*Musée Rural 'A Schiewesch'; Maison 47, Binsfeld;* ☏ *97 98 20; www.museebinsfeld.lu;* ⏰ *Easter–Oct 14.00–18.00 Tue–Sun, Nov–Mar 14.00–18.00 Sat–Sun; adult/child €4*) Two restored 300-year-old farmhouses here have been converted into another of those fascinating ethnic museums Luxembourg does so well, giving an insightful glimpse into past rural life. The collection consists of over 1,000 objects large and small, shoehorned into 20 rooms. This is an old-fashioned museum showcasing an old-fashioned world – the kind they don't make 'em like any more, and all the more endearing for it. It's fascinating, even if the homemade mannequins modelling the traditional costumes are getting dog-eared, and sport manic stares that make them a little scary. Out in the barn is a collection of antique

farm machinery, including ploughs and threshing machines. The only downside is a lack of explanations, not just in English, but in *any* language. This causes no problem when it comes to recognising old bedpans and anvils, but you need to exercise your imagination to figure out the terrifying veterinarian instruments – or perhaps the squeamish among us are better off left in the dark.

To get there, bus 685 runs hourly from Troisvierges, from where there are trains elsewhere. Refreshments are available in the Café Am Musée, next door.

Asselborn Mill (*Moulin d'Asselborn;* ☎ *99 86 16; www.hotelvieuxmoulin.lu;* ⊕ *10.00–12.00 & 14.00–18.00 daily; adult/child €3/1.50 or €5/3 inc Writing Museum*) This picturesque little watermill was allegedly first mentioned in texts in 1490, making it possibly the oldest in the country (and the existence of a previous mill on the site has been traced back to 1036). It's also a restaurant and hotel (see *Where to stay and eat*, page 215, for details and directions), but you don't have to eat or sleep here to visit the museum (buy tickets at reception). Inside a selection of old equipment explains the milling process. Remember to make a circuit of the outside as well to appreciate it fully – it's the gorgeous setting that really makes this place.

There is some moderately easy walking to be done in the vicinity – ask at reception for a map. The recommended route is a 12km hike that takes between three and four hours. It follows an hourglass loop with the mill at its 'waist', so can easily be broken into two. Head in the recommended clockwise direction otherwise you'll spend your entire time searching behind you for clues (red arrows on a white background). It's a pleasantly varied hike through mixed pine forest (home to foxes, deer and buzzards), and across open fields of wheat and barley, patrolled by serenading skylarks. If you do it in one go, the hotel can rustle up a packed lunch.

Writing Museum/Former Classroom (*Musée des Ecritoires/Ancienne Salle de Classe; Maison 164, Asselborn;* ☎ *99 86 16; www.relaispostal.lu;* ⊕ *on request; adult/child €3/1.50, or €5/3 inc Mill Museum*) This one-room collection above the restaurant of the Relais Postal covers the history of writing and is full of inkwells, pens and letter-opening knives, with an audio commentary in English. There is also a reconstruction of an old school room, with rows of wooden desks.

Cornelyshaff (*83 Haaptstrooss, Heinerscheid;* ☎ *92 17 451; www.cornelyshaff.info;* ⊕ *early until late daily; free*) The large building housing this multi-function 'tourist centre' looks like it used to be a barn. In fact, it has had various uses over the years: farm, brewery, café and distillery. It was even at one time an immigration office. Nowadays, in addition to the on-site hotel and restaurant/bar, there's an information centre, a shop selling local produce, a bakery, and the Ourdaller microbrewery. On the last Saturday of the month, there's an artisans' **market** (*Mar–Nov 10.00–16.00*) behind the main building, selling honey, locally smoked salmon, wild boar sausage, herbal remedies, woollen garments, jewellery and so forth. In theory you can visit the brewery on market days, but in practice the 'man with the key' doesn't always show up. You can also tour it at any time by calling ahead (*€5pp with tasting*).

For an easy pastoral walk starting and ending at Cornelyshaff, pick up their leaflet for the **Rondwee Biolandbau** (Organic agriculture circuit). This 6.7km loop (two hours at a stroll), takes you through the fields, across rolling countryside with wide views and the song of skylarks in the air (in spring and summer at least), for the most part following paved (but practically traffic-free) lanes. The route passes the Croix du Vent, a cross sculpture juxtaposed against nearby wind turbines. This is the site of the former church of Buchenburg, a village thought to have been abandoned because of plague around the time of the Thirty Years War (1618–48). In 1792 the church itself – believed to have been constructed 'before AD822' – was demolished and rebuilt 1.5 km away in Heinerscheid. The return passes through an organic farm – hence the trail's name.

Three Borders Monument (*Monument Trois Frontières, 2km east of Lieler*) A field in the heart of nowhere is an unusual location for a tribute to the European Union, but this particular spot is less than 100m from Germany and right on the Belgian frontier. Pre-dating Schengen by a decade, the monument was installed in 1977 to commemorate the 20th anniversary of the founding of Europe. Appropriately, half the surrounding park is in Belgium, the rest in Luxembourg – the brook running through the middle marks the border.

What makes this interesting is where you are. The meeting point of the three nations is 100m away on the other side of the road, but rather inconveniently it sits smack in the middle of the river Our, denying you the opportunity to be in three countries simultaneously – unless you brought galoshes. If two and a near miss will suffice, there's a bridge on the German/Belgian frontier, and you can stare back into Luxembourg a massive (but rather moist) 2m away. Markers by the riverbanks tell you where to look. The bridge itself has had a makeover since the previous edition of this guide. The old rickety wooden contraption has become an impressive steel and concrete structure, named after Georges Wagner (1900–94), a former chairman of the European Union for the Eifel and Ardennes, whose idea it was to put the original crossing here in 1977. For a short multi-national hike there's also a 2km marked trail looping through the countryside, taking in all three countries – it takes half an hour to complete. Head to the right on the far side of the bridge (in Germany), then bear around to the left onto the track leading into the forest. Around 750m north, head back downhill to the left, over the next bridge (into Belgium), then follow the road back to Luxembourg.

You'll need your own transport to get here, and there are no facilities once you arrive. Head for the hamlet of Lieler in the top right-hand corner of the country, and keep driving downhill until you see the monument by the road.

BASTOGNE

The town of Bastogne in Belgium, 12km over the border from Luxembourg, is a near-essential detour on any tour of the north for those interested in World War II history. First documented in the 7th century AD, the town's history paralleled that of the rest of the Grand Duchy for more than a millennium – it was after all part of Luxembourg until the emergence of Belgium as an independent state sliced the country in half. But it kept its head more or less below the parapet until 16 December 1944, when Hitler launched his last-gasp counter-offensive through the Ardennes. Shortly afterwards, Brigadier General Anthony Clement McAuliffe (1898–1975) arrived with the US 101st Airborne Division to defend the town and halt the Nazi advance. The fighting was fierce, and the Americans found themselves surrounded. Then on 22 December, when a German delegation arrived to ask for the American surrender, the general uttered the immortal single-word reply, 'Nuts!' This stubbornness proved the turning point of the campaign, and a few days later General Patton's forces broke through to relieve the town. The townsfolk were so proud of McAuliffe's efforts on their behalf they renamed their main square in his honour – this is one place where Patton is only the second-most revered American. For a dramatised reconstruction of the events, watch the 1949 Hollywood movie *Battleground,* set in Bastogne.

GETTING THERE AND AROUND Bus
537 departs from Ettelbruck station (hourly from Monday to Saturday, less often on Sunday), and takes one hour to reach Bastogne. The route also passes through Wiltz (18 minutes from Bastogne). Total travel time from Luxembourg City (take the **train** to Ettelbruck and switch to the bus) is around 1½ hours. **Driving** from the capital takes about an hour. Once in Bastogne, most sights are within an easy ten-minute walk of place McAuliffe, with the exceptions of the Centre of World War Two Memories and the Mardasson Memorial, for which you'll need your own transport, or to be prepared for a 20-minute walk each way. There are no urban bus services.

TOURIST INFORMATION
Maison du Tourism pl McAuliffe; +32 61 212 711; www.si-bastogne.be; ⊕ 09.00–12.30 & 13.00–18.00 daily. Has leaflets & information on Bastogne & the surrounding area. You can buy a General Patton figurine to take home if you want.

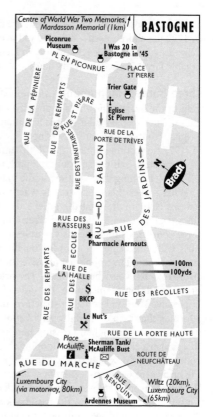

BASTOGNE

Centre of World War Two Memories, Mardasson Memorial (1km)
Piconrue Museum
I Was 20 in Bastogne in '45
PL EN PICONRUE
PLACE ST PIERRE
RUE DE LA PÉPINIÈRE
RUE DES REMPARTS
RUE DES TRINITAIRES
RUE ST PIERRE
Trier Gate
Eglise St Pierre
RUE DE LA PORTE DE TRÈVES
RUE DU SABLON
RUE DES JARDINS
N
RUE DES BRASSEURS
RUE DES ÉCOLES
RUE DES JARDINS
RUE DES
Pharmacie Aernouts
RUE DES REMPARTS
RUE DE LA HALLE
RUE DES ÉCOLES
BKCP
0 — 100m
0 — 100yds
RUE DES RÉCOLLETS
Le Nut's
RUE DE LA PORTE HAUTE
Place McAuliffe
Sherman Tank/ McAuliffe Bust
ROUTE DE NEUFCHÂTEAU
RUE DU MARCHE
RUE RENQUIN
Luxembourg City (via motorway, 80km)
Wiltz (20km), Luxembourg City (65km)
Ardennes Museum

🏠 **WHERE TO STAY** This guide is about Luxembourg, so why not stay in Wiltz or Clervaux and make this a day trip?

🍴 **WHERE TO EAT** There are numerous cafés, brasseries and restaurants lining the main square. They will feed you whatever you need from *croques* through to pizza or multi-course dinners. Most are open daily, though a few may close one or two

GAMES WITH FRONTIERS

We don't have a word in English to describe them, which is hardly surprising since between the UK, Ireland, Canada, the US, Australia and New Zealand we cannot muster up a single one between us. In fact, of the larger English-speaking nations, only South Africa can chip in, with an impressive five (but then they can use the Dutch/Afrikaans word). On the other hand tiny Luxembourg has three. What am I talking about? In German it is called a *Dreiländereck* – 'three-country corner' – a place where three nations' borders all meet at a single point. Unfortunately, Luxembourg also contrives to have all of its examples located in the centres of rivers and streams, denying you the chance to dance around them and be in three places at once.

days a week. Bars often serve lighter meals all day, although the *menu du jour* may only be available from 12.00 until 14.00.

✕ **Le Nut's** 3 pl McAuliffe; ✆ +32 61 689 669; ⊕ 09.00–22.00 daily. Apologies to the grammar police, but that rogue apostrophe in the name is their doing, not mine. This place stands apart from many on the main square because it's in-keeping with the 'General' theme. It's a standard Belgian brasserie, bright & loud with shiny brass fittings, plus photos & other war memorabilia on the walls. Food ranges from *croques* to spaghetti, or you can opt for the 'GI Menu', & choose from the Calibre 30 (25cm of grilled sausage), Calibre 50 (50cm of the same), or for real gluttons, the Barracuda: 1m of tubular meat (seriously). Wash these down with local Bastogne Pale Ale, sold in 75cl bottles that serve 3. €–€€

OTHER PRACTICALITIES

✚ **Pharmacie Aernouts** rue du Sablon 145; ✆ +32 61 211 429; ⊕ 09.00–12.30 & 13.30–19.00 Mon–Fri, 09.00–13.00 Sat
$ **BKCP Bank** rue du Sablon 79; ✆ +32 61 215 401; www.bkcp.be; ⊕ 09.00–13.00 & 14.00–16.30 Mon–Fri

✉ **Post office** pl McAuliffe 40; ✆ +32 22 012 345; ⊕ 09.00–12.30 & 13.30–18.00 Mon–Fri, 09.00–12.30 Sat

WHAT TO SEE AND DO The most prominent feature on the main square, place McAuliffe, next door to the tourist office, is a **Sherman tank**, a visible reminder of the town's not-so-distant past. Beside the tank is a **bust** of General McAuliffe himself.

Ardennes Museum (*Musée Au Pays d'Ardennes; 20 rue de Neufchâteau;* ✆ *+32 61 214 911;* ⊕ *09.30–17.00 daily; adult/child €3/free*) Finding this small museum near the main square isn't difficult: aim for the large sign saying 'original museum'. It contains three cluttered display rooms. One shows local rural artefacts including butter- and cheese-making equipment, clog-making tools, ploughs and a 'lemonade drawout' machine (no, I have no idea either – and I've seen it). The second room is dedicated to the natural history of the Ardennes, and contains various stuffed animals and fish that would have been frolicking in the forests and rivers around Bastogne had they not been hooked out by anglers or gunned down by hunters. The final room pays inevitable homage to the war, with the usual souvenirs picked up in the wake of the fighting.

Piconrue Museum (*Musée en Piconrue; 2 pl en Piconrue;* ✆ *+32 61 215 614; www.piconrue.be;* ⊕ *10.00–18.00 Tue–Sun; adult/child €4/1.50*) This gallery is mainly devoted to changing temporary exhibitions, but has a small permanent collection of religious art. The building is interesting in its own right as it has a glassed-in central courtyard with a large tree at its heart. The museum is also home to the Maison des Légendes – the House of Legends – a permanent exhibit on local myths and legends (fairies, wood nymphs, that sort of thing).

I Was 20 in Bastogne in '45 (*J'avais 20 ans en '45 à Bastogne; Espace Quartier Latin, pl St Pierre;* ✆ *+32 61 502 002; www.bastogne.be/20ansen45;* ⊕ *May–Sep 10.00–18.00 daily, Oct–Apr 10.00–18.00 Mon–Thu & Sat–Sun, last admission 17.00; adult/child €6.50/5, children under 8 free*) Given their fleeting nature, I wouldn't normally include a temporary exhibition in a guidebook, but this has been extended until 'at least' the end of 2012, and will hopefully remain longer. There's a good reason for its popularity: it's a magnificent, haunting exhibit on Bastogne's experiences in World War II, from the occupation until liberation, with focus on the battle for Bastogne. Subtitled 'the Battle of the Ardennes recollected by those who were there', several rooms show video interviews with elderly folk who were children during the occupation, and they speak about their hopes, fears and general innocence during those dark times. Many interviews were conducted by today's children. Other interviewees were soldiers (both German and American), members of the resistance, or self-confessed collaborators. For a balanced view, several rooms tell events from the German side, showing they were basically as scared as everyone else. Perhaps the most telling room – 'The Hell of the Ardennes' – contains nothing but bare tree stumps, with a loud soundtrack of gunfire, exploding shells and confused shouting. Of course it can only hint at the real hell, but is nonetheless a powerful re-creation. If you have the chance to visit this excellent exhibition, do.

Trier Gate (*Porte de Trèves; rue Porte de Trèves;* \ *+32 61 213 287;* ⏲ *by appointment only*) The Porte de Trèves, a massive, square, sandstone tower by the St Peter Church, is all that remains of Bastogne's medieval ramparts – the rest were levelled by the French in 1688. It now contains a small history museum.

Centre of World War Two Memories (*Centre de la Mémoire de la IIème Guerre Mondiale; Colline du Mardasson, off N874, 1km northwest of Bastogne;* \ *+32 61 211 413*) At the time of writing the former **Bastogne Historical Center** was closed and scheduled for redevelopment and expansion into this new museum, like its predecessor dedicated to honouring and preserving the memory of those who gave their lives on both sides during the war. It is supposed to open before the end of 2012, but don't hold your breath, as work didn't appear to have started as of summer 2011.

Mardasson Memorial (*Mémorial du Mardasson; Colline du Mardasson, off N874, 1km northwest of Bastogne;* ⏲ *always open; free*) Beside the site of the Centre of World War Two Memories is a giant memorial dedicated to the 'eternal friendship between the American and Belgian peoples'. Inaugurated in 1950, it's in the form of a five-pointed star, 31m in diameter and 12m high, around which are the names of the 50 US states. You can climb the spiral staircase to the roof for a view. The crypt, in the hillside below the monument, has three altars: one each for the Catholic, Protestant and Jewish faiths.

Historical route You can also trace a historical route around the Bastogne region, stopping at 16 memorials and sights, including several of those mentioned above. Pick up a leaflet from the tourist office, but you'll need your own transport: it's 80km in total.

Appendix 1

LANGUAGE

Three languages have equal status in Luxembourg: Luxembourgish (known locally as *Lëtzebuergesch*), French and German. Native-born Luxembourgers are trilingual, and are brought up speaking all three. Being able to master a few words of Luxembourgish is always appreciated, although it's less widely understood in Luxembourg City where there are many migrant workers and foreign-born locals, who often prefer using French. English is widely spoken throughout the country, however, particularly in the capital and in major tourist centres.

As a consistent and unified spelling of Luxembourgish was only introduced in 1984 when it became an official national language, you may well encounter slight variations in how some words are written. Note that nouns are capitalised in Luxembourgish and German, but not in French.

PRONUNCIATION

French Many people will already be somewhat familiar with French pronunciation, but there are a few well-known stumbling blocks that (according to French people at least) English-speakers 'always' get wrong:

- **eu** is close to an English 'err' (unlike its German equivalent; see below);
- **é** is similar to 'ay' as in 'day' and is pronounced when it is at the end of a word (in contrast to an unaccented e);
- **ou** is pronounced like the 'oo' in 'boot';
- **u** is similar to the above, but the mouth should be more rounded, so it becomes closer to 'you';
- **ç** is always pronounced as a soft 'c' (ie: like an 's') no matter what the following vowel;
- **h** is always silent;
- **j** is pronounced 'zh', as in 'pleasure' (also in Luxembourgish);
- **r** should always be rolled, almost like a short purring action (also in German and Luxembourgish);
- when a syllable ends in **n** it transforms the preceding vowel into a nasal grunting sound – hence 'vin' (wine) does not rhyme with the English 'tin', but is instead closer to 'van', and uttered partly through the nose.
- Unlike in German, other accents in French do not generally transform the pronunciation of vowels, but instead usually denote missing letters that have fallen out of use, or letters that have changed over the course of time.

German German vowel sounds are the most likely to catch English speakers out, although there are several other differences to watch out for, and umlauts (the 'double dot' accents) do have an effect on the way vowels should be spoken:

- **au** is like the 'ow' in 'cow';
- **ä** is close to the short 'e' in 'let';
- **äu** and **eu** are both pronounced like 'oy' in 'coy';
- **ei** is pronounced like 'eye';
- **ö** sounds like the 'er' sound in the English 'fur';
- **oo** is more like the 'oh' sound in 'go', but slightly longer, almost like the 'ough' in 'bought';
- **ü** sounds like the 'oo' in 'zoo', but with more rounded lips – not dissimilar to the unaccented 'u' in French;
- **b** and **d**; at the end of words, sound more like 'p' and 't' respectively;
- **ch** has only one direct equivalent in English: imagine how a Scot would say 'loch' (or just say it, if you happen to be Scottish!);
- **j** is always pronounced like 'y' in 'you';
- **sch** is similar to the English 'sh'
- **v** is closer to an English 'f', particularly at the start of a word;
- **w** is hard, and sounds like an English 'v'.

Luxembourgish Luxembourgish, meanwhile, is a law unto itself, and very difficult for foreigners to get spot on, not least of all because there are dialectal variations even within this small country. One simple word may be pronounced in three different ways depending on whether you are talking to someone from the north, the south or the city! The situation is in no way made easier by the lack of a coherent spelling system until recent years. Because of the complications involved, a close attempt at Luxembourgish will usually be enough to win you friends.

One vowel sound to watch out for that appears in Luxembourgish, but not in German, is **ë**. It falls midway between the German **ä** and **ö**.

VOCABULARY

Essentials	Luxembourgish	French	German
Good morning	*Gudden moïen*	*Bonjour*	*Guten Morgen*
Good afternoon	*Bonjour*	*Bonjour*	*Guten Tag*
Good evening	*Gudden owend*	*Bonsoir*	*Guten Abend*
Good night	*Gutt nuecht*	*Bonne nuit*	*Gute Nacht*
Hello	*Moïen*	*Bonjour*	*Hallo*
Goodbye	*Äddi/Awar*	*Au revoir*	*Auf Wiedersehen*
My name is …	*Ech heesche …*	*Je m'appelle …*	*Ich heisse …*
What is your name?	*Wéi heescht dir?*	*Comment vous appelez-vous?*	*Wie heissen Sie?*
How are you?	*Wéi geet et iech?*	*Comment allez-vous?*	*Wie geht es Ihnen?*
Well thanks	*Merci, gudd*	*Bien, merci*	*Gut, danke*
Pleased to meet you	*Ech si frouh, iech kennezeléieren*	*Enchanté(e)*	*Es freut mich, Sie kennenzuleren*
Please	*Wanneg gelift (w.e.g.)*	*S'il vous plait (s.v.p.)*	*Bitte*
Thank you	*Merci (villmols)*	*Merci (beaucoup)*	*Danke (schön)*
You're welcome	*Gär geschidd*	*Je vous en prie*	*Bitte/Bitte sehr*
Pardon	*Pardon*	*Pardon*	*Verzeihen Sie bitte*
Excuse me	*Entschëllegt*	*Excusez-moi*	*Entschuldigung*
Cheers!	*Prost!*	*Santé!*	*Prost!*
Yes	*Jo*	*Oui*	*Ja*
No	*Neen*	*Non*	*Nein*
Maybe	*Vläicht*	*Peut-être*	*Vielleicht*
OK	*An der rei*	*D'accord*	*In Ordnung*

I don't understand	Ech verstin iech net	Je ne comprends pas	Ich verstehe nicht
Do you speak English?	Schwätzt du engulsch?	Parlez-vous l'anglais?	Sprechen Sie Englisch?
Please speak more slowly	Schwätzt w.e .g. méi lues	Parlez plus lentement s'il vous plaît	Bitte langsamer spechen
Do you understand?	Verstidd der?	Comprenez-vous?	Verstehen Sie?
Can you help me?	Ként der mir héllefen?	Pourriez-vous m'aider?	Können Sie mir helfen?
I like ... very much	Ech hun ... ganz gär	J'aime beaucoup ...	Ich mag ... sehr
I don't like ...	Ech hun ... net gär	Je n'aime pas ...	Ich mag nicht
Do you like?	Hues Du dat gär?	Aimez-vous?	Gefällt es Ihnen?

Questions

How?	Wëi?	Comment?	Wie?
What?	Wat?	Quoi?	Was?
Where?	Wou?	Où?	Wo?
What is it?	Wat et?	Qu'est-ce que?	Was ist das?
Which?	Wat fir?	Quel(le)?	Welche (r, s)?
When?	Wann?	Quand?	Wann?
Why?	Wuerfir?	Pourquoi?	Warum?
Who?	Wien?	Qui?	Wer?

Numbers

0	null	zero	null
1	eent	un(e)	eins
2	zwee	deux	zwei/zwo
3	dräl	trois	drei
4	véier	quatre	vier
5	fënnef	cinq	fünf
6	sechs	six	sechs
7	siwen	sept	sieben
8	aacht	huit	acht
9	néng	neuf	neun
10	zéng	dix	zehn
11	elef	onze	elf
12	zwielef	douze	zwölf
13	dräizeng	treize	dreizehn
14	véierzéng	quatorze	vierzehn
15	fofzéng	quinze	fünfzehn
16	siechzéng	seize	sechzehn
17	siwwenzéng	dix-sept	siebzehn
18	uechtzéng	dix-huit	achtzehn
19	nonzéng	dix-neuf	neunzehn
20	zwanzéng	vingt	zwanzig
21	eenanzwanzéng	vingt et un	einundzwanzig
30	drëssig	trente	dreissig
40	véirzeg	quarante	vierzig
50	fofzeg	cinquante	fünfzig
60	siechzeg	soixante	sechzig
70	siwenzeg	septante*	siebzig
80	uechtzech	quatre-vingts	achtzig
90	nonzeg	nonante*/	neunzig

| 100 | honnert | cent | hundert |
| 1,000 | dausend | mille | tausend |

*Not standard French, but used in francophone countries

Time

What time is it?	Wéi spéit ass et?	Quelle heure est-il?	Wie spät ist es?
It's ...	Et ass ... Auer	Il est ... heures	Es ist ... Uhr
... in the morning	moies	du matin	morgens/vormittags
... in the evening	owes	du soir	abends
today	haut	aujourd'hui	heute
tonight	hënnt	ce soir	heute abend
tomorrow	muer	demain	morgen
yesterday	géscht(er)	hier	gestern
morning	moien	matin	Morgen/Vormittag
evening	owend	soir	Abend

Days

Monday	Méindeg	lundi	Montag
Tuesday	Dënschdeg	mardi	Dienstag
Wednesday	Mëttwoch	mercredi	Mittwoch
Thursday	Donneschdeg	jeudi	Donnerstag
Friday	Freideg	vendredi	Freitag
Saturday	Samschdeg	samedi	Samstag/Sonnabend
Sunday	Sonndeg	dimanche	Sonntag
Public holiday	Feierdag	jour de fête	Feiertag
Hour	Stonn	heure	Stunde
Day	Deg	jour	Tag
Week	Woch	semaine	Woche
Month	Mount	mois	Monat

Months

January	Januar	janvier	Januar
February	Februar	février	Februar
March	Mäerz	mars	März
April	Abrëll	avril	April
May	Mee	mai	Mai
June	Juni	juin	Juni
July	Juli	juillet	Juli
August	August	août	August
September	September	séptembre	September
October	Oktober	octobre	Oktober
November	November	novembre	November
December	Dezember	décembre	Dezember

Getting around

I'd like ...	Ech géing gär ...	Je voudrais ...	Ich möchte ...
a one-way ticket	Billje	un billet aller simple	einfache Fahrkarte
a return ticket	e Billje fir zeréck	un retour	Rückfahrkarte
I want to go to ...	Ech géing gär op ... goen	Je voudrais aller à ...	Ich möchte nach ... fahren
How much is it?	Wivill kascht et?	C'est combien?	Wie viel kostet das?

What time does it leave?	Um wivill Auer fiirt en?	À quelle heure il part?	Um wie viel Uhr fährt es?
delayed	verspéidung	retardé	verspätet
cancelled	annuléiert	annulé	storniert/annulliert
first/second class	éischt/zweeten Klass	première/deuxième classe	erste/zweite Klasse
reduced fare	reduzéierte Billje	billet à tariff réduit	Fahrkarte mit Ermäßigung
platform	Quai	quai	Gleis
ticket office	Guichet	guichet	Fahrkartenschalter
left-luggage locker	Consigne	consigne	Gepäckschliessfach
timetable	Horaire	horaire	Fahrplan
station	Gare	gare	Bahnhof
bus stop	Arrêt	arrêt	Bushaltestelle
train	Zuch	train	Zug
boat	Boot	bateau	Boot
car	Won	voiture	Auto
motorbike/moped	Töff	moto/vélomoteur	Motorrad
bicycle	Velo	vélo	Fahrrad
arrival/departure	Arrivée/départ	arrivé/depart	Ankunft/Abfahrt
next	nächst	prochain(e)	nächster/n/s
Have a good journey	Gudd Rees	Bon voyage	gute Reise
Is this the road to …?	Ass dat hei de Wee fir op …?	Ce-ci est le chemin à …?	Ist dies der Weg nach …?
service station	Tankstell	station-service	Tankstelle
petrol	Benzin	essence	Benzin
unleaded	bläifräi	sans plomb	bleifrei
I have broken down	Ech hun eng Panne	Ma voiture est tombée en panne	Ich habe eine Panne
straight ahead	riichtaus	tout droit	geradeaus
turn left	lénks	tournez à gauche	abbiegen links
turn right	riets	tournez à droit	abbiegen rechts
behind	hannert	derrière	hinter
in front of	viischt	devant	vor
opposite	géintiwwer	en face de	gegenüber
entrance	Agang	entrée	Eingang/Einfahrt
exit	Auswee	sortie	Ausgang/ Ausfahrt

EMERGENCY

Help!	Hëllef!	Au secours!	Hilfe!
Call a doctor	Ruff en Dokter	Appelez un médecin	Rufen Sien einen Arzt an
There's been an accident	Do ass en Ongléck geschidd	Il y a eu un accident	Er gab einen Unfall geschehen
Police	Police	police	Polizei
Fire	Feier	incendie	Feuer/Brand
Ambulance	Ambulanz	ambulance	Krankenwagen
Thief	Déif	voleur	Dieb
Hospital	Klinik/Spidol	hôpital	Krankenhaus
I am ill	Ech si krank	Je suis malade	Ich bin krank

toilets – men/women	*Toilette – männer/fraen*	*toilettes – hommes/femmes*	*Toiletten – Herren/Damen*
not in service	*futti*	*hors service*	*ausser Betrieb*
push	*dreiwen*	*poussez*	*drücken*
pull	*zéien*	*tirez*	*ziehen*

Accommodation

Do you have a room?	*Huet Dir nach en zemmer fräi?*	*Avez-vous une chambre?*	*Haben Sie ein Zimmer frei?*
I'd like a ...	*Ech hätt gär eng ...*	*Je voudrais une ...*	*Ich möchte ein ...*
single room	*Eenzelzëmmer*	*chambre pour une personne*	*Einzelzimmer*
double room	*Duebelzëmmer*	*chambre double*	*Doppelzimmer*
a room with two beds	*Zëmmer mat zwee Better*	*chambre à deux lits*	*Zimmer mit zwei Betten*
Bathroom/shower	*Buedzëmmer/Dusch*	*salle de bains/douche*	*Badezimmer/Dusche*
How much is it per night?	*Wivill kascht d'Nuecht?*	*Quel est le prix par nuit?*	*Wie viel kostet es pro Nacht?*
Is breakfast included?	*Is muereskaffi abegraff?*	*Le petit déjeuner est compris?*	*Is das Frühstück inbegriffen?*

Food

Do you have a table for ... people?	*Hut Dir en Dësch fir ... Leit?*	*Avez-vous une table pour ... personnes?*	*Haben Sie einen Tisch für ... Personen?*
menu	*Menuskaart*	*carte, menu*	*Speisekarte*
wine menu	*Wäikaart*	*carte des vins*	*Weinkarte*
local produce	*Regionalprodukter*	*produits du terroir*	*Produkte aus der Gegend*
to reserve	*reservéien*	*réserver*	*reservieren*
I am a vegetarian	*Ech si Vegetarier*	*Je suis végétarien(ne)*	*Ich bin Vegetarier(in)*
starter	*Entrée*	*hors d'oeuvre*	*Vorspeise*
main course	*Plat*	*plat*	*Hauptspeise*
dessert	*Dessert*	*dessert*	*Nachtisch/Dessert*
Please bring me ...	*Bréngt mer wanneg gelift ...*	*Apportez-moi s'il vous plaît ...*	*Bringen Sie mir doch bitte ...*
a fork/knife/spoon	*Forschett/Messer/Läffel*	*fourchette/ couteau/ cuillère*	*Gabel/Messer/Löffel*
delicious	*këstlech*	*délicieux*	*lecker/köstlich*
Please may I have the bill	*D'rechnung wanneg gelift*	*L'addition s'il vous plaît*	*Die Rechnung, bitte*
to pay	*betalen*	*payer*	*bezahlen*
open	*opp*	*ouvert*	*geöffnet*
closed	*zou*	*fermé*	*geschlossen*
breakfast	*Mereskaffi*	*petit déjeuner*	*Frühstück*
lunch	*Mëttegiessen*	*déjeuner*	*Mittagessen*
supper	*Nuetiessen*	*diner*	*Abendessen*
eat/drink	*iessen/drénken*	*manger/boire*	*essen/trinken*

Basics

| bread | *Brout* | *pain* | *Brot* |
| butter | *Botter* | *beurre* | *Butter* |

cheese	Kéis	fromage	Käse
eggs	Eër	oeufs	Ei
pepper	Peffer	poivre	Pfeffer
salt	Salz	sel	Salz
sugar	Zocker	sucre	Zucker

Fruit

apple	Apel	pomme	Apfel
banana	Banan	banane	Banane
grape	Drauf	raisin	Traube
pears	Bir	poire	Birne

Vegetables

carrot	Muert	carrotte	Karotte
garlic	Knuewelek	ail	Knoblauch
onion	Zwiwwel	oignon	Zwiebel
pepper (sweet)	Paprika	poivron	Paprika
potato	Gromper	pomme de terre	Kartoffel
salad	Zalot	salade	Salat
tomato	Tomat	tomate	Tomate

Fish

fish	Fësch	poisson	Fisch
mussels	Mullen	moules	Muscheln
salmon	Salem	saumon	Lachs
trout	Frëll	truite	Forelle

Meat

meat	Fleesch	viande	Fleisch
beef	Rëndfleesch	boeuf	Rindfleisch
chicken	Poulet	poulet	Huhn/Hänchen
ham	Ham	jambon	Schinken
lamb	Lamm	agneau	Lamm
pork	Schwäin	porc	Schweinefleisch
sausage	Zoossiss	saucisson	Wurst

Drinks

drinks	Gedrénks	boissons	Getränke
beer	Béier	bière	Bier
coffee	Kaffi	café	Kaffee
orange juice	Orangejus	jus d'orange	Orangensaft
milk	Mëllech	lait	Milch
tea	Té	thé	Tee
water sparkling/ flat	Spruddelwaasser/ Waasser	eau pétillante/ plate	Wasser mit Kohlensäure/ ohne Kohlensäure
wine	Wäin	vin	Wein

Shopping

| I'd like to buy ... | Ech géing gär ... kafen | Je voudrais acheter ... | Ich möchte ... kaufen |
| How much is it? | Wivill kascht dat? | C'est combien? | Wie viel kostet das? |

It's too expensive	*Et ass ze deier*	*C'est trop cher*	*Es ist mir zu teuer*
I'll take it	*Ech huelen et*	*Je le prends*	*Ich nehme es*
Please may I have ...	*Gitt mer wanneg gelift ...*	*Donnez-moi s'il vous plait ...*	*Ich möchte gerne ...*

Communications

I am looking for ...	*Ech sichen ...*	*Je cherche ...*	*Ich suche ...*
post office	*Post*	*poste*	*Post/Postamt*
market (square)	*Maart*	*(place du) marché*	*Markt(platz)*
church	*Kiersch*	*église*	*Kirche*
tourist office	*Tourismus*	*office du tourisme*	*Fremdenverkehr ... amt/Tourismbüro*
town hall	*Geméng*	*hôtel de ville*	*Rathaus*

Health

doctor	*Dokter*	*médécin*	*Arzt*
prescription	*Ordonnance*	*ordonnance*	*Verschreibung*
pharmacy	*Apdikt*	*pharmacie*	*Apotheke*
I am ...	*Ech sin ...*	*Je suis ...*	*Ich bin ...*
asthmatic	*Asthmatiker*	*asthmatique*	*Asthmatiker*
epileptic	*Epileptiker*	*épileptique*	*Epileptiker*
diabetic	*Zockerkrank*	*diabétique*	*Diabetiker*
I'm allergic to ...	*Ech sin Allergiker ...*	*Je suis allergique aux ...*	*Ich bin allergisch auf ...*
antibiotics	*Anitbiotikken*	*antibiotiques*	*Antibiotika*
aspirin	*Aspro*	*aspirine*	*Aspirin*
nuts	*Nëss*	*noix*	*Nüsse*
bees	*Beien*	*abeilles*	*Bienen*

Travel with children

Is there a ...?	*Get et e ...?*	*Est-ce qu'il y a ...?*	*Gibt es ein/eine/ einen ...?*
baby changing room	*Raum fir d'Kanner frësch ze man*	*bébé-change*	*Babywickelraum*
children's menu	*Kannermenu*	*menu pour enfant*	*Kinderspeisekarte*
Do you have ...?	*Hut Dir ...?*	*Avez-vous ...?*	*Haben Sie ...?*
nappies	*Wëndelen*	*couches de bébé*	*Windeln*
potty	*Potti*	*pot*	*Töpfchen*
highchair	*e Kannerstull*	*chaise haute*	*Hochstuhl*

Appendix 2

FURTHER INFORMATION

BOOKS For everything you need to know about travelling around Luxembourg, you've picked up the right book. Most of the other titles mentioned here are hard to find outside Luxembourg.

Language

Christophory, Jules *English–Lëtzebuergesch Dictionary* Lycée Michel Rodange, 1996
Christophory, Jules *Who's Afraid of Luxembourgish?* Editions Paul Bauler, 1979. A trilingual Luxembourgish/French/English phrasebook.

Living in Luxembourg

Bunt, Vivane *Family Guide*. A booklet containing 60 tips for new residents.
Hello – The Insider's Guide to Luxembourg. Published annually, this booklet has listings (but not reviews – you'll need this guide for that) of accommodation, food shops, bars, gay-friendly clubs, music venues and more.
Just Arrived – Luxembourg Guide for Residents Ville de Luxembourg. A French–English directory of just about everything published by the Luxembourg City government. It's especially handy if you've just arrived and haven't got to grips with the Yellow Pages. If you need to know where to find Tie Rack in Kirchberg, look no further.
Living in Luxembourg A guide updated annually by the American Women's Club of Luxembourg (AWC). It's available in most of Luxembourg City's bookshops.

Cooking and culture

Hausemer, Georges & Hoffmann, Guy *Luxembourg Culinaire – Cuisine, Country & People* Editions Guy Binsfeld, 1997. If you can't get enough of that *judd mat gaardebounen* and want to recreate it at home, this is the definitive guide to both the national culture and local cuisine. As well as hundreds of glossy photos it includes around 100 typical and traditional recipes.
Reid, Andrew *Luxembourg: The Clog-Shaped Duchy: A Chronological History of Luxembourg from the Celts to the Present Day* AuthorHouse, 2005. Does exactly what the title suggests, providing an interesting and in-depth look at the history and people of the Grand Duchy.

There are also all manner of heavy and glossy books on Luxembourgish subjects from castles to the countryside. They won't give you any practical advice, but they might look nice on your coffee table if your arms are strong enough to carry any of these often-weighty tomes.

Other Editions Guy Binsfeld (*www.editionsguybinsfeld.lu*) is Luxembourg's largest publisher, and produces many titles of interest to tourists from walking maps to coffee-table photo extravaganzas. Visit the website for a full listing. Three books with self-explanatory

A2

titles for outdoors enthusiasts are *Mountain Bike Tour, Luxembourg 171 Rambling Routes* and *Rambling Without Frontiers.*

WEBSITES

www.352luxmag.lu News in English about Luxembourg, plus a weekly downloadable magazine.

www.agendalux.lu Run by the national tourist office, this will tell you what's on and where.

www.architectour.lu Has suggestions for themed self-drive architectural tours.

www.autobus.lu (in French) Bus transport information for Luxembourg City.

www.bedandbike.lu Useful information about cycle tours.

www.chapter1.lu Luxembourg's only English-language bookshop.

www.gastronomie.lu Contains a directory of local restaurants.

www.hiking-in-luxembourg.co.uk Useful web portal with links to sites about hiking and cycling in Luxembourg.

www.lcto.lu Official website of the Luxembourg City Tourist Office.

www.luxembourg.co.uk Run by the Luxembourg Tourist Office in London. It's informative enough that many Luxembourgers also come here for information.

www.miselerland.lu (in French/German) General information about the Moselle region's products, with suggested bike tours.

www.mobiliteit.lu For public transport information throughout Luxembourg (bus and train).

www.mullerthal-trail.lu General information about hiking in the Little Switzerland area.

www.nightrider.lu (in French/German) After-hours 'taxi' transport around the Grand Duchy.

www.restaurant.lu (in French) Contains reviews of a great many Grand Duchy dining experiences.

www.statermuseeen.lu Provides information on all things museum-related.

travelluxembourg.org Contains a wealth of information on the Grand Duchy, with useful facts, ideas and addresses.

www.vins-cremants.lu This site tells you everything about the local wine industry.

www.visitluxembourg.lu or **www.ont.lu** Official website of the Luxembourg National Tourist Office. Has a wealth of information on where to go, what to see and where to stay.

www.wort.lu/en News in English.

Index

Page numbers in **bold** indicate major entries; those in *italic* indicate maps